# FOURTH EDITION

**3**

## Series Director: **Diane Larsen-Freeman**

# Grammar Dimensions

## Form • Meaning • Use

Stephen H. Thewlis

**HEINLE**
**CENGAGE Learning™**

Australia • Brazil • Japan • Korea • Mexico • Singapore • Spain • United Kingdom • United States

HEINLE
CENGAGE Learning™

**Series Director: Diane Larsen-Freeman:
Grammar Dimensions 3: Form, Meaning, and
Use, Fourth Edition**
Stephen H. Thewlis

Publisher: Sherrise Roehr

Consulting Editor: James W. Brown

Acquisitions Editor, Academic ESL:
   Tom Jefferies

Director of Content Development:
   Anita Raducanu

Director of Product Marketing: Amy Mabley

Executive Marketing Manager: Jim McDonough

Senior Field Marketing Manager:
   Donna Lee Kennedy

Editorial Assistants: Katherine Reilly,
   Emily Dedinger

Senior Production Editor:
   Maryellen Eschmann-Killeen

Senior Print Buyer: Mary Beth Hennebury

Development Editors:
   Amy Lawler, Sarah Barnicle

Production Project Manager: Chrystie Hopkins

Production Services: Pre-Press PMG

Interior Designer: Lori Stuart

Cover Designer: Studio Montage

Cover Image: ©Digital Vision/Getty/RF

For product information and technology assistance, contact us at
**Cengage Learning Customer & Sales Support, 1-800-354-9706**

For permission to use material from this text or product,
submit all requests online at **cengage.com/permissions**
Further permissions questions can be emailed to
**permissionrequest@cengage.com**

Library of Congress Control Number: 2006909605

ISBN-13: 978-1-4130-2742-6

ISBN-10: 1-4130-2742-3

International Student Edition

ISBN-13: 978-1-4130-2755-6

ISBN-10: 1-4130-2755-5

**Heinle**
25 Thomson Place
Boston, MA 02210
USA

Cengage Learning is a leading provider of customized learning solutions with office locations around the globe, including Singapore, the United Kingdom, Australia, Mexico, Brazil, and Japan. Locate your local office at:
**international.cengage.com/region**

Cengage Learning products are represented in Canada by
Nelson Education, Ltd.

Visit Heinle online at **elt.heinle.com**
Visit our corporate website at **cengage.com**

Credits appear on pages C1–C2, which constitutes a continuation of the copyright page.

Printed in China by China Translation & Printing Services Limited
4 5 6 7 11 10

# CONTENTS

# Appendices    A-1

# Answer Key (for Puzzles and problems only)    A-12

# Credits    C-1

# Index    I-1

# A Word from Diane Larsen-Freeman, Series Editor

Before **Grammar Dimensions** was published, teachers would ask me, "What is the role of grammar in a communicative approach?" These teachers recognized the importance of teaching grammar, but they associated grammar with form and communication with meaning, and thus could not see how the two easily fit together. **Grammar Dimensions** was created to help teachers and students appreciate the fact that grammar is not just about form. While grammar does indeed involve form, in order to communicate, language users also need to know the meaning of the forms and when to use them appropriately. In fact, it is sometimes not the form, but the *meaning* or *appropriate use* of a grammatical structure that represents the greatest long-term learning challenge for students. For instance, learning when it is appropriate to use the present perfect tense instead of the past tense, or being able to use two-word or phrasal verbs meaningfully, represent formidable challenges for English language learners.

The three dimensions of *form*, *meaning*, and *use* can be depicted in a pie chart with their interrelationship illustrated by the three arrows:

Helping students learn to use grammatical structures accurately, meaningfully, and appropriately is the fundamental goal of **Grammar Dimensions.** It is consistent with the goal of helping students to communicate meaningfully in English, and one that recognizes the undeniable interdependence of grammar and communication.

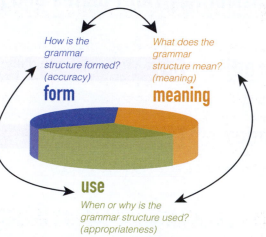

How is the grammar structure formed? (accuracy)
**form**

What does the grammar structure mean? (meaning)
**meaning**

**use**
When or why is the grammar structure used? (appropriateness)

To learn more about form, meaning, and use, read **The Grammar Book: An ESL/EFL Teacher's Course,** Second Edition, by Marianne Celce-Murcia and Diane Larsen-Freeman. ISBN: 0-8384-4725-2.

To understand more about teaching grammer effectively, read **Teaching Language: From Grammer to Grammaring** by Diane Larsen-Freeman. ISBN: 0-8384-6675-3.

Enjoy the Fourth Edition of **Grammer Dimensions**!

THE GRAMMAR BOOK

An ESL / EFL Teacher's Course
SECOND EDITION

MARIANNE CELCE-MURCIA
DIANE LARSEN-FREEMAN

# Welcome to *Grammar Dimensions*, Fourth Edition!

The **clearest**, most **comprehensive** and **communicative** grammar series available! The fourth edition of *Grammar Dimensions* is more **user-friendly** and makes teaching grammar more **effective** than ever.

## GRAMMAR DIMENSIONS IS COMPREHENSIVE AND CLEAR.

*Grammar Dimensions* systematically addresses the three dimensions of language—form, meaning, and use—through clear and comprehensive grammar explanations and extensive practice exercises. Each unit methodically focuses on each students' dimension and then integrates what they have learned in end-of-unit activities. In addition, grammatical structures are recycled throughout the series allowing students to practice and build upon their existing knowledge.

## GRAMMAR DIMENSIONS IS COMMUNICATIVE.

*Grammar Dimensions* includes a large variety of lively communicative and personalized activities throughout each unit, eliciting self-expression and personalized practice. Interactive activities at the start of each unit serve as diagnostic tools directing student learning towards the most challenging dimensions of language structure. Integrated activities at the end of each unit include reading, writing, listening, and speaking activities allowing students to practice grammar and communication in tandem. New research activities encourage students to use authentic Internet resources and to reflect on their own learning.

## GRAMMAR DIMENSIONS IS USER-FRIENDLY AND FLEXIBLE.

*Grammar Dimensions* has been designed to be flexible. Instructors can use the units in order or as set by their curriculum. Exercises can be used in order or as needed by the students. In addition, a tight integration between the Student Book, the Workbook, and the Lesson Planner makes teaching easier and makes the series more user-friendly.

## GRAMMAR DIMENSIONS IS EFFECTIVE.

Students who learn the form, meaning, and use of each grammar structure will be able to communicate more accurately, meaningfully, and appropriately.

## New to the Fourth Edition

- **NEW and revised grammar explanations** and examples help students and teachers easily understand and comprehend each language structure.

- **NEW and revised grammar charts and exercises** provide a wealth of opportunities for students to practice and master their new language.

- **NEW thematically and grammatically related Internet and *InfoTrac®College Edition* activities** in every unit of books 2, 3, and 4 develop student research using current technologies.

- **NEW Reflection activities** encourage students to create personal language goals and to develop learning strategies.

- **NEW design, art, and photos** make each activity and exercise more engaging.

- **NEW Lesson Planners** assist both beginning and experienced teachers in giving their students the practice and skills they need to communicate accurately, meaningfully, and appropriately. All activities and exercises in the Lesson Planner are organized into step-by-step lessons so that no instructor feel overwhelmed.

## SEQUENCING OF *GRAMMAR DIMENSIONS*

In *Grammar Dimensions* students progress from the sentence level to the discourse level, and learn to communicate appropriately at all levels.

| *Grammar Dimensions* Book 1 | *Grammar Dimensions* Book 2 | *Grammar Dimensions* Book 3 | *Grammar Dimensions* Book 4 |
|---|---|---|---|

Sentence level → Discourse level

|  | **Book 1** | **Book 2** | **Book 3** | **Book 4** |
|---|---|---|---|---|
| **Level** | High-beginning | Intermediate | High-Intermediate | Advanced |
| **Grammar level** | Sentence and sub-sentence level | Sentence and sub-sentence level | Discourse level | Discourse level |
| **Primary language and communication focus** | Semantic notions such as *time* and *place* | Social functions, such as *making requests* and *seeking* permission | Cohesion and coherence at the discourse level | Academic and technical discourse |
| **Major skill focus** | Listening and speaking | Listening and speaking | Reading and writing | Reading and writing |

# Guided Tour of *Grammar Dimensions* 3

Unit goals **provide a roadmap** for the grammar points students will work on.

"**Opening Task**" can be used as a **diagnostic warm-up** exercise to explore students' knowledge of each structure.

"**Focus**" sections present the **form, meaning,** and/or **use** of a particular structure helping students develop the skill of "**grammaring**"—the ability to use structures accurately, meaningfully, and appropriately.

**Clear grammar charts present** rules and explanation preceded by examples, so teachers can have students work inductively to try to discover the rule on their own.

**Purposeful exercises** provide a wealth of opportunity for students to practice and personalize the grammar.

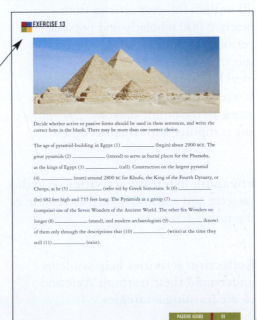

"Use Your English" (fondly known as the purple pages) offer communicative activities that **integrate grammar with reading, writing, listening, and speaking skills.** Communicative activities consolidate grammar instruction with enjoyable and meaningful tasks.

Research activity using *InfoTrac® College Edition* and the Internet encourages students to read articles on carefully selected topics and use this information to reflect on a theme or on information studied in each unit. *InfoTrac® College Edition*, an Online Research and Learning Center, appears in Grammar Dimensions 2, 3, and 4 and offers over 20 million full-text articles from nearly 6,000 scholarly and popular periodicals. Articles cover a broad spectrum of disciplines and topics—ideal for every type of researcher. Instructors and students can gain access to the online database 24/7 on any computer with Internet access.

**Engaging listening activities** on audio cassette and audio CD further reinforce the target structure.

**Reflection** activities help students understand their learning style and create learning strategies.

## Supplements

These additional components help teachers teach and student learn to use English grammar structures accurately.

### The Lesson Planner

The lesson planner facilitates teaching by providing detailed lesson plans and examples, answer keys to the Student Book and Workbook, references to all of the components, and the tapescript for the audiocassette activities. The Lesson Planner minimizes teacher preparation time by providing:

- Summary of main grammar points for the teacher
- Information for the teacher on typical student errors
- Step-by-step guidelines for every focus box, exercise, and activity
- Suggested correlations between exercises and activities in the Use Your English pages
- Suggested timing for each exercise and each lesson
- Lead-in suggestions and examples for focus boxes
- Suggestions for expansion work follow most exercises
- Balance of cognitive and communicative activities
- Explanation for the teacher of the purpose of each activity, in order to differentiate cognitive from communicative emphasis
- Occasional methodology notes to anticipate possible procedural problems.

### Assessment CD-ROM with ExamView Pro Test Generator

The Assessment CD-ROM allows instructors to **create customized quizzes and tests** quickly and easily from a test bank of questions. Monitoring student understanding and progress has never been easier! The answer key appears with instructor copies of each quiz or test created.

### Audio Program

Audio cassettes and CDs **provide listening activities for** each unit so students can practice listening to **grammar structures.**

### Workbook

Workbooks **provide additional exercises** for each grammar point presented in the student text. Also offers editing practice and questions types found on many language exams.

### Web site

Features additional grammar practice activities: elt.thomson.com/grammardimensions.

# Empirical and Experiential Support for the *Grammar Dimensions* Approach

## Opening Task Activities

The approach to teaching grammar used in the *Grammar Dimensions* series is well-grounded empirically and experientially. The Opening Task in each unit situates the learning challenge and allows students to participate in and learn from activity right from the beginning (Greeno 2006). In addition, students don't enter the classroom as empty vessels, waiting to be filled (Sawyer 2006). By observing how students perform on the Opening Task, teachers can analyze for themselves what students know and are able to do and what they don't know or are not able to do. Teachers can thus select from each unit what is necessary for students to build on from what they already bring with them.

## Consciousness-Raising Exercises and Focus Boxes

Many of the exercises in *Grammar Dimensions* are of the consciousness-raising sort, where students are invited to make observations about some aspect of the target structure. This type of activity promotes students' noticing (Schmidt 1990), an important step in acquiring the grammar structure. The Focus Boxes further encourage this noticing, this time very explicitly. Explicit formulations of the sort found in the Focus Boxes can lead to implicit acquisition with practice (DeKeyser 1998). Moreover, certain learners (those with analytic learning styles) benefit greatly from explicit treatment of grammar structures (Larsen-Freeman and Long 1991).

## Productive Practice and Communicative Activities

However, noticing by itself is insufficient. In order to be able to use the grammar structure, students need productive practice (Gatbonton and Segalowitz 1988; Larsen-Freeman 2003). Therefore, many of the exercises in *Grammar Dimensions* are of the output practice sort. Furthermore, each unit ends with communicative activities, where attention to the grammar is once again implicit, but where students can use the grammar structure in "psychologically authentic" or meaningful ways. Psychological authenticity is very important in order for students to be able to transfer what they know to new situations so that they can use it for their own purposes (Blaxton 1989) and so they are not left to contend with the "inert knowledge problem," (Whitehead 1929) where they know about the grammar, but can't use it.

## The Three Dimensions of Grammar: Form, Meaning, and Use

Finally, applied linguistics research (Celce-Murcia and Larsen-Freeman 1999) supports the fundamental premise underlying *Grammar Dimensions*: that knowing a grammar structure means being able to use it accurately, meaningfully, and appropriately. Form focus or meaning focus by itself is insufficient (Larsen-Freeman 2001); all three dimensions—form, meaning, and use—need to be learned.

# References

Blaxton, T. (1989). Investigating dissociations among memory measures: Support for a transfer-appropriate processing framework. *Journal of Experimental Psychology: Learning, Memory, and Cognition 15 (4): 657-668.*

Celce-Murcia, M. and D. Larsen-Freeman. (1999). *The grammar book: An ESL/EFL teacher's course.* Second Edition. Boston: Heinle & Heinle.

De Keyser, R. (1998). Beyond focus on form: Cognitive perspectives on learning and practicing second language grammar. n C. Doughty and J. Williams (eds.), *Focus on Classroom Second Language Acquisition.* Cambridge: Cambridge University Press, 42–63.

Gatbonton, E. and N. Segalowitz. (1988). Creative automatization: Principles for promoting fluency within a communicative framework. *TESOL Quarterly 22 (3): 473–492.*

Greeno, J. (2006). Learning in activity. In R. K. Sawyer (ed.), *The Cambridge handbook of learning sciences.* Cambridge: Cambridge University Press, 79–96.

Larsen-Freeman, D. (2001). Teaching grammar. In M. Celce-Murcia (ed.), *Teaching English as a Second or Foreign Language.* Third edition. Boston: Heinle & Heinle, 251–266.

Larsen-Freeman, D. (2003). *Teaching language: From grammar to grammaring.* Boston: Heinle & Heinle.

Larsen-Freeman, D. and M. Long. (1991). *An introduction to second language qcquisition research.* London: Longman.

Sawyer, R. K. (2006). Introduction: The new science of learning. In R. K. Sawyer (ed.), *The Cambridge handbook of learning sciences.* Cambridge: Cambridge University Press, 1–16.

Schmidt, R. (1990). The role of consciousness in second language learning. *Applied Linguistics 11 (2), 129–158.*

Whitehead, A. N. 1929. *The aims of education.* New York: MacMillan.

# Acknowledgments from the Series Director

This fourth edition would not have come about if it had not been for the enthusiastic response of teachers and students using all the previous editions. I am very grateful for the reception *Grammar Dimensions* has been given.

I am also grateful for all the authors' efforts. To be a teacher, and at the same time a writer, is a difficult balance to achieve . . . so is being an innovative creator of materials, and yet, a team player. They have met these challenges exceedingly well in my opinion. Then, too, the Thomson Heinle team has been impressive. I am grateful for the leadership exercised by Jim Brown, Sherrise Roehr, and Tom Jefferies. I also appreciate all the support from Anita Raducanu, Amy Mabley, Sarah Barnicle, Laura Needham, Chrystie Hopkins, Mary Beth Hennebury, and Abigail Greshik of Pre-Press Company. Deserving special mention are Amy Lawler and Yeny Kim, who never lost the vision while they attended to the detail with good humor and professionalism.

I have also benefited from the counsel of Marianne Celce-Murcia, consultant for the first edition of this project, and my friend. Finally, I wish to thank my family members, Elliott, Brent, and Gavin, for not once asking the (negative yes-no) question that must have occurred to them countless times: "Haven't you finished yet?" As we all have discovered, this project has a life of its own and is never really finished! And, for this, I am exceedingly grateful. Happy Grammaring all!

# A Special Thanks

The series director, authors, and publisher would like to thank the following reviewers whose experienced observations and thoughtful suggestions have assisted us in creating and revising *Grammar Dimensions*.

Michelle Alvarez
*University of Miami*
Coral Gables, Florida

Edina Pingleton Bagley
*Nassau Community College*
Garden City, New York

Jane Berger
*Solano Community College,*
California

Mary Bottega
*San Jose State University*

Mary Brooks
*Eastern Washington University*

Christina Broucqsault
*California State Polytechnic*
 *University*

José Carmona
*Hudson Community College*

Susan Carnell
*University of Texas at Arlington*

Susana Christie
*San Diego State University*

Diana Christopher
*Georgetown University*

Gwendolyn Cooper
*Rutgers University*

Julia Correia
*Henderson State University*
Arkadelphia, Arkansas

Sue Cozzarelli
*EF International, San Diego*

Catherine Crystal
*Laney College, California*

Kevin Ccross
*University of San Francisco*

Julie Damron
*Interlink at Valparaiso*
 *University, Indiana*

Glen Deckert
*Eastern Michigan University*

Eric Dwyer
*University of Texas at Austin*

Nikki Ellman
*Laney College*
Oakland, California

Ann Eubank
*Jefferson Community College*

Alice Fine
*UCLA Extension*

Alicia Going
*The English Language Study*
 *Center, Oregon*

Molly Gould
*University of Delaware*

Maren M. Hargis
*San Diego Mesa College*

Penny Harrold
*Universidad de Monterrey*
Monterrey, Mexico

Robin Hendrickson
*Riverside City College*
Riverside, California

Mary Herbert
*University of California, Davis*
 *Extension*

Jane Hilbert
*ELS Language Center,
Florida International
University*

Eli Hinkel
*Xavier University*

Kathy Hitchcox
*International English
Institute, Fresno*

Abeer Hubi
*Altarbia Alislamia Schools
Riyadh, Saudi Arabia*

Joyce Hutchings
*Georgetown University*

Heather Jeddy
*Northern Virginia
Community College*

Judi Keen
*University of California,
Davis,* and *Sacramento
City College*

Karli Kelber
*American Language Institute,
New York University*

Anne Kornfield
*LaGuardia Community
College*

Kay Longmire
*Interlink at Valparaiso
University, Indiana*

Robin Longshaw
*Rhode Island School of Design*

Robert Ludwiczak
*Texas A&M University
College Station, Texas*

Bernadette McGlynn
*ELS Language Center, St.
Joseph's University*

Billy McGowan
*Aspect International, Boston*

Margaret Mehran
*Queens College*

Richard Moore
*University of Washington*

Karen Moreno
*Teikyo Post University,
Connecticut*

Gino Muzzetti
*Santa Rosa Junior College,
California*

Mary Nance-Tager
*LaGuardia Community
College, City University of
New York*

So Nguyen
*Orange Coast College
Costa Mesa, California*

Karen O'Neill
*San Jose State University*

Mary O'Neal
*Northern Virginia
Community College*

Nancy Pagliara
*Northern Virginia
Community College*

Keith Pharis
*Southern Illinois University*

Amy Parker
*ELS Language Center, San
Francisco*

Margene Petersen
*ELS Language Center,
Philadelphia*

Nancy Pfingstag
*University of North
Carolina, Charlotte*

Sally Prieto
*Grand Rapids Community
College*

India Plough
*Michigan State University*

Mostafa Rahbar
*University of Tennessee at
Knoxville*

Dudley Reynolds
*Indiana University*

Dzidra Rodins
*DePaul University
Chicago, Illinois*

Ann Salzman
*University of Illinois at
Urbana-Champaign*

Jennifer Schmidt
*San Francisco State
University*

Cynthia Schuemann
*Miami-Dade Community
College*

Jennifer Schultz
*Golden Gate University,
California*

Mary Beth Selbo
*Wright College, City Colleges
of Chicago*

Mary Selseleh
*American River College
Sacramento, California*

Stephen Sheeran
*Bishop's University,
Lenoxville, Quebec*

Kathy Sherak
*San Francisco State
University*

Sandra E. Sklarew
*Merritt Community College
Oakland, California*

Keith Smith
*ELS Language Center, San
Francisco*

Helen Solorzano
*Northeastern University*

Jorge Vazquez Solorzano
*Bachillerato de la Reina de
Mexico*
S. C., Mexico, D. F.,
Mexico

Christina Valdez
*Pasadena City College
Pasadena, California*

Danielle Valentini
*Oakland Community College
Farmington Hills,
Michigan*

Amelia Yongue
*Howard Community College
Columbia, Maryland*

# OVERVIEW OF THE ENGLISH VERB SYSTEM
## Time and Tense

## UNIT GOALS

- Review the English verb system

- Keep tenses in the same time frame

- Change the time frame correctly within a passage

## OPENING TASK
### Comparing Past, Present, and Future

■ **STEP 1**

Work with a partner: Student A, look at the following information about Bob Lee, a typical American college student. Student B, look at the information on the next page about Bob's grandfather, Robert Lee. Student A, tell Student B about Bob's life. Student B, tell Student A about Robert's life.

**BOB LEE**

**Born:** 1987

**Family:** Two brothers and one sister, living with mother; parents divorced; Bob lives in a college dorm

**Occupation:** currently a sophomore, studying biology, plans to be a doctor

**Regular activities:** school, part-time job in the library, time with girlfriend, visiting family some weekends and during school vacations

**Hobbies or favorite sports:** basketball, skiing, computers, music, TV

**Visits to foreign countries:** Mexico (once), Canada (twice)

**Special skills or abilities:** computers, university chorus

**Probable activity at this moment:** studying for biology midterm

### ROBERT LEE

**Born:** 1930  **DIED:** 1992

**Family:** Five brothers, four sisters; only one sister and brother survived childhood; father died of tuberculosis when Robert was 14 years old

**Occupation:** factory worker, never finished high school

**Regular activities:** job (12-hour days); helping mother; family life, church

**Hobbies or favorite sports:** radio, baseball (on factory team)

**Visits to foreign countries:** none

**Special skills or abilities:** baseball, harmonica playing

**Probable activity when Bob was born:** working at the factory

## ■ STEP 2

Now work together to create a story for Roberta, Bob's granddaughter. Fill in some information below and then tell another pair of students about how you think Roberta's life will be.

### ROBERTA CHONG-DAVIS

**Born:** 2035

**Family:** _____

**Occupation:** _____

**Regular activities:** _____

_____

**Hobbies or favorite sports:** _____

_____

**Visits to foreign countries or planets:** _____

_____

**Special skills or abilities:** _____

_____

**Probable activity at this moment 100 years from today:** _____

_____

## FOCUS 1    Overview of the English Verb System

The form of any verb in English is made up of two things: time frame and aspect.

| | |
|---|---|
| **Time frame** tells **when** something took place. There are three basic time frames: **present, past,** and **future.** | **Aspect** tells **how** the verb is related to that time, or gives some other information about the quality of the action. (See Unit 2.) |

There are four kinds of aspect, and each one has a basic meaning.

| ASPECT | MEANING |
|---|---|
| simple | **at** that time |
| progressive | **in progress during** that time |
| perfect | **before** that time |
| perfect progressive | **in progress during and before** that time |

When we combine the three time frames and the four aspects, we get twelve possible combinations of forms. These forms are called **tenses,** and the name of each tense tells which time frame and which aspect are being used. The charts in Appendix 1, on pages A-1 to A-4, show in more detail the three basic time frames and the tenses that are used in each.

| ASPECT ➤ Time Frame ▼ | SIMPLE | PROGRESSIVE | PERFECT | PERFECT PROGRESSIVE |
|---|---|---|---|---|
| | | | TENSES | |
| Present | *simple present* study/studies give/gives | *present progressive* am/is/are studying am/is/are giving | *present perfect* has/have studied has/have given | *present perfect progressive* has/have been studying has/have been giving |
| Past | *simple past* studied gave | *past progressive* was/were studying was/were giving | *past perfect* had studied had given | *past perfect progressive* had been studying had been giving |
| Future | *simple future* will study will give | *future progressive* will be studying will be giving | *future perfect* will have studied will have given | *future perfect progressive* will have been studying will have been giving |

## EXERCISE 1

Read the following numbered passages and identify the time frame of each. Is it present time, past time, or future time?

1. (a) Matt had a terrible headache. (b) His tongue was dry, and his eyes were burning. (c) He had been sneezing constantly for nearly an hour. (d) He hated springtime. (e) For most people spring meant flowers and sunshine, but for Matt it meant allergies.

2. (a) I really don't know what to do for vacation. (b) My vacation starts in three weeks, and (c) I'm trying to decide what to do. (d) I've been to Hawaii and New York. (e) It's too early in the year to go camping in the mountains. (f) I've been working hard at the office and I really need a break. (g) I've saved enough money to have a really nice trip. (h) I just can't decide where to go or what to do.

3. (a) The changing world climate will mean changes in food production. (b) Scientists think that summers throughout North America will become much hotter and drier than they are now. (c) Crops that require a lot of water will be less economical to grow. (d) Society will have to develop different energy sources, (e) since fossil fuels, such as coal and oil, may have become depleted by the end of the next century.

4. (a) "Social Darwinism" was a popular theory of the nineteenth century. (b) It compared social and economic development with biological evolution. (c) According to this theory, competition between rich people and poor people was unavoidable. (d) The poor were like dinosaurs who were dying out because they had lost the battle for survival—economic survival.

5. (a) Scientific research often has an important social impact. (b) In recent years scientists have discovered that Vitamin B can prevent certain kinds of childhood blindness. (c) As a result, programs have been established that provide education and dietary supplements to children in developing countries.

## EXERCISE 2

Choose three of the passages in Exercise 1, and underline each complete verb phrase (the verb plus any auxiliary—*have, do, is*, etc.—that shows the tense of the verb). Name the tense of each verb phrase you have underlined.

## EXERCISE 3

Check your knowledge of irregular verb forms by completing the chart on page 4. You may work with other students. When you finish, check your work using Appendix 6, Irregular Verbs, on page A-10.

# UNIT 1

Irregular Verbs

## Group 1

| BASE FORM | PAST TENSE FORM | PAST PARTICIPLE FORM |
| --- | --- | --- |
| become | became | become |
| begin | began | begun |
| bend | bent | bent |
| bet | bet | bet |
| bind | bound | bound |
| bite | bit | bit |
| bleed | bled | bled |
| blow | blew | blown |
| break | broke | broken |
| bring | brought | brought |
| build | built | built |
| buy | bought | bought |
| catch | caught | caught |
| choose | chose | chosen |
| come | came | come |
| cost | cost | cost |
| cut | cut | cut |
| dig | dug | dug |
| do | did | done |
| draw | drew | drawn |
| drink | drank | drunk |
| drive | drove | driven |
| eat | ate | eaten |
| fall | fell | fallen |
| feed | fed | fed |
| feel | felt | felt |
| fight | fought | fought |
| find | found | found |
| fit | fit | fit |
| fly | flew | flown |
| forbid | forbade | forbidden |
| forget | forgot | forgotten |
| forgive | forgave | forgiven |
| freeze | froze | frozen |
| get | got | got |

## Group 2

| BASE FORM | PAST TENSE FORM | PAST PARTICIPLE FORM |
| --- | --- | --- |
| go | went | gone |
| grind | ground | ground |
| grow | grew | grown |
| hang | hung | hung |
| have | had | had |
| hear | heard | heard |
| hide | hid | hidden |
| hit | hit | hit |
| hold | held | held |
| hurt | hurt | hurt |
| keep | kept | kept |
| know | knew | known |
| lead | led | led |
| leave | left | left |
| lend | lent | lent |
| let | let | let |
| lose | lost | lost |
| make | made | made |
| mean | meant | meant |
| meet | met | met |
| pay | paid | paid |
| put | put | put |
| quit | quit | quit |
| read | read | read |
| ride | rode | ridden |
| ring | rang | rung |
| rise | rose | risen |
| run | ran | run |
| say | said | said |
| see | saw | seen |
| seek | sought | sought |
| sell | sold | sold |
| send | sent | sent |
| set | set | set |
| shake | shook | shaken |
| shine | shone | shone |
| shoot | shot | shot |
| shut | shut | shut |

## Group 3

| BASE FORM | PAST TENSE FORM | PAST PARTICIPLE FORM |
| --- | --- | --- |
| sing | sang | sung |
| sink | sank | sunk |
| sit | sat | sat |
| sleep | slept | slept |
| slide | slid | slid |
| speak | spoke | spoken |
| speed | sped | sped |
| spend | spent | spent |
| split | split | split |
| spread | spread | spread |
| spring | sprang | sprung |
| stand | stood | stood |
| steal | stole | stolen |
| stick | stuck | stuck |
| sting | stung | stung |
| strike | struck | struck |
| swear | swore | sworn |
| sweep | swept | swept |
| swim | swam | swum |
| swing | swung | swung |
| take | took | taken |
| teach | taught | taught |
| tear | tore | torn |
| tell | told | told |
| think | thought | thought |
| throw | threw | thrown |
| understand | understood | understood |
| wake | woke | woken |
| wear | wore | worn |
| weave | wove | woven |
| weep | wept | wept |
| win | won | won |
| wind | wound | wound |
| write | wrote | written |

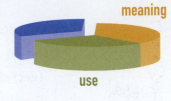
## FOCUS 2  Keeping Tenses in the Same Time Frame

In general, we choose a particular time frame and then choose from among the tenses within that time frame in order to describe events.

| EXAMPLES | EXPLANATIONS |
|---|---|
| (a) My roommate Charley **had** a dance party last Friday night. I **was working** that night, so I **didn't get** home until 10:00, and by then everyone **had** already **started** dancing. | Use past tenses to describe things that happened at a specific time in the past. |
| (b) My roommate Charley **has** a dance party every Friday night. I **work** on Friday nights, so I **don't get** home until 10:00, and by then everyone **has** already **started** dancing. | Use present tenses to describe things that are happening now, are related to now, or happen again and again. |
| (c) My roommate Charley **is going to have** a dance party next Friday night. I **will be working** next Friday night, so I **won't get** home until 10:00, and by then everyone **will** already **have started** dancing. | Use future tenses to describe events that are going to happen at some time in the future. |

## EXERCISE 4

Decide what time frame each of these passages should be written in, and then write the appropriate verb form in the blanks.

1. I hear we (a) ___will be___ (be) playing games at Charley's party next week. I hope there (b) ___will be___ (be) dancing as well! I (c) ___will have completed___ (have completed) my dance class by then.

*future.*

2. Jeff (a) ___had___ (have) an interesting experience yesterday afternoon. As he (b) ___was walking___ (be walking) from his house to the grocery store, he (c) ___saw___ (see) someone he (d) ___had gone___ (have gone) to high school with.

*past*

3. Matt (a) _____has_____ (have) a terrible time getting to work every day. When he (b) _____is driving_____ (be driving) to work he often (c) _____gets_____ (get) caught in terrible traffic jams. Even though he only (d) _____lives_____ (live) a few miles from the office, it sometimes (e) _____takes_____ (take) nearly an hour to get to work.

*present*

4. The Imperial City of Rome (a) _____was_____ (be) badly damaged by fire during the first century AD. At the time it (b) _____had been believed_____ (be believed) that the Emperor Nero (c) _____was playing_____ (be playing) a violin while the city (d) _____burned_____ (burn) to the ground.

*past*

5. Scientists (a) _____are_____ (be) worried that the world climate (b) _____are changing_____ (be changing). They (c) _____believes_____ (believe) this change (d) _____has resulted_____ (have resulted) from an increase in the amount of carbon dioxide ($CO_2$) in the earth's atmosphere. Whenever "fossil fuels" such as coal or oil (e) _____is burned_____ (be burned), the amount of $CO_2$ (f) _____increases_____ (increase). This (g) _____causes_____ (cause) the atmosphere to retain more heat. There (h) _____is_____ (be) proof that this process already (i) _____has begun_____ (have begun). Scientists (j) _____have discovered_____ (have discovered) that the average temperature of the world's oceans (k) _____has risen_____ (have risen) by one degree in the last twenty years.

*present*

6. John (a) _____will leave_____ (leave) for Paris on Tuesday. He (b) _____will be staying_____ (be staying) with a local family for the first few weeks. After that, he probably (c) _____will find_____ (find) a small apartment of his own.

*future*

# Changing the Time Frame Within a Passage

use

Although the time frame often stays the same within a passage, an author sometimes changes the time frame.

| EXAMPLES | EXPLANATIONS |
|---|---|
| | The author does this in order to: |
| (a) There **are** many examples in history of increasing military power causing a decreasing standard of living. Rome **was** unable to feed both its army and its population. Great Britain **declined** steadily from its economic position in the early part of this century. | move from a general statement to specific examples |
| (b) **One hundred years ago** the life expectancy in the United States **was** about 65. **Nowadays**, it **has increased** by an average of ten years. **In the next century**, if current trends continue, people **should be able to live** until their nineties. Interestingly enough, however, **a hundred years ago** the number of people who were over 100 **was** less than 1 percent of the population. That figure **has not changed** substantially, even **today**. | show contrast between one time and another |
| (c) I saw an elderly lady yesterday. **You don't see her kind much anymore**. She was wearing a black dress and she was carrying an umbrella. **Most elderly ladies I know don't carry umbrellas, and pants are more common than dresses**. As she walked down the street, I thought about how much life has changed since she was my age. | make a statement of general truth |

## EXERCISE 5

Mark the following passages with a slanted line (/) to show where the time frame changes. The first one has been done for you as an example.

1. My brother called me up yesterday. / I always know he needs to borrow money when he calls, because I never hear from him at any other time. / We spoke about this and that for a few minutes. He asked about my job and my family. We talked about his problems with his boss. / These are typical topics before he finally asks for a loan. / This phone call was no exception. He needed fifty dollars "until pay day." / Somehow, when payday comes he never remembers to pay back the loan.

2. I'll be really happy when the summer is over./I don't like hot weather, and I can't stand mosquitoes. There's a lot of both of those things in the summer./Last summer I tried to escape by going on a trip to Alaska. The heat wasn't bad, but the mosquitoes were terrible!/Next year I think I'll consider a vacation in Antarctica./I understand it's really cold there in July.

3. For more than fifty years scientists around the world have all used a single system to measure the strength (or "magnitude") of earthquakes./The Richter Scale was developed by Charles Richter in 1935. It was designed so scientists could compare the strength of earthquakes in different parts of the world. It was not designed to measure damage in earthquakes, but only intensity./This is because a less powerful earthquake in a heavily populated area can cause more damage than a stronger earthquake in an unpopulated area.

## EXERCISE 6

Discuss each change of time frame that you found in Exercise 5 with a partner. Why did the author change the time frame? There may be more than one reason. Share your explanation with the rest of the class.

## EXERCISE 7

Underline the complete verb phrases (verb plus auxiliaries) in the passages in Exercise 5 and name the tense of each verb phrase.

# Use Your English

speaking/writing

**ACTIVITY**  **1**  speaking/writing/listening

■ **STEP 1**   Work with a partner. Describe a typical day in your life. Tell your partner about the things you do, where you go, and how you typically spend your time. Mention at least five regular activities.

■ **STEP 2**   Next, describe a typical day in your life five years ago. Mention at least five activities that you did on a regular basis.

■ **STEP 3**   Your partner should use this information to decide what three things in your life have changed the most in the last five years, and report this information to the rest of the class. Make a similar report to the class about the changes in your partner's life.

**ACTIVITY** **2**  listening

CD Track 1

Listen to these descriptions about two people—one who is no longer living and one who is still alive. Based on the time frame and verb tenses used in the descriptions, decide which person is still living and which person is deceased.

## ACTIVITY 3 speaking/writing

Congratulations! You've just won a million dollars in a lottery. BUT . . . you have to spend all the money in a single week. AND . . . you can't spend more than $50,000 for any single purchase. (In other words, you can't just buy a million-dollar house. You have to make at least twenty separate purchases.) If you don't spend it all, you won't get any of it.

**STEP 1** What are your plans? In a brief essay, or in an oral presentation, answer this question: **How you will spend the money?**

**STEP 2** It's the end of the week. How did you spend your money? Change the verb tenses of your essay or presentation to answer this question: **How did you spend the money?**

## ACTIVITY 4 writing/speaking

Newspaper headlines represent a special kind of English. They usually omit a lot of important grammatical information. Test how well you know the basic sentence elements of English by "translating" these headlines into complete sentences. Compare your "translations" to those of another student.

**Example:** BABY FOUND IN BUS STATION
*A baby has been found in the bus station.*

---

STOCK MARKET CRASHES

U.S. POPULATION MOVING WEST

NEW BUDGET TERMED "DISASTER"

U.S. TO PROTEST NUCLEAR TESTING

PRESIDENT TO VISIT CHINA

DROUGHT EXPECTED TO WORSEN

BIG WHITE HOUSE SHAKE-UP

NEW PLAN TO IMPROVE BUS SERVICES

TEST SCORES IMPROVING IN PUBLIC SCHOOLS

LINK FOUND BETWEEN DIET AND HEART DISEASE

CANCER REPORTED INCREASING

MAJOR DECREASE IN INTERNATIONAL STUDENTS IN U.S.

---

## ACTIVITY 5 research on the web

In Activity 3 you were asked to imagine how you would spend a million dollars. How do you think your choices compare to real people who won that kind of money?

**STEP 1** Log onto *InfoTrac® College Edition* and do a keyword search of "lottery winners' behavior". There are several articles in *People Weekly* (for example) that tell what happened to real lottery winners after their good fortune. How did their real life experiences compare to the way you imagined yours would be? Compare two or three winners' stories to your own.

**STEP 2** With a partner or in a small group name three things that lottery winners typically do with their winnings. Name two or three disadvantages to becoming suddenly wealthy.

## ACTIVITY 6 language strategy activity

Now that you have finished this first unit and have some ideas about your areas of strength and weakness, look briefly through all the units of this book and the Table of Contents on pp. iii–xi in order to identify:

- one unit you would like the whole class to study.
- one unit you would enjoy studying by yourself.
- one unit you think you could study together with another student in the class.
- one unit you feel you already understand well enough to explain to another student.

# OVERVIEW OF THE ENGLISH VERB SYSTEM
## Aspect

## UNIT GOALS

- Review aspect in English verbs
- Review the simple tenses
- Use progressive, perfect, and perfect progressive aspects appropriately

## OPENING TASK

### A Picture Is Worth a Thousand Words

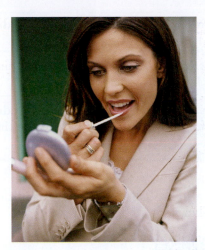

## STEP 1

With a partner, discuss each of these photographs and together write sentences about them. Your sentences should answer these questions.

- What has just happened? Why do you think so?
- What is happening now? Why do you think so?
- What is going to happen next? Why do you think so?

## STEP 2

Once you have described all the pictures, compare your descriptions with two other pairs of students. Do you all agree? Did you use the same verb tenses in your descriptions?

## STEP 3

Report any interesting similarities and differences to the rest of the class.

## FOCUS 1    Overview of Aspect

The basic aspect meanings listed on page 2 in Unit 1 indicate the time relationship between one verb and another.

| ASPECT | MEANING | EXAMPLE |
|---|---|---|
| simple | **at** that time | (a) The police **arrested** the protesters at 2:45 P.M. |
| progressive | **in progress during** that time | (b) They **were blocking** the street when they were arrested. |
| perfect | **before** that time | (c) They **had stopped** traffic for over an hour. |
| perfect progressive | **in progress during** and **before** that time | (d) They **had been protesting** the president's decision when the arrests started. |

We also use aspect to describe additional distinctions about an action or situation:

| EXAMPLES | EXPLANATIONS |
|---|---|
| | Aspect indicates whether the action or situation: |
| (e) The protester **disrupted** the politician's speech. | • happens just once |
| | OR |
| (f) Protesters **have been disrupting** politician's speeches as long as politicians **have been making** them. | • happens continuously or repeatedly |
| (g) The police **are arresting** the protester, but perhaps he'll escape. | • is still happening |
| | OR |
| (h) The police **have arrested** the protester, so he won't be able to escape. | • is completed |
| (i) Shopkeepers **are storing** some of their breakable items on the floor until the threat of earthquake aftershocks has passed. | • is temporary |
| | OR |
| (j) Shopkeepers in earthquake areas **store** expensive, breakable items on the lower shelves in order to lessen the possibility of damage. | • is permanent |

## EXERCISE 1

Analyze one of these paragraphs with a partner. Identify the basic time frame. Then say which meaning is expressed by the aspect in the underlined verb phrases.

1. By the time John gets on Flight 53 to Paris the day after tomorrow, he <u>will have accomplished</u> a great deal in a short period of time. He <u>will have moved out</u> of the apartment where he <u>has been living</u> for the last couple of years. He will have said some long, sad good-byes. He <u>will certainly be thinking</u> about all the friends he <u>will no longer see</u> every day.

2. When the earthquake hit San Francisco in 1989, Jeff <u>was</u> still at his office. He <u>had been trying</u> to finish a project. He <u>had been working</u> on it for over a week, and he was almost done. He <u>was just making</u> some final changes when the building started to move. When the quake <u>started</u>, he quickly <u>got</u> under his desk. He <u>was</u> glad that he <u>had</u> once <u>read</u> an article on what to do in earthquakes. He <u>had studied</u> the article carefully, so he <u>knew</u> exactly what to do.

3. Denise <u>is</u> quite a stylish dresser. She <u>thinks</u> that it <u>is</u> important to be neat and well-dressed, and she always <u>wants</u> to look her best. Every morning before she <u>leaves</u> for work, she <u>looks</u> at herself in the mirror. She <u>checks</u> to make sure that she <u>has combed</u> her hair and <u>hasn't put</u> her makeup on too heavily. She <u>makes</u> sure that she <u>is wearing</u> makeup colors that <u>go</u> nicely with the clothes she <u>is</u> wearing. She <u>checks</u> to see that her slip <u>isn't showing</u>, and her stockings <u>are</u> straight. She <u>makes sure</u> that the shoes she <u>has chosen</u> <u>match</u> the color of her dress and her coat. She <u>likes</u> feeling confident and attractive, and she <u>feels</u> that taking an extra minute in front of the mirror <u>is</u> worth the time.

**Simple Tenses**

use

| EXAMPLES | EXPLANATIONS |
|---|---|
| | Use simple tenses: |
| (a) Social psychology **is** the study of the factors that **influence** group behavior.<br>(b) The people of ancient Rome **spoke** Latin.<br>(c) A criminal **will** always **return** to the scene of the crime. | • to express general ideas, relationships, and truths |
| (d) Denise always **checks** her appearance in the mirror before she leaves for work.<br>(e) James Fennimore Cooper **wrote** for three hours every day except Sunday.<br>(f) People **will commute** to the moon by spaceship at the end of the next century. | • to describe habitual or recurrent actions |
| (g) Scientists **report** that they have identified the cause of AIDS.<br>(h) When the protesters **decided** to disrupt the meeting they had already heard about the president's decision.<br>(i) Roberta Chong-Davis **will visit** the moon someday. | • to establish time frame |
| (j) Denise **worries** that she won't look professional.<br>(k) One hundred years ago many people **felt** that a woman's place was in the home, not the office.<br>(l) If Bob is late for dinner, his mom **will worry** about him. | • to describe mental perceptions or emotions |
| (m) Bob **has** two brothers and a sister.<br>(n) Robert's hobbies **consisted** of playing baseball and the harmonica.<br>(o) Roberta's job **will require** regular travel to the moon. | • to express possession or logical relationship |

## EXERCISE 2

Work with the same partner that you did for the Opening Task of Unit 1. But instead of describing Bob Lee and his family, describe your own lives, and those of your grandfathers and what may be true for your granddaughters. Each of you should write at least two sentences that describe the lives of each generation.

## FOCUS 3 — Progressive Aspect

**use**

Progressive tenses (present progressive, past progressive, and future progressive) are made by using forms of

$$Be + Verb + \textit{-ing}$$

| EXAMPLES | EXPLANATIONS |
|---|---|
| | Use progressive aspect instead of simple aspect to describe: |
| (a) Other people **are** always **waiting** when Jeff **gets** to the bus stop. (They're already waiting **before** he gets there.) | • actions already in progress versus actions that happen afterwards |
| (b) Jeff **reads** the morning paper when he **gets** to the bus stop. (He reads his paper **after** he gets there.) | |
| (c) When Denise **entered** the room, the other employees **were working,** but when she left the room, they **laughed.** (They were working **before** she entered, but they laughed **after** she left.) | |
| (d) Victor **studies** English, but he **is not studying** at the moment. | • actions at a specific time (**now** or **then**) versus habitual or recurring actions |
| (e) John **lived** in France for a year, but he certainly **wasn't living** there when they had the election. | |
| (f) Those protesters **are** always **asking** for changes in the government. | • repeated actions |
| (g) Denise **is** still **working** to finish the report. | • uncompleted actions |
| (h) Those protesters **are being** very noisy, but they **are** angry, so I guess it's understandable. | • actions rather than states |

## EXERCISE 3

Why is progressive aspect used in these sentences? There may be more than one possible reason.

**Example:** He is studying for an examination now.
*action in progress now, uncompleted action*

1. Peter was reading a magazine when Denise saw him.
2. Don't call Jeff after 10:00 PM because he will be sleeping.
3. They were selling Girl Scout cookies from house to house yesterday afternoon.
4. Whenever I see John, he is always reading a book.
5. Matt will be visiting friends all over the country during the summer.
6. Denise was thinking about a solution to her problem, so I didn't interrupt her.
7. Charley was living with his cousin for a while.
8. Are you having trouble with this assignment?
9. Our teacher will be staying at the Bates Motel during the conference.
10. I am trying to explain this, so please pay attention.

## EXERCISE 4

Decide whether simple or progressive aspect should be used in these sentences. Both choices may be correct.

1. Please turn down the radio. I _____ (study) for a test.
2. Peter _____ (read) the newspaper when the phone rang.
3. I'm afraid those demonstrators might (a) _____ (get) in trouble with the police because they (b) _____ (march) without official permission.
4. Bambang still _____ (not study) as much as his parents want him to.
5. Rebecca _____ (speak) Russian. I wonder where she learned it?
6. Columbus (a) _____ (look) for a shorter route to Asia when he (b) _____ (discover) the New World by mistake.
7. When Columbus (a) _____ (reach) Cuba, he (b) _____ (think) it was India.
8. I _____ (try) to help you. Please listen carefully.
9. I (a) _____ (study) in the library when I (b) _____ (hear) the news about the latest suicide bombing.
10. Matt will probably _____ (sleep) if you wait until midnight to try to call him.

# FOCUS 4    Perfect Aspect

**use**

Perfect Tenses (present perfect, past perfect, and future perfect) are made by using forms of:

### *Have* + Verb (past participle usually ends in *-ed* or *-en*)

The basic meaning of the perfect aspect is this: the action described using the perfect aspect began before other action or another point in time, and it continues to have influence.

| EXAMPLES | EXPLANATIONS |
|---|---|
| | Use perfect aspect instead of simple aspect to describe actions: |
| (a) Peter **had finished** the project when Denise **talked** to him. (The project was finished before she talked to him.)<br>(b) Peter **finished** the project after Denise **talked** to him. (She talked to him first, and then he finished the project.) | • that happen before another action |
| (c) He has a report to present tomorrow. He **has reviewed** the figures, but he **hasn't prepared** the PowerPoint presentation yet. | • that focus on whether they are completed or uncompleted |
| (d) I **have finished** my work so now I'm watching TV.<br>(e) I **have** just **had** a snack, so I don't want any dinner. | • that are related to the present moment |
| (f) Robert Lee **has worked** in a factory for thirty-five years. (He still works there.)<br>(g) Robert Lee **worked** in a factory for thirty-five years. (He doesn't work there anymore.) | • that began in the past but still continue now |

## EXERCISE 5

Why is perfect aspect used in these sentences? There may be more than one reason.

1. Please don't take my plate. I haven't finished my dessert.
2. You are too late; the doctor has just left the office.
3. He had forgotten to leave a key, so we couldn't get into the office.
4. She will already have left before you receive her farewell letter.
5. I've done my homework for tomorrow.
6. Biff hadn't even finished high school when he joined the Army.
7. The teacher has canceled the grammar test, so we won't need to study tonight.
8. It has rained every January for the last ten years, so I don't think it's a good idea to plan a picnic.

## EXERCISE 6

Decide whether perfect or simple aspect should be used in these sentences.

1. John _____ (say) goodbye to his classmates at school when he started packing for his trip.
2. Jonas Salk _____ (conduct) many unsuccessful experiments when his efforts finally resulted in the discovery of a vaccine for polio.
3. The United States _____ (have) the same form of government for more than two hundred years.
4. Bob _____ (visit) Mexico five times so far. He really likes traveling there.
5. When Bambang (a) _____ (come) to the United States, he (b) _____ (not be) away from his parents for more than a few days.
6. By the time Roberta Chong-Davis is 50 years old, she will probably _____ (travel) to the moon several times.
7. I _____ (not sleep) well since those noisy people moved into the apartment next door.
8. Columbus (a) _____ (complete) three voyages to islands in the Caribbean when he (b) _____ (realize) that the islands (c) _____ (not be) part of India.
9. We _____ (live) in this house since 1986.
10. Victor _____ (study) very hard for the TOEFL* test, so I hope he does well!

*TOEFL is a registered trademark of the Educational Testing Service (ETS). This publication is not endorsed or approved by ETS.

## Perfect Progressive Aspect

use

Perfect progressive tenses (present perfect progressive, past perfect progressive, and future perfect progressive) are made by using forms of:

*Have + Been + Verb + -ing*

| EXAMPLES | EXPLANATIONS |
|---|---|
| | Use perfect progressive aspect instead of perfect aspect to describe: |
| (a) Peter **has been working** on that project all day. He still hasn't finished it. | • actions that are uncompleted (a) instead of completed (b) |
| (b) Peter **has worked** on that project for three hours. Now he can do something else. | |
| (c) You **have been talking** for the last hour. Please give someone else a chance to use the phone. | • actions that are continuous (c) instead of repeated (d) |
| (d) Denise **has talked** to Peter several times about his lack of effort. | |

### EXERCISE 7

Decide whether perfect or perfect progressive aspect should be used in these sentences. More than one answer may be correct.

1. It _has been raining_ (rain) ever since we got here. I wish it would stop!

2. Matt _had worked_ (work) on that computer virus for nearly a year before he realized that nothing could destroy it.

3. I'm very pleased. I _have found_ (find) the picture you mentioned in the newspaper.

4. Lately John _has found_ (find) life without Mary more and more difficult.

5. Gladstone _has been cooking_ (cook) all afternoon. I hope the food will be as delicious as it smells.

6. Jeff (a) _has been looking_ (look) for his car keys for over an hour, when he realized that he (b) _had left_ (leave) them in the car.

7. I _have been trying_ (try) to solve the problem for over an hour. I give up!

8. Next January 31, Jeff and Matt _has been living_ (live) together as roommates for five years.

9. The protesters (a) _had come_ (come) to city hall once a year ever since I (b) _have come_ (move) here.

10. I _have been trying_ (try) to reach him several times by phone, without success.

## EXERCISE 8

Write the appropriate form for the verbs in the following paragraph. The first three have been done for you as examples.

My roommate Charley (1) ____had____ (have) a dance party last Friday night. I (2) __was working__ (work) that Friday night, so I (3) ___didn't get___ (not get) home until 10:00. By the time I (4) ____got____ (get) there, everyone (5) __had started__ (start) dancing. When I (6) ___walked___ (walk) into the room, everybody (7) ___shouted___ (shout) "Welcome home!" because I (8) __just arrived__ (just arrive), and they (9) __was keeping__ (keep) dancing. I (10) ____went____ (go) into the kitchen to find something to eat. There (11) ____were____ (be) several other people in the kitchen. They (12) ____sit____ (sit) by an open window. We (13) __were talking__ (talk) and (14) ___laughing___ (laugh) for a while. Just when I (15) __had been__ (be) ready to start dancing myself, there (16) ____was____ (be) a knock at the door. I (17) ____went____ (go) to answer it and (18) __discovered__ (discover) our neighbor, who (19) __was complaining__ (complain) about the noise. He (20) ____asked____ (ask) us to turn the music down. We (21) ___obeyed___ (obey), of course. And although the party (22) ____got____ (get) a little quieter, we still (23) ____had____ (have) fun.

## EXERCISE 9

Rewrite the paragraph in Exercise 8 in a present time frame. Keep the time relations between the verbs the same by maintaining the same aspect differences as in the paragraph in Exercise 8.

My roommate Charley (1) ____has____ (have) a dance party every Friday night. I (2) __am working__ (work) Friday night these days, so I (3) ___don't get___ (not get) home until 10:00. On most Fridays, by the time I (4) ____get____ (get) there, everyone (5) __has started__ (start) dancing. When I (6) ___walk___ (walk) into the room everybody (7) ___shouts___ (shout) "Welcome home!" because I (8) __have just arrived__ (just arrive), and they (9) ____keep____ (keep) dancing. I generally (10) ____go____ (go) into the kitchen to find something to eat. Usually, there (11) ____are____ (be) several other people in the kitchen. They (12) __are sitting__ (sit) by an open window. We (13) ____talk____ (talk) and (14) ____laugh____ (laugh) for a while. Just when I (15) ____am____ (be) ready to start dancing myself, there (16) ____is____ (be) almost always a knock at the door. I (17) ____go____ (go) to answer it, and (18) __discover__ (discover) our neighbor, who (19) __complains__ (complain) about the noise. He (20) ____asks____ (ask) us to turn the music down. We (21) ____obey____ (obey), of course. And although the party (22) ____get____ (get) a little quieter, we generally still (23) ____have____ (have) fun.

## EXERCISE 10

Rewrite the paragraph in Exercise 8 in a future time frame. Keep the time relations between the verbs the same by maintaining the same aspect differences as in the paragraph in Exercise 8.

My roommate Charley (1) _is going to have_ (have) a dance party next Friday night. He has done this so often that I think I know exactly what's going to happen. I (2) _will be working_ (work) next Friday night, so I (3) _won't get_ (not get) home until 10:00. By the time I (4) _will get_ (get) there, I'm sure that everyone (5) _will have started_ (start) dancing already. When I (6) _will walk_ (walk) into the room everybody (7) _will shout_ (shout) "Welcome home!" because I (8) _will have just arrived_ (just arrive), but they probably (9) _will keep_ (keep) dancing. I probably (10) _will go_ (go) into the kitchen to find something to eat, and undoubtedly there (11) _will be_ (be) several other people in the kitchen. They (12) _will sit_ (sit) by an open window. If next Friday is like most of these parties, we (13) _will talk_ (talk) and (14) _laugh_ (laugh) for a while, and just when I (15) _will be_ (be) ready to start dancing myself, there most likely (16) _will be_ (be) a knock at the door. I (17) _will go_ (go) to answer it, and (18) _will discover_ (discover) our neighbor. He (19) _will compl_ (complain) about the noise, and (20) _will ask_ (ask) us to turn the music down. We (21) _will obey_ (obey), of course. Although the party (22) _will get_ (get) a little quieter, we undoubtedly still (23) _will have_ (have) fun.

## EXERCISE 11

Work with a partner. Compare the tenses you used in Exercises 8, 9, and 10. Did you use the same aspect for each verb in all three exercises? What does this tell you about how tenses work together in a particular time frame? Discuss these questions with your partner, and report your ideas to the rest of the class.

## EXERCISE 12

Talk about your own life. Complete these sentences with true information about yourself. Compare your answers with other students. Did you all use the same verb forms?

1. Until I came to this country, I . . .

2. I often think about my problems when . . .

3. I had never seen . . . before I . . .

4. The next time I see my family they . . .

5. I am usually unhappy if . . .

6. When I was growing up, I . . .

7. I have been studying English since I . . .

8. Lately, I . . .

9. Once I have completed my education, I . . .

10. I have never . . . but I plan to do it someday.

# Use Your English

Listen to the following conversations and put a check next to any statements that can be correctly inferred from each conversation.

CD Tracks
2, 3, 4, 5

## Conversation 1

—— (a) Mary doesn't want a roommate.

—— (b) Mary doesn't have a roommate at the moment, but she's looking for one.

—— (c) John doesn't want a roommate.

—— (d) John doesn't have a roommate at the moment, but he's looking for one.

## Conversation 2

—— (a) Peter is looking the contract over at this moment.

—— (b) Peter is not looking the contract over at this moment.

—— (c) Denise is looking the contract over at this moment.

—— (d) Denise is not looking the contract over at this moment.

## Conversation 3

—— (a) The janitor finished washing the floors before Angela's arrival.

—— (b) He finished washing the floors after Angela's arrival.

—— (c) The janitor emptied the trash before Angela's arrival.

—— (d) He emptied the trash after Angela's arrival.

—— (e) The janitor finished the windows before Angela's arrival.

—— (f) He finished the windows after Angela's arrival.

## Conversation 4

—— (a) Bob works at the steel mill now.

—— (b) Bob doesn't work at the steel mill now.

—— (c) Dave works at the steel mill now.

—— (d) Dave doesn't work at the steel mill now.

**ACTIVITY 2** writing

Revise your descriptions of the photographs in the Opening Task on pages 12 and 13 by using the past time frame. Start your descriptions like this: *When this picture was taken . . .*

**ACTIVITY 3** reading

Look at the front page of a newspaper. Find three examples of each of the three time frames (present, past, and future). They may be in the same article or three different articles.

**ACTIVITY 4** speaking

Bring in three interesting photographs from a newspaper or magazine. Make a brief presentation about these photos to the class. Describe what is happening, what has happened, and what is going to happen. Then give three reasons why you think the photo is interesting.

## ACTIVITY 5    writing/speaking

Describe a routine that you typically follow. Then describe one time when you did not follow that routine, and tell what happened. For example, perhaps you usually take the bus to school. What time do you get there? What are people on the bus doing when you get on? What happened on the day when you decided to walk to school because the bus was late, or on the day when your classmate offered to take you for a ride in his cousin's brand-new car?

## ACTIVITY 6    research on the web

Do a keyword search in *InfoTrac® College Edition* under "protestors" and pick a recent article that seems interesting. Prepare a brief report on the protestors:

- What were they protesting?
- What actions did they take?
- Did the police become involved?
- Were arrests made?
- What had the protestors been doing that caused their arrest?

Prepare a brief presentation for the class, or write a short description of the protest, its causes and consequences.

## ACTIVITY 7    language strategy

How are you progressing in English? In your notebook, create a 3-column chart, with sections for your accomplishments, goals, and strategies. Using the steps listed below, fill in the chart.

| ACCOMPLISHMENTS | GOALS | STRATEGIES |
|---|---|---|
| 1. | 1. | 1. |
| 2. | 2. | 2. |
| 3. | 3. | 3. |

**STEP 1**

Describe how your ability to communicate in English has changed since you began your studies. What kinds of things were you able to accomplish a year ago, and what can you do now that is different?

**Examples:**

1. *A year ago, I couldn't understand spoken English very well. My listening comprehension has improved a lot. I understand most things people say to me.*
2. *A year ago I needed to use a dictionary for almost every word. Now my vocabulary is much larger.*

Think of three areas where your skills have improved. Write sentences describing those things under the column marked Accomplishments in your chart.

**STEP 2**

Next, describe some things that you still can't do, but you want to be able to do. Think of at least three things you can't or don't do now, but want to be able to do by the end of this course.

**Examples:**

1. *I don't talk to my friends on the telephone because I have a hard time understanding them. I want to be able to talk on the telephone.*
2. *I can't do well on the TOEFL test. My scores on Part 2 are a little low. I want to get a good score on the TOEFL.*

Write sentences describing those skills under the column marked Goals.

**STEP 3**

Compare your accomplishments and goals to those of other people in the class. As a group, think of three strategies for increasing your language abilities and achieving your goals, and write them under the column marked Strategies. Present your list of strategies to the rest of the class.

# ADVERBIAL PHRASES AND CLAUSES

## UNIT GOALS

- Identify phrases and clauses

- Correctly position adverbs

- Correctly position adverbial phrases and clauses

## OPENING TASK

### Who? What? Which? Where? When? Why? How?

■ **STEP 1**

Newspaper reporters say that all basic news information about people and events can be summarized by asking and answering only the seven "Universal Questions" (Who? What? Which? Where? When? Why? How?). Summarize the following newspaper article by writing *Wh*-questions. Write as many questions as you need to in order to summarize all the important information.

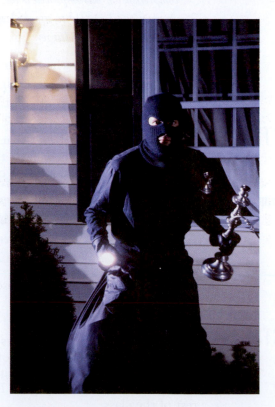

## Ski Mask Bank Robber Strikes Again

VANCOVER, BC— Columbia Savings and Loan was struck by a bank robber for the third time this year. An unidentified man in a blue ski mask entered the bank during the busiest time of the day and demanded money from the cashier.

Although three security officers were on duty, the thief was able to escape on foot. Bank officials estimate total losses of over ten thousand dollars. Police have been interviewing witnesses in hopes of getting a more complete description of the thief.

Similar robberies in other parts of the city have led police to suspect that the same person might be responsible for all three robberies. Authorities are concerned about the fact that robberies have increased a great deal in the last three months. As a result, bank officials say, they will begin to install metal detectors in order to prevent people from entering banks with guns.

## ■ STEP 2

Give your questions to a partner. Your partner should try to reconstruct the article by writing answers to your questions. Do the same with your partner's list of questions.

## ■ STEP 3

Compare your partner's answers with your questions and with the article. Your partner should do the same with your answers. Is any important information missing from your answers? Was there anything that you did not know how to ask about? Were there questions that you could not answer?

## FOCUS 1 | Identifying Phrases and Clauses

**form**

Phrases are groups of related words.

| EXAMPLES | EXPLANATIONS |
|---|---|
| (a) **An unidentified man** in a blue ski mask has been robbing **city banks** for several months. | **Noun phrases:** noun + determiner and modifiers *Who, whom,* and *what* ask about noun phrases. |
| (b) An unidentified man in a blue ski mask **has been robbing** city banks for several months. | **Verb phrases:** auxiliaries + verb *What . . . do . . .* asks about verb phrases. |
| (c) An unidentified man **in a blue ski mask** has been robbing city banks for several months. | **Prepositional phrases:** preposition + noun phrase **Adjective prepositional phrases** give more information about nouns. *Which* asks about adjective phrases. |
| (d) An unidentified man in a blue ski mask has been robbing city banks **for several months.** | **Adverbial prepositional phrases** give more information about verbs. *Where, when, how, why, how long, how often,* and *how much* ask about adverbial phrases. |

Clauses are groups of related words that contain both a subject and a verb.

| EXAMPLES | EXPLANATIONS |
|---|---|
| (e) **A man robbed the bank.** | **Independent clauses** can function as sentences. |
| (f) Have you heard **that a man robbed the bank?** | **Dependent clauses** cannot function as sentences. |
| (g) A man robbed the bank **that we visited yesterday.** | **Adjective clauses** (also called relative clauses) give more information about noun phrases. |
| (h) A man robbed the bank **before the police could arrive to catch him.** | **Adverbial clauses** give more information about verb phrases. |

The following chart shows how different kinds of *Wh*-questions focus on different parts of the sentences and can be answered with either phrases or clauses.

| | **WH-QUESTIONS** | **PHRASES** | **CLAUSES** |
|---|---|---|---|
| Who/Whom | **Who** reported the crime to the police? | **The security manager** did. | **Whoever is responsible for security** reported it. |
| | **Who(m)** did the police arrest? | They arrested **the old man**. | They arrested the man **who they found hiding in the alley**. |
| What | **What** have you told the reporters? | I told them my **experience**. | I told them **that the investigation is still not finished**. |
| What . . . do | **What did** the police **do**? | They **tried to catch the thief**. | They hoped **that they would find the criminal**. |
| Which | **Which teller** was robbed? | It was the teller **with the blonde hair**. | The teller **who was interviewed by the police** was. |
| Where | **Where** did the thief go? | He went **down the street, towards the park**. | The thief went **where the police couldn't find him**. |
| When | **When** did they finish the investigation? | They finished it **on Tuesday at 3:00**. | They finished it **when they had collected all the evidence**. |
| How | **How** did the thief get away? | He got away **on foot**. | The thief disappeared **as if he had become invisible**. |
| How _____ | **How busy** was the bank yesterday? | It was **busier than usual**. | It was **so busy that nobody noticed the thief**. |
| How long | **How long** has that officer been on the police force? | He's been a policeman **for a long time**. | He has been a policeman **since he first moved to the city**. |
| How often | **How often** has this bank been robbed? | It's been robbed **from time to time**. | It's been robbed **as often as any other bank has been robbed**. |
| How much | **How much** money did the thief take? | He took **too much to count**. | He took **so much that they haven't determined the entire amount**. |
| Why | **Why** did you go to the bank? | I went **for some money**. | I went to the bank **because I needed money**. |
| | | I went to the bank **to cash a check**. | I went to the bank **so that I could cash a check**. |

## EXERCISE 1

There is a popular American TV quiz show called *Jeopardy*. Contestants are given answers, and they must provide a question for each answer. Play *Jeopardy* with a partner. Here are some answers. For each answer, decide what form it is (phrase or clause) and make up a suitable question.

**Examples:**    Answer 1: *by studying (phrase):*

Question 1: *How can I get a good score on the TOEFL® Test*?*

Answer 2: *once I get a good score on the TOEFL Test (clause):*

Question 2: *When will you begin your university studies?*

1. the president
2. He went to the movies.
3. I am.
4. in 2004
5. at noon
6. from Japan
7. for fun
8. after I finish school
9. because he needs money
10. because of the TOEFL test
11. by practicing
12. My sister can.
13. in order to learn English
14. to find a good job
15. the old man
16. until he passes the TOEFL test
17. to my brother
18. a book and a pen
19. too expensive
20. as long as I am a student
21. so he can buy books

## EXERCISE 2

Each of these sentences consists of two or more clauses. Put brackets around each clause, as shown in the example.

**Example:**    [Although John is a little homesick], [he still plans to stay in France for at least a year].

1. Matt likes to get up early most days, but he prefers to sleep late on weekends.

2. Denise has a lot of work that has to get done, so she won't consider taking a vacation.

3. Because they feel war is too destructive, many people are opposed to military solutions for international problems.

4. I once met a man who looked just like a friend of mine.

5. John is looking for an additional job that he can do in his spare time because he needs some extra money.

6. I know an old lady who swallowed a fly.

7. Although I have many friends, I still enjoy meeting people that I've never met before.

8. Last night after dinner Peter wrote to an old friend who(m) he went to school with.

*TOEFL is a registered trademark of the Educational Testing Service (ETS). This publication is not endorsed or approved by ETS.

## FOCUS 2 — Basic Adverbial Position

Adverbials are words, phrases, and clauses that answer questions like *how, how often, how much, where, when,* and *why.*

| EXAMPLES | EXPLANATIONS |
|---|---|
| (a) Biff **never** goes **downtown anymore.** | adverbs |
| (b) Biff exercises **as often as possible** at the **gym on Saturdays.** | adverbial phrases |
| (c) Biff works out **because he wants to improve his physique.** | adverbial clauses |

Most adverbial information follows the verb phrase (verb + object) and usually appears in a basic order (some other variations are possible).

| VERB PHRASE | MANNER | PLACE | FREQUENCY | TIME | PURPOSE OR REASON |
|---|---|---|---|---|---|
| what . . . do | how | where | how often | when | why |
| (d) *Biff lifts weights* | *vigorously* | *at the gym* | *every day* | *after work* | *to fight stress.* |

Some adverbs can come before the verb or between the auxiliary and the main verb.

| EXAMPLES | EXPLANATIONS |
|---|---|
| (e) Gladstone **often** goes on strange diets<br>(f) He has **never** lost more than a few pounds. | **Adverbs of frequency:**<br>affirmative: *always, often, usually, sometimes*<br>negative: *seldom, rarely, hardly ever, never* |
| (g) He has **rigorously** avoided sweets for more than a year. | **Adverbs of manner:**<br>*rigorously, quickly, completely,* etc. |
| (h) He **recently** lost fifty pounds. | **Indefinite adverbs of time:**<br>*recently, typically, previously, finally,* etc. |

Read the following passage then follow these directions:

1. Circle the verb in every sentence.

2. Underline the adverbs, adverbial phrases, and adverbial clauses.

3. Decide whether the meaning of each adverbial is frequency, manner, place, time, or reason/purpose.

The first paragraph has been done for you as an example.

Biff Bicep                    Gladstone Gulp

frequency

manner

Biff Bicep and Gladstone Gulp are close friends. (1) They (are) always (trying) to change the way they look because neither one is very pleased with his appearance, (2) but they do it differently.

Biff Bicep is a serious body-builder. (3) He tries to increase the size of his muscles by lifting weights at a gym near his house. (4) He usually goes there at the same time every day. (5) He drinks special vitamin supplements to gain weight and (6) works out vigorously twice a day—in the morning and in the afternoon. (7) He usually starts out on an exercise bike to warm up his muscles. Then he moves on to his exercises. (8) He exercises his upper body on Mondays, Wednesdays, and Fridays. (9) On Tuesdays, Thursdays, and Saturdays, he does exercises to develop the muscles of his lower body. (10) He never works out on Sundays, so his muscles can have a chance to rest.

Gladstone Gulp is a serious dieter. (11) He always seems to be trying to lose weight by going on special weight-reducing diets whenever he feels too heavy. (12) He usually drinks a special diet drink at breakfast and lunch. (13) Sometimes he doesn't eat anything after breakfast in order to save a few calories. (14) He also tries not to snack in between meals. (15) As a result, he is usually really hungry when he gets home, and (16) so he often goes directly to the kitchen to find something to eat. Although he is a serious dieter, he's not a terribly successful one. (17) He has never permanently lost more than a few pounds. (18) He's always looking for a magic way to lose weight without having to diet or exercise.

## EXERCISE 4

Add the adverbials in parentheses to each sentence. There may be more than one possible position.

**Example:** He gains back the lost weight. (quickly) (usually)

He usually gains the lost weight back quickly.

Usually he quickly gains back the lost weight.

1. Gladstone Gulp goes on a new diet. (because he feels heavy) (every few months)

2. He uses diet pills. (to increase his metabolism) (regularly)

3. He rides an exercise bicycle. (occasionally) (to use up calories) (very hard)

4. He trades diet plans. (with his friend Biff) (sometimes)

5. He reads about every new diet. (in magazines) (carefully) (whenever he can)

6. He doesn't follow their directions. (carefully) (always)

7. He drinks a special vitamin supplement. (usually) (to make sure he gets proper nutrition)

## EXERCISE 5

Interview a classmate and find out something that he or she does:

1. every day
2. for his or her health
3. very well
4. before bedtime
5. outdoors
6. occasionally
7. better than anyone else in his or her family
8. automatically
9. with considerable difficulty
10. after class

Write complete sentences about these activities and report them to the class.

## FOCUS 3  Position and Order of Adverbial Phrases

When there is more than one adverbial phrase in a clause, the order usually follows these guidelines.

| EXAMPLES | EXPLANATIONS |
|---|---|
| (a) AWKWARD: He exercises vigorously at the gym **every Monday, Wednesday, and Friday after work.** <br><br> (b) BETTER: He exercises vigorously at the gym **after work every Monday, Wednesday, and Friday.** | Shorter adverbial phrases usually come before longer adverbial phrases. Since the frequency phrase is long, it is better to have it follow the time phrase. |
| (c) Many people frequently eat dinner **in neighborhood restaurants in Toronto.** <br><br> (d) NOT: Many people frequently eat dinner **in Toronto in neighborhood restaurants.** | When there are two adverbial phrases of the same kind (place, time, etc.), the more specific adverbial phrase always comes first. |
| (e) AWKWARD: He washes his car **carefully in the driveway with a special soap once a week.** <br><br> (f) BETTER: **Once a week,** he **carefully** washes his car **in the driveway with a special soap.** | It is not common to have more than two or three adverbials after the verb phrase. If there are several adverbials, then one is usually moved to the beginning of the sentence. |

## ◼ EXERCISE 6

Identify the meaning (*place, frequency, reason, time, etc.*) and form (*adverb, adverb phrase, adverbial clause*) of the underlined adverbials in the numbered sentences in the article on the next page. Tell why you think they appear in the order that they do. There may be several possible reasons, so discuss your ideas with a partner. The first one has been done for you as an example.

**Example:** (a) manner, adverb, (b) place, adverbial prepositional phrase, (c) time, adverbial clause, (d) time, adverbial phrase.

  **Reasons:** adverbials follow general manner, place, and time order.

# Bizarre Attack by Wild Pigs on Rampage

*Buttonwillow, GA*—Mary Morris is a lucky woman tonight. (1) She is resting (a) <u>comfortably</u> (b) <u>at her Buttonwillow home</u> (c) <u>after doctors released her from Button-willow Hospital</u> (d) <u>earlier this afternoon.</u> Early this morning she was involved in one of the strangest automobile accidents in local history. Her car was attacked by a herd of wild pigs.

(2) "I was driving (a) <u>on a dirt road</u> (b) <u>along the river,</u> (c) <u>just like I always do,</u>" she told reporters in an impromptu news conference at the hospital, (d) <u>"when I hit a muddy patch of road.</u> I got out of the car to try to push it out of the mud. (3) (a) <u>While I was doing that</u> a herd of pigs (b) <u>suddenly</u> came (c) <u>out of the bushes</u> (d) <u>to attack me.</u> There were so many of them that I was completely surrounded, but I was able to get back into the car. (4) I (a) <u>finally</u> scared them (b) <u>back into the bushes</u> (c) <u>by blowing the horn.</u> (5) Then I sat (a) <u>there</u> (b) <u>for several hours</u> (c) <u>before I felt safe enough to leave the car</u> and (d) <u>could look for some help.</u>" Ms. Morris was treated for gashes on her legs and shock. She was given a tetanus shot, and released later in the day.

Scientists are a little puzzled as to why the pigs might have attacked in the first place. Animal psychologist Dr. Lassie Kumholm suggested that it may have been because one of the females in the herd could have just given birth near where the car got stuck. (6) (a) <u>Sometimes</u> pigs can (b) <u>suddenly</u> become aggressive (c) <u>quite quickly</u> (d) <u>if their young are threatened.</u> This herd of pigs is a well-known nuisance. (7) They have (a) <u>repeatedly</u> caused minor damage (b) <u>in the area</u> (c) <u>for the last several years,</u> but this is the first time they have been known to actually attack humans. (8) (a) <u>On several occasions</u> local property owners have sent petitions (b) <u>to county offices</u> (c) <u>to complain about the problem.</u>

## Putting Adverbial Phrases at the Beginning of a Sentence

form

use

| EXAMPLES | EXPLANATIONS |
|---|---|
| | Most adverbials can also appear at the beginning of a clause or sentence for the following reasons. |
| (a) **Once a week**, Jeff carefully washes his car in the driveway with a special soap. | • if there are several other adverbs or adverbial phrases, or if the object of the verb phrase is very long |
| (b) **In the suitcase**, Matt found an extra wool sweater that had been knitted by his grandmother. | |
| (c) NOT: Matt found an extra wool sweater that had been knitted by his grandmother **in the suitcase**. | |
| (d) **Carefully and slowly**, Jeff carried the heavy tray of fragile glasses to the table. | • in order to emphasize adverbial information |
| (e) Matt and Jeff have a beautiful apartment. **Along one wall**, there are big windows with a marvelous view. | • to show logical relationships between sentences. |
| (f) Matt was born in 1965. **In 1988**, he moved to San Francisco. | |
| (g) John became quite fluent in French. **As a result**, he was able to get a job with a company that exports computer parts to West Africa. | |

Most adverbials can be placed at the beginning of the sentence without making other changes in word order, but some require a question word order when they are put at the beginning of the sentence.

| EXAMPLES | EXPLANATIONS |
|---|---|
| **Normal Position:** | • negative adverbs of frequency (*never, seldom, rarely*) |
| (h) Gladstone **seldom loses** more than a few pounds. | |
| **Emphatic Position:** | |
| (i) **Seldom does** Gladstone **lose** more than a few pounds. | |

Make these sentences more emphatic by moving the adverbial to the beginning of the sentence. Be sure to change the word order if necessary.

1. I have rarely seen such a mess.
2. Gladstone is often so hungry that he eats an entire cake.
3. He usually doesn't lose control.
4. We will never finish this project.
5. Steve seldom feels unhappy for very long.
6. Denise printed out the letter of complaint quickly and efficiently and sent it special delivery to Mr. Green.

## FOCUS 5 — Position of Adverbial Clauses

use

Most adverbial clauses appear after the main clause, but many can also come before the main clause.

| EXAMPLES | EXPLANATIONS |
| --- | --- |
| (a) **As if it were the easiest thing in the world**, Biff did a triple backflip and ended with a handstand. <br><br> (b) **As soon as John got to the airport**, he began to have second thoughts about going to France. | • to emphasize the adverbial clause |
| (c) **Until Jeff moved to San Francisco**, he had never seen the ocean. He had never been to a disco or eaten Chinese food. He had never even fallen in love. <br><br> (d) **Whenever John thought about Mary**, he began to feel guilty. He would imagine her sitting sadly at home alone, writing him long letters. He felt that he wasn't missing her as much as she was missing him. | • to establish a context that applies to several sentences |
| (e) I usually read the paper **before** I take a shower. <br><br> (f) **After** I read the paper, I usually take a shower. <br><br> (g) **If** you wash the dishes, **then** I'll dry them and put them away. | • to show sequence <br><br><br><br><br><br> *(Chart continued on next page)* |

Certain adverbial clauses almost always appear after the main clause.

| EXAMPLES | EXPLANATIONS |
|---|---|
| (h) Matt works out **where** Biff works out.<br>(i) AWKWARD: **Where** Biff works out, Jeff works out.<br>(j) **Wherever** he goes, Matt makes new friends and has wonderful adventures. | • adverbial clauses of place except those that begin with *wherever* or *everywhere* |
| (k) John worked all summer **so (that)** he would have enough money to study in France.<br>(l) AWKWARD: So that he would have enough money to study in France, John worked all summer. | • adverbial clauses of result with *so that* |
| (m) Matt visited his grandmother **for he knew she had been sick.**<br>(n) NOT: **For he knew she had been sick,** Matt visited his grandmother. | • adverbial clauses of reason with *for* |

Punctuation of adverbial clauses depends on their position in a sentence.

| EXAMPLES | EXPLANATIONS |
|---|---|
| (o) **After I took the examination,** I ate lunch.<br>(p) I ate lunch **after I took the examination.** | Adverbial clauses before the main clause are followed by a comma. No extra punctuation is necessary if they appear after the main clause. |
| (q) **Since you don't have much money,** I'll pay for dinner.<br>(r) I'll pay for dinner **since you don't have much money.** | |

Work with a partner to answer these questions about the sentences below. The first sentence has been done as an example.

a.   Does the adverbial clause in these sentences appear before or after the main clause?

b.   Decide which of the reasons listed in Focus 5 can be used to explain why the author chose to put the adverbial clauses in this order.

1.  Because Biff enjoys vigorous exercise, he tends to pursue sports that build up his muscles.

    a. _before_____     b. _to emphasize the adverbial clause_____

2.  On the other hand, Gladstone practices exercises like yoga because for him exercise is a means of relaxation.

    a. _after_____     b. _to show sequence_____

3.  Both Biff and Gladstone want to lose weight because they want to feel and look better.

    a. _after_____     b. _____

4.  Because Mary Morris may have stopped her car too close to a newborn piglet, she became the victim of a bizarre attack.

    a. _before_____     b. _to emphasize the adverbial clause_____

5.  When the ski-mask robber entered the bank, he showed the teller a gun and demanded money.

    a. _before_____     b. _emphase_____

6.  Columbia Savings and Loan had already been robbed three times when the ski-mask robber appeared yesterday.

    a. _after_____     b. _____

7.  The bank manager told the press about the robbery so that the public would become aware of the need for more security.

    a. _aft_____     b. _____

8.  Since he first agreed to work on the project in 1985, he has spent more than twenty years trying to educate people about global warming.

    a. _be_____     b. _____

# Use Your English

## ACTIVITY  1 speaking/writing

### ■ STEP 1

Find out some basic information about another student in the class by asking some of the seven "Universal Questions" that were described in the Opening Task. Here are some suggested topics.

| | |
|---|---|
| Who: | name, family background |
| What: | hobbies, special interests, plans for the future |
| Where: | home town, current living situation |
| When: | date of birth, date of arrival in this country, date of expected completion of English studies |
| How Long: | length of time in this country, amount of previous English study |
| How Often: | regular activities, hobbies |
| How Much: | special skills, abilities, and interests |
| Why: | reasons and goals for studying English, joining this class, leaving home |

### ■ STEP 2

Report the information to the rest of the class in a short written paragraph or oral presentation.

## ACTIVITY 2 speaking

An "ulterior motive" is a hidden reason for doing a good thing. For example, helping a friend who is in trouble is a good thing to do, but if your real reason for doing it is because you want that person to lend you money later, your motive may make your action a bad one.

### ■ STEP 1

In a small group discuss the following situations. For each situation identify some "pure motives"—reasons for doing the action that would make it a good or generous act—and some "ulterior motives"—hidden reasons that would make the act a selfish one.

- loaning someone money
- not telling a friend some bad news
- being friendly and obedient to a rich relative
- working harder than anyone else at your job

### ■ STEP 2

Based on your discussion decide whether people's actions should be judged by what they do (their actions) or why they do it (their motivations). Present your opinion and your reasons to the rest of the class.

**ACTIVITY 3** writing/speaking

Which form of motivation is more common in your day-to-day activities: extrinsic motivation or intrinsic motivation?

| *Extrinsic motivation* is **purpose**. You do something in order to achieve something else, such as studying business in order to get a high-paying job in the future. | *Intrinsic motivation* is **cause**. You do something because you like the activity itself, such as studying business because you love being a student and enjoy economic theory. |
| --- | --- |

■ **STEP 1**   Decide whether your basic motivation for each of the activities listed below is extrinsic or intrinsic. Identify additional things you do because of intrinsic motivation. Make a four column chart in your notebook. In the first column in your chart, write three things you do because of intrinsic motivation.

| | | |
| --- | --- | --- |
| studying English | watching TV | cleaning the house |
| driving a car | reading newspapers | doing homework |
| cooking | exercise | shopping |

■ **STEP 2**   Interview three other students in the class to find out things they do because of intrinsic motivation. Write the information in the chart in your notebook. Use one column for each student.

■ **STEP 3**   Form a group with two or three other students whom you did not interview, and compare all the information you have gathered. As a group, decide on answers to the following question and present your ideas to the rest of the class.

What are the three most common characteristics shared by all things that people do because of intrinsic motivation? For example, do intrinsically motivated activities result in self-improvement? Are they pleasurable? Do people feel unhappy if they don't have an opportunity to pursue these activities?

# ACTIVITY 4 — listening

CD Tracks 6, 7

■ **STEP 1**  Listen to the two recorded news broadcasts. Based on what you hear write as many questions as you can with *Who, What, Where, When Why* and *How* about each broadcast and give them to a partner to answer. You may need to listen to the broadcasts more than once in order to ask and answer the questions.

■ **STEP 2**  Compare your questions and answers with those of another pair of students. As a group try to write a summary of one of the news stories.

# ACTIVITY 5 — speaking

The world seems to be divided into two kinds of people: morning people (who do their best work early in the day) and night people (who are sleepy in the morning, and are most productive in the late afternoon or even late at night). Which kind are you? Interview a partner to find out which kind of person he or she is.

■ **STEP 1**  Find out **how** your partner does each activity in the chart below at the time of day listed. (Some examples have been provided.) Ask about two additional activities.

■ **STEP 2**  Decide on whether your partner is a morning person or a night person, and report your findings to the rest of the class.

| WHEN? / WHAT? | EARLY MORNING: HOW? | AFTER LUNCH: HOW? | LATE AT NIGHT: HOW? |
|---|---|---|---|
| vigorous exercise | Slowly | Well, but not if he's hungry | Easily, but it keeps him awake |
| balancing your checkbook | | | |
| thinking up original ideas | | | |
| relaxed reading for pleasure | | | |
| concentrated reading for work or school | | | |
| social activity and conversation | | | |

## ACTIVITY 6 research on the web

Which means of weight control do you follow?  The one used by Biff Bicep or the one used by Gladstone Gulp?  Use *InfoTrac® College Edition*, to enter "diet and exercise" and scan a few articles to see which system the experts recommend for weight control.  Prepare a list of the three advantages and three disadvantages of each approach and decide which one is most appropriate for your individual personality.  Report your ideas to the rest of the class, or compare them with those of a partner.

## ACTIVITY 7 language strategy

Language teachers recommend that students keep a journal or language learning log to record their progress, goals, and questions. Studies have proven that students who do this learn more quickly and effectively. Here is one example of a language learning log format. Fill out your log at least once a week during this course.  Turn it in or discuss it with your teacher or with another student in the class.

### LANGUAGE LEARNING LOG

Section 1. MISTAKES, CORRECTIONS, AND EXPLANATIONS

Write down **five mistakes** that you made in either writing or speaking in the last week. For each mistake write the correct form. In your own words, explain what was wrong with your original sentence.

**Examples:**
Mistake: I exercise usually three times a week.
Correction: I usually exercise three times a week
Explanation: Usually must go before the verb.

Section 2. QUESTIONS

Write **three questions** you have about any aspect of grammar that you have read, heard, or studied in the last week. Your teacher will return your journal with an explanation of your questions.

**Examples:** Where do adverbial clauses usually appear?
How many adverbs can I use in a single sentence?
My friend said "Never have I seen such a mess!" Is that correct word order? Why does he use question word order?

# PASSIVE VERBS

## UNIT GOALS

- Review passive form and meaning
- Know when to include the agent
- Use *get* passives
- Choose between passive and active

## OPENING TASK

### Has the Earth Been Visited by Beings from Outer Space?

Stonehenge is a circle of giant stones. It is located far away from anything else in the middle of a plain in southern England.

The Nazca Lines are a group of huge pictures drawn in the desert of western Peru that can only be seen from an airplane.

Certain structures around the world have very mysterious origins. Many people believe that these places are clear proof that beings from other planets have visited the Earth, because no one can explain exactly how or why they were constructed.

### ■ STEP 1

Two of the most famous of these mysterious structures are Stonehenge and the Nazca Lines. Read about one of them in the chart on the next page and then answer the questions.

How were they constructed?

| STONEHENGE | THE NAZCA LINES |
|---|---|
| • The giant stones were transported from a great distance from an unknown place.<br><br>• The stones are too heavy to be lifted upright or to be placed on top of each other.<br><br>• A large number of people would probably be required to construct such a large structure, more people than were probably living in prehistoric Britain.<br><br>• The distances between the stones are very precise, accurate to the millimeter. | • The pictures can only be seen from the air. The people who built the designs could not actually see them.<br><br>• A large number of people would be required to construct such large pictures. There definitely isn't enough water for so many people there, because it is one of the driest places on earth.<br><br>• The designs are very precise. One image is a perfect spiral, accurate to the millimeter. |

Why were they constructed?

| STONEHENGE | THE NAZCA LINES |
|---|---|
| • Some stones seem to point to certain stars.<br><br>• Some stones seem to have some connection with the position of the sun at certain times of year.<br><br>• Some stones may have had some connection with human sacrifices. | • Some pictures seem to have some mathematical or geometrical meaning.<br><br>• Some pictures represent flowers and animals that are not found anywhere near the location of the lines.<br><br>• Some designs look like symbols that are used to direct modern aircraft. |

When were they constructed?

| STONEHENGE | THE NAZCA LINES |
|---|---|
| • It was already considered to be a mysterious place when Britain was occupied by the Romans in the first century BCE.<br><br>• There is no historical record of its construction. | • They weren't discovered until people started flying over the area in airplanes.<br><br>• They predate Inca civilization by at least two thousand years. |

## ■ STEP 2

Form a group consisting of one student who read about the same mysterious place as you did and two students who read about the other mysterious place. Compare your answers.

## ■ STEP 3

In your group discuss this question: Are these structures proof that the Earth has been visited by beings from some other planet? Why or why not? Share your ideas with the rest of the class.

form

## FOCUS 1 — Review of Passive Verb Forms

| EXAMPLES | EXPLANATIONS |
|---|---|
| (a) The Nazca Lines **were discovered** by airplane pilots.<br><br>(b) They **weren't discovered** until the 1930s.<br><br>(c) How **were** such huge designs **built**? | ***be* + past participle ( + *by* phrase)**<br>Form all passive verbs in the same way. Only the *be* auxiliary changes form. There is often no information about who or what performed the action, but when there is, it appears as a *by* phrase. |
| (d) Stonehenge **was** constructed of rocks that came from many miles away.<br><br>(e) The Nazca Lines **were** made by removing soil and rocks to expose the different-colored soil underneath. | **Change *be* auxiliary to indicate:**<br>• singular or plural |
| (f) Stonehenge **was** constructed long before Britain **was** invaded by the armies of Rome.<br><br>(g) The Nazca Lines **weren't** discovered until the 1930s because they **weren't** seen by people on the ground. | • affirmative or negative |
| (h) Mysterious structures **are** found in a number of places in the world.<br><br>(i) Some **were** discovered this century.<br><br>(j) Perhaps the reasons for their existence **will be** discovered with further research.<br><br>(k) Many theories explaining their existence **have been** proposed.<br><br>(l) While they **were being** built, civilization was still very young. | • time frame (*present, past, future*) and aspect (*simple, perfect, progressive*) |
| (m) The Nazca Lines **may be** destroyed, if further protection **can't be** provided.<br><br>(n) Preservation efforts for all such mysterious structures **ought to be** started without delay.<br><br>(o) Both Stonehenge and the Nazca Lines **might have been** used to predict astronomical events. | • modal information (*prediction, ability, advisability, possibility*, etc.) |

## EXERCISE 1

Find eight examples of passive verb forms in the information provided on page 47 and underline them. Decide whether each form is:

a. singular or plural

b. affirmative or negative

c. present, past, or future time frame

d. simple, perfect, or progressive aspect

## EXERCISE 2

Write the passive forms for the verbs provided below.

**Example:** construct (singular, present progressive) is being constructed

1. forget (plural, past perfect) _____

2. establish (singular, simple past) _____

3. manufacture (singular, simple present) _____

4. obtain (singular, simple present) _____

5. require (plural, simple future) _will be required_____

6. discover (plural, present perfect) _have been discovered._____

7. make (singular, present progressive) _is ~~in~~ being made._____

8. leave (plural, past perfect) _had been left_____

9. build (singular, simple past) _~~is past~~ Was built_____

10. produce (singular, simple present) _is ~~presented~~ being produced____

11. send (singular, future perfect) _will have been sent_____

12. notice (plural, past progressive) _was being noticed_____

13. need (singular, simple future) _~~is~~ will be needed_____

14. forget (plural, present perfect) _have been forgotten._____

15. study (plural, present progressive) _are being studied_____

## EXERCISE 3

Use the information provided below to construct passive sentences.

**Example:** The Chinese invented gunpowder.

Gunpowder _____was invented_____ in China.

1. Pakistanis speak Urdu, Punjabi, Sindhi, Baluchi, Pashtu, and English.

   Urdu, Punjabi, Sindhi, Baluchi, Pashtu, and English _are spoken_ in Pakistan.

2. The people of Sri Lanka have mined gems for centuries.

   For centuries gems _had been mined_ in Sri Lanka.

3. The French consider snails a great delicacy.

   Snails _are considered_ a great delicacy in France.

4. People throughout Asia eat rice.

   Rice _is eaten_ throughout Asia.

5. Argentineans consume more beef per capita than in any other country.

   More beef _is consumed_ per capita in Argentina than in any other country.

6. Ancient Egyptians worshiped cats.

   Cats _were worshiped_ in ancient Egypt.

7. The Japanese have developed a new system of high-resolution television.

   A new system of high-resolution television _have been developed_ in Japan.

8. Americans invented the games of baseball and basketball.

   The games of baseball and basketball both _were invented_ in America.

## EXERCISE 4

Working with a partner, make up five additional passive sentences about products or accomplishments of a national or cultural group that you are familiar with.

## EXERCISE 5

Choose eight verbs from Exercise 2. Make an original passive sentence for each verb.

## FOCUS 2    Passive Meaning: Agent Versus Receiver

### Agent and Receiver in Active Sentences

| SUBJECT | ACTIVE VERB | OBJECT | EXPLANATION |
|---|---|---|---|
| agent <br> (a) An employee | action <br> found | receiver <br> a wallet outside the office. | The agent is the doer of an action. The receiver is the person or thing that is affected by the action. In active sentences the agent is the subject of the sentence. The receiver is the object. |

### Agent and Receiver in Passive Sentences

| SUBJECT | PASSIVE VERB | (BY + NOUN PHRASE) | EXPLANATION |
|---|---|---|---|
| receiver <br> (b) A wallet | action <br> was found outside the office. | (agent) | In passive sentences the receiver is the subject and the agent is often not mentioned. When it is included, it occurs in a prepositional phrase with *by*. |
| (c) The wallet | was found | by an employee. | |

## EXERCISE 6

Read the article on page 52 about the Nazca Lines. Underline all the passive constructions that you find. For each example of the passive that you can find, circle the **receiver**. If the **agent** is mentioned, draw a square around it. The first sentence of each paragraph has been done as an example.

## THE MYSTERY OF THE NAZCA LINES

(1) The Nazca Lines were not discovered until the 1930s, when they were first noticed by airplane pilots flying over Peru's Atacama Desert. (2) They consist of huge pictures, several kilometers in size, that were drawn in the desert. (3) They portray such things as birds, spiders, and abstract geometrical designs. (4) These pictures were made more than three thousand years ago by removing stones and dirt over large areas to expose the differently colored soil beneath.

(5) The amazing thing about the Nazca Lines is that none of these pictures can be seen by people on the ground. (6) They are so huge that they can only be seen from a great height. (7) The pictures were constructed with amazing precision. (8) How such measurements were made still hasn't been satisfactorily explained. (9) It seems impossible that the primitive construction techniques that existed three thousand years ago could have been used to create such gigantic, perfectly constructed designs.

(10) Why were these gigantic pictures made? (11) Were they intended as gifts for the gods, as some people have suggested? (12) Or, as others believe, were they created as "direction signs" for visitors from other planets? (13) No one knows. (14) One thing is known: The reasons and methods of their construction have been destroyed by time, but the pictures have been preserved for at least two thousand—and maybe even three thousand—years!

## ■ EXERCISE 7

Write one active sentence and one passive sentence for each set of agent, receiver, and verb.

**Example:**    **Agent:** the maid; **Receiver:** the money; **Verb:** find
            **active:** The maid found the money.
            **passive:** The money was found by the maid.

1. **Agent:** pilots; **Receiver:** the Nazca Lines; **Verb:** discover

2. **Agent:** Ancient Romans; **Receiver:** Stonehenge; **Verb:** can not explain

3. **Agent:** Lee Harvey Oswald; **Receiver:** John F. Kennedy; **Verb:** assassinate

4. **Agent:** beings from outer space; **Receiver:** the Earth; **Verb:** visit

5. **Agent:** parents; **Receiver:** their children; **Verb:** teach good manners

6. **Agent:** society; **Receiver:** social minorities; **Verb:** discriminate against

## FOCUS 3 — When to Include the Agent

use

Because we most often use passive verbs to describe situations when the agent is not the primary focus, we usually do not include the agent (*by* + noun phrase) in passive sentences. However, sometimes it is necessary to include the agent.

| EXAMPLES | EXPLANATIONS |
|---|---|
| | Include the agent: |
| (a) Many important scientific discoveries have been made **by women**. | • when the agent gives us additional new information. |
| (b) Radioactivity, for example, was discovered **by Marie Curie** in 1903. | • when information about the agent is too important to omit. |
| (c) This music was written **by a computer**. <br> (d) That picture was painted **by a monkey**. | • when the agent is surprising or unexpected. |

### EXERCISE 8

Identify the agent in each of these sentences and decide if it is necessary. Correct any sentences by omitting unnecessary *by* phrases.

**Example:** That symphony was written by a composer in the nineteenth century

*Not necessary. (That symphony was written in the nineteenth century.)*

1. The Nazca Lines were constructed by an unknown civilization approximately two thousand years ago.

2. The lesson was assigned by the teacher for next week.

3. This picture was painted by Picasso when Picasso was 12 years old.

4. My briefcase was taken by someone, but it was found and turned in to the Lost and Found Office by someone in my English class.

5. Many foreign students don't need scholarships because they are being supported by friends or relatives.

6. I would never guess that these poems were translated by children.

# FOCUS 4    The *Get* Passive

## Forming the *Get* Passive

| EXAMPLES | EXPLANATIONS |
|---|---|
| (a) Matt rides to work with a neighbor who works nearby. He **gets picked up** at the bus stop every morning. | In spoken or informal English, we can use *get* instead of *be* as the passive auxiliary. |
| (b) Matt **gets dropped off** in front of his office. | |
| (c) He **should be getting picked up** in a few minutes. | |
| (d) **Did** Matt **get** picked up yesterday? | Questions and negatives require *do* if the verb phrase does not contain a form of *be* or a modal auxiliary. |
| (e) He **didn't get** dropped off at the usual place. | |
| (f) He **might not have gotten picked up** by the usual person. | |

## Using *Get* Passive Sentences

| EXAMPLES | EXPLANATIONS |
|---|---|
| (g) George W. Bush **was** elected president by the electoral college after the Supreme Court ruled in his favor in 2000. | The *get* passive is more common with animate (living) subjects, than with inanimate (nonliving) ones. |
| (h) He **got** elected even though he did not get a majority of the popular vote. | |
| (i) The hospital **was built** in the 1930s. | |
| (j) NOT: The hospital **got built** in the 1930s. | |
| (k) Mariko **got married** last Saturday. | The *get* passive emphasizes the action rather than the state. |
| (l) She **has** never **been married** before. | |

## EXERCISE 9

Decide whether *be* or *get* is more appropriate in these sentences. Sometimes either form could be correct.

**Examples:** North America _____was_____ settled by several European countries.

John's car ____got/was____ damaged, so he had to take public transportation.

1. The Nazca Lines _____was_____ discovered in the 1930s.

2. Charlie _____was_____ arrested on his way home from the football game.

3. New medicines are _____being_____ developed that seem effective in fighting cancer.

4. That's really dangerous. If your leg _____gets_____ broken, don't blame me.

5. I don't think John and Mary will ever _____got_____ married. They're too different.

6. Don't put that fish in the same aquarium with the others. It might _____be_____ eaten by the larger ones.

| FOCUS 5 | Special Cases: Verbs with No Passive Forms and Other Verbs with No Active Forms |
|---------|------------------------------------------------------------------------------|

| EXAMPLES | EXPLANATIONS |
|----------|--------------|
| (a) Few changes **have occurred** at Stonehenge over the years.<br><br>(b) The discovery of the Nazca Lines **happened** in the 1930s.<br><br>(c) Some Nazca lines **seem** to be in the shape of flowers.<br><br>(d) The purpose of the Nazca lines **has disappeared** under the sands of the Atacama Desert. | Some verbs don't have a passive form because they do not take direct objects. This category includes verbs such as:<br><br>*occur, happen, take place . . .*<br>*appear, seem, look . . .*<br>*emerge, vanish, disappear, appear . . .* |
| (e) NOT: A ceremonial function was had by these pictures.<br><br>(f) NOT: Some animals are resembled by the pictures. | Even verbs that take objects, when they describe states, do not occur in the passive. |
| (g) The drawing of the Nazca lines ⎰ began ⎱ more than 2000 years ago.<br>⎱ was begun ⎰ | Some verbs describe changes of state and can occur in the active with a passive meaning. |
| (h) Jeff **was born** in Kansas.<br><br>(i) NOT: Jeff's mother **bore** him in Kansas. | A few passive verbs do not have active forms. |
| (j) The Nazca Lines **are located** (exist) in the Atacama Desert of Peru.<br><br>(k) They **located** (found) the Atacama Desert on a map. | Some passive verbs have different meanings in passive and active. |

## EXERCISE 10

Here is a list of some verbs that do not have passive forms. Choose five verbs and write a sentence for each one. Compare your sentences with those of other students.

| appear | consist of | seem | look | occur |
|--------|-----------|------|------|-------|
| take place | resemble | happen | collide | emerge |
| disappear | vanish | | | |

| FOCUS 6 | Choosing Passive Versus Active |
| --- | --- |

use

The active voice is more common than the passive, but in some situations, the passive form should be used.

| EXAMPLES | EXPLANATIONS |
| --- | --- |
| (a) Denise's computer **was stolen** from her office. | Use passive instead of active:<br>• if the agent is unknown. |
| (b) The new library **was finished** about a year ago. | • if the agent is not the focus. |
| (c) I had an accident yesterday. This other car went through a red light and hit me. My car **was** completely **destroyed.** | • if the agent is obvious from context. |
| (d) Did you hear the news? Matt **was injured** slightly in the earthquake, but Jeff was O.K. | • to focus on the receiver. |
| (e) Passengers **are asked** to refrain from smoking.<br>(f) The audience **will be encouraged** to participate.<br>(g) Something **should be done** about the drug problem.<br>(h) The present perfect tense **is used** to describe actions in the past that are related to the present in some way.<br>(i) Water **is formed** by combining hydrogen and oxygen. | • to make general explanations, statements and announcements, or in scientific and technical writing. |

## EXERCISE 11

Why do you think the author used passive verbs in the following sentences? There may be more than one possible reason.

**Example:** No one is permitted to enter the office while the votes are being counted.
*general announcement*

1. Reagan was first elected president of the United States in 1980.
2. There is a lot of controversy about the Nazca Lines, especially about why they were built and how they were constructed.
3. They weren't even noticed until people started flying over the area in planes.
4. Was it John's brother who got arrested at the demonstration?
5. The house was broken into while the family was away.

Read this excerpt from an introductory sociology textbook. Choose one paragraph, and underline all the passive constructions that you find. With a partner, decide why the author chose to use passive constructions.

## CHAPTER 3  SOCIAL MINORITIES AND DISCRIMINATION

### *INTRODUCTION*

(1) In most societies, certain social minorities are sometimes discriminated against by society as a whole. (2) Discrimination may occur because of a group's race, religion, ethnic or cultural background, sexual orientation, or even the language that they speak in their homes. (3) Such groups are sometimes denied basic rights, legal protections, or access to the same facilities as the general public. (4) In many societies, discrimination is slowly being eliminated—at least in terms of legal and governmental policies. (5) But these changes have not come quickly or easily.

(6) The United States, for example, has made a great deal of progress in eliminating discrimination against some of its social minorities. (7) As recently as the 1950s blacks and whites were not allowed to get married in many southern states. (8) They were forced to use separate drinking fountains, rest rooms, and even schools and libraries. (9) However, as a result of active protest and political demonstration such discriminatory laws were changed, and segregation based on race is no longer permitted.

(10) But other groups have been less successful. (11) Women have made many gains in American society, but they are still paid less than men for the same kinds of work. (12) Gay people still face enormous legal and social discrimination. (13) They are not allowed to serve in the army or join organizations like the Boy Scouts; in many states they can be fired from their jobs if employers learn of their sexual orientation. (14) They do not have the same kind of basic legal protection for family relationships and property that the rest of society takes for granted. (15) Courts may still take children away from homosexual parents, or deny inheritance rights to lifelong partners when one partner dies.

(16) Conditions for all minorities in the United States seem to be improving, although it will be a long time before social attitudes catch up with the progress that has been made in legal protections.

P. 58   INTRODUCTION TO SOCIOLOGY   SECOND EDITION

Decide whether active or passive forms should be used in these sentences, and write the correct form in the blank. There may be more than one correct choice.

The age of pyramid-building in Egypt (1) ___began___ (begin) about 2900 BCE. The great pyramids (2) ___were intended___ (intend) to serve as burial places for the Pharaohs, as the kings of Egypt (3) ___were called___ (call). Construction on the largest pyramid (4) ___started___ (start) around 2800 BC for Khufu, the King of the Fourth Dynasty, or Cheops, as he (5) ___was referred to___ (refer to) by Greek historians. It (6) ___is___ (be) 482 feet high and 755 feet long. The Pyramids as a group (7) ___comprised___ (comprise) one of the Seven Wonders of the Ancient World. The other Six Wonders no longer (8) ___stand___ (stand), and modern archaeologists (9) ___know___ (know) of them only through the descriptions that (10) ___are written___ (write) at the time they still (11) ___existed___ (exist).

Decide whether active or passive forms should be used in these sentences, and write the correct form in the blank. There may be more than one correct choice.

The Taj Mahal in Agra, India, (1) ___built___ (build) for the Moghul Emperor Shah Jahan. It (2) ___was designed___ (design) to (3) ___serve___ (serve) as a tomb for his beloved wife. Many people (4) ___consider___ (consider) the Taj to be the most beautiful building in the world. The entire structure (5) ___is made___ (make) of white marble and semiprecious stones. Shah Jahan originally (6) ___intended___ (intend) for a second Taj (7) ___located___ (locate) across the river from the first one. The second Taj was supposed to (8) ___copy___ (copy) the original Taj in every detail except one: The second Taj, which Shah Jahan (9) ___planned___ (plan) as his own tomb, was supposed to (10) ___consist___ (consist) of black marble and semiprecious stones, instead of the same white marble that (11) ___was used___ (use) for the first Taj. Shah Jahan (12) ___was imprisoned___ (imprison) by his own son and (13) ___died___ (die) before he (14) ___got___ (get) a chance to (15) ___implement___ (implement) his plan. His vision of two twin Taj Mahals, one white and one black, never (16) ___be accomplished___ (accomplish).

## ACTIVITY 1 reading/speaking

The article in Exercise 12 discussed discrimination against social minorities in the United States. Share your ideas and opinions about discrimination with other students.

■ **STEP 1** Read the article again and discuss these questions with a partner or in a small group:

1. What is the main idea of this article?

2. What are some common reasons for discrimination mentioned in the article?

3. What examples does the article give of successful progress in eliminating discrimination in the United States?

4. What examples does the article provide about discrimination against women? Can you think of other examples?

5. The article discusses legalized discrimination and social discrimination. Name one example of each kind of discrimination against gay people.

| | |
|---|---|
| Koreans in Japan | Catholics in Northern Ireland |
| Turks in Germany | people with physical disabilities |
| Arabs in France | people with certain political beliefs |
| Chinese in Southeast Asia | people with certain physical characteristics |
| Jews in Eastern Europe | (fat people, short people, left-handed |
| Hindus in Sri Lanka | people, etc.) |

■ **STEP 2** Listed below are examples of some other social groups that sometimes face discrimination. Identify one example that you are familiar with and describe that discrimination to another student.

■ **STEP 3** With your partner think of one additional example and describe the discrimination that this group faces to the rest of the class.

■ **STEP 4** Discuss whether there are situations in which legal or social discrimination can ever be justified. Report the results of your discussion to the rest of the class.

## ACTIVITY 2 writing

Go to the library, on *InfoTrac® College Edition*, or on the Internet. Use a search engine like Google® or Yahoo® and find enough information to write a brief report on the history of a famous structure or public monument. Include facts about its design, construction, and function, and why it is famous. Use the passive voice at least three times in your report. Pick one of these examples, or choose one of your own.

| | |
|---|---|
| The Eiffel Tower (Paris) | Latin American Tower (Mexico City) |
| The Golden Gate Bridge (San Francisco) | The Imperial Palace (Tokyo) |
| The Statue of Liberty (New York) | The Temple of Heaven (Beijing) |
| Angkor Wat (Cambodia) | The Chunnel (between England and France) |
| The Parthenon (Athens) | The Sydney Opera House (Australia) |

## ACTIVITY 3 writing

Have you ever had a day that was so unlucky that it made you wish that you had never even gotten out of bed? What happened? Was it unlucky because of what happened to you or because of something you did? Were you the "agent" or the "receiver" of your unlucky events? Write a paragraph that describes what happened on that day.

## ACTIVITY 4 listening

CD Track 8

**STEP 1**  Listen to the news broadcast and, in your notebook, write a one-sentence summary of what the news broadcast is about.

**STEP 2**  Read the following questions and then listen to the news broadcast again. Answer the questions in complete sentences.

1. What was announced today?

2. When did Velasquez probably paint the portrait?

3. How did the painting get into the closet?

4. Why didn't officials know about the painting's existence?

5. Who authenticated the painting?

6. What is being done now, as a result of this discovery?

7. How much is the painting worth?

■ **STEP 3** Compare your answers with a partner's. Listen to the news broadcast a third time to check answers that you disagree on or are unsure about. Share your final answers with the rest of the class.

## Activity 5 research on the web

Go on the Internet and use a search engine like Google® or Yahoo® to find out how one or more of the common items listed below are manufactured. If you prefer, you can talk about some other item you are familiar with. Report your findings to the rest of the class.

glass    molasses    silicon chips    rope    porcelain    paper

## ACTIVITY 6 reflection

Read a newspaper or listen to a national TV or radio news broadcast in English and write down three examples of passive verbs that you hear. Try to identify the receiver and the agent, if it is stated, and suggest why the passive form was used. If possible, have a partner listen independently to the same broadcast or read the same newspaper and then compare your answers.

# UNIT 5

# ONE-WORD AND PHRASAL MODALS

## UNIT GOALS

- Review modal forms and uses

- Identify and use one-word and phrasal modals

- Understand formal and informal uses of modals

## OPENING TASK

### Identifying the Pros and Cons of Immigration

Every year hundreds of thousands of people leave their native country and go to live permanently to another country. Some are political refugees; others hope to find better economic opportunities for themselves and their families. Some come to their new country legally, and others are forced to enter or stay illegally. But for everyone the move to a new country often involves a lot of difficulties.

## STEP 1

Read this list of reasons why people immigrate to a new country and the list of difficulties people sometimes face after they immigrate. Check reasons why you would consider immigrating to another country and the difficulties that you think you might face. Then add one more reason and difficulty that are true for you.

| REASONS | DIFFICULTIES |
|---|---|
| —— People can't make enough money to feed their families. | —— People have to learn a new language. |
| —— People aren't allowed to practice their religion. | —— People aren't able to forget their old customs. |
| —— People have to serve in the army for a long time. | —— Their children won't grow up the way they did. |
| —— People are expected to choose a profession or a spouse that their parents (or government) tell them to. | —— People have difficulty finding work or have to take low-paying jobs because they can't speak the language well. |
| _____ | _____ |
| _____ | _____ |

## STEP 2

Consider present immigrant unrest in countries like France or England and elsewhere. Do you think large-scale immigration is a good idea? What is the impact on the people who move to a new country and on the country itself? Discuss your ideas with several classmates. Decide on three reasons in favor of immigration and three reasons opposing immigration. Present your ideas to the rest of the class.

## FOCUS 1  Review of Modal Forms

Many one-word modals correspond to one or more phrasal modals with a similar meaning.

| ONE-WORD MODALS | | PHRASAL MODALS | |
|---|---|---|---|
| can/could | may/might | be able to | be allowed to |
| will/would | shall/should | be going to | have to, have got to |
| must | | ought to, be supposed to, had better | |

| MODAL | AFFIRMATIVE STATEMENTS | NEGATIVE STATEMENTS | QUESTIONS/ SHORT ANSWERS |
|---|---|---|---|
| **One-Word Modals** *can/could may/might will/would shall/should* | (a) Victor **can** speak Spanish. | (b) He **cannot** speak it at the school where he studies English. | (c) Where **can** he speak it? <br> (d) Can he speak it at home? Yes, he probably **can**. |
| | (e) Victor **should** always speak English at school. | (f) He **shouldn't** speak Spanish with his classmates. | (g) **Should** he speak Spanish in school? No, he **shouldn't**. |
| **Phrasal Modals with *Be*** *be able to be going to be about to be supposed to be allowed to* | (h) Victor **is able to** speak Spanish. | (i) He **is not supposed** to speak Spanish in English class. | (j) **Is he allowed to** speak it at home? Yes, he probably is. |
| | (k) Victor **was able to** speak Spanish with his family. | (l) He **wasn't supposed** to speak Spanish at school. | (m) When **was** he **allowed to** speak Spanish? After class. |
| **Phrasal Modals without *Be*** *have to used to* | (n) Victor **has to** speak English in class. | (o) He **does not have to** speak it at home. | (p) **Does** he **have to** speak it at home? No, he **doesn't**. |
| | (q) Victor **had to** speak English with his teacher. | (r) He **didn't have to** speak it with his family. | (s) Where **did** he **have to** speak it? At school. |
| | (t) He **used to** speak only Spanish. | (u) He **didn't use to** speak English at all. | (v) **Did** he **use to** speak English? No, he **didn't**. |

*Continued*

| MODAL | AFFIRMATIVE STATEMENTS | EXPLANATION |
|---|---|---|
| *have got to* *had better* *ought to* | (w) He has got to speak English with his teacher. (x) He had better not speak Spanish in class. (y) He ought to try speaking English at home, too. | These modals do not usually appear in questions or negative sentences. One-word modals are used instead. |

## EXERCISE 1

Victor Sanchez immigrated to the United States six months ago and is busy trying to learn English. Read these sentences about Victor's study habits. The forms of the modals are incorrect. Identify the problems and correct the sentences.

**Example:** Has Victor to speak English?

_Does Victor have to speak English?_

1. Victor hasn't to do his homework.

2. Does Victor able to speak Spanish at home?

3. Can Victor speak Spanish? Yes, he can speak.

4. Where he is allowed to speak Spanish?

5. Why he can't speak Spanish at school?

6. Ought Victor to speak Spanish at school?

7. Had Victor better speak English at school?

8. Used Victor to speak Spanish?

9. Does Victor allowed to speak Spanish in school? No, he doesn't allowed.

10. Why he should speak English in school? Why he shouldn't Spanish?

## FOCUS 2

# Social Uses of One-Word and Phrasal Modals

Most basic social interactions use modals.

| USE | ONE-WORD MODALS | EXAMPLES | PHRASAL MODALS | EXAMPLES | SPECIAL NOTES |
|---|---|---|---|---|---|
| Making requests | *would* <br><br> *could* <br><br> *will* <br> *can* | (a) **Would** you open the window? <br> (b) **Could** you turn down the radio? <br> (c) **Will** you pass the salt? <br> (d) **Can** you loan me a dollar? | | | The one-word modals are listed here in order of most polite or formal to most informal. |
| Asking for, giving, or denying permission | *may* <br> *can* | (e) **May** I come in? <br> (f) Of course you **can**! <br> (g) You **can't** smoke here. | *be allowed to* | (h) You're **allowed to** bring a friend. <br> (i) You're **not allowed to** smoke here. | *May* is considered more polite than *can*. |
| Giving invitations | *will* <br> *would* <br> *can* | (j) **Will** you come for dinner? <br> (k) **Would** you like to join us? <br> (l) **Can** you come to my party? | | | |
| Making offers | *will* <br> *shall* | (m) **I'll** do the dishes. <br> (n) **Shall** I help with the dishes? | *would . . . like* | (o) **Would** you **like** me to do the dishes? | Use *shall* to make offers of action by the speaker. |

use

## FOCUS 2

### Social Uses of One-Word and Phrasal Modals

*Continued*

| USE | ONE-WORD MODALS | EXAMPLES | PHRASAL MODALS | EXAMPLES | SPECIAL NOTES |
|---|---|---|---|---|---|
| Making promises or expressing intention | *will* | (p) **I'll** do it <br> (q) I promise **I'll** do it. <br> (r) **I'll** do it, no matter what! | *be going to* | (s) **I'm going to** finish this, I promise. <br> (t) **I'm going to** finish this whether you want me to or not. | *Be going to* expresses a stronger intention than *will*. <br><br> See Unit 15, Focus 3, for more information on this difference. |
| Making suggestions | *shall* <br> *could* <br><br> *can* <br><br> *might* | (u) **Shall** we go out to dinner? <br> (v) We **could** get Chinese food. <br> (w) You **can** try that new restaurant. <br> (x) Victor **might** try harder to speak English outside of class. | | | Use *shall* to suggest actions that involve both the speaker and the listener. |

**FOCUS 2**

## Social Uses of One-Word and Phrasal Modals

*Continued*

| USE | ONE-WORD MODALS | EXAMPLES | PHRASAL MODALS | EXAMPLES | SPECIAL NOTES |
|---|---|---|---|---|---|
| Expressing advice | *could* | (y) Victor **could** study harder. | *ought to* | (bb) You **ought to** do your homework every night. | These forms are listed in increasing order of necessity. |
| | *should* | (z) Victor **should** study every day. | *had better*<br>*had better not* | (cc) You **had better** start working harder if you want to pass this class. | *Ought to* is rarely used in negative statements or questions. |
| | | (aa) He **shouldn't** speak Spanish at home. | | (dd) You **had better not** skip class. | *Had better* is an emphatic form. It is often used as a threat. It is used in affirmative and negative sentences, but it is not used with questions. Notice that the negative form is *had better not*, NOT *hadn't better*. |
| | | | *be supposed to* | (ee) You're **supposed to** do your homework every night. | |
| | | | | (ff) You're **not supposed to** ask your roommate to help you with the homework. | |
| Obligation, and necessity/ prohibition | *must* | (gg) We **must** leave before 5:00. | *have to* | (ii) You **have to** leave before 5:00. | *Have to* and *must* have different meanings in negative sentences:<br>*must not* = prohibition;<br>*don't have to* = lack of necessity. |
| | | (hh) You **mustn't** tell a lie | | (jj) You **don't have to** work late if you don't want to. | |
| | | | *have got to* | (kk) You've **got to** stop spending so much money. | *Have got to* is not used in questions or negatives. |

# EXERCISE 2

Identify the social uses expressed by the modals in the sentences below the chart.
Write the number of the sentences in the chart to show how it is being used.

For each modal use write one additional sentence of your own. The first three
sentences have been identified for you as examples.

| USE | FORM |
|---|---|
| Making requests<br>Sentence #: _____ | Your own example _Can you help me with my homework?_ |
| Asking for, giving, or denying permission<br>Sentence #: _1_ | Your own example |
| Giving invitations<br>Sentence #: _3_ | Your own example |
| Making offers<br>Sentence #: _2_ | Your own example |
| Making promises or expressing intentions<br>Sentence #: _____ | Your own example |
| Making suggestions<br>Sentence #: _____ | Your own example |
| Expressing advice, obligation, necessity, or prohibition<br>Sentence #: _____ | Your own example |

1. May I have some cheese?
2. Shall I open a window?
3. Can you come to my party?
4. Would you join us for dinner?
5. We could have Chinese food tonight.
6. We might try the Hong Kong Café.
7. You mustn't forget John's birthday.
8. We don't have to study over the weekend.
9. You shouldn't stay up so late.
10. You ought to try harder in speech class.
11. Could you please turn down the radio?
12. Would you like me to help you with your homework?
13. Shall we go to Las Vegas for a vacation?
14. I'm going to pass the TOEFL® Test, no matter what it takes!
15. I'll pay you back next Tuesday.
16. You'd better not leave.
17. I can do that for you.
18. Victor can't speak Spanish in his English class.

# FOCUS 3

## Common One-Word and Phrasal Modal Meanings

Modals also express important meanings.

| MEANING | ONE-WORD MODALS | EXAMPLES | PHRASAL MODALS | EXAMPLES | SPECIAL NOTES |
|---|---|---|---|---|---|
| Expressing general possibility | *can* | (a) Immigrating to a new country **can** be very difficult. | | | See Unit 17 for more information |
| | *will* | (b) Immigrating to a new country **will** usually require a lot of life-style changes. | | | |
| Expressing impossibility | *can't* | (c) It **can't** be easy to get U.S. citizenship! | | | See Unit 17 for more information |
| | *couldn't* | (d) You **couldn't** be thinking about going back home already! | | | |
| Describing future events | *will* | (e) Victor **will** get his green-card next year. | *be going to* | (g) Steve's **going to** move to Canada if the Republicans win the next election. | *Shall* is very formal in American English. *Will* is preferred |
| | *shall* | (f) We **shall** apply for an immigrant visa next year. | *be about to* | (h) He's **about to** apply for citizenship. | *Be going to* is discussed in Unit 15. *Be about to* is used to describe events in the immediate future. |

**FOCUS 3** Common One-Word and Phrasal Modal Meanings

*Continued*

| MEANING | ONE-WORD MODALS | EXAMPLES | PHRASAL MODALS | EXAMPLES | SPECIAL NOTES |
|---|---|---|---|---|---|
| Making predictions | *could* | (i) We **could** get our visas next week. | *ought to* | (n) It **ought to** take about a year to get the visa. | Listed in order of increasing probability. |
| | *might* | (j) It **might** take a little longer than that. | *be going to* | (o) It's **going to** take another month. | *Ought to* is rarely used in negative statements or questions. |
| | *may* | (k) We **may** have to wait a while | | | See Focus 4 and Focus 5 for more information |
| | *should* | (l) It **should** be ready in three months. | | | |
| | *will* | (m) It **will** be ready tomorrow. | | | |
| Making logical inferences | *must* | (p) People **must** get tired of waiting for their visas. | *have to* | (r) Getting a work permit **has to** be difficult! | These phrasal modals are not used in negative inferences or in questions |
| | | (q) Victor hasn't applied for a work permit; he **must not** need to work. | *have got to* | (s) Getting a visa **has got to** take a lot of determination! | |
| Describing abilities | *can* *could* | (t) Victor **can** speak English now, but he **couldn't** speak it a year ago. | *be able to* | (u) Victor **was able to** ask his question in English, but he **wasn't able to** understand the answer. | Differences in meaning and use of these forms are discussed in more detail in Unit 24 |
| Describing habitual actions in the past | *would* | (v) When Victor lived in El Salvador, he **would** dream of moving to Canada. | *used to* | (w) Immigrant visas **used to** be much easier to get. | Using *would* and *used to* implies that the situation no longer happens |

Identify the meanings expressed by the modals in these sentences. Write the number of the sentences in the chart to show how it is being used.

For each modal meaning, write one additional sentence of your own. The first three sentences have been identified for you as examples.

| MEANING | FORM |
|---|---|
| General possibility Sentence #: __1__ | Your own example ____Getting an immigrant visa can be____ very tricky! |
| Impossibility Sentence #: __2__ | Your own example _____ |
| Future time Sentence #: _____ | Your own example _____ |
| Prediction Sentence #: _____ | Your own example _____ |
| Logical inference Sentence #: _____ | Your own example _____ |
| Ability Sentence #: __3__ | Your own example _____ |
| Habitual actions in the past Sentence #: _____ | Your own example _____ |

1. It can be quite rainy this time of year.
2. You couldn't be hungry! You just ate.
3. I couldn't understand American TV programs a year ago.
4. I used to get frustrated when I watched TV.
5. Those naughty children will misbehave if you give them a chance.
6. I will be there at 5:00.
7. I may have to leave early.
8. Antonio got A's in all his classes. He has to be very smart.
9. I've been able to make friends in every country I've lived in.
10. It can't be midnight already! It seems like we just got here.
11. We should be there in twenty minutes unless there's a traffic jam.

12. Naomi must not have to worry about money. She buys really expensive clothes.

13. I'll graduate next June.

14. It might be too late to call John. He usually goes to bed early.

15. I would always have trouble going to sleep on the night before school started when I was a child.

## ◼◼ EXERCISE 4

How are the modals being used in each of these sentences? Decide whether they express: request, permission, invitation, offers, promises, suggestions, advice, obligation, necessity, possibility or impossibility, future time, predictions, logical inferences, abilities, or past habitual actions.

**Examples:** Can I ask you a question? _____request_____

Can you speak Spanish? _____ability_____

1. Will you open the door? _____

2. Will the office be open tomorrow? _____

3. I can't hear you. _____

4. You can't smoke here; it's a church. _____

5. You shouldn't smoke; it's bad for your health. _____

6. You really ought to see a doctor. _____

7. The doctor has just finished with another patient; he ought to be ready to see you in just a minute. _____

8. You walked twenty miles today? You must be tired! _____

9. You must leave at once if you don't want to miss the train. _____

10. I may be late tonight, so plan on eating dinner without me. _____

11. Can I speak to Dr. Martinez? _____

12. You may not leave before the teacher tells you to. _____

13. I'm interested in buying that car, but it could be too expensive.

_____

14. Could you pass the butter? _____

15. Could you read when you were 5 years old? _____

## EXERCISE 5

Underline the one-word and phrasal modals in this paragraph. (There may be more than one modal in each sentence.) Then identify the meaning or use for each modal (permission, necessity, etc.—see Exercise 4 for options. The first sentence has been done for you as an example.

**Example:** (1) *necessity*

I'm not looking forward to this afternoon, because I <u>have to go</u> to the Immigration Office. (2) I have a problem with my work permit and I can't get a social security number. (3) I'm supposed to be there at three o'clock, and I mustn't be more than five minutes late, or they'll cancel my appointment. (4) So I guess I had better leave plenty of time to get there. (5) The bus is supposed to come every ten minutes, but it's often late. (6) I know that I shouldn't be nervous, but I really don't like the Immigration Office. (7) The officer is

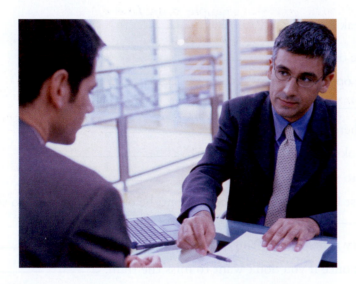

going to tell me that I have to keep better track of my documents. (8) I know that I'm supposed to keep a record of every visit, but sometimes I just can't find the time. (9) After my appointment I won't be able to go home for three hours, because I have to go back to my job. Here I am only a janitor at a chemical company instead of being a supervisory laboratory technician like I was in my country. (10) I know I'm going to be happy when I finally get my green card!

## EXERCISE 6

Write a sentence with a one-word modal about each of the following topics:

**Example:** an activity to avoid if you want to be healthy
<u>You should avoid foods that are high in fat.</u>

1. a daily responsibility
2. the best way to keep in touch with friends far away

3. advice for a lazy student

4. something you know how to do well

5. a possible event in the future

6. something that is against school rules

7. something you don't know how to do

## EXERCISE 7

Work with a partner. Use the phrasal modals below to ask your partner questions about daily life and activities. For each of the phrasal modals listed below ask:

   a. one *yes/no* question.

   b. one *wh-* question.

Report your partner's answers in full sentences.

The first one has been done for you as an example, using *have to*.

**Example:** have to: *Do you have to take the bus to get to school?*
*No I don't. I get a ride with a friend.*
*What time do you have to leave home?*
*About fifteen minutes before class.*
*My partner doesn't have to leave her house until just before class because she gets a ride in a friend's car.*

1. have to

2. be allowed to

3. be supposed to

4. be able to

5. be going to

## EXERCISE 8

Restate the ideas you wrote about in Exercise 6 by using phrasal instead of one-word modals. Are there any modal meanings that cannot be expressed with phrasal modals?

**Example:** You should avoid foods that are high in fat.
*You ought to avoid foods that are high in fat.*

**FOCUS 4** | **Choosing One-Word Versus Phrasal Modals**

use

Certain modal meanings and uses can only be expressed by one-word modals.

| USE | EXAMPLES |
|---|---|
| Requests | (a) **Would** you help me? |
| | (b) **May** I have some cheese? |
| | (c) **Can** you turn down the radio? |
| Some predictions | (d) We **might** not have enough money. |
| | (e) We **could** fail the quiz if we don't study. |
| Invitations | (f) **Can** you come to my party? |
| | (g) **Would** you join us for dinner? |
| Suggestions | (h) We **could** have Chinese food tonight. |
| | (i) We **might** try the Hong Kong Café. |
| Expressions of general possibility or impossibility | (j) A criminal **will** always return to the scene of the crime. |
| | (k) He **couldn't** have a TOEFL score of 600! He doesn't understand anything I say. |

In cases where both one-word and phrasal modals can be used, phrasal modals are preferred in the following situations.

To clarify modal meaning:

| EXAMPLES | EXPLANATIONS |
|---|---|
| | This one-word modal has two possible meanings: |
| (l) Charlie **may not** bring a date. | It's **possible** that he **won't** bring a date. |
| | He **doesn't have permission to bring** a date. |
| (m) Charlie **isn't allowed to** bring a date. | This phrasal modal has only one possible meaning: |
| | He **doesn't have permission to** bring a date. |

To combine two modal meanings in the same verb phrase:

| EXAMPLES | EXPLANATIONS |
|---|---|
| (n) A teacher **must be able to** explain things clearly. <br> (o) NOT: She ***must can*** explain things clearly. | Two one-word modals cannot be combined. |
| (p) Poor people **shouldn't have to** pay the same taxes as rich people. <br><br> (q) **I may be able to** get some extra tickets. | We can combine a one-word and phrasal modal. In such cases the one word modal always comes first. |
| (r) A firefighter **has to be able to** carry at least 250 pounds. <br> (s) You **ought to be able to** speak French if you want a job in Paris. <br> (t) **I'm going to have to** leave in a minute. | We can also combine two phrasal modals. |

## ▪ EXERCISE 9

What are the duties of citizenship? Decide whether people in society (a) **should have to do** or (b) **shouldn't have to do** the things listed below. Add three more ideas of your own of what people should have to do and shouldn't have to do. Compare your sentences to those of a partner.

**Examples:** (a) *People should have to send their children to school.*

(b) *They shouldn't have to follow one particular religion.*

1. send their children to school
2. follow one particular religion
3. go to work wherever the government sends them
4. work without pay on community projects
5. always obey their leaders
6. be required to vote in elections
7. report criminals to the police
8. get permission to leave the country
9. serve in the army
10. pay taxes

## EXERCISE 10

What modal meanings are being expressed by the following sentences?

**Example:** Don't leave your passport anywhere that the children are going to be able to reach. (*future activity, ability*)

1. We're going to have to leave the country if our government gets any more repressive.

2. If the immigration officer asks for another document, we aren't going to be able to get our visa today.

3. The customs agent isn't going to permit anyone to go behind the counter.

4. Most people have to be able to feel their private property is protected in order to live without worry.

5. Citizens have got to be allowed to vote if the government is going to stay legitimate.

6. Some people feel that anyone who wants to become an American citizen ought to be able to speak English.

7. Children under 18 years old aren't supposed to be allowed to immigrate without their parents' permission.

8. You don't have to be able to speak the language of a country in order to want to live there.

## EXERCISE 11

Combine the modal meanings given below.

**Example:** You _might be allowed to_ bring a guest. (possibility, permission)

1. Use a one-word and phrasal modal combination:
   a. I _____ speak with the visa officer. (necessity, permission)
   b. Noncitizens _____ to get drivers licenses. (advisability, permission)
   c. Students _____ speak English in class. (advisability, necessity)

2. Use two phrasal modals:
   a. A prospective immigrant _____ describe the system of government of the new country. (necessity, ability)
   b. I _____ come to the immigration meeting.
   c. In order for a society to be healthy, people _____ speak freely. (necessity, ability)
   d. You _____ speak French if you want a job in Paris. (advisability, ability)

## EXERCISE 12

Pretend you are planning to immigrate to a new country. Make sentences that combine the following modal meanings.

**Example:** future possibility and permission

*I may be allowed to run for political office after I get my new citizenship.*

1. advisability and ability
2. necessity and ability
3. future possibility and ability

4. advisability and necessity
5. necessity and permission
6. advisability and permission

## FOCUS 5  Formal and Informal Use of Modals

use

There are differences in the level of formality between some one-word and phrasal modals.

| | MORE FORMAL | | LESS FORMAL | |
|---|---|---|---|---|
| **Ability**<br>*be able to/can* | (a) | I'm **not able to** speak to you now. | (b) | I **can't** speak to you now. |
| **Future activity**<br>*be going to/will* | (c) | I **will** work a little longer. | (d) | I'm **going to** work a little longer. |
| **Necessity**<br>*must/have to, have got to* | (e) | We **must** go. | (f) | We **have to** go. |
| | | | (g) | We ('ve) **got to** get out of here! |
| **Advisability**<br>*should/ought to* | (h) | You **should** tell your parents. | (i) | You **ought to** tell your parents. |

## EXERCISE 13

With a partner, discuss the following topics using informal language. Compare the modals you used with those in your partner's sentences.

1. a daily responsibility
2. the best way to keep in touch with friends far away
3. advice for a lazy student
4. a possible event or occurrence next year

Choose one or two sentences and change them to more formal language to tell your teacher or the rest of the class.

# Use Your English

Below are descriptions of three people who have applied for citizenship in a new country. In a small group, pretend that you are a committee who has to decide which one should be given a residence visa. (You can only choose one!) Follow these steps:

■ **STEP 1** Examine the applicants' reasons for wanting to immigrate. Decide whether they will be able to fulfill the basic duties of citizenship in the new country.

■ **STEP 2** As a group, decide which applicant most deserves the residence visa and which one least deserves it.

■ **STEP 3** Present your decision and your reasons to the rest of the class.

| APPLICANT A | APPLICANT B | APPLICANT C |
|---|---|---|
| • belongs to a religion that is discriminated against in his or her country and will probably be imprisoned or executed because of those beliefs | • wants to earn higher wages and send the money back to relatives in the home country | • was jailed for political activity in college and is now being threatened by the secret police |
| • plans on maintaining the family's religion and language | • has skills that are needed badly in the new country | • doesn't agree with the politics or government of the new country and doesn't believe in paying taxes |
| • will not allow children of the family to go to public schools in the new country | • does not intend to vote or become involved in the politics of the new country | • is engaged to someone from the new country |
| • has few job skills and may need to be supported by public welfare | • believes in obeying the law, but will try to avoid national service | • has skills that are badly needed in the new country |

## ACTIVITY 2   reading/speaking

The first requirement for many new immigrants is to find work in the new country. This is often difficult to do because of language and cultural differences. Below are three advertisements for jobs available in clerical administration, computer programming, and sales.

■ **STEP 1**    For each job, identify

1. the things that an applicant must be able to do.
2. the things he or she should be able to do (although may not be absolutely required).
3. some things that are neither required nor recommended, but are still characteristics that the "perfect candidate" might have.
4. what an interested candidate has to do in order to apply for the position.

■ **STEP 2**    Would any of these jobs interest you? Why or why not? Compare your ideas to those of other students in the class.

---

**PROGRAM ASSISTANT**

Provide clerical and admin. support to five public program coord. involved in developing educational materials and providing training for hazardous waste workers.

QUALIFICATIONS: exper. operating word processing software and laser-printer hardware. Skill in establishing and maintaining master computer and paper files of program information. Interpersonal skills required to commun. with numerous instructors and staff on various university campuses. Organizational skills to estab. priorities. Related exper. working in a public service/public program atmosphere pref'd. SALARY: $1799-2124/mo. with excel. benefits. Send detailed résumé to:

Personnel Office
Box 1012, 1066 Hastings St.
San Francisco, CA

**LAW FIRM PROGRAMMER/ ANALYST**

Exciting opportunities exist in our office as we continue to develop, install, refine, and enhance automated solutions to law firm information processing. If you are a professional with 5 years of programming experience, have a background in 4 computer languages, and have business software development exp., we'd like to hear from you. We seek individuals who strive for excellence in their work product, who prefer a challenging, fast-paced environment, and who are service oriented. Excellent communication skills are a must!
Send résumé and salary history to:

Human Resources
PO Box 7B-23R
San Francisco, CA

**SALES CAREER OPPORTUNITY**

College Textbook Sales McGruder-Hall Western Region Office has immediate openings for 2 Assoc. Sales Reps. These positions involve both office sales support & selling textbooks to professors on college campuses. Qualifications include:

* 4 yr. College Degree
* Exc. Communications Skills
* Strong Organization Skills w/ Ability to Prioritize Multiple Tasks
* Desire to Move into Outside Sales Position
* Strong Motivation to Succeed
* Willingness to Travel

We offer excellent salary & benefits package. Please send résumé to:

Sales Manager
McGruder-Hall Inc.
5561 Francisco St., Ste. 738
SF, CA 94133

No Phone Calls Please

ACTIVITY **3**  writing

Write your own want ads advertising the qualifications and skills necessary for these occupations. First decide on necessary and desirable qualifications, and then tell interested people what they should do in order to apply.

| | |
|---|---|
| English teacher | United Nations translator |
| firefighter | police officer |
| executive secretary/administrative assistant | computer programmer |

ACTIVITY **4**  reading/speaking

Look in the want ads of your local newspaper and find two examples of jobs that you think you would like. Describe the positions to the rest of the class, and tell why you think you would be a good candidate for the jobs.

ACTIVITY **5**  listening

CD Tracks
9, 10

**STEP 1**  Listen to the two following conversations. Write down the topic of each conversation. For each conversation notice any modals that the speakers used and the context for using them.

**STEP 2**  Listen to the conversations again and list at least two examples of modals that you heard in each conversation. What meanings did these modals communicate in Conversation 1? In Conversation 2?

**STEP 3**  Compare your findings to those of other students.

- What differences in level or formality could you hear?
- Based on what you heard, think of one question you want to ask your teacher about using modals in English.

## ACTIVITY 6    research on the web

Go to the Internet and log onto the Web site of the Migration Policy Institute (www.migrationinformation.org). Click on "Global Data" and choose a country whose migration patterns you are interested in finding out about. Browse through the statistics there and prepare a brief report about the migration patterns in that country. How have they changed over time? Are there any surprising features? Report your findings to the rest of the class.

## ACTIVITY 7    reflection

What does it mean to "speak another language"? Read the skills listed below and decide whether each skill is in category A or category B.

*Category A:* A person **must** be able to do this in a new language in order to say that he or she "speaks the language."

*Category B:* A person only **should** be able to do this if he or she is a native speaker of the language.

Write the letter of the category in the space provided, and for each category think of one more skill of your own.

1. _____ read a newspaper
2. _____ understand native speakers perfectly when they speak to each other
3. _____ understand native speakers when they speak to foreigners
4. _____ have a perfect accent
5. _____ never make mistakes
6. _____ discuss abstract philosophy
7. _____ take care of day-to-day needs
8. _____ read and understand literature and poetry
9. _____ speak correctly enough that people can understand what you mean
10. A _____
11. B _____

Based on your definition, do you consider yourself to be fluent in English? Explain.

# INFINITIVES

## UNIT GOALS

- Review the form of infinitives and gerunds and the meaning of infinitives

- Understand and use sentences with verbs followed by infinitives

- Use infinitives as the subjects of sentences

## OPENING TASK

### The "To Do" List

Getting ready to go on a long trip requires a lot of preparation. In two days John Tealhome is leaving to spend a year studying in France. On the next page is his list of the things that he needs to do before he goes, the things that he would like to ask his girlfriend Mary to do and the things he wants his roommate Charlie to do for him.

| TO DO | Check with Mary | Check with Charlie |
|---|---|---|
| • buy Mary a present | • Does she really understand why I'm going? | • remind about helping move boxes to Mary's parents' garage |
| • ~~say good-bye to Prof Montaigne~~ | | • ~~check with landlord about cleaning deposit~~ |
| • ~~buy address book~~ | • Is she still planning to visit? When? | • clean the kitchen |
| • ~~buy suitcase~~ | • move boxes to her parents' garage | • change name on the bill for the electric company |
| • buy new jacket | • ~~drive me to airport?~~ | |
| • get small gifts for my host family | • have farewell dinner? Where? | • ~~get address of his old girlfriend (ballet dancer)? don't tell Mary!~~ |
| • have farewell dinner with Mom & Dad | | • get money he owes me |
| • get traveler's checks | | |
| • reconfirm ticket and get seat assignment | | |

## ■ STEP 1

**Look at John's "To Do" list and discuss these questions with a partner.**

- What things does John still need to do?
- What things does he need Mary to do?
- What things does he want Charlie to do?
- What thing does he want Charlie not to do?
- Has he forgotten to do anything?
- How ready do you think John really is?
- If he doesn't have time to get everything done, what things should he be sure to do, and what things could he decide not to do without creating problems?

## ■ STEP 2

**Present your answer to the last question to the rest of the class.**

**form**

## FOCUS 1 | Overview of Infinitives and Gerunds

Infinitives and gerunds are formed from verb phrases.

| EXAMPLES | EXPLANATIONS |
|---|---|
| (a) We need **to use** infinitives in certain situations. | Infinitives are formed by adding *to* before a verb (*to* + verb). |
| (b) Other situations require **using** gerunds. | Gerunds are formed by adding *-ing* to a verb (verb + *ing*). |

Gerunds and infinitive phrases function like noun phrases.

| EXAMPLES | EXPLANATIONS |
|---|---|
| | They can be used: |
| (c) **Using gerunds and infinitives** can be tricky. | • as subjects |
| (d) **To know which form is correct** requires some experience. | |
| (e) Some verbs require **using gerunds.** | • as objects of verbs |
| (f) With other verbs, you'll need **to use infinitives.** | |
| (g) This unit and the following one will focus **on using** infinitives and gerunds. | • as objects of prepositions |
| (h) By the end, you should feel confident **about choosing** the correct form most of the time. | |
| (i) But once you understand the principles, it's not **difficult to decide on the correct form.** | • with adjective phrases |

Underline the infinitive and gerund phrases in this passage. Tell how three of the forms you have identified are used in the sentence.

**Example:** Norman likes <u>to collect stamps.</u>

*Used as object of verb likes*

(1) Norman likes to collect stamps. (2) He likes getting them from anywhere, but he is particularly interested in collecting stamps from Africa. (3) He has tried to get at least one stamp from every African country. (4) This hasn't always been easy to do. (5) He has tried writing to the post offices of various countries, but they haven't always responded to his request. (6) A friend suggested looking in commercial stamp catalogs for hard-to-find stamps, and Norman has had pretty good luck finding rare or unusual stamps there. (7) He has also begun corresponding with stamp collectors in other countries and has asked them to send him stamps when they first come out. (8) They are usually happy to do it and have urged him to do the same thing for them. (9) He enjoys learning about other countries and finds that collecting stamps is a good way to do this.

## FOCUS 2    Infinitives

| EXAMPLES | EXPLANATION |
| --- | --- |
| (a) John wants **to study at the Sorbonne** while he is in Paris. <br><br> (b) He's afraid **to take the entrance examination** because he thinks his French isn't good enough. | Infinitives usually refer to the possibility of an action occurring. The action has not yet happened. |

Infinitives can contain the same information as any verb phrase.

| EXAMPLES | EXPLANATIONS |
| --- | --- |
| (c) John decided **to go** to Paris. <br> (d) Mary decided **not to go** with him. <br> (e) They want **to spend** John's last weekend in the country together so they decided **not to go** out with their friends. | **Affirmative/Negative** <br> Affirmative infinitive: *to* + verb <br> Negative infinitive: *not to* + verb |
| (f) John needs **to pack** his clothes. <br> (g) His clothes need **to be packed.** <br> (h) John intends **to become** active in student government, and hopes **to be elected** to the student council. | **Active/Passive** <br> Active infinitive: *to* + verb <br> Passive infinitive: *to* + *be* + past participle |
| (i) John would prefer **to have left** yesterday, but Mary would prefer next week. <br> (j) He hopes **to be studying** at the Sorbonne by January. | **Perfect/Progressive Aspect** <br> Perfect infinitive: *to* + *have* + past participle <br> Progressive infinitive: <br>    *to* + *be* + present participle |
| (k) Charlie plans **to have done** the things John asked him to do when John leaves for the airport (He'll do the things before John leaves for the airport.) <br> (l) Charlie plans **to be doing** the things John asked him to do when John leaves for the airport. (Charlie will start doing the things just before or when John leaves.) <br> (m) Charlie plans **to do** the things John asked him to do when John leaves for the airport. (John will start doing them after John leaves.) | Aspect tells us when the infinitive happens in relation to the main verb. |

## EXERCISE 2

Complete the sentences by expressing the idea in the infinitive as a verb phrase. Be sure to include all the information about time, aspect, and active or passive in your verb phrase.

**Example:**  I hope **to be elected** to the student council.

I hope <u>I will be elected to the student council.</u>

1. Charlie claims **to have paid** John the money he owes him.

    Charlie claims that he _____.

2. John expected Charlie **to have** already **talked** to the landlord.

    John expected that Charlie _____.

3. Mary reminded John **not to forget** his passport.

    Mary said, "_____."

4. John expected Charlie **to be cleaning** their apartment when he came home.

    John expected that Charlie would _____.

5. Mary is never happy **to be left alone** on a Saturday night.

    If Mary _____, she is never happy.

## EXERCISE 3

Complete the sentences by expressing the underlined clause as an infinitive phrase. Be sure to include all the information about time, aspect, and active or passive in your infinitive phrase.

**Example:**  John hopes that he <u>will pass the entrance exam for the Sorbonne in two months</u>.

He hopes  <u>to pass the entrance exam in two months</u> .

1. John has the hope that <u>he will have finished all his tasks</u> by his departure date.

    John hopes _____ by his departure date.

2. John's French teacher requires that all <u>students stop talking when class begins</u>.

    John's French teacher requires all students _____.

3. The doctor told John: "<u>Don't take this medicine more than twice a day</u>."

    The doctor reminded John _____.

4. John thought that <u>Charlie would be cleaning their apartment</u> when he got home.

    John expected Charlie _____ when he got home.

5. When John is bothered while he is doing his packing, he doesn't like it.

    John never likes _____.

## ◼ EXERCISE 4

Interview a partner to get two or three answers for each of these questions.

**Examples:** What things do your teachers expect you **to do**?

*They expect me to speak up in class.*

What things do your teachers expect you **not to do**?

*They expect me not to copy my homework from other students.*

1. What things does your partner's family expect him or her **to do**?

    _____

    What things do they expect him or her **not to do**?

    _____

2. How does your partner like **to treat** people he or she has just met?

    _____

    How does your partner like **to be treated** by his or her teachers?

    _____

3. What things do your partner's teachers expect him or her **to do** at the beginning of class?

    _____

    What things do teachers expect your partner **to have done** before the beginning of class?

    _____

4. What does your partner plan **to do** when school ends?

    _____

    What does your partner plan **to be doing** when school ends?

    _____

## Noun or Pronoun Plus Infinitive

| EXAMPLES | IMPLIED MEANING | EXPLANATIONS |
|---|---|---|
| (a) Norman wants **to collect foreign stamps**.<br><br>(b) Norman wants **us to collect foreign stamps**. | **Norman** will collect the stamps.<br>**We** will collect the stamps. | Sometimes it is necessary to identify who is performing the action described by the infinitive. |
| (c) Rare stamps are easy **to identify**. | They're easy for everyone to identify. | *to* + verb: The performer of the infinitive is usually the same as the subject of the main verb or "everybody." |
| (d) Rare stamps are easy **for experts to identify**.<br><br>(e) The stamp was difficult **for Norman to obtain**. | They're only easy for experts to identify; not for other people.<br><br>Norman had difficulty, but other collectors didn't. | (*for*) + noun phrase + *to* + verb: The performer of the infinitive can be a noun or an object pronoun (*him, us, etc.*). |

| EXAMPLES | EXPLANATIONS |
|---|---|
| (f) Norman **reminded us to give** him the stamps.<br><br>(g) NOT:<br>Norman **reminded to give** him the stamps. | Certain main verbs require using noun or pronoun + infinitive. (See Focus 5.) |
| (h) Infinitives are difficult **for students to understand**.<br><br>(i) NOT:<br>Infinitives are difficult **students to understand**. | With certain verbs (see Focus 6) and adjectives, the noun/pronoun + infinitive **must** occur with *for*. |

In these sentences identify who performs the action described by the highlighted infinitive.

**Examples:** Mary was expecting John **to be** ready before now.

*John*

Norman was asked **to bring** his African collection to the stamp club.

*Norman*

1. Norman claims **to be speaking** for the entire club.

    _____

2. This airline requires people **to get** their seat assignments before going to the airport.

    _____

3. Professor Montaigne requested her students **to bring** their books to class.

    _____

4. John's sister promised **to stay** after the party.

    _____

5. John intends **to pass** the entrance examination for the Sorbonne by Christmas.

    _____

6. John asked his friend **to give** him his old girlfriend's phone number.

    _____

7. Norman wasn't allowed **to stay up** late when he was a child.

    _____

8. John's parents encouraged all their children **to study** in another country while they were in college.

    _____

## FOCUS 4 · Verbs Followed by Infinitives: Pattern 1

**Verbs Followed by Infinitives: Pattern 1**

| EXAMPLES | EXPLANATIONS |
|---|---|
| (a) **John decided to go** shopping but he **neglected to bring** his credit card. | With certain verbs the infinitive immediately follows the main verb. |
| (b) Charlie **tried to comfort** Mary, but she **refused to accept.** | |
| (c) Charlie **seemed to have** too much work, but he **was** only **pretending to be** busy. | |

### ■ EXERCISE 6

There are seventeen Pattern 1 verbs in the following paragraph. Underline them and write the base verbs in the blanks.

(1) The Acme Stamp Company <u>agreed</u> to send Norman some stamps, but when he got them they didn't <u>appear</u> to be in good condition. (2) The company claimed to be reputable, but Norman still felt the stamps were bad. (3) He didn't care to pay good money for bad stamps and he felt that he deserved to get a refund. (4) So he decided to phone the company directly. (5) He demanded to speak to the manager. (6) The manager pretended to be concerned, but he hesitated to make any firm promises about refunds. (7) The company offered to exchange the stamps, but Norman refused to accept the offer. (8) All the stamps from that company seemed to be of poor quality. (9) The company also tended to be very slow in filling orders. (10) Norman has learned to make sure a company is reputable before placing a large order with them. (11) He neglected to do this with the Acme Stamp Company. (12) Norman still hopes to get a refund. (13) He is waiting to see if the company will give him one before he files a formal complaint with the post office.

*agree*
*appear*
_____
_____
_____
_____
_____
_____
_____
_____
_____
_____
_____
_____
_____
_____

## EXERCISE 7

Complete these sentences with infinitive phrases. Express your real opinion. Compare your answers with those of other students.

**Example:**  An honest person should never pretend . . .
_to be something that he or she really isn't._

1. A good parent should never neglect _____.
2. Most children in elementary school learn _____.
3. Most poor people can't afford _____.
4. The world situation today seems _____.
5. Shy students sometimes hesitate _____.
6. Selfish people rarely offer _____.
7. A good friend should never refuse _____.
8. Criminals deserve _____.
9. Most children hope _____.
10. In general, good students tend _____.
11. Most American teenagers can't wait _____.
12. Most good teachers seem _____.
13. An honest person should never agree _____.
14. Excellent athletes often appear _____.

## EXERCISE 8

Interview a partner and find out about five of the following topics. Report your information to the rest of the class in full sentences.

**Example:**  _My partner often neglects to do her homework._

1. a responsibility he or she often neglects to do
2. something he or she learned to do in English class
3. something he or she can't afford to do
4. a kind of assistance that he or she would never hesitate to accept
5. something he or she would refuse to do, no matter how much he or she were paid to do it
6. a reward he or she thinks he or she deserves to receive
7. how he or she tends to behave in a room full of strangers
8. something he or she pretended to do as a child
9. how people in this class appeared to be on the first day of school
10. a famous person he or she would never care to meet

**form**

## FOCUS 5 — Verbs Followed by Infinitives: Pattern 2

Pattern 2: Verb + Noun/Object Pronoun + Infinitive

| EXAMPLES | EXPLANATIONS |
|---|---|
| (a) Other stamp collectors have **advised Norman to order** stamps from catalogs. <br><br> (b) They **warned him not to spend** a lot of money unless he could **trust the stamp company to send** genuine stamps. | Some verbs are followed by a noun/object pronoun plus infinitive. They describe situations where the subject causes or influences someone or something else to perform the action described by the infinitive. |

Verbs that occur only with this pattern are:

| | | | | |
|---|---|---|---|---|
| advise | convince | hire | persuade | tell |
| allow | encourage | invite | remind | trust |
| cause | forbid | order | require | urge |
| command | force | permit | teach | warn |

 **EXERCISE 9**

Create sentences using the cues given.

**Examples:** (advise/study) *John's parents advised him to study French.*

(force/cancel) *The heavy fog forced the airport to cancel all flights.*

1. remind/pay
2. warn/not forget
3. convince/help
4. hire/work
5. require/pay
6. forbid/marry
7. invite/join
8. teach/speak
9. allow/leave
10. order/send
11. urge/vote
12. trust/spend
13. tell/eat
14. encourage/ask
15. force/leave

## FOCUS 6 — Verbs Followed by Infinitives: Pattern 3

**Pattern 3: Verb (+ Noun Phrase) + Infinitive**

| EXAMPLES | EXPLANATIONS |
|---|---|
| (a) John **expects to leave** in an hour, and he **expects Mary to come** with him.<br><br>(b) Norman **wants to get** stamps from every country, and he **wants us to help** him. | Many verbs can be followed by either an infinitive or a noun phrase plus infinitive. |
| (c) Mary's father **arranged for John to get** a cheap ticket.<br><br>(d) He never **intended for Mary to be** unhappy. | A few verbs of this kind must use *for* before the noun phrase. Verbs that follow this pattern are: *arrange, intend, consent, afford.* |

### ■ EXERCISE 10

Interview other students in the class about one of the following topics. Report your answers in full sentences to the class.

**Examples:** *Jamal likes to do the dishes, but he prefers someone else to do the cooking.*

*Hamdi needs to write a statement of purpose for her university application, but she needs a native English speaker to check over her grammar.*

1. things they **like to do** versus things they **like someone else to do**
2. things they **expect to do** versus things they **expect someone else to do**
3. things they have **asked to do** versus things they have **asked someone else to do**
4. things they **need to do** versus things they **need someone else to do**
5. things they have **arranged to do** versus things they have **arranged for other people to do**

## EXERCISE 11

Combine these sentence pairs by replacing *this* with an infinitive phrase made from the information in the first sentence.

**Example:**  John will spend a year in France. Mary doesn't want **this**.
*Mary doesn't want John to spend a year in France.*

1. John will write a long letter once a week. Mary has requested **this**.
2. John might postpone his trip until next year. Mary would prefer **this**.
3. She will try to visit him while he's there. She has decided **this**.
4. She was upset by the news of his plans. He didn't expect **this**.
5. John got a very cheap ticket. Mary's father arranged **this**.
6. John didn't apply for a passport. He neglected **this**.
7. John will report to the police when he arrives. French law requires **this**.
8. Mary will begin to study French herself. John has encouraged **this**.
9. Mary feels hurt that John is leaving. John never intended **this**.

## FOCUS 7 | Using Infinitives with Passive Verbs

| EXAMPLES | EXPLANATIONS |
|---|---|
| (a) **People warned Norman not to pay** a lot of money for stamps from unfamiliar companies. <br><br> (b) **Norman was warned not to pay a** lot of money. | Pattern 2 and Pattern 3 verbs (except those that require *for*) can be used in passive sentences. |

### EXERCISE 12

Complete these sentences with infinitives. Use real information that expresses your true opinion. Compare your ideas with those of other students in the class.

1. Most people can be trusted . . .

   _____

2. Children should be allowed . . .

   _____

3. All teachers should be encouraged . . .

   _____

4. Noisy people should be told . . .

   _____

5. Teenagers should be warned . . .

   _____

6. Students should be expected . . .

   _____

7. Guests should be invited . . .

   _____

8. Rich people should be required . . .

   _____

# FOCUS 8    Infinitives as Subjects of a Sentence

| AWKWARD | BETTER | EXPLANATIONS |
|---|---|---|
| (a) **To collect stamps is fun.** | (b) **It's fun to collect stamps.** | Infinitive phrases can be used as subjects in a sentence. We usually begin such sentences with *it* and put the infinitive phrase at the end of the sentence. |
| (c) **To have been introduced to Professor Montaigne is an honor.** | (d) **It's an honor to have been introduced to Professor Montaigne.** | |
| (e) **For John to study in France is a good idea.** | (f) **It's a good idea for John to study in France.** | |

## ▪▪ EXERCISE 13

Complete these sentences with ideas that express your true opinion. Compare your answers with those of other students.

1. It's always a good idea . . .

    _____

2. It's enjoyable . . .

    _____

3. It's never wise . . .

    _____

4. It's every parent's dream . . .

    _____

5. It's never a teacher's responsibility . . .

    _____

6. It's sometimes difficult . . .

    _____

7. It's usually necessary . . .

    _____

8. It's seldom easy . . .

    _____

# Use Your English

## ACTIVITY 1 writing

In the Opening Task on pages 86 and 87 you examined the things on John Tealhome's mind a couple of days before his departure for a year overseas. Have you ever left for a long trip? How prepared and well organized were you two days before your departure?

**STEP 1**  Make a list like John's that indicates the things you still needed to do, and some of the things that you needed other people to do for you. Compare your list and John's. Who was better organized?

**STEP 2**  Write a paragraph describing your experience. Did you have a chance to do everything you needed or wanted to do? Was there anything you forgot to do? What advice would you give someone preparing for a similar trip?

## ACTIVITY 2 speaking

Do parents treat boys and girls differently?

**STEP 1**  Interview some classmates and find out what things children in their culture are taught to do when they are growing up.

| | BOYS ARE ENCOURAGED TO . . . | BOYS ARE ENCOURAGED NOT TO . . . | GIRLS ARE ENCOURAGED TO . . . | GIRLS ARE ENCOURAGED NOT TO . . . |
|---|---|---|---|---|
| Examples | *be brave* *defend their sisters* | *cry* *play with dolls* | *be neat and tidy play with dolls* | *play roughly* *get dirty* |
| Student 1 | | | | |
| Student 2 | | | | |
| Student 3 | | | | |

**STEP 2**    Compare the responses of the people you interviewed. What differences are there? What might be the reasons for some of these differences? What things are taught to all children regardless of their gender or culture?

# ACTIVITY 3    speaking

**A superstition** is a folk belief about lucky or unlucky events. For example, in some cultures the number 13 is considered to be an unlucky number. Friday the thirteenth is supposed to be a particularly unlucky day. Some people don't want to attend a party or sit at a table where there are thirteen people. Many buildings, especially hotels, do not have a thirteenth floor. Other superstitions still affect basic manners in society. Because of an old superstition, it is considered polite to say "God bless you" when someone near you sneezes, even to someone you do not know.

**STEP 1**    Work with other students to develop a presentation for the rest of the class about some modern superstitions and how people act as a result of those superstitions. Identify some things that people try to do and some things they try not to. You may wish to compare the superstitions of several different cultures. Are there any superstitions that are universal? Why do you think superstitions come into being?

**STEP 2**    Present your ideas to the rest of the class.

■ **STEP 1**    Read the questions below, and then listen to the conversation between two students for information to answer them in complete sentences.

■ **STEP 2**    Compare your answers with another student's. Listen to the conversation a second time to confirm or clarify any questions you're not sure of.

1. What information should the students expect to be tested on?

_____

2. What were they told not to study?

_____

3. What had the man been planning to do tonight?

_____

4. Why wasn't the man in class yesterday?

_____

5. What had he been told to do in order to improve his chance for graduate school?

_____

6. Why doesn't he want a paid position at the library?

_____

## ACTIVITY 5 — research on the web

"Collectibles" can sometimes be worth a lot of money. In this unit you read about someone who collects stamps. There are many other kinds of objects that people like to collect, and they can sometimes command high prices. Go into *InfoTrac*® *College Edition* and type the keywords "treasures in the attic" or "collectibles". Scan articles to make a list of some of the other things that are considered "collectibles." Or, if you have a favorite collectible of your own, do some research to see whether your collection is worth much money. Present your findings to the rest of the class or write a short report for your teacher.

## ACTIVITY 6 — reflection

### STEP 1

Below is a list of some possible strategies for learning to speak English. Decide whether the listed strategy is something that language learners should try to do or something that they should try *not* to do in order to learn more effectively.

- Try to use new vocabulary in writing and conversation.
- Stop to look up every unfamiliar word in the dictionary.
- Be very careful not to make any mistakes.
- Guess at the meaning of unfamiliar words by using other clues in the sentence.
- Become discouraged if you don't understand 100 percent of everything you hear.
- Always think of your ideas in your own language first, and then translate them word-by-word into English.
- Listen for the general idea in conversations.
- Look for opportunities to speak English as often as possible.
- Go over your mistakes on homework and try to understand why you made them.
- Go over your mistakes on homework and write the correct answer.
- Find ways to punish yourself if you make a mistake.
- Don't speak unless you are sure the answer is correct.

### STEP 2

List three more strategies language learners should try to use, and three strategies they should try not to do.

### STEP 3

Compare your list with several other students', and present any interesting similarities and differences to the rest of the class.

# GERUNDS

- Understand the form and meaning of gerunds

- Understand and use sentences with verbs followed by gerunds

- Learn some basic principles about when to use an infinitive and when to use a gerund

## OPENING TASK
### Leisure Time

How do you like to spend your free time?  Researchers have found that most people fit into one of two categories: Do-ers and Be-ers.

**DO-ERS** like doing things during their free time. They have hobbies and activities that keep them busy. They plan their free time. A good vacation is one that lets them do many different things and have many new experiences.

**BE-ERS** prefer not doing things. They like to spend an afternoon relaxing, reading a magazine, or just doing nothing at all—sleeping, daydreaming. They don't plan their free time; they just let it happen. A good vacation is one that makes them feel relaxed.

## STEP 1

In this chart, list ways you spend your free time. Describe some things you do (or don't do) on a typical "day off." Two examples for each category have been provided. Add five more that are true for you.

| ACTIVITIES I ENJOY DOING IN MY FREE TIME (I DO THEM, AND I ENJOY THEM). | ACTIVITIES I ENJOY *NOT* DOING IN MY FREE TIME (*I DON'T DO* THEM, AND I ENJOY NOT DOING THEM). | ACTIVITIES I DON'T ENJOY DOING IN MY FREE TIME (I DO THEM, BUT I DON'T ENJOY THEM). |
|---|---|---|
| 1. reading the paper | 1. not getting up early | 1. doing chores (cleaning and laundry) |
| 2. talking with friends | 2. not driving to work | 2. taking work home from the office |
| 3. | 3. | 3. |
| 4. | 4. | 4. |
| 5. | 5. | 5. |
| 6. | 6. | 6. |
| 7. | 7. | 7. |

## STEP 2

Describe the activities in your chart to a partner. Your partner should decide whether you appear to be a *do-er* or a *be-er*. What category does your partner seem to be in? Present your findings about each other to the rest of the class.

## FOCUS 1    Gerunds

| EXAMPLES | EXPLANATIONS |
| --- | --- |
| (a) Norman enjoys **collecting stamps**. He doesn't mind **paying a lot of money** for rare ones.<br><br>(b) Mary isn't happy about John's **leaving** for a year.<br><br>(c) I hate **having** to do chores on the weekend! | Gerunds are nouns or noun phrases that are formed by adding *-ing* to the simple form of the verb. In general they refer to an action that is already happening or has been completed. |

Gerund phrases can contain the same information as any verb phrase.

| EXAMPLES | EXPLANATIONS |
| --- | --- |
| (d) I enjoy **staying in bed** on Sunday mornings.<br><br>(e) I like **not getting up** early.<br><br>(f) Peter likes **having a responsible job,** but he hates **not having enough free time** for his family. | **Affirmative/Negative**<br>Affirmative gerund: verb + *-ing*<br>Negative gerund: *not* + verb + *-ing* |
| (g) Matt and Jeff enjoy **inviting friends** for dinner.<br><br>(h) Matt and Jeff enjoy **being invited** to their friends' homes for dinner.<br><br>(i) Denise likes **giving orders,** but she hates **being told** what to do. | **Active and Passive**<br>Active gerund: verb + *-ing*<br>Passive gerund: *being* + verb |
| (j) Bambang was nervous about **taking** tests.<br><br>(k) Bambang was happy about **having gotten** a good grade on his exam. | **Simple/Perfect Aspect**<br>Simple gerund: verb + *-ing*<br>Perfect gerund: *having* + past participle<br>We don't often use perfect gerunds, and there is no progressive gerund. |

## EXERCISE 1

Complete the sentences by expressing the idea in the gerund as a verb phrase.

**Example:** I enjoy **not doing** anything on Sunday mornings.

*I don't do anything on Sunday* _____, and I enjoy that.

1. I hate being asked to do laundry on the weekend.

   When _____, I hate it.

2. I really appreciate your having cleaned the kitchen while I was taking my Saturday afternoon nap.

   I really appreciate that _____.

3. Denise suspects Peter of sleeping on the job.

   Denise suspects that _____.

4. We didn't plan for their having problems over the weekend.

   We didn't plan for the fact that _____.

5. I think he resents not being invited to the picnic.

   I think he resents the fact that _____.

## EXERCISE 2

Complete the sentences by expressing the underlined clause as a gerund phrase. Be sure to include all the information in the verb phrase in your gerund phrase.

**Example:** <u>I don't ever do any homework on Saturday nights</u>, and I enjoy that.

I enjoy <u>not doing (never doing) any homework on Saturday nights</u>.

1. <u>When I am asked for my suggestions about ways to improve my language skills</u>, I like it.

   I like _____.

2. Your teacher really appreciates <u>that you have been so careful with this homework</u>.

   Your teacher really appreciates _____.

3. Mary suspected that <u>John was planning to contact Charlie's old girlfriend</u>.

   Mary suspected _____.

4. The teacher didn't plan for the fact <u>that the students had completely forgotten the grammar rules</u>.

   The teacher didn't plan on _____.

5. I think John is disappointed <u>that he wasn't selected for the scholarship</u>.

   I think that John is disappointed about _____.

## EXERCISE 3

Interview a partner and find out two or three things for each of these topics.

**Example:** Things your partner enjoys doing:

*What things do you enjoy doing on Sunday mornings?*

*I enjoy reading the paper.*

Things your partner enjoys not doing:

*What things do you enjoy not doing on Sunday mornings?*

*I enjoy not getting up early.*

1. Things your partner enjoys **doing** on the weekends.

    Things your partner enjoys **not doing** on the weekends.

2. Things your partner hates **doing**.

    Things your partner doesn't mind **other people doing**.

3. Things or services your partner likes **giving to other people**.

    Things or services your partner likes **other people giving to him or her**.

4. Things that attending a college typically requires **doing**.

    Things that attending a college typically requires **having done**.

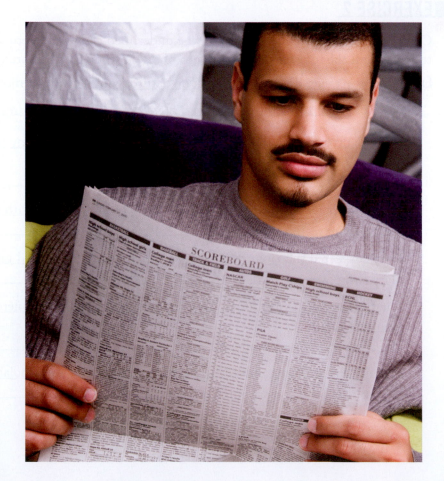

# FOCUS 2 | Noun or Pronoun Plus Gerund

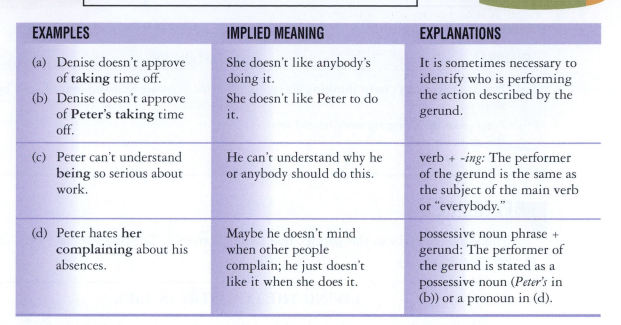

| EXAMPLES | IMPLIED MEANING | EXPLANATIONS |
|---|---|---|
| (a) Denise doesn't approve of **taking** time off. <br> (b) Denise doesn't approve of **Peter's taking** time off. | She doesn't like anybody's doing it. <br> She doesn't like Peter to do it. | It is sometimes necessary to identify who is performing the action described by the gerund. |
| (c) Peter can't understand **being** so serious about work. | He can't understand why he or anybody should do this. | verb + -ing: The performer of the gerund is the same as the subject of the main verb or "everybody." |
| (d) Peter hates **her complaining** about his absences. | Maybe he doesn't mind when other people complain; he just doesn't like it when she does it. | possessive noun phrase + gerund: The performer of the gerund is stated as a possessive noun (*Peter's* in (b)) or a pronoun in (d). |

## EXERCISE 4

In these sentences, underline the gerund and draw a line to the person who performs the action it describes. Circle that person.

**Examples:** Is there any way we can delay taking the test?

No politician will ever admit not having a solution to the budget problem.

1. Jeff enjoys playing with his puppy on the weekends.

2. I really appreciate your helping us get ready for the party.

3. Peter has considered looking for a job that has less stress.

4. Matt could never imagine taking work home from the office.

5. Mary resents John's spending a year overseas.

6. Denise will never excuse his having behaved so rudely.

7. John wanted to postpone leaving for the trip, but he didn't anticipate not being able to change his ticket.

8. We'll really miss Norman's singing and dancing in the stamp club talent show.

## FOCUS 3  Verbs Followed by Gerunds: Pattern 1

Pattern 1: Verb + Gerund

| EXAMPLES | EXPLANATION |
|---|---|
| (a) Denise Driven **can't help thinking** about work all the time. | Some verbs are followed immediately by a gerund. |
| (b) Peter **gave up bringing** work home from the office because it took time away from his family. | |

### EXERCISE 5

Underline the verbs in this passage that follow Pattern 1. The first two have been done for you.

---

**LIVING THE LOW-STRESS LIFE**

(1) Psychologists <u>recommend</u> reducing the amount of stress in one's life. (2) They <u>suggest</u> allowing time for activities you enjoy and avoiding activities that cause stress. (3) Some people deny having too much stress in their lives and would never consider changing their work habits. (4) Other people admit working harder than they would really like to. (5) But psychologists feel that everyone could benefit from the low-stress life, not only individuals themselves, but also their friends and families.

(6) Most people can't help having a certain amount of stress, no matter how relaxed they are. (7) But here are a few very simple, basic changes in daily activities that will greatly decrease the amount of stress in your life.

• (8) You can give up scheduling every minute of your day and keep some "open space" in your plans on a daily basis.

• (9) You should avoid making promises to do things you don't really want to do and quit doing activities that you don't find enjoyable.

• (10) You can practice making time each day for relaxation. (11) Such changes include not doing work activities on the weekend and spending time with loved ones or doing activities you enjoy instead.

(12) Initially these changes may be difficult, because we are taught to feel lazy if we aren't working, and you may resist changing old patterns. (13) But if you keep on following the basic principles listed above, it will get easier to keep doing it.

---

### EXERCISE 6

Use five verbs that you found in Exercise 5 to describe some of your own leisure habits. Talk about things that you regularly avoid doing and things that you do regularly and intend to keep on doing.

## FOCUS 4 — Verbs Followed by Gerunds: Pattern 2

Pattern 2: Verb +  { Gerund
                    { Noun Phrase + Infinitive

| EXAMPLES | | EXPLANATION |
|---|---|---|
| **Gerund**<br>(a) Psychologists **advise reducing** stress in one's diet.<br>(c) They **urge giving up** activities that you don't enjoy. | **Infinitive**<br>(b) My psychologist **advised me to reduce** the level of stress in my life.<br>(d) He **urged me to give up my** weekends at the office. | Some verbs are followed by a gerund when referring to "everybody," and by an infinitive when referring to a specific person. |

### EXERCISE 7

For each of these Pattern 2 verbs listed below write two sentences—one with a noun phrase and one without. If you wish, you can write a single sentence that uses both patterns.

**Example:** advise

*Most people advise taking a long hot bath if you want to relax but my doctor advised me to have a nice cup of tea instead.*

1. require

_____

_____

2. encourage

_____

_____

3. urge

_____

_____

4. advise

_____

_____

5. forbid

_____

_____

**FOCUS 5** | **Verbs Followed by Gerunds: Pattern 3**

Pattern 3: Verb (+ Noun Phrase) + Gerund

| EXAMPLES | EXPLANATION |
|---|---|
| (a) **I don't mind being** lazy on the weekend, but my roommate **dislikes my doing** so.<br><br>(b) **I dislike doing chores** on the weekend, but **I don't mind your doing** them. | Many verb-gerund combinations can be used with or without noun phrases. |

Common verbs that follow this pattern are:

| | | | | |
|---|---|---|---|---|
| anticipate | delay | don't mind | imagine | resent |
| appreciate | deny | enjoy | miss | tolerate |
| consider | dislike | excuse | postpone | understand |

### EXERCISE 8

Complete these sentences with true information. Use gerunds in your answers, and if the highlighted verb can be used with a noun phrase, try to use a noun phrase in your answer.

1. I usually **avoid** . . .

2. When I was a child I used to **imagine** . . .

3. My English teacher **recommends** . . .

4. I would like to **quit** . . .

5. I am **considering** . . .

6. Honest people shouldn't **tolerate** . . .

7. To be a good soccer player it's necessary to **practice** . . .

8. A teacher's responsibility **includes** . . .

9. Becoming a really good speaker of a foreign language **requires** . . .

10. I **appreciate** guests . . .

Combine these sentence pairs by replacing "**this**" with a gerund phrase made from the first sentence.

**Example:** John will spend a year in France. Mary resents **this**.

Mary resents John's spending a year in France.

1. John sings a funny song whenever he sees her. Mary will miss **this**.

   _____

   _____

2. He wants to become really fluent in French. Mary doesn't really understand **this**.

   _____

   _____

3. He applied to the program without consulting Mary. She resents **this**.

   _____

   _____

4. She will not have a chance to talk with him every day. She's not looking forward to **this**.

   _____

   _____

5. John is leaving in two weeks. He is quite excited about **this**.

   _____

   _____

6. John needs at least three weeks to get a passport. He didn't anticipate **this**.

   _____

   _____

7. This will make his departure even later than expected. John wanted to avoid **this**.

   _____

   _____

## FOCUS 6 — Gerunds in Other Positions in a Sentence

Gerunds can be used in other places in the sentence where noun phrases normally appear.

**Subjects of a sentence**

| EXAMPLES | EXPLANATION |
| --- | --- |
| **Gerund Subjects**<br>(a) **Collecting stamps** is fun.<br>(b) AWKWARD: It's fun **collecting stamps**. | Unlike infinitive subjects, gerund subjects usually begin a sentence and are not usually used with *it* constructions. |
| **Infinitive Subjects**<br>(c) It's fun **to collect** stamps.<br>(d) AWKWARD: **To collect stamps** is fun. | |

**Objects of prepositions and two-word verbs**

| EXAMPLES | EXPLANATION |
| --- | --- |
| (e) John is excited **about moving** to France.<br>(f) John is exhausted **from staying up** all night.<br>(g) I'm exhausted **from staying up** all night.<br>(h) I'm **looking into studying** overseas. | Gerunds can follow prepositions and two-word (phrasal) verbs. |

## EXERCISE 10

Complete these sentences with information that describes your true feelings about these topics. Compare your answers to those of other students in the class.

1. Talking to strangers . . .
2. Eating ice cream . . .
3. I'm nervous about . . .
4. I'm never afraid of . . .
5. My friends are concerned about . . .
6. I would like to give up . . .
7. Growing older . . .
8. I get tired of . . .

## FOCUS 7 — Choosing Infinitives Versus Gerunds

There is a basic difference in meaning between infinitives and gerunds that can help us choose the correct form in many cases.

| EXAMPLES | EXPLANATIONS |
|---|---|
| (a) I plan **to study** all weekend, so I guess I can relax this afternoon. | Infinitives usually refer to the possibility of an action occurring. The action has not happened yet. |
| (b) I don't enjoy **studying** all weekend, but we have a big examination on Monday. | Gerunds usually refer to an action that has already started or has already been experienced. |
| (c) I **want to swim** in the pool all afternoon.<br>(d) I **intend to take** the TOEFL® test at the end of the semester. | Verbs of desire (*hope, wish, plan, want*, etc.) imply that the speaker hasn't experienced the action yet, but may in the future. They are typically followed by infinitives. |
| (e) I **enjoy swimming** on warm Saturday afternoons.<br>(f) I can't stand **using** my weekends to do chores.<br>(g) I can't stand **to use** my weekends to do chores. | Certain verbs of emotion (*enjoy, appreciate*, etc.) imply that the speaker has already experienced the cause of that emotion. They are typically followed by gerunds. Other verbs of emotion (*like, love, hate, can't stand*) can be followed by gerunds **or** infinitives without much difference in meaning. |

Some verbs have an important difference in meaning depending on whether they are followed by an infinitive or a gerund.

| VERB | EXAMPLES | IMPLIED MEANING |
|---|---|---|
| *forget* | (h) **I forgot to meet** them. | I didn't meet them because I forgot about our appointment. |
| | (i) **I forgot meeting** them. | I met them, but I didn't remember that I did. |
| *try* | (j) **We tried to clean** the kitchen, but we ran out of soap. | We couldn't clean it. |
| | (k) **We tried cleaning** the kitchen, but there was still a bad smell. | We cleaned it, but that didn't solve the problem. |
| *remember* | (l) John **remembered to mail** the postcard to Mary. | He remembered, and then went to the mailbox. |
| | (m) John **remembered mailing** the postcard. | He mailed the postcard, and remembered it later. |
| *stop* | (n) Gladstone **stopped eating bacon** last month. | He doesn't eat it anymore. |
| | (o) Gladstone **stopped to eat** because he was so hungry. | Gladstone took a break and ate. |

In the chart below, review the basic patterns and common verbs in each pattern. Work with a partner and try to write as many additional verbs for each pattern as you can remember without looking through this unit. A few have been done for you.

| VERBS THAT TAKE INFINITIVES | | | VERBS THAT TAKE GERUNDS | | |
|---|---|---|---|---|---|
| **Pattern 1** | **Pattern 2** | **Pattern 3** | **Pattern 1** | **Pattern 2** | **Pattern 3** |
| *appear* | *advise* | *expect* | *can't help* | *encourage* | *appreciate* |
| *refuse* | *remind* | *arrange* | *keep on* | *urge* | *anticipate* |
| *seem* | | | | | *dislike* |
| | | | | | |
| | | | | | |
| | | | | | |
| | | | | | |
| | | | | | |
| | | | | | |
| | | | | | |
| | | | | | |
| | | | | | |

■■ **EXERCISE 12**

Fill in the blank with the gerund or infinitive form of the word in parentheses. There may be more than one correct answer.

1. If you want to lose weight, you should try _____ (avoid) all sweets. That might be better than going on a diet.

2. I know Bambang was at the party, but I don't remember _____ (talk) to him.

3. On his way home from the stamp club meeting, Norman stopped _____ (pick up) a few things at the store.

4. Suddenly, all the people at the party began _____ (talk) at the same time.

5. My sister has never been able to quit _____ (smoke).

6. Ruth couldn't enjoy the movie because she forgot _____ (bring) her glasses with her.

7. Nowadays, children have stopped (a) _____ (play) traditional children's games and seem (b) _____ (prefer) (c) _____ (play) video games instead.

8. I'll try _____ (eat) any kind of food once.

## EXERCISE 13

Fill in the blanks with the correct form of the verbs in parentheses. There may be more than one correct answer.

Before the invention of radio and television, people spent much of their leisure time (1) _____ (do) activities that required (2) _____ (do) or (3) _____ (make) something. They practiced (4) _____ (play) a musical instrument or studied (5) _____ (sing). Most people learned (6) _____ (keep) busy by (7) _____ (try) (8) _____ (improve) their abilities in some way or by (9) _____ (practice) a skill. People who couldn't afford (10) _____ (spend) much money on hobbies often started (11) _____ (collect) simple objects, such as matchbook covers or stamps, or even things like buttons or bottle caps. Of course, most people spent a lot of time (12) _____ (read) and (13) _____ (write) letters to friends. Children played games in which they pretended (14) _____ (be) pirates or cowboys or people they remembered (15) _____ (read) about in books. Many women were extremely clever at (16) _____ (make) and (17) _____ (decorate) articles of clothing. Men often kept busy by (18) _____ (make) toys for children or (19) _____ (carve) small sculptures out of wood.

## EXERCISE 14

Fill in the blanks with the correct form of the verbs in parentheses. There may be more than one correct answer, so be prepared to explain why you chose the answer you did.

Since the invention of radio and television, leisure-time activities have changed. Nowadays, people don't find it as easy (1) _____ (fill) their time with such productive activities. Television has encouraged many people (2) _____ (stop) (3) _____ (work) on their hobbies. Children are spending more and more time (4) _____ (watch) TV or (5) _____ (play) video games. As a result, traditional children's games that have been played for hundreds of years are beginning (6) _____ (forget). Traditional skills such as embroidery, sewing, and woodcarving are failing (7) _____ (be passed) on from parent to child. People seem (8) _____ (prefer) activities that allow them (9) _____ (be) passive observers rather than active participants. If these traditional forms of recreation keep (10) _____ (disappear) at the current rate, many of the things that people used to enjoy (11) _____ (do) will only be found on television documentaries about how people tried (12) _____ (spend) their leisure time in the days before television.

# Use Your English

## ACTIVITY 1 speaking

In the Opening Task on page 106 you were asked to decide whether you are a **do-er** or a **be-er** in the way that you spend your free time.

■ **STEP 1** Form a group with other people who are in the same category as you. Together come up with a list of the five or ten best ways to spend a rainy afternoon.

■ **STEP 2** Compare your list of activities with that of a group from the other category What does this tell you about the differences between **do-ers** and **be-ers?**

## ACTIVITY 2 speaking

Choose a partner that you know pretty well.

■ **STEP 1** Describe two or three things you can't imagine him or her ever doing. Then identify two or three things you expect your partner to do on a routine basis. Explain your reasons. What is it about your partner that makes you think he or she would behave that way? Your partner should then do the same thing with you.

■ **STEP 2** Were you or your partner surprised by any of the things you heard? For example, did your partner tell you that he couldn't imagine your doing something that you actually do quite frequently? Or perhaps your partner mentioned an expectation that you would never consider doing. Report any surprises to the rest of the class.

## ACTIVITY 3 Writing

We all have bad habits that we would like to stop doing, and things that we know we should do, but don't. New Year's Eve is a popular time to make resolutions about ways to improve our behavior.

■ **STEP 1**     Make a list of "New Year's Resolutions."
What are some things you would like to stop doing? (For example, *watching so much TV.*) What are some things you would like to start doing? (For example, *getting more exercise.*)

■ **STEP 2**     Compare your New Year's Resolutions to those of other people in the class. Are there any common categories or characteristics?

## ACTIVITY 4 Speaking

Prepare a short talk for the rest of the class on one of these topics:

• Your likes and dislikes: activities that you don't mind, can't stand, love, hate, resent, and enjoy or things about other people that you can't stand but many other people don't seem to mind (for example: *I can't stand friends being too serious about their work, and having no other interests in life*), and things about other people that you don't mind, but many other people can't stand (for example: *I don't mind people being late*).

• Your future plans: activities that you anticipate doing or hope or intend to do—and things that would make you postpone or delay those activities or consider not doing them.

## ACTIVITY 5 — listening

**STEP 1**    Read the questions below. Then listen for the information to answer them from the radio program about leisure time in the United States.

CD Track 12

1. What amount of time per week are people expected to work in the U.S., Germany, and Japan?

2. What is the average amount of annual vacation for workers in the U.S., Germany, and Japan?

3. What do Americans typically do on the weekend?

4. What is the third reason mentioned for the decreasing amount of free time?

5. Give two examples of "working vacations."

**STEP 2**    Compare your answers with a partner's, and then listen to the program again to confirm any information you're not sure of.

## ACTIVITY 6 — research on the web

Go to *InfoTrac® College Edition* and type in the keywords "leisure time Americans." Choose an article and read it. Decide how similar American access to and use of leisure time is to your own. Are you similar to or different from "typical" Americans? Report three things that surprised you in the article. Compare your answers to those of two or three other students. Present your group's ideas to the rest of the class.

## ACTIVITY 7 — reflection

Work with two or three other students and make a list of at least five things that good language learners should try to do and at least five things that they should avoid doing when attempting to learn a new language. Present your ideas to another group and together come up with a list of "do's and don't's" for people trying to learn and practice a new language. You may want to work as a whole class to develop a poster to display in your classroom.

# INTENSIFIERS (*Very, Too, Enough,* Etc.) AND DEGREE COMPLEMENTS (*So That, Such That,* Etc.)

## UNIT GOALS

- Use intensifiers such as *very, too,* and *enough*

- Use the word *not* with intensifiers

- Correctly form *so that* and *such that* clauses

- Use *too* and *(not) enough* plus infinitive phrases

## OPENING TASK

### How Much Is Too Much? Are You A Workaholic?

The word *workaholic* is used to describe people who like their jobs so much that they are "addicted" to them. They are not just very interested in their jobs; they're too interested in them. They often neglect other responsibilities (to their families, to their own physical health, etc.) in order to concentrate on their jobs and do them well. The word *workaholic* has an interesting history. It is derived from the word *alcoholic*, which is used to describe a person who is addicted to alcohol. And like alcoholics, an organization has been formed to help people recover from their addiction to work.

### ■ STEP 1

Read these questions developed by an organization called Workaholics Anonymous (based on the famous principles of Alcoholics Anonymous) and decide whether you or someone you know is a workaholic.

## HOW DO I KNOW IF I'M A WORKAHOLIC?

1. Do you get more excited about your work than about family or anything else? No

2. Are there times when you can charge through your work and other times when you can't?

3. Do you take work with you to bed? on weekends? on vacation? No

4. Is work the activity you like to do best and talk about most? No

5. Do you work more than 40 hours a week? No

6. Do you turn your hobbies into money-making ventures?

7. Do you take complete responsibility for the outcome of your work efforts?

8. Have your family or friends given up expecting you on time? No

9. Do you take on extra work because you are concerned that it won't otherwise get done?

10. Do you underestimate how long a project will take and then rush to complete it? Yes

11. Do you believe that it is okay to work long hours if you love what you are doing? Yes

12. Do you get impatient with people who have other priorities besides work? important

13. Are you afraid that if you don't work hard you will lose your job or be a failure? Yes

14. Is the future a constant worry for you even when things are going very well?

15. Do you do things energetically and competitively including play? mood

16. Do you get irritated when people ask you to stop doing your work in order to do something else? annoyed or too bad

17. Have your long hours hurt your family or other relationships?

18. Do you think about your work while driving, falling asleep or when others are talking? Yes

19. Do you work or read during meals? No

20. Do you believe that more money will solve the other problems in your life?

© Workaholics World Service Organization 2005

## ■ STEP 2

In recent years the suffix *-aholic* has been applied to other things. Although you will not find these words in a dictionary, you may hear them in conversations or on television, or read them in popular magazines. In addition to workaholics, people can sometimes be *sportaholics* (too interested in sports), *shopaholics* (spend too much time and money shopping), *TVaholics* (too much watching television and not enough doing anything else), or even *chocaholics* (people who can't live without chocolate). What other kinds of "*-aholic*" people can you think of? You have read about workaholics. Work with a partner and invent at least one other term for people who carry their enthusiasm about something too far. Present your term and definition to the rest of the class.

**meaning**

| FOCUS 1 | Describing How Much or To What Degree |

We can answer *how* questions about degree or intensity with **intensifiers** or **degree complements**.

| | **INTENSIFIERS**<br>*very, too, quite, extremely, etc.* | **DEGREE COMPLEMENTS**<br>*so/such . . . that . . .*<br>*too/enough . . . to . . .* |
|---|---|---|
| How devoted is Denise? | (a) Denise is **extremely devoted** to her job. | (b) Denise is **so devoted** to her job **that** she spends her weekends at the office. |
| How hard a worker is she? | (c) She's **quite a hard worker,** and even spends her weekends at the office. | (d) She is **such** a hard worker **that** she has no time for a personal life outside her job. |
| How interested is Peter in his job? | (e) Peter is **extremely bored** with his job. | (f) Peter is **too** interested in other things **to make** his job the focus of his life. |
| How quickly does he work? | (g) He works **rather slowly.** | (h) Peter works steadily **enough to** avoid being fired. |

### EXERCISE 1

Underline the intensifiers in the following passage. The first sentence has been done for you.

(1) Denise Driven is a <u>very</u> dedicated employee, but she's <u>a little too</u> serious. (2) Although she's <u>extremely</u> hard working and <u>quite</u> efficient, she's also <u>rather</u> competitive and <u>not very</u> friendly. (3) She comes in to work an hour earlier than anyone else and is always the last one to leave. (4) At the end of the day she's <u>really too</u> tired for other activities. (5) She has no hobbies and few friends. (6) She's actually <u>a bit</u> dull, since she's <u>not really</u> interested in anything but her job.

(7) Peter Principle is a rather easygoing fellow. (8) Although he works fairly hard, and is reasonably serious about his work, his job is not the most important thing in his life, and he likes to have time to pursue other interests. (9) He lives a fairly normal life. (10) He likes spending time with his children, and he is quite active in the Lions Club. (11) He is also a rather accomplished musician. (12) He plays the clarinet in a jazz band with some of the other people from the office. (13) Peter and Denise really don't get along. (14) She thinks he's a little lazy and "insufficiently motivated." (15) He thinks she's a rather humorless workaholic who is "not very nice." (16) It's somewhat difficult to decide who's right.

## EXERCISE 2

Underline the degree complements in the following paragraph. For each degree complement make a *how* question.

**Example:** Denise is <u>too serious to be able to appreciate Peter's laid-back point of view</u>.
**How question:** *How serious is Denise?*

Denise Driven and Peter Principle still aren't getting along. (1) Denise is <u>so rushed</u> at work these days that she doesn't have any free time. (2) She has <u>too little energy</u> at the end of the workday to have any hobbies. (3) She's feeling a little lonely, but she's <u>too busy to make any close friends</u>. (4) Peter has suggested that she take some time off, but she always says that there's too much going on at work for her to take a vacation. (5) Nothing moves fast <u>enough</u> for her to feel satisfied. (6) Even her administrative assistant works <u>too</u> slowly to keep up with all the projects she is involved with. (7) Peter, on the other hand, still works hard <u>enough</u> to avoid being fired. (8) But, unlike Denise, he isn't <u>so</u> dedicated to his job that he is willing to give up everything else in order to get ahead. (9) He loves his family <u>enough</u> to make their needs his most important priority. (10) He's just not competitive <u>enough</u> about his job for Denise to consider him a threat to her authority.

**Intensifiers**

form    meaning

use

| MEANING | MORE FORMAL INTENSIFIERS | LESS FORMAL (CONVERSATIONAL) INTENSIFIERS |
|---|---|---|
| An excessive degree | (a) That's **too** expensive. | (b) She's **way too** serious. |
| A great degree | (c) Denise is **quite** busy.<br>(d) She's **extremely** dedicated.<br>(e) She works **very** hard. | (f) Denise is **really** busy.<br>(g) She works **so** hard!<br>(h) She's **awful(ly)** serious. |
| A moderate degree | (i) He's a **rather** accomplished musician.<br>(j) It's **somewhat** difficult to decide who is right.<br>(k) He's **fairly** hard-working.<br>(l) He does his job **reasonably** well.<br>(m) He works hard **enough**. | (n) Peter's **pretty** dedicated.<br>(o) Denise is **kind of** depressed.<br>(p) He's **sort of** easygoing. |
| A small degree | (q) He gets **slightly** annoyed.<br>(r) She's **a bit** competitive.<br>(s) Work can sometimes be **a little** monotonous. | (t) He's **a tad** lazy. |
| An insufficient degree | (u) He doesn't work hard **enough**. | (v) Peter doesn't get paid **near(ly)** enough. |

**The position of intensifiers in a sentence**

| EXAMPLES | EXPLANATIONS |
|---|---|
| (w) Denise works **extremely hard**.<br>(x) Peter works **steadily enough**. | All intensifiers come before the adjective or adverb, except *enough*, which comes after. |
| (y) Denise is **a very dedicated** worker.<br>(z) She is **quite a dedicated** worker. | In noun phrases, intensifiers come between the determiner (*a, the, some,* etc.) and the adjective, except for *quite*, which comes before the determiner. |

Use the intensifiers from Focus 2 to describe the skills and activities listed below. After each example, make statements that are true for you.

1. **a skill you are proud of**: something you do well to a moderate degree

   **Example:** I'm a pretty good tennis player.

   *I'm a pretty good cleaner.*

2. **a favorite food**: a kind of food you like to a great degree

   **Example:** I'm extremely fond of popcorn.

   *I love Ka-Nom-Jeen-Num-Ngearw very much.*

3. **something that is not enjoyable for you, but you don't hate**: an activity you dislike to a small degree

   **Example:** Doing homework can be slightly boring.

   *I'm a bit jokking.*

4. **an ability you want to develop**: a skill you have in an insufficient degree

   **Example:** I don't speak English fluently enough.

   *I'm not good singer enough.*

5. **a bad habit**: something you do to an excessive degree

   **Example:** I eat too much ice cream.

   *I'm too lazy to do homework.*

6. **a special talent**: something you do well to a great degree

   **Example:** I'm a really good musician.

   *My character is quite beatiful.*

Are the following sentences written in formal or informal style? If they are in informal/conversational style, change the intensifier to make the sentence more formal. If they are in formal style, change the intensifier to make the sentence less formal. There are several possible answers, so be prepared to explain why you chose the answer you did.

**Examples:**   That project is so hard! (*Informal*)

**More formal:** <u>That project is very hard.</u>

I'm rather busy at work, so I won't be able to attend your party. (*Formal*)

**Less formal:** <u>I'm pretty busy . . .</u>

1. I'm feeling kind of sick today.
2. I'm somewhat confused by all your instructions.
3. She's really unfriendly.
4. He's quite annoyed about the missed deadlines.
5. I'm sort of busy right now.
6. It's rather hot in this office, don't you think?
7. Peter works pretty hard.
8. Denise is pretty serious.
9. That boss is awfully hard to satisfy.

# FOCUS 3 — *Too* Versus *Very*

| *VERY*—A GREAT DEGREE | *TOO*—AN EXCESSIVE DEGREE<br>(so much of something that it is not good) |
|---|---|
| (a) This project is **very** difficult, but maybe I'll be able to finish it by the deadline. | (b) This project is **too** difficult. I can't finish it. |
| (c) Denise is **very** serious about her work. She's a good worker. | (d) Denise is **too** serious about her work. She's a workaholic. |

## EXERCISE 5

Complete these sentences using *too* or *very*.

1. We got there _____too_____ late. All the other people had left.

2. I'm _____very_____ busy, but I think I can finish the report for you.

3. Denise works _____too_____ hard for her own good. She's going to get sick if she's not careful.

4. Denise works _____very_____ hard because she's ambitious and wants to get ahead.

5. Don't bother to invite Denise to the party. She's _____too_____ serious to have *infinitive down/too* any fun!

6. She gave the instructions _____very too_____ quickly for me to hear well, but I'm _____very_____ sure that she wanted this finished before the end of the day.

7. Children are growing up _____too_____ quickly these days. They try to act like adults while they're still kids!

8. We arrived at the meeting _____very_____ late, but there was still a little business to discuss.

9. I really like Peter. I think he's _____very_____ intelligent and has a great personality!

10. I really don't like Denise. I think she's _____too_____ serious about work.

## FOCUS 4 — Using Intensifiers with *Too*

| EXAMPLES | EXPLANATION |
| --- | --- |
| (a) It's **way too** difficult! <br> (b) It's **really too** hot. <br> (c) It's **a little too** expensive. <br> (d) It's **a bit too** late. | We use a few intensifiers with *too* to indicate how excessive something is. |

### EXERCISE 6

Complete these sentences, using an intensifier with *too*.

**Examples:**  You just missed the plane. You ___arrived a bit too late.___

I can't quite reach the top shelf. It ___is a little too high.___

1. I don't have quite that much money. It ___is a little too expensive,___ .
2. I wish she would smile sometimes. She ___is a little too service person.___ .
3. There's no way I can help you finish that report. I ___'m too stupid,___
4. Only a couple of students passed the test. The test was ___too hard,___ .
5. I can't drink that coffee. It's ___too sweet,___ .

### EXERCISE 7

Pick five things from the list below that you don't like. Add two other things that aren't on the list. Give reasons for your dislike, using *too* and an intensifier.

**Examples:**  I don't like workaholics. They're really too serious.

I don't like dogs. They're a little too friendly.

| babies | workaholics | doing homework |
| --- | --- | --- |
| dogs | diamond necklaces | being away from my family |
| cats | summer weather | rap music |
| spinach | sports cars | police officers |
| liberals | conservatives | |

I don't like summer weather at MI. It's too hot.
I don't like sports cars. It's a little too dangerous.
I don't like babies. They're too easy crying.
I don't like rap music. It's too difficult to understand.
I don't like being away from my family. I feel
a little too lonely.

## FOCUS 5 — Using Intensifiers with *Not*

These intensifiers (*too, very, so, really, quite*) can be used in negative sentences to "soften" a statement or make it more indirect or polite.

| EXAMPLES | IMPLIED MEANING |
|---|---|
| (a)  Peter's new co-worker is **not too bright**. | He's **rather stupid**. |
| (b)  Sometimes Peter doesn't work **very hard**. | Sometimes he's **lazy**. |
| (c)  Please **don't** drive **so fast**. | You drive **too fast**. |
| (d)  She's **not really interested** in sports. | She's **somewhat bored** with sports. |
| (e)  I'm **not quite sure** I trust Denise. | I **distrust** Denise. |

### EXERCISE 8

Make these sentences more polite by replacing or adding intensifiers that use *not*. There may be more than one way to "soften" your comment.

**Examples:**  This movie's pretty boring. <u>It's not too interesting.</u>

He dances rather badly. <u>He doesn't dance too well.</u>

1. She's quite unfriendly.
   <u>She's not quite friendly.</u>

2. The boss is somewhat unhappy with you.
   <u>The boss isn't too happy with you.</u>

3. I hate homework.
   <u>I don't quite love homework.</u>

4. Matt is a terrible cook.
   <u>Matt isn't quite a good cook.</u>

5. Denise dislikes listening to other people's problems.
   <u>Denise doesn't really enjoy listening to other people's problems that much.</u>

6. This office is too crowded for me.
   <u>This office doesn't have enough room for me</u>

# FOCUS 6 — Degree Complements with *Too* and *Enough*

## *Too* + infinitive phrase

| | EXAMPLES |
|---|---|
| *too* + adjective | (a) Some teenagers are **too immature to make** really wise decisions. |
| *too* + adverb | (b) They grow **too quickly** for clothes **to fit** for very long. |
| *too much/little* + noncount noun | (c) They have **too much pride to ask** for advice from their elders.<br>(d) They have **too little patience to wait** for complete freedom. |
| *too many/few* + count noun | (e) They have **too many people**, such as teacher and parents, telling them what to do **to feel** truly independent.<br>(f) They have **too few chances to exercise** responsibility. |
| verb + *too much/little* | (g) Teenagers think they **know too much** to listen to their parents and **too little to be responsible** for their actions. |

## *Enough* + infinitive phrase

| | EXAMPLES |
|---|---|
| adjective + *enough* | (h) Most teenagers are **responsible enough to do** a good job. |
| adverb + *enough* | (i) They work **hard enough to get** the same pay as adults. |
| verb + *enough* | (j) They have **learned enough to make** wise decisions. |
| *enough* + noun | (k) Parents often give their teenagers **enough responsibility to prepare** them for adult life. |

Restate each pair of sentences with a statement of degree using *too* or *enough*.

**Examples:** Denise is very serious about her career. She doesn't understand why Peter is so relaxed.

*Denise is too serious about her career to understand why Peter is so relaxed.*

Peter isn't terribly serious about his job. He doesn't want to spend every weekend at the office.

*Peter isn't serious enough about his job to want to spend every weekend at the office.*

1. Denise has lots of responsibilities. She can't take a vacation right now.

   *Denise has too much resposibilities to take a vacation right now.*

2. The pace of work is extremely hectic. Denise can't do her best work.

   *The pace of work is so busy hectic for Denise to do her best work.*

3. Denise's assistant works very slowly. Denise can't catch up on her correspondence.

   _____

4. Mr. Green hasn't assigned Denise much additional support. Denise can't meet the contract deadline.

   _____

5. Denise is very proud. She doesn't want to ask her boss for more help.

   _____

6. Denise isn't nice to Peter. He won't offer to help her with the contract.

   _____

7. There is always a little free time. Peter spends it on his friends, his music, and his family.

   _____

8. Peter plays the clarinet quite well. He could be a professional musician.

   _____

9. He doesn't like Denise. He won't help her meet her contract deadline.

   _____

10. Work is not that important. Peter doesn't make it the focus of his life.

    _____

## FOCUS 7    Implied Meanings of *Too* and *Not Enough*

The implied meaning of the infinitive phrase depends on which degree word we have chosen and the situation we are using it in.

| EXAMPLES | POSSIBLE IMPLIED MEANINGS |
|---|---|
| (a)  Mr. Green is **too old to worry** about losing his hair. | He doesn't worry about losing his hair. OR He worries about it, but he shouldn't. |
| (b)  Mr. Green **is not young enough to wear** the latest fashions. | He doesn't wear the latest fashions. OR He wears those fashions, but he shouldn't. |
| (c)  He is **wise enough to listen** to both sides in the argument. | He listens to both sides. |
| (d)  He is **wise enough not to take sides** in the argument. | He doesn't take sides. |

### EXERCISE 10

Choose the correct implied meaning for these degree complements.

1. Teenagers are too young to buy alcoholic beverages.
   a. They can buy alcoholic beverages.
   b. They can not buy alcoholic beverages.
2. Peter does not work hard enough to be promoted.
   a. He will be promoted.
   b. He won't be promoted.
3. Mr. Green is wise enough to avoid taking sides in the argument.
   a. He avoids taking sides in the argument.
   b. He never avoids taking sides in the argument.
4. Teenagers think they are smart enough not to make mistakes.
   a. They think they might make mistakes.
   b. They think they won't make mistakes.

## EXERCISE 11

Decide whether you agree with the following statements about teenagers. Use *too* or *enough* and an infinitive to give your opinion about things that 15-year-olds are old enough or too young to do.

Fifteen-year-olds are old enough . . .
Fifteen-year-olds are too young . . .

**Examples:**  Fifteen-year-olds are old enough to drive.
  Fifteen-year-olds are too young to live in their own apartments.

1. They should be able to drive.
2. They shouldn't live in their own apartments.
3. They can fall in love.
4. Schools should let them choose what classes they want to take.
5. Teachers should talk to them as adults.
6. They shouldn't be able to buy alcohol or cigarettes.
7. Their parents should give them some financial responsibility.
8. The law shouldn't treat them as adults.
9. They shouldn't be police officers or soldiers.
10. Society shouldn't give them total freedom.

## EXERCISE 12

Do you have all the money or all the free time you wish you had? Are there some things you are **not** able to do because you don't have enough resources or time, or because you have too many responsibilities?

  Write sentences that describe five activities you can't do, and what keeps you from doing them.

**Examples:**  I don't have enough time to read novels.

  I'm too poor to take a vacation this summer.

Using this chart, interview a partner about what things he or she thinks people are old enough to do at the age of 15, and what things he or she thinks people are still too young to do. Then ask your partner to think of one other thing that people are old enough to do at age 15, and one more thing they're still too young to do. Report some of your partner's opinions and reasons he or she feels that way to the rest of the class. Some examples have been provided for you.

| ACTIVITIES | OLD ENOUGH OR TOO YOUNG? | WHY? |
|---|---|---|
| Marry and raise a family | too young | They are not mature enough to take that responsibility. They should be in their twenties. |
| Decide on a future career | old enough | They already know the kinds of things they like to do and the kinds of things they are good at. |
| Drive a car | | |
| Go on dates without a chaperone | | |
| Make wise decisions about life | | |
| Live independently outside their parents' home | | |
| Pay taxes | | |
| Serve in the army | | |
| Get a full-time job | | |
| Get a part-time job | | |
| Take care of young children | | |
| Write poetry | | |
| Be a professional athlete | | |
| Vote in national elections | | |
| Control their own money | | |
| Become parents | | |
| | too young | |
| | old enough | |

## EXERCISE 14

Working with a partner, ask and answer the following "foolish" questions. Answer the question with a *yes* or *no*, and give a reason for your answer using *too*. Then try to restate your answer using *enough*. Ask your partner five more "foolish" questions of your own.

**Examples:** Can you swim to Hawaii?

No. It's too far for someone to swim.

No. Nobody is strong enough to swim to Hawaii.

1. Do you have any great-great-grandchildren?
2. Can you walk 150 miles in a single day?
3. Is $50 a fair price for a cup of coffee?
4. Can dogs read?
5. Do banana trees grow wild in Russia?
6. Can one person lift a grand piano?
7. Can you learn to speak English fluently in a week?
8. Can a hundred-year-old woman still have babies?
9. Do you remember what you did on your first birthday?
10. Can you eat fifty hamburgers in a single meal?

## EXERCISE 15

Working with a partner, ask and answer these questions. Give your real opinions. Use *enough* in your answer.

**Example:** Why don't some people do well on the TOEFL® Test?*

Because they don't know enough English to get a high score.

1. How much money do you need for a happy life?
2. How well do you speak English?
3. When should children move out of their parents' home?
4. When should people get married?
5. How quickly or slowly should a person drive on a turnpike or freeway?
6. What's an ideal age to retire?
7. What kind of person should be president?
8. What is an important characteristic for a basketball player?
9. Why can't monkeys learn to speak languages?

*TOEFL is a registered trademark of the Educational Testing Service (ETS). This publication is not endorsed or approved by ETS.

## FOCUS 8 — Degree Complements with *So* and *Such*

*So* + *Such* + *That* clauses

|  | EXAMPLES |
|---|---|
| *so* + adjective | (a) Denise is **so serious** about her work that she rarely takes a vacation. |
| *so* + adverb | (b) Peter plays the clarinet **so well** that he once considered being a professional musician. |
| *so* + *many/few* + (count noun) | (c) Denise has **so many projects** that her assistant can't finish them fast enough.<br>(d) She has **so few outside interests** that most people consider her rather boring. |
| *so* + *much/little* + (noncount noun) | (e) The project took **so much time** that Denise had to spend her weekend in the office.<br>(f) They have **so little time** to get the job done that they'll have to spend the weekend in the office. |
| *such* + (*a/an*) + (adjective) + noun | (g) The disagreement between Peter and Denise has become **such a serious problem** that they are not speaking to each other.<br>(h) Denise gives her assistant **such large amounts** of work that he is thinking about quitting. |

In spoken English and less formal written English the *that* in *so/such* constructions can be omitted.

| (i) I'm so busy **that** I could die. | OR (j) I'm so busy I could die. |
|---|---|
| (k) Denise is such a serious person **that** she probably doesn't know how to have fun. | OR (l) Denise is such a serious person she probably doesn't know how to have fun. |

## EXERCISE 16

Identify the degree complements in the following passage by underlining the result clauses where *that* has been omitted. The first paragraph has been done for you as an example.

**Tall Tales** story

(1) In American English we use the term tall tale to describe stories that are so exaggerated <u>they become funny.</u> (2) No one really believes that they're true. (3) That's part of the fun. (4) The point of a tall tale is to tell such incredible lies <u>everyone ends up laughing.</u> (5) American folklore is filled with examples of tall tales.

(6) One famous tall tale is the story of the winter when the weather was so cold everything froze.

(7) Each day things got a little colder. (8) First, the usual things froze: water, plants, pipes, machinery. (9) Then it got worse. (10) It was such a cold winter <u>dogs and cats froze when they went outside,</u> and birds fell out of the sky, frozen solid. (11) Then it got even worse. (12) It got so cold <u>people's words froze</u> whenever they tried to talk. (13) You couldn't hear a single sound. (14) Of course, people like to talk, no matter how cold it is. (15) So people kept talking and their words kept freezing just as soon as they came out of their mouths.

(16) Then suddenly the cold weather came to an end. (17) One day it was so cold <u>nobody could carry on a conversation</u> because the words just froze right up, and the next day it was warm enough to wear shorts. (18) The change in weather was so great and so sudden <u>everything became unfrozen</u> all at the exact same minute. (19) All those frozen words thawed out at once, and the resulting noise was so loud <u>everyone became deaf.</u>

## EXERCISE 17

Make statements of degree about the underlined items in the following pairs of sentences by using *so* and *such*.

**Examples:** There are <u>many plants</u> in the rainforest with possible medical uses. Scientists fear we may lose valuable medical resources if they are destroyed

There are <u>so</u> many plants in the rainforest with possible medical uses <u>that</u> scientists fear we may lose valuable medical resources if they are destroyed.

1. The world's forests are being destroyed at a <u>rapid rate.</u>

   We can't ignore the problem any longer.

2. The world population is growing <u>quickly.</u>

   We can't continue our old habits.

3. We have <u>few alternative materials.</u>

   We haven't stopped using trees for fuel.

4. There has been <u>a rapid growth</u> in population.

   There are no other places for people to live except the rainforests.

5. Some countries have <u>few other natural resources.</u>

They are forced to use the rainforests for economic development.

6. The problems appear <u>impossible</u> to solve.

Some countries haven't even begun to look for a solution.

7. The United Nations considers deforestation <u>a problem.</u>

They are trying to establish conservation programs throughout the developing world.

8. The loss of the rainforests is <u>a major global threat.</u>

The future of mankind may be at stake.

## EXERCISE 18

Give true answers to these questions using *so/such*.

**Example:** What kind of student are you?

I'm such a good student that I always do my homework before class.

1. What kind of student are you?
2. How quickly or slowly do you walk or drive?
3. Have you ever wanted something a great deal? How badly did you want it?
4. Did you ever eat a huge amount of food? What happened?
5. How high are the Himalayan Mountains?
6. Did you have a good time on your first birthday?
7. How tall was the tallest person you've ever seen?
8. How hard is the TOEFL® test?
9. What happened in the most boring class you've ever been to?
10. How wonderful is your grammar teacher?

# Use Your English

## ACTIVITY  1 writing

- **STEP 1** In Exercise 16 you read an unbelievable story called a **tall tale**. Work with a group to invent a tall tale or unbelievable story of your own to tell to the rest of the class. The more unbelievable the story is, the funnier it will be.

- **STEP 2** The class should decide which group told the "tallest tale."

## ACTIVITY 2 speaking/writing

Tell about a time when you or someone you know lost their temper, made a foolish mistake, or said or did something without realizing it. Here are some examples:

- The driver of the bus I was riding got so mad and shouted so loudly that his false teeth actually flew out of his mouth.
- My brother was so excited to get to Hawaii that he left his sweater and overcoat on the plane. He was pretty cold when he returned to Chicago.
- I was once in such a hurry to get to work that I left the house wearing one black shoe and one brown shoe.

Use one of the following situations, or think of some of your own:

- *I was once so happy that . . .*
- *My sister was so hungry that . . .*
- *A student I know once got so nervous in class that . . .*

- *When I was a child, I was once so frightened that . . .*
- *I once experienced such frustration that . . .*
- *I was once so angry that . . .*

## ACTIVITY 3 listening/speaking/writing

When are adult children old enough to move away from home? Different cultures have different opinions about when (and if) this should happen. Interview people from three or four different countries. What is the average age at which people move away from home? What do other people think if someone leaves home at a much younger or much older age than the average? Are there different standards for men and women? Make a report on what you have discovered.

## ACTIVITY 4 — writing

Write a short (one-page) essay that describes how you feel about the importance of work in your life. Here are some questions you may wish to answer:

- Is work more or less important than other things in your life?
- Could you ever become a workaholic? Why or not not?
- Who would you rather work with, Denise Driven or Peter Principle? Why?

## ACTIVITY 5 — writing

There's a popular saying in America that it's not possible to be too rich, too good-looking, or too thin. Write a short (one-page) essay about the topic:

- Do you agree? Are there some qualities or characteristics that no one can have too much of? If so, what are they? Why do you feel that nobody can have too much of those qualities?
- Do you disagree? Is there a negative aspect to being extremely good-looking, wealthy, or fashionably slim?

## ACTIVITY 6 — listening/writing

CD Track 13

**STEP 1** Listen to the lecture on the destruction of tropical rainforests. Use the outline below to organize the information from the lecture.

I. Economic impact of rapid population growth
  A.
  B.
II. Result of economic impact on rainforests
III. Problems with reforestation
IV. Primary reasons to maintain existing rainforest areas
  A.
  B.

**STEP 2** Write a one- or two-sentence summary of the lecture.

## ACTIVITY 7 research on the web

■ **STEP 1**

Using the Internet, go to the home page for Workaholics Anonymous (http://www.workaholics-anonymous.org). Read the information of the Web site under "About" regarding workaholism and decide whether you or someone you know is a workaholic. Based on what you read on the Web site, decide on three pieces of advice you would recommend to someone who is suffering from workaholism.

■ **STEP 2**

Use an Internet engine such as Google® or Yahoo® or Ask® and search some of the other -aholic conditions that were mentioned in the opening task (sportaholics, shopaholics, chocoholics). Which conditions are "serious" and have organizations like WA or AA to help sufferers, and which ones seem just for fun? Report your findings to the rest of the class.

## ACTIVITY 8 reflection

One way good language learners increase their vocabulary is by listening to how native speakers talk. Slang expressions change quickly and vary in usage by age. Intensifiers are one area where you can hear great differences between young and old and different regions of the same country. Slang intensifiers are popular with American teenagers. One current slang intensifier is "hecka" or "hella" to mean "very."

Listen to teenagers talking, either on TV or in real life and note the slang intensifiers that they use. Report one slang intensifier that you heard to the rest of the class. Tell where you heard it and how it was used. Your teacher may (or may not!) be able to tell you the meaning. If you know any teenager, ask them what they think are the current styles for intensifiers.

# UNIT 9

# MODIFYING NOUN PHRASES
## Adjectives and Participles

## UNIT GOALS

- Put adjective modifiers in the correct order

- Form and understand the meaning of present and past participle modifiers

- Use other noun modifiers in the proper order

## OPENING TASK
### Going to a Flea Market

Many Americans are fond of going to "flea markets" or "garage sales," where private individuals sell things that they no longer need. Such items are called "secondhand." People are attracted to these sales because it is often possible to find valuable antiques and collectibles for sale rather cheaply.

## STEP 1

The objects shown here were all found on sale at a flea market or garage sale. Match the objects with the descriptions, and guess how much the person who bought them paid for them.

- One slightly used, antique, blue Moroccan dish
- An interesting antique wooden clock
- A really beautiful old Italian glass bowl
- A fascinating collection of rare, used English textbooks

## STEP 2

Think of two things you own that you don't want anymore. Write a short description of each thing. Show your descriptions to your classmates. Try to find classmates who want to buy your things, and find two things you want to buy from classmates.

## FOCUS 1 — Overview of Word Order in Noun Phrases

A noun phrase consists of a determiner and noun plus all its modifiers. Determiners can be articles, demonstratives, possessives, or quantifiers.

| TYPES OF NOUN PHRASES | PARTS OF NOUN PHRASES |
|---|---|
| *determiner + noun*<br>(a) **the** books; **these** books<br>(b) **my** books; **some** books | **Kinds of determiners**<br>articles, demonstratives,<br>possessives, quantifiers |
| *determiner (+ modifiers) + noun)*<br>(c) some **extremely interesting, really beautiful used** books<br>(d) some interesting, really beautiful used **grammar** books | **Kinds of modifiers**<br>adjectives and participles (with or without intensifiers)<br>other nouns |
| *determiner (+ modifiers) + noun + (modifying phrases and clauses)*<br>(e) some interesting, really beautiful used grammar books **with red covers**<br>(f) some interesting, really beautiful used grammar books **printed in China** with red covers<br>(g) some interesting, really beautiful used grammar books printed in China with red covers **that we studied last semester** | **Kinds of modifying phrases and clauses**<br><br>prepositional phrases<br><br>participle phrases<br><br><br>relative clauses |

Although it is rare to have more than three or four modifiers for a single noun phrase, this is the usual order for different categories of modifiers.

| DETERMINER | INTENSIFIERS | ADJECTIVES AND PARTICIPLES | NOUN MODIFIER | NOUN | MODIFYING PHRASES |
|---|---|---|---|---|---|
| the/a/an | really | old/new | stone | wall | next to the river |
| some/no | very | interesting | university | campus | described |
| my/your | slightly | well-known | | | in the brochure |
| each/every | | | | | |
| these/those | | | | | |

# EXERCISE 1

From the chart below, make five noun phrases that use more than one modifier. Then write a sentence for each noun phrase. You can use singular or plural forms of the nouns. Compare your sentences to the examples and to those of several other students.

| DETERMINERS | INTENSIFIERS | ADJECTIVES AND PARTICIPLES | NOUN MODIFIERS | NOUNS |
|---|---|---|---|---|
| a | very | little | stone | teacher |
| some | rather | experienced | English | statue |
| your | extremely | cute | circus | animals |
| the | quite | famous | university | watches |
| this | wonderfully | relaxing | pocket | professor |
| those | really | expensive | three-week | vacation |
| | somewhat | good | grammar | |
| | | pleasant | | |
| | | ugly | | |

**Examples:** I like this really expensive pocket watch.
Only your very experienced English teachers will know the answer.
Many very famous university professors are not very *good* teachers.

1. _____

_____

2. _____

_____

3. _____

_____

4. _____

_____

5. _____

_____

# FOCUS 2 | Order of Descriptive Adjectives

Different categories of descriptive adjectives **usually** occur in the following order.

| EVALUATION/ OPINION | APPEARANCE | AGE | COLOR | ORIGIN |
|---|---|---|---|---|
| good | *size/measure* | old | red | *geographical* |
| bad | big | young | green | French |
| ugly | small | new | blue | Mexican |
| interesting | low | antique | striped | Japanese |
| nice | high | | bright green | *material* |
| intelligent | heavy | | dark blue | wooden |
| | | | deep purple | vegetable |
| | *shape* | | | cotton |
| | round | | | brass |
| | square | | | |
| | triangular | | | |
| | *condition* | | | |
| | chipped | | | |
| | broken | | | |
| | rotten | | | |

Within a category there is some possible variation.

| EXAMPLES | EXPLANATIONS |
|---|---|
| (a)  a **big, round, shiny** apple <br> (b)  a **big, shiny, round** apple <br> (c)  a **shiny, big, round** apple | Adjectives of **appearance** usually follow the order in (a): **size, shape, condition**. But other orders are also possible. |
| (d)  a **Japanese silk** fan <br> (e)  a **silk Japanese** fan | Adjectives of **origin** usually follow the order in (d): **geographical, material**. But other orders are also possible. |

## EXERCISE 2

Put the descriptive adjectives in these noun phrases in the correct category in the chart below or your notebook. Not every category is used in each noun phrase. The first one has been done for you as an example.

Here are some things that were for sale at the flea market:

1. handsome, small, well-polished Italian leather shoes
2. a big shiny new red racing bicycle
3. a cute little brown puppy
4. some beautiful old Thai silk pajamas
5. a round antique brass tea tray
6. a painted Japanese wooden screen
7. an interesting recent French physics textbook
8. a funky, broken-down old chair

| CATEGORY | 1 | 2 | 3 | 4 | 5 | 6 | 7 | 8 |
|---|---|---|---|---|---|---|---|---|
| **EVALUATION/ OPINION** | handsome | | | | | | | |
| **APPEARANCE** | | | | | | | | |
| size | small | | | | | | | |
| shape | — | | | | | | | |
| condition | well-polished | | | | | | | |
| **AGE** | — | | | | | | | |
| **COLOR** | — | | | | | | | |
| **ORIGIN** | | | | | | | | |
| geographical | Italian | | | | | | | |
| material | leather | | | | | | | |
| **NOUN** | shoes | | | | | | | |

## EXERCISE 3

Add the modifiers in the correct order to the following passages. The first one has been done for you as an example.

My friend Wolfgang is a shopaholic. Whenever he goes out of the house he

returns with some (1) ___strange new___ (new, strange) "bargain." He rarely

buys any (2) _____ (useful, really) items. Once he came home with

some (3) _____ (bright, flannel, purple) blankets. "They match my

(4) _____ (pretty, French, new) curtains," he said. But those curtains were

still in their (5) _____ (plastic, original) wrappings. He was so busy

shopping that he hadn't had time to hang them up.

Fortunately, Wolfgang refuses to buy anything secondhand. I can imagine all

the (6) _____ (useless, incredibly ugly, antique) "art objects" he would

bring home. He already has (7) _____ (brand-new, European, expensive,

plenty of, brightly colored) shirts and sweaters. But that doesn't stop him from buying

more. He just piles them into his (8) _____ (little, dark, bedroom, over-

crowded) closet. He has some (9) _____ (Italian, nice, handmade) shoes

that I have never even seen him wearing.

He's running out of space to put things. He has such a (10) _____

(new, nice) apartment with lots of storage space, but his closets look like some

(11) _____ (old, poor) shopkeeper's (12) _____

(frightening, terrible) nightmare!

## EXERCISE 4

Are these sentences correct or incorrect? If they are incorrect, identify the problem and correct it.

1. I bought a green, old, pretty vase at the flea market.
2. He's a university, brand-new dormitory resident.
3. It's an antique, genuine, black, old-fashioned umbrella.
4. Would you like some of these delicious, little, chocolate candies?
5. Would you like to hear about my summertime, exciting, vacation plans?

**form**

| FOCUS 3 | **Participle Modifiers** |
|---|---|

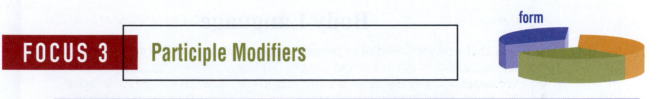

| EXAMPLES | EXPLANATIONS |
|---|---|
| (a) **The interesting man** told **fascinating** stories about his adventures in Sumatra.<br><br>(b) **The interested woman** listened carefully. She was **fascinated** by the man's stories about his adventures in Sumatra. | Present and past participles can be used like descriptive adjectives to describe nouns. |

| VERB | PRESENT PARTICIPLE | PAST PARTICIPLE | EXPLANATIONS |
|---|---|---|---|
| study | studying | studied | Present participles are formed by adding *-ing* to the verb. |
| forget | forgetting | forgotten | Past participles are formed by adding *-ed* to regular verbs or by using the third form (*-en* form) of irregular verbs. For a review of irregular past participle forms see Appendix 6. |

## EXERCISE 5

Underline all the participles in the following passage, and tell what noun they describe. The first paragraph has been done as an example.

**Examples:** (1) revealing—present participle, describes "information"
(2) hidden—past participle, describes "emotions"
(3) widespread—past participle, describes "reactions"
(4) exciting—present participle, describes "situations"; increased—past participle, describes "heart rates"
(5) no participle modifiers in this sentence

# Body Language

(1) Unconscious facial expressions and "body language" often give <u>revealing</u> information to other people. (2) Many people's "<u>hidden</u>" emotions are actually quite visible to anyone who knows how to read people's faces. (3) Some reactions are so <u>widespread</u> in all cultures that there seems to be a physical basis for them. (4) All people react in the same way to certain <u>exciting</u> situations by breathing more rapidly and experiencing <u>increased</u> heart rates. (5) Facial expressions of basic emotions, such as anger, surprise, and amusement, appear to be universal.

(6) Other reactions are not so universal. (7) Many, but not all, individuals respond to an embarrassing situation by blushing (when the face and neck turn bright red). (8) Some people show that they are bored by growing less active and becoming sleepy or inattentive. (9) Others respond to boring situations by becoming more active and showing such physical signs as jiggling feet or wiggling fingers. (10) But for other people, such reactions may be unintended indications of nervousness or anxiety, not boredom. (11) When someone experiences a confusing situation, he or she may unconsciously try to hide that confusion by smiling, thus making what is known as "the stupid grin." (12) But another person might respond by looking angry.

(13) There are not only variations in this "silent language" between different individuals, but there are also important differences between cultures. (14) Certain kinds of "silent language" give one particular message in one culture, but a conflicting message in another culture. (15) For example, eye contact (looking directly into the eyes of the person you are speaking to) has very different meanings in different cultures. (16) In American culture, if you do not look directly into someone's eyes while talking, the listener will think that you are dishonest. (17) If someone is described as "shifty-eyed" it means that he or she cannot be trusted. (18) But in many Asian cultures, avoiding eye contact is a sign of politeness and respect, and prolonged eye contact (which indicates sincerity in American culture) means aggression or hostility, and is seen as a threatening behavior. (19) Mistaken "body language" can often result in even more misunderstanding than using the wrong word or incorrect grammar.

**FOCUS 4** — **Meanings of Present and Past Participles**

| EXAMPLES | EXPLANATIONS |
|---|---|
| (a) a **loving** mother (She loves her children.) | Present participles modify **agents.** The agents do or perform the actions described by the participle. |
| (b) a **well-loved** mother (She is loved by her children.) | Past participles modify **receivers.** The receivers are affected by the action described by the participle. |

## EXERCISE 6

Paraphrase these sentences by choosing the correct participle for the cues given.

**Example:** Most of my friends enjoy reading novels.

Most of my friends are _____interested_____ (interest) in reading novels.

Novels are _____interesting_____ (interest) to most of my friends.

1. The audience didn't understand the lecture.
   a. The audience was _____ (confuse).
   b. The lecture was _____ (confuse).

2. The students didn't do well on the exam.
   a. The exam results were _____ (disappoint).
   b. The students were _____ (disappoint).

3. Children who watch scary movies may not be able to sleep afterwards.
   a. (Frighten) _____ children may not be able to go to sleep.
   b. (Frighten) _____ movies may keep children from sleeping.

4. That was quite a delicious snack.
   a. The snack was quite _____ (satisfy).
   b. We were quite _____ (satisfy).

5. Most students enjoy studying grammar.
   a. Most students are _____ (interest) in grammar.
   b. Grammar is _____ (interest) to most students.

## EXERCISE 7

Use present or past participles to complete these definitions.

**Example:** Information that reveals thoughts can be described as _____revealing_____ information.

Emotions that people hide can be described as _____hidden_____ emotions.

1. Situations that excite people can be described as _____ situations.

2. Temperatures that rise can be described as _____ temperatures.

3. A situation that embarrasses people can be described as an _____ situation.

4. Results that people can prove in experiments can be described as _____ results.

5. News that depresses people can be described as _____ news.

6. Individuals whom some bad news depresses can be described as _____ individuals.

7. A question that puzzles people can be described as a _____ question.

8. People that are puzzled by a question can be described as _____ people.

## FOCUS 5 | Adding Information to Participles

### Noun + Participle

| EXAMPLES | EXPLANATIONS |
|---|---|
| (a) a **man-eating** tiger <br> (a tiger that eats people) <br><br> (b) a **trend-setting** fashion <br> (a fashion that sets a trend) <br><br> (c) a **fire-breathing** dragon <br> (a dragon that breathes fire) | Present participles usually describe the agent. You can also identify the receiver of the action by adding nouns. |
| (d) a **flea-bitten** dog <br> (a dog that is bitten by fleas) <br><br> (e) a **manmade** lake <br> (a lake that was made by people) <br><br> (f) a **male-dominated** society <br> (a society that is dominated by males) | Past participles usually describe the receiver. You can add nouns to past participles when you want to identify the agent as well. <br><br> Some noun-participle combinations appear without hyphens. |

### Adverb + Participle

| EXAMPLES | EXPLANATIONS |
|---|---|
| (g) a **fast-moving** train <br> (a train that moves fast) <br><br> (h) some **homegrown** tomatoes <br> (tomatoes that were grown at home) <br><br> (i) a **much-visited** attraction <br> (an attraction that is visited a lot) | You can add adverbs to both past and present participles to include important additional information to the participles. <br><br> Some special cases appear without hyphens. |

### Special Cases

| EXAMPLES | EXPLANATIONS |
|---|---|
| (j) a **blue-eyed** baby <br> (a baby with blue eyes) <br><br> (k) a **long-legged** ballet dancer <br> (a dancer with long legs) | You can make "past participles" from some adjective-noun combinations to describe certain kinds of physical characteristics. |
| (l) a **barely concealed** dislike <br><br> (m) a **deeply depressed** individual | Adverb-participle combinations, especially adverbs ending with -*ly* appear without hyphens |

## EXERCISE 8

Use the information in these sentences to make participles.

**Example:** The story is loved very much. It's a ___much-loved___ story.

1. In that incredible jump, the sky-diver defied death.

   The sky-diver made a _____ jump.

2. I bought this cake at a store.

   It's a _____ cake.

3. Gladstone Gulp bought a machine to reduce his weight.

   It's a _____ machine.

4. They trained the new employee well.

   She became a _____ employee.

5. That poor kitten is starved for love.

   It's a _____ kitten.

6. They filmed the movie with a camera that they held by hand.

   It was filmed with a _____ camera.

7. Look at that man with the long hair!

   Look at that _____ man!

8. Learning grammar can consume a lot of time.

   It can be a _____ activity.

## EXERCISE 9

Write original sentences that describe at least five of the following.

1. the most boring teacher you have ever had
2. the most self-satisfied politician you have ever heard of or read about
3. The most surprised reaction you have ever seen
4. The most amazing thing you have ever seen
5. The most worried person in your family
6. The most modern-thinking political leader you know
7. The behavior of the most bored student you have ever known
8. The most irritating habit your best friend has

## EXERCISE 10

Choose the correct participle form for these sentences from the cues given. The first paragraph has been done for you as an example.

Problems in communication can happen when some of the conscious and unconscious actions of the (1) _____nonspoken_____ (nonspeak) part of a language are misunderstood. There can sometimes be (2) _____confusing_____ (confuse) situations between teachers and students in the classroom.

Teachers in American classrooms, for example, may often become (3) _____ (annoy) when students don't volunteer answers to general questions in class. Silence in American classrooms often means that the students are (4) _____ (bore), (5) _____ (disinterest), or (6) _____ (uninvolve) in the class activity. Similarly, teachers interpret eye contact from students as a sign that the lesson is (7) _____ (interest) and (8) _____ (involve) for them, and that they are actively (9) _____ (engage) in the learning process.

Students are sometimes (10) _____ (confuse) about the best way to show that they are paying attention. In an American classroom, asking questions is one good way to do this, but students from other cultures may be (11) _____ (embarrass) by having to admit that they are (12) _____ (confuse). Sometimes they feel (13) _____ (worry) that asking questions may be interpreted as (14) _____ (teacher-challenge) behavior or as a somewhat (15) _____ (insult) suggestion that the teacher has not explained things clearly enough.

The best way to solve these misunderstandings is to talk about them in class. Both American teachers and international students alike are often very (16) _____ (surprise) to find out about their sometimes (17) _____ (mistake) assumptions about what classroom behavior means in different cultures.

**form**

## FOCUS 6    Modifiers That Follow Noun Phrases

| PARTICIPIAL PHRASES | PREPOSITIONAL PHRASES | EXPLANATION |
|---|---|---|
| (a) The man **speaking to John** told him some shocking information. | (b) The man **with John** told him some shocking information. | Prepositional phrases occur after the noun. |
| (c) The woman **surrounded by reporters** is a world-renowned expert on nonverbal communication. | (d) The woman **next to the window** is a world-renowned expert on nonverbal communication. | Participial phrases can occur before or after the noun, but there is a difference in function. |

| EXAMPLES | EXPLANATIONS |
|---|---|
| (e) The man **speaking to John** told him some shocking information. | Participial phrases usually come after the noun if they identify the noun (tell which particular noun we are talking about). |
| (f) **Speaking to the man,** John found out some shocking information. | They can come before the noun if that noun has already been identified and the participle describes more about the noun. |

### ▌ EXERCISE 11

Underline the modifying phrases in this article. Draw an arrow to indicate the noun each phrase modifies. Circle the noun. The first two sentences have been done for you as an example.

(1) One aspect of nonverbal communication frequently mentioned by researchers discussing cross-cultural differences is the varying size of the "conversation bubble" in each culture. (2) This bubble is the amount of physical distance maintained between people engaged in different kinds of conversation. (3) Americans having polite social conversations usually stand about an arm's length apart. (4) Closer distances are permitted only between people having a more intimate relationship. (5) Unless you are a very close friend or family member, moving closer than an arm's length is usually interpreted as overly aggressive (either socially or sexually). (6) People growing up in Latin cultures tend to have a smaller conversation bubble than people coming from Northern European cultures. (7) As a result, North Americans or Northern Europeans sometimes come across as a little cold or unfriendly to people raised in Latin countries such as Italy, Spain, or Latin America. (8) In general, Middle Eastern cultures tend to have the smallest conversation bubble, while Northern Asian and Northern European cultures tend to have the largest.

# Use Your English

Go to a flea market, thrift shop, garage sale, or even a department store. Write brief descriptions of things you find there that fit these categories:

- something really cheap
- something that costs more than $25
- something you might like to own

- something funny
- something ugly

ACTIVITY  **speaking**

Play *Adjective Tennis* with a partner. Here's how it's done:

■ **STEP 1**    One person thinks of a noun phrase (a noun plus a determiner) and a modifier.

■ **STEP 2**    The other person puts the modifier in its correct position and gives another modifier for the first person to add to the noun phrase. The modifier has to make sense. For example, if the noun is radio, intelligent is not an acceptable modifier.

■ **STEP 3**    The person who can't think of an appropriate modifier, or who puts it in the wrong place, loses. Keep going until one person puts an adjective in the wrong place or can't think of something new to add. You may want a third student to act as your referee.

**Example:**   Student 1:   a ball . . . tennis
Student 2:   a **tennis** ball . . . old
Student 1:   an **old** tennis ball . . . rubber
Student 2:   an old **rubber** tennis ball . . . dirty
Student 1:   a **dirty** old rubber tennis ball . . . incredibly
Student 2:   an **incredibly** dirty old rubber tennis ball . . . huge
Student 1:   an incredibly dirty, **huge** old rubber tennis ball . . . etc.

# ACTIVITY 3 speaking/writing

Examine this list of common emotions and choose two or three:

| | | | |
|---|---|---|---|
| boredom | embarrassment | depression | confusion |
| annoyance | worry | amusement | excitement |

■ **STEP 1**  For each emotion identify two or three situations that cause you to feel that emotion. Next identify two or three typical physical (body language) or psychological (hidden) reactions you have when you feel each of the emotions. The first one has been done as an example.

| BORING SITUATIONS: | BORED REACTIONS: |
|---|---|
| 1. long meetings | 1. I yawn, get sleepy, fidget |
| 2. gossip about people I don't know | 2. I think about other things |
| 3. talking about things that don't interest me | 3. I draw pictures in my notebook |

■ **STEP 2**  Compare your responses and the situations that cause those responses with those of other students in the class. Discuss these questions:

- Are there universal unconscious body language reactions to certain emotions?
- Which category showed more individual variation: the reactions or the situations?
- Do some cultures express emotions more readily than others?

■ **STEP 3**  Present your ideas to the rest of the class, or write answers to the discussion questions for your teacher to read and correct.

# ACTIVITY 4 speaking/writing

Think of three characteristics that make someone fascinating and three characteristics that make someone boring. Compare your answers with those of several other people and make a list of characteristics that everyone agrees on. Present your list to the class.

**ACTIVITY 5** **speaking**

Are facial expressions universal? This is a chart used to teach a common "vocabulary" of facial expressions to deaf students. Examine these expressions in a small group made up of people from different cultures (if possible). In your culture are there any feelings expressed by different facial expressions than the ones shown? How are facial expressions different in other cultures? Present your ideas to the class.

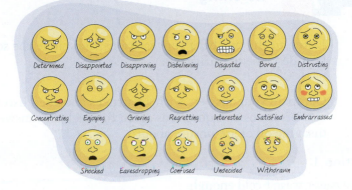

Determined · Disappointed · Disapproving · Disbelieving · Disgusted · Bored · Distrusting
Concentrating · Enjoying · Grieving · Regretting · Interested · Satisfied · Embarrassed
Shocked · Eavesdropping · Confused · Undecided · Withdrawn

**ACTIVITY 6** **speaking**

Below are some other facial expressions. The emotions they portray have been omitted. Choose four or five expressions.

■ **STEP 1**    Use adjectives or participles to describe these expressions. Be ready to explain why you have chosen the description that you did.

*(continued)*

■ **STEP 2**    Compare your answers with those of several other students in the class. Did you interpret any of the expressions differently? Do those differences tell you anything about facial expressions in other cultures?

■ **STEP 3**    Report any significant differences or insights to the class.

**ACTIVITY 7 listening**

CD Tracks
14, 15

■ **STEP 1**    Listen to the two brief conversations, and circle the sentences that best describe the situation.

■ **STEP 2**    Compare your answers with a partner's and then listen to the conversations and questions again to check any answers that you disagree on or are unsure about.

**Conversation 1**

1.  a.  The water wasn't cold enough.
    b.  She wanted a glass of water.

2.  a.  She wanted iced water.
    b.  She didn't want iced water.

3.  a.  The tea was too warm.
    b.  The tea was too small.

**Conversation 2**

1.  a.  The girl's grandmother is the one who teaches physics.
    b.  The girl's grandmother is the one who is retired.

2.  a.  He's trying to organize a lecture program for senior citizens.
    b.  He's trying to organize a lecture program for physics.

3.  a.  The girl's mother is the one who teaches physics.
    b.  The girl's mother is the one who teaches biology.

## ACTIVITY 8 research on the web

 Go to the Internet and use an Internet search engine such as Google® or Yahoo®. Enter the keywords "body language" or "nonverbal communication". There are several "dictionaries" of nonverbal patterns. Scan through a few of the sites you find there and pick one that you think would be interesting and helpful to other students in the class. Present the site to the rest of the class and tell why you chose it.

## ACTIVITY 9 reflection

Facial expressions, eye contact, and other examples of body language communicate meaning as powerfully as words, and they vary widely from culture to culture.

■ **STEP 1**   Observe Americans speaking to each other in different situations. Identify at least one gesture (this can be a body movement or hand signal) and one facial expression that you think are being used to communicate meaning in the conversation. Write a brief description of the nonverbal behavior and what you think the meaning of it was.

■ **STEP 2**   Think of one example of non-verbal behavior used by people in your culture that is different from that in the United States. It could be something obvious like bowing or shaking hands in certain situations or something more subtle, such as eye contact or maintaining a certain physical distance during a conversation.

■ **STEP 3**   Work with three or four other students to choose two or three "typical" American gestures that every student of English should learn. Practice them as a group and teach them to the rest of the class. You may also want to demonstrate the non-verbal behavior from your own culture. Explain its meaning to the class.

# COMPARATIVES

## UNIT GOALS

- **Correctly express various degrees of similarity and difference**

- **Correctly use different complex comparisons of amount**

- **Understand and use formal and informal statements of comparison**

## OPENING TASK

### Comparing Developing and Developed Countries

Here is some statistical information about four countries that were once British colonies. Use the information to discuss the following questions with a partner or in a small group.

- What are some things that Bangladesh and Pakistan have in common? What are some differences?

- What are some things that Canada and the United States have in common? What are some differences?

- What are some differences between developed and developing countries? Are there similarities? What are they?

---

**People's Republic of Bangladesh**

| | |
|---|---|
| **Area:** | 144,000 sq. km. |
| **Population:** | 147,365,352 |
| **% under 15 years old** | 33% |
| **Growth rate:** | 2.09% |
| **Life expectancy** | 62 years |
| **Languages:** | (national) Bangla; (official) English |
| **Religion:** | Muslim 83%, Hindu 16% |
| **Literacy rate:** | males 54%, females 32% |
| **GDP:** (Gross domestic product) | $304.3 billion |
| **Per capita GDP:** (gross domestic product per person) | $2,100 per year |
| **% of population below poverty line** | 45% |
| **Politically independent since:** | 1947 from Britain; 1971 from Pakistan |

---

## Islamic Republic of Pakistan

| | |
|---|---|
| **Area:** | 803,940 sq km. |
| **Population:** | 165,803,560 |
| **% under 15 years old** | 39% |
| **Growth rate:** | 2.09% |
| **Life expectancy** | 63 |
| **Languages:** | (national) Urdu, (official) English, (regional) Punjabi, Sindhi, Pashtu, Baluchi |
| **Religion:** | Sunni Muslim 77%, Shi'a Muslim 20%, other 3% |
| **Literacy rate:** | males: 62%  females 35% |
| **GDP:** (Gross domestic product) | $393.4 billion |
| **Per capita GDP:** (gross domestic product per person) | $2,400 per year |
| **% of population below poverty line** | 32% |
| **Politically independent since:** | 1947 from Britain |

## United States of America

| | |
|---|---|
| **Area:** | 9,631,420 |
| **Population:** | 298,444,215 |
| **% under 15 years old** | 20.4% |
| **Growth rate:** | 0.91% |
| **Life expectancy** | 78 |
| **Languages:** | English |
| **Religion:** | Protestant 52%, Catholic 24%, Mormon 2%, Jewish 1%, Muslim 1%, other 10%, none 10% |
| **Literacy rate:** | 99% |
| **GDP:** (Gross domestic product) | $12.36 trillion |
| **Per capita GDP:** (gross domestic product per person) | $41,800 per year |
| **% of population below poverty line** | 12% |
| **Politically independent since:** | 1776 from Britain |

## Canada

| | |
|---|---|
| **Area:** | 9,984,670 sq km |
| **Population:** | 33,098,932 |
| **% under 15 years old** | 18% |
| **Growth rate:** | 0.9% |
| **Life expectancy** | 80.2 years |
| **Languages:** | English, French |
| **Religion:** | Roman Catholic 43%, Protestant 23%, other Christian 4.4%, Muslim 1.9%, other and unspecified 11.8%, none 16% |
| **Literacy rate:** | 99% for both males and females |
| **GDP:** (Gross domestic product) | $1.114 trillion |
| **Per capita GDP:** (gross domestic product per person) | $34,000 per year |
| **% of population below poverty line** | 16% |
| **Politically independent since:** | 1867 from Britain |

**FOCUS 1**  **Comparisons of Degree: Adjectives and Adverbs**

| EXAMPLES | MEANING | FORM |
|---|---|---|
| | MORE:  X > Y | X *is* (intensifier) $\begin{cases} \text{adjective} + er \\ more + \\ \quad \text{adjective} \\ more + \\ \quad \text{adverb} \end{cases}$ *than Y.* |
| (a) Pakistan **is much larger than** Bangladesh is. <br> (b) The people of Pakistan are **somewhat more literate than** the people of Bangladesh. <br> (c) Bangladesh is growing **slightly more quickly than** Pakistan is. | large difference ↕ small difference | *much* <br> *considerably* <br> *substantially*  } intensifiers <br> *somewhat* <br> *slightly/a bit* |
| (d) Pakistan's post-colonial history is **just as recent as** Bangladesh's is. | THE SAME; X = Y | X *is* (intensifier) *as* $\begin{cases} \text{adjective} \\ \text{adverb} \end{cases}$ *as Y.* <br><br> *exactly* <br> *just*  } intensifiers |
| (e) Pakistan's female literacy rate is **almost as low as** Bangladesh's. | LESS: X < Y | X *is* (intensifier) *as* $\begin{cases} \text{adjective} \\ \text{adverb} \end{cases}$ *as Y.* <br><br> small difference  *almost* <br> *nearly*  } intensifiers |
| (f) Pakistan is **not as crowded as** Bangladesh is. <br> (g) Bangladesh is **not nearly as large as** Pakistan. | small difference ↕ large difference | X *is not* (intensifier) *as* $\begin{cases} \text{adjective} \\ \text{adverb} \end{cases}$ *as Y.* <br><br> *quite* <br> *nearly*  } intensifiers |
| (h) Bangladesh is growing **slightly less rapidly than** Pakistan. <br> (i) Bangladesh is **substantially less prosperous than** Pakistan is. | small difference ↕ large difference | X *is* (intensifier) *less* $\begin{cases} \text{adjective} \\ \text{adverb} \end{cases}$ *than Y.* <br><br> *slightly/a bit* <br> *somewhat* <br> *substantially/* } intensifiers <br> *considerably* <br> *much* |

## EXERCISE 1

In the following chart, write statements of comparison about the United States and Canada. Use the information on page 167. Use intensifiers to make accurate statements.

| MEANING | FORM | COMPARATIVE STATEMENT |
|---|---|---|
| MORE | *. . . er than* | The area of Canada is somewhat larger than the area of the United States. |
|  | *more . . . than* | _____ |
| THE SAME | *as . . . as* | _____ |
| LESS | *nearly as . . . as* | _____ |
|  | *not as . . . as* | _____ |
|  | *less . . . than* | _____ |

## EXERCISE 2

Read the paragraph on the next page comparing Pakistan and Bangladesh and fill in the chart. For each feature listed, note whether it is greater in Pakistan or in Bangladesh, and whether the difference is large or small.

| FEATURE | GREATER IN PAKISTAN OR BANGLADESH? | SMALL OR LARGE DIFFERENCE? |
|---|---|---|
| Population | Pakistan | small |
| Area | Pakistan | large |
| Population density |  |  |
| Standard of living |  |  |
| Population growth |  |  |
| GDP |  |  |
| Educational development |  |  |
| Prosperity |  |  |

(1) Although the population of Bangladesh is slightly less than that of Pakistan, its land area is considerably smaller. (2) This means that the population density of Pakistan is not nearly as great as that of Bangladesh, and as a result, the general standard of living is substantially higher. (3) Although the population of Pakistan is not growing quite as quickly as Bangladesh's, its GDP is somewhat higher, and as a result, it will be a very long time before the standard of living for Bangladeshis becomes as high as for Pakistanis. (4) Educational development is not quite as high in Bangladesh as in Pakistan; economic development is somewhat lower, and, as a result, people in Bangladesh are generally less prosperous.

## EXERCISE 3

Make comparative statements about the countries below using the information provided. Use appropriate intensifiers to describe whether the difference is large or small. Compare your statements to those of a partner.

**Example:** *The literacy rate in Brunei is slightly lower than in Bulgaria.*
*Brunei's per capita GDP is considerably higher than Bulgaria's.*

|  | BRUNEI | BULGARIA |
|---|---|---|
| Per capita GDP | $23,600 | $8200 |
| Population | 372,631 | 7,450,349 |
| Literacy rate | 94% | 98.6% |

|  | JAMAICA | JAPAN |
|---|---|---|
| Per capita GDP | $4100 | $29,400 |
| Population | 2,731,832 | 127,417,244 |
| Literacy rate | male 84.1% females 91.6% | 99.5% |

| | SOUTH KOREA | TURKEY |
|---|---|---|
| Per capita GDP | $19,200 | $7,400 |
| Population | 48,422,644 | 69,600,559 |
| Literacy rate | 98% | males 84.1%<br>females 78.7% |

## EXERCISE 4

Interview a partner to obtain the following information, and then make statements that compare you and your partner.

**Example:** *My partner is substantially older than I am.*
*I am much younger than my partner.*

*1894 Feb July 8th*
*90-13.*

| QUESTIONS | YOUR PARTNER | YOU |
|---|---|---|
| How old | 37 23. | 18 19. |
| How long studying English | 2 years | 12 years. |
| When he/she usually goes to sleep | 11 o'clock | 12 o'clock |
| How often he/she goes to the movies | once/mouth | once twice   twice/month |
| How quickly he/she thinks English skills are improving | | |
| How big his/her family? | 10. | 3. |

| | |
|---|---|
| **FOCUS 2** | **Comparisons of Amount: Noun Phrases** |

| EXAMPLES | MEANING | FORM |
|---|---|---|
| (a) Pakistan has **much more land area than** Bangladesh does. | **MORE: X > Y** | X + VP + (intensifier) + *more* NP *than* Y (*does*)* |
| (b) Pakistan has **somewhat more people than** Bangladesh. | large difference ↕ small difference | *much/many considerably/ substantially slightly somewhat* } intensifiers |
| (c) One has **as much representation as** the other. | **THE SAME: X = Y** | X + VP + (intensifier) + *as much/many* NP *as* Y (*does*)* |
| (d) Pakistan sends **just as many representatives** to the U.N. **as** Bangladesh does. | | *exactly just* } intensifiers |
| (e) Bangladesh has **almost as many people under 15 years old as** Pakistan. | **LESS: X < Y** | X + VP + (intensifier) *as much/many* NP *as* Y (*does*)* |
| (f) Pakistan does not have **quite as many people living in poverty as** Bangladesh does. | small difference | *almost nearly* } intensifiers |
| (g) Bangladesh doesn't have **nearly as much land area as** Pakistan. | small difference large difference | X + *not* + VP + (intensifier) *as much/many* NP *as* Y (*does*)*<br><br>*quite nearly* } intensifiers |
| (h) Bangladesh has **slightly fewer people than** Pakistan. | | X + VP + (intensifier) *fewer/less* NP *than* Y (*does*)* |
| (i) Bangladesh has **much less land than** Pakistan does. | small difference ↕ large difference | *slightly somewhat substantially/ considerably much/many* } intensifiers |

*NP = Noun Phrase    VP = Verb Phrase

## EXERCISE 5

In the following chart, write statements of comparison about the United States and Canada. Use the information on page 167. Use intensifiers to make accurate statements.

| MEANING | FORM | COMPARATIVE STATEMENT |
|---|---|---|
| MORE | *more . . . than* | The United States had substantially more people than Canada. |
| THE SAME | *as much/many . . . as* | |
| LESS | *almost as much/many . . . as* | |
| | *not* + VERB + *as much/ many . . . as* | |
| | *fewer/less . . . than* | |

## EXERCISE 6

Read the paragraph comparing Pakistan and Bangladesh starting below. Underline the first comparison statement in each sentence and rewrite it. Then say whether the difference is big or small.

**Example:** Bangladesh has <u>somewhat fewer people than Pakistan</u>.
*Bangladesh's population is less than Pakistan's. It is a small difference.*

(1) Although Bangladesh has somewhat fewer people than Pakistan, it has considerably less land area. (2) This means that Pakistan does not have nearly as many people per square kilometer as Bangladesh does, and as a result, there is much less pressure on basic resources such as roads and water supply. (3) As a rule, people in Bangladesh have somewhat fewer opportunities for economic improvement than people in Pakistan. (4) Bangladesh has just about as many literate women as Pakistan, but it has fewer people living above the poverty line, and so there is somewhat less political and economic stability in Bangladesh than there is in Pakistan. (5) However, Pakistan has more regional ethnic groups than Bangladesh does, and there are more incidents of ethnic unrest in Pakistan than there are in Bangladesh. (6) Thus, Bangladesh has fewer extreme political conflicts than Pakistan.

# EXERCISE 7

Make comparative statements about the countries below using the information provided. Use appropriate intensifiers to describe whether the difference is large or small. Compare your statements to those of a partner.

**Examples:** *Luxembourg has somewhat more official languages than Libya.*
*Libyans don't make nearly as much money as people in Luxembourg.*

|  | **LUXEMBOURG** | **LIBYA** |
|---|---|---|
| Per capita GDP | $58,900 | $6,700 |
| Number of official languages | 3 | 1 |
| Total GDP | $27.27 billion | $37.48 billion |
| % of population living in poverty | NA | NA |

|  | **SWITZERLAND** | **SWAZILAND** |
|---|---|---|
| Per capita GDP | $33,800 | $5,100 |
| Number of official languages | 3 | 2 |
| Total GDP | $251.9 billion | $6.018 billion |
| % of population living in poverty | 0 | 40% |

|  | **TAIWAN** | **THAILAND** |
|---|---|---|
| Per capita GDP | $25,300 | $8,100 |
| Number of official languages | 1 | 1 |
| Total GDP | $576.2 billion | $524.8 billion |
| % of population living in poverty | 1% | 10% |

## EXERCISE 8

Interview a partner to obtain the following information, and then make statements that compare you and your partner.

**Examples:** a. *My partner has taken the TOEFL® Test\* several more times than I have.* (5 times)
b. *I have taken the TOEFL test fewer times than my partner.* (2 times)

| QUESTIONS | YOUR PARTNER | YOU |
|---|---|---|
| 1. Times he or she has taken the TOEFL test | 5 | 2 |
| 2. Rooms in your partner's house or apartment | | |
| 3. Languages your partner understands | | |
| 4. Number of children he or she has or would like to have | | |
| 5. Countries he or she has visited | | |
| 6. Number of family members | | |

1. a. _____
   b. _____

2. a. _____
   b. _____

3. a. _____
   b. _____

4. a. _____
   b. _____

5. a. _____
   b. _____

6. a. _____
   b. _____

\* TOEFL is a registered trademark of the Educational Testing Service (ETS). This publication is not endorsed or approved by ETS.

**form**   **meaning**

| FOCUS 3 | **Comparisons of Similarity and Difference: Noun Phrases** |
|---|---|

Comparisons can also be made in terms of **similarity** and **difference,** in addition to amount and degree.

| EXAMPLES | MEANING | FORM |
|---|---|---|
| (a) Pakistan uses **exactly the same official language as** Bangladesh. | **IDENTICAL:** X = Y | X + VP + (intensifier) + *the same* NP *as* Y (*does*)* <br> X *and* Y + VP (intensifier) + *the same* NP* |
| (b) Pakistan and Bangladesh use the **same official language.** | | *exactly* *precisely* } intensifiers |
| (c) Pakistan has very **much the same life expectancy rate as** Bangladesh (does). | **SIMILAR:** X ~ Y | X + VP + (intensifier) *the same* NP* *as* Y (*does*). <br> X *and* Y + VP + (intensifier) *the same* NP.* |
| (d) Pakistan and Bangladesh have **almost the same growth rate.** | great similarity ↕ small similarity | *very much* *basically* *almost* *somewhat* } intensifiers |
| (e) Bangladesh does**n't** have **quite the same population as** Pakistan (does). | **DIFFERENT:** X ≠ Y | X + *not* + VP + (intensifier) + *the same* NP *as* Y (*does*).* <br> X *and* Y + *not* VP + (intensifier) *the same* NP.* |
| (f) People in Pakistan and Bangladesh do **not** have **at all the same culture.** | small difference ↕ large difference | *quite* *nearly* *at all* } intensifiers |
| (g) Bangladesh has a **slightly different growth rate from** Pakistan. | | X + VP + (intensifier) + *different* + NP *from/than* Y.* <br> X *and* Y + VP + (intensifier) + *different* + NP* |
| (h) People in Pakistan and Bangladesh have **very different cultures.** | small difference ↕ large difference | *slightly/a bit* *somewhat* *substantially/* *considerably* *much/very* } intensifiers |

*NP = Noun Phrase    VP = Verb Phrase

## EXERCISE 9

Underline the statements of similarity and difference in the following passage. For each comparative structure you find, (a) identify the **things** that are being compared, and (b) decide whether the comparison describes things that are **identical, similar, or different**. The first two sentences have been done for you as an example.

**Example:** *1. (a) different kinds of English; (b) similar*
*2. (a) things like vocabulary and pronunciation; (b) different*

### REGIONAL VARIETIES OF ENGLISH

(1) Although English is spoken in many countries, English speakers don't all speak quite the same kind of English. (2) Things like vocabulary and pronunciation are often substantially different. (3) The differences between some varieties of English are easy to identify. (4) No one would mistake Indian English for Australian English. (5) The pronunciation features of these two "Englishes" are quite different. (6) British English is substantially different from American English, not only in terms of accent, but also spelling and vocabulary—especially slang.

(7) But the differences between some regional varieties are more subtle. (8) For example, many people think that Canadian and American varieties of English are exactly the same, but in fact, there are some differences, and not all words are pronounced alike. (9) In America the vowel sound in the word *"out"* is pronounced differently from that in *"boot."* (10) But in Canada many people pronounce *shout* basically like *shoot*. (11) To most people Canadian English and American English seem very much alike. (12) But the careful listener will be able to find a number of examples of the ways Americans speak the language differently from their northern neighbors.

## EXERCISE 10

Based on your own knowledge and the statistical information you read about in the Opening Task (pages 166–167), make statements about general similarities and differences between developing countries and developed countries. Describe one characteristic of developing countries that is likely to be (a) identical, (b) similar, (c) somewhat different, and (d) very different from developed countries.

## EXERCISE 11

Interview a partner about how he or she typically likes to spend a vacation. Identify two things about your partner's vacation likes and dislikes that are (a) identical, (b) similar, (c) somewhat different, and (d) very different from yours.

## FOCUS 4 — Comparisons of Similarity and Difference: Verb Phrases

| EXAMPLES | MEANING | FORM |
|---|---|---|
| (a) Canadians pronounce most words **just the same as** Americans (do). | **IDENTICAL OR SIMILAR** | X + VP* + (intensifier) + *the same as* Y (*does*). <br> X *and* Y + VP + (intensifier) + *the same* |
| (b) Canadians and Americans pronounce most words **very much the same**. | | X + VP* (intensifier) *like* Y (*does*). <br> X *and* Y + VP + (intensifier) *alike*. |
| (c) Canadian English sounds **almost like** American English (does). | identical ↕ similar ↕ less similar | *exactly/just* <br> *almost* <br> *very much* <br> *quite/much* <br> *somewhat*  } intensifiers |
| (d) American and Canadian English sound **very much alike**. | | |
| (e) Some Canadian words aren't pronounced **exactly like** American words (are). | **DIFFERENT** | X + *not* + VP* + (intensifier) *like* Y (*does*). <br> X *and* Y + *not* + VP* (intensifier) *alike*. |
| (f) Australian English and Indian English do **not sound at all alike**. | small difference ↕ large difference | *exactly* <br> *quite* <br> *much* <br> *at all*  } intensifiers |
| (g) Canadians do **not** pronounce *out* **quite the same as** Americans (do). | | X + *not* + VP* + (intensifier) *the same as* Y (*does*) <br> X *and* Y + not + VP* + (intensifier) *the same*. |
| (h) Americans and Canadians don't pronounce out **at all the same**. | small difference ↕ large difference | *quite* <br> *a bit* <br> *at all*  } intensifiers |
| (i) Canadians pronounce English **a bit differently from** Americans. | | X + VP* + (intensifier) *differently from/than* Y <br> X *and* Y + VP* + (intensifier) *differently*. |
| (j) Australians and Americans pronounce English **quite differently**. | small difference ↕ large difference | *a bit* <br> *somewhat* <br> *quite*  } intensifiers |

*VP = Verb Phrase

## EXERCISE 12

Use the information you read in Exercise 9 and your own experience to make statements of similarity and difference using the cues below. Use intensifiers to indicate whether these differences are large or small.

**Examples:** Indians/Australians/pronounce English/like
*Indians don't pronounce English at all like Australians.*

Canadians/Americans/pronounce English/alike
*Canadians and Americans don't pronounce English quite alike.*

1. British/American/use slang expressions/differently
2. No two countries/speak a common language/the same
3. Spanish in Spain/in Latin America/differently from
4. The word *color*/in Britain/in America/is spelled/not alike
5. Many Canadians pronounce the vowel in *shout/shoot* /the same as
6. Grammar/in regional varieties of English/alike

| FOCUS 5 | Informal Usage of Comparisons |

**use**

There are differences between formal (written) and informal (spoken) English when making comparative statements.

| LESS FORMAL/CONVERSATIONAL STYLE | MORE FORMAL/WRITTEN STYLE |
|---|---|
| (a) The culture of Pakistan is **different than** Bangladesh. | (b) The culture of Pakistan is **different from** that of Bangladesh. |
| (c) Canadians pronounce certain words **differently than** Americans. | (d) Canadians pronounce certain words **differently from** Americans. |
| (e) Pakistan had **much the same** colonial history **that** Bangladesh **did.** | (f) Pakistan had **much the same** colonial history **as Bangladesh.** |

## EXERCISE 13

Change these informal comparisons to their more formal variations.

1. Canadian English follows the same grammatical rules that American English does.
2. My partner usually spends his vacations differently than me.
3. The social values of Korea are quite different than Kuwait.
4. Many people in developing countries have a lower per capita income than many people in developed countries.
5. My brother has almost the same hobbies that I do.

# Use Your English

## ACTIVITY 1 speaking

How can you tell if someone is from another country? What are some things people do differently when they come from another culture?

■ **STEP 1**  Working with a partner from another culture, talk about how you know when someone is a foreigner. If you can, be sure to ask two or three Americans how they know when someone is from another country.

■ **STEP 2**  Identify some general or universal differences in behavior, dress, etc. that are true for all cultures. Some examples of generic differences are: speaking with an accent, clothing styles, and so on.

## ACTIVITY 2 writing/speaking

Have you ever met someone who reminds you of someone else? What characteristics and actions were similar? In what ways were the two people different? In a brief essay or oral presentation, tell about these two people.

## ACTIVITY 3 listening

Listen to the conversation between Kim and Bob about a class in Anthropology. See if you can get enough information to answer the questions on the quiz that Professor Jordan gave them the next day. If necessary you can listen to the conversation more than once.

CD Track 16

Anthropology 112: Cultural Geography Quiz #3
1. Define "language family."
2. Define "culture family."
3. What two examples of culture families were mentioned in the lecture?
4. What is the relationship between culture and economic and political problems in developing countries?

## ACTIVITY 4   reading/speaking

In this unit you have examined some information on the economic differences between developing and developed countries. Based on the information in this unit as well as your own knowledge, discuss the questions below in a small group.

- Which do you think is a more common source of conflict between nations: economic differences or cultural differences? Can you give examples to support your opinion?
- What do the differences and similarities between developed and developing countries mean for world peace and global development?

## ACTIVITY 5   research on the web

Go onto the Internet and find the *Info Please Almanac* at http://www.infoplease.com/countries.html. Click under "Countries of the World" and find out information about two countries that you are interested in. Look for information about differences in population, geography, and economics and make a brief report that compares these two countries. You may also try looking for this information by using an Internet search engine such as Google® or Yahoo® and entering the key words, "countries of world". Your teacher will tell you whether the report should be written or oral.

## ACTIVITY 6   reflection

Work with another student. Talk about your strengths and weaknesses as an English language learner. What skills are you particularly good at? What do you find most challenging? What about your partner's skills profile? Together, come up with at least three differences between you and your partner and three ways that each of you can use your strengths to assist your partner in strengthening his or her weak spots.

## UNIT GOALS

- Correctly understand and use different coordinating conjunctions

- Correctly understand and use different sentence connectors

- Correctly understand and use different subordinating conjunctions

## OPENING TASK

### Improving Your Writing

Bambang Soetomo asked his English teacher to point out grammatical problems in his essay about culture shock.

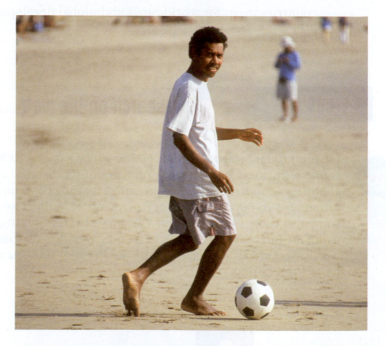

### ■ STEP 1

With a partner, go over the essay and the teacher's comments. What suggestions would you give to Bambang in order to improve his writing? Can you correct his essay?

### ■ STEP 2

Compare your corrected essay to the sample with possible corrections in Exercise 1 on page 187.

My experience with culture shock

Every person has experience with culture shock. However I am no exception. And I have experience with culture shock. Although I have lived in the United States for almost 1 year. I still often feel homesick and I miss my family. When I first came to the U.S., I was very comfortable and because everything was new everything was interesting for me. I enjoyed my independence from my parents. I enjoyed to experience new food and making new friends. Everything was strange, nevertheless I enjoyed the new experiences.

FRAG
RUN-ON
RUN-ON
AWKWARD
AWKWARD

Soon I got used to many differences. Even though I was used to them. Still I wasn't comfortable. Little by little I grew tired of the differences. Because the things in America weren't new to me anymore. The differences weren't interesting they were boring. However I began to miss things in Indonesia. For example, food, my friends, the warm climate. I became depress and homesick. I stayed in my room, because I was tired of speaking English all the time. Even though I studied however my grades weren't so good.

FRAG
FRAG
AWKWARD
RUN-ON
FRAG

So I visited my advisor. He told me about culture shock. I learned that every person has this kind of experience and it can't be avoid. I learned that this culture shock is temporary but universal. My advisor told me I must to keep busy and talk about my culture shock with my friends. This was good advice, as a result, my culture shock became less and in spite I sometimes still miss my life in Indonesia. I don't feel depression the same as before.

RUN-ON
AWKWARD
RUN-ON
AWKWARD

## FOCUS 1 | Overview of Connectors

Connectors show logical relationships between clauses in a sentence, between sentences within a paragraph, or even between paragraphs.

| EXAMPLES | EXPLANATIONS |
|---|---|
| (a) Matt grew up in Kansas, **but** he now lives in San Francisco.<br><br>(b) Bambang **not only** misses his family, **but** he **also** wishes a few friends were in America with him. | There are three categories of connectors: **Coordinating conjunctions** connect two similar grammatical structures, such as noun phrases, prepositional phrases, or independent clauses. |
| (c) Matt grew up in Kansas. **However,** he now lives in San Francisco.<br><br>(d) Bambang misses his family. **In addition,** he wishes that a few friends were in America with him. | **Sentence connectors** show the logical connection between sentences. |
| (e) **Although** Matt grew up in Kansas, he now lives in San Francisco.<br><br>(f) **In spite of his homesickness,** Bambang still tried to concentrate on his studies.<br><br>(g) **In addition to missing** his family, Bambang wishes that a few friends were in America with him. | **Subordinating conjunctions** connect a dependent noun clause, a noun phrase, or a gerund phrase with the main clause. |

Relationships expressed by these connectors can be divided into four general categories: **additive, contrastive, cause and effect,** and **sequence.** See the chart on pages 185–186.

| MEANING | FORM | | |
|---|---|---|---|
| | COORDINATING CONJUNCTIONS | SENTENCE CONNECTORS* | SUBORDINATING CONJUNCTIONS |
| **ADDITIVE** | | | |
| Addition | (a) Bambang misses his family, **and** they miss him. | (b) Bambang misses his family, too. He **also** misses his friends. **In addition**, he is having culture shock. **Besides**, he's homesick. | (c) **In addition to** missing his family, Bambang misses his friends. |
| Emphasis/ Intensifying | (d) **Not only** does Bambang miss his family, **but** he is **also** experiencing culture shock. | (e) **Furthermore**, he's not doing well in school. **In fact**, he failed two midterms. **Actually**, he's quite depressed. **Indeed**, he's thinking about going home. | (f) **Besides** being depressed, he's having trouble in school, **not to mention** feeling lonely all the time. |
| **CONTRASTIVE** | | | |
| Contrast | (g) Everyone experiences culture shock, **but** it eventually passes. | (h) Some people have severe culture shock. Others, **however**, just feel a mild depression. Bambang's culture shock is almost over; yours, **on the other hand**, may just be beginning. Mild culture shock is a universal experience. Deep depression, **in contrast**, is not. | (i) Some people have severe culture shock, **while** others just feel a mild depression. **Whereas** some people have severe culture shock, others just feel a mild depression. |
| Concession (yes . . . but) | (j) The advisor told him culture shock can't be avoided, **yet** it is fortunately temporary. | (k) Bambang feels homesick. **Even so**, he will stay until he finishes his studies. Bambang studies hard. **Nevertheless**, he isn't getting good grades. **In spite of this**, he is still trying to improve. | (l) **Although** he feels homesick, Bambang will stay until he finishes his studies. He isn't getting good grades, **even though** he studies hard. **In spite of** experiencing culture shock/**In spite of the fact that** he still experiences culture shock, Bambang has decided not to go home. |

*Continued on next page*

\* Need an example using *moreover*. See #23 on page 185.

*Continued from previous page*

## FORM

| MEANING | COORDINATING CONJUNCTIONS | SENTENCE CONNECTORS | SUBORDINATING CONJUNCTIONS |
|---|---|---|---|
| **CAUSE AND EFFECT**<br>Reason | (m) Bambang went to see his advisor, **for** he was worried about his grades. | (n) Bambang was worried about his grades. **With this in mind,** he went to see his advisor. | (o) He found it difficult to concentrate, **due to** being depressed. **Because/Since** Bambang was worried about his grades, he went to see his advisor. |
| Result | (p) He was depressed, **so** he went to see his advisor. | (q) Bambang was worried about his grades. **Accordingly,** he went to see his advisor. His advisor told him that culture shock is universal. He **consequently** felt much better about his depression. **As a result,** he decided not to go home early. He **therefore** canceled his plane reservation. | (r) **As a result** of feeling depressed, he decided to talk with his advisor. He made an appointment **so that** he could find out about leaving school early. **In order to** find out more about culture shock, he decided to read some articles about it. |
| Conditional | (s) The advisor told Bambang to keep busy, **or (else)** he would become more depressed. | (t) Bambang didn't want to go home early. **Then** he would feel that he had failed. **Under such circumstances,** he might even feel worse than he had in America. | (u) His advisor told him to get a lot of exercise, **providing/if** he could do that without neglecting his studies. |
| **SEQUENCE**<br>Sequence | (v) He made an appointment, **and** he went directly to see his advisor. | (w) **First,** one must recognize culture shock. **Then** one must deal with it. **Eventually** everyone gets over it. **Soon** they start to feel more comfortable in the new culture. | (x) Bambang felt much better **after** he talked with his advisor. **When** he found out about culture shock, he was glad he hadn't decided to leave **before** talking with his advisor. |

## EXERCISE 1

Identify the form and meaning of the highlighted connectors. The first sentence has been done for you as an example.

**Examples:** and—*form: coordinating conjunction;* **meaning:** *additive*
since—*form: subordinating conjunction;* **meaning:** *reason*

### My Experience with Culture Shock

(1) Every person who has lived in a new culture has had some experience with culture shock, **and** I am no exception, **since** I, too, have had an experience with culture shock. (2) **Although** I have lived in the United States for almost one year, sometimes I still feel homesick, and still miss my family. (3) When I **first** came to the U.S., I was very excited. (4) **Because** everything was new, everything was interesting. (5) I enjoyed my independence from my parents; I **also** enjoyed experiencing new situations and making new friends. (6) **Although** everything was a little strange, I **nevertheless** enjoyed these new experiences. (7) **Eventually** I got used to many of the differences, **but even though** I was used to them, I still wasn't comfortable. (8) **In fact,** little by little I grew tired of the differences. (9) **Because** the things in America weren't new to me anymore, the differences weren't interesting. (10) **Indeed,** they had **actually** become boring. (11) **As a result,** I began to miss things about Indonesia, such as food, friends, and the warm tropical climate, more and more. (12) I **soon** became depressed and homesick. (13) I stayed in my room, **because** I was tired of speaking English all the time. (14) **Even though** I studied hard, my grades weren't good. I wanted to go home. (15) **Because of** these feelings, I decided to see my advisor, **so that** I could get some advice about returning home without finishing my studies. (16) He told me two important things about culture shock. (17) **First,** I learned that any person in a new culture has a similar kind of experience, **and** that culture shock can't be avoided. (18) **Furthermore,** I learned that culture shock is not only universal, but also temporary. (19) **As a result of** his advice, I realized that I should be patient, and that I shouldn't go home just yet. (20) My advisor **also** suggested that I try to keep busy and talk about my culture shock with my friends. (21) I followed this good advice, **and as a result,** my culture shock has become less troublesome. (22) **In spite of the fact that** I sometimes still miss my life in Indonesia, I don't feel as depressed as I did. (23) **Moreover,** I no longer want to return home before I finish my studies. I know that I can adjust to this new life.

## EXERCISE 2

Circle the appropriate connector from the options in parentheses. There may be more than one correct choice.

Both Canada and the United States have large minorities that speak languages other than English. Canada has a large French-speaking minority. The United States, (1) (*on the other hand, furthermore, consequently, yet*) has a large Spanish-speaking minority. (2) (*But, However, So*) the ways the two countries deal with this fact are rather different.

Canada has adopted a policy of bilingualism and has two official languages. All students study both languages in school. (3) (*Moreover, Nevertheless, Therefore*) all official government activities are conducted in both languages.

However, in the United States there is a movement to make English the only official language. (4) (*So, So that, As a result*), some people may be officially discouraged from using languages other than English at work. In some parts of the country, there are very few facilities available to people who can't speak English, (5) (*and, but, yet, so*) (6) (*under such circumstances, on the other hand, in addition to*) Spanish speakers may be required to provide their own translators in such places as hospitals or government offices. (7) (*In spite of, Even though, Consequently*) all students in the public schools are taught English, (8) (*but, and, for, no connector*) English-speaking students are not usually required to study Spanish.

These differences in bilingualism may result from geography. In Canada, the French speakers are actually a majority in certain parts of the country, primarily in the Province of Quebec. In the United States, (9) (*however, on the other hand, in spite of this, therefore*) Spanish-speaking communities are spread around the country. Large numbers of Spanish speakers are found in New York, Florida, New Mexico, and California. (10) (*As a result, Under such circumstances, In addition, Besides*) there are substantial numbers in many other states and large cities. (11) (*Although, However, In spite of*) they do not constitute a majority in any single region.

Complete these sentences using information provided in Exercises 1 and 2.

1. In addition to missing his family, Bambang . . .

   _____

2. In spite of sometimes still missing his family, . . .

   _____

3. Before he talked to his advisor about culture shock, . . .

   _____

4. Bambang now understands that his depression was the result of culture shock.
   Because of this, . . .

   _____

5. Bambang sometimes does poorly on tests, even though . . .

   _____

6. Bambang sometimes does poorly on tests, in spite of . . .

   _____

7. Canada has an official policy of bilingualism. The United States, however, . . .

   _____

8. Canada has an official policy of bilingualism. Consequently, . . .

   _____

9. As a result of Canada's official policy of bilingualism, . . .

   _____

10. Canada's French-speaking minority is concentrated in a particular part of the
    country. Consequently, . . .

    _____

11. Canada's French-speaking minority is concentrated in a particular part of the
    country. Nevertheless, . . .

    _____

12. Since all government business is conducted in both languages, . . .

    _____

# FOCUS 2    Using Coordinating Conjunctions to Connect Parallel Forms

Unlike other connectors, coordinating conjunctions (*and, but, or, nor,* and *yet*) can join any **parallel** grammatical structures.

| EXAMPLES | STRUCTURES BEING JOINED |
|---|---|
| (a) **Jeff** and **Matt** are **roommates** and **best friends**. | nouns |
| (b) They **live** and **work** in San Francisco. | verbs |
| (c) They are **poor** but **hard-working** young men. | adjectives |
| (d) Every Saturday they clean their apartment **quickly** but **thoroughly**. | adverbs |
| (e) They hurry **down the street** and **around the corner** to do their shopping. | prepositional phrases |
| (f) They're always in a hurry **to go bike riding** or **to take their dog to the park**. | infinitives |
| (g) On Saturday nights they like **dancing at discos** and **going to nightclubs** to meet friends. | gerunds |
| (h) They enjoy living together because **they have many common interests,** and **it's cheaper than living alone.** | clauses |

| EXAMPLES | EXPLANATIONS |
|---|---|
| (i) Jeff likes neither **dancing** nor **swimming**. <br> (j) Matt **is** originally from Kansas but now **lives** in San Francisco. | **Parallel Structure (correct):** In formal written English, structures joined by coordinating conjunctions should have the same grammatical form. |
| (k) NOT: Jeff likes both **vacations** and **working**. <br> (l) NOT: Matt **comes** originally from Kansas, but now **living** in San Francisco. | **Nonparallel Structure (not correct)** |

## EXERCISE 4

Circle the coordinating conjunctions in this passage and underline the elements that each one connects. The first paragraph has been done for you as an example.

(1) <u>Matt</u> (and) <u>Jeff</u> first came to San Francisco in 1990, after they had graduated from college. (2) Both of them had grown up in small towns. (3) <u>Jeff was from Wisconsin,</u> (and) <u>Matt grew up in Kansas,</u> (but) <u>neither one enjoyed living in a small town</u>. (4) There wasn't enough <u>freedom</u> (or) <u>excitement</u> for their tastes. (5) Each one decided to move to San Francisco because he had heard <u>that it was a beautiful city,</u> (and) <u>that it was filled with interesting people</u>.

(6) When they first met, they were surprised and delighted to discover how many things they had in common and how similar their interests were. (7) Jeff liked weightlifting, and so did Matt. (8) Matt loved opera, and Jeff did too. (9) Jeff wasn't entirely comfortable with "big-city" life, nor was Matt, but neither one missed living in a small town at all. (10) They both liked dogs and wanted to have one for a pet, so they decided to look for an apartment and live together. (11) They both thought it would be cheaper and more fun to have a roommate.

(12) However, when they moved in together and began living with each other, they found that there were also a lot of differences between them. (13) Jeff was very neat, but Matt wasn't. (14) He preferred to let the dirty dishes pile up until there were "enough" to bother with, and he did not pick up his clothes or keep things neat. (15) Jeff, on the other

hand, always wanted things to be washed immediately, even if there were only one or two dishes. (16) Matt liked staying out late every Friday night, but Jeff always wanted to get up early on Saturday mornings to clean the house and to finish chores so they could spend the afternoon relaxing or playing with their new puppy in the park. (17) They soon realized that they would either have to start making compromises or start looking for separate apartments, which neither Matt nor Jeff wanted to do. (18) Fortunately, their similarities outweighed their differences, and they settled into a pleasant life together.

## FOCUS 3  Problems Using Coordinating Conjunctions

| REDUNDANT | LESS REDUNDANT | EXPLANATION |
|---|---|---|
| (a) Jeff enjoys cleaning, **but he doesn't like to clean** on Saturday mornings. | (b) Jeff enjoys cleaning, **but not** on Saturday mornings. | When using coordinating conjunctions, repeated information should be omitted unless doing so makes the meaning unclear. |
| (c) Jeff didn't like life in a small town, and Matt **didn't like it either.** | (d) Jeff didn't like life in a small town, and Matt **didn't either.** | |
| (e) Matt and Jeff get phone calls **from their parents and from their friends** almost every week. | (f) Matt and Jeff get phone calls **from their parents and friends** almost every week. | |

| EXAMPLES | EXPLANATIONS |
|---|---|
| (g) Bambang Soetomo studies **hard, but** he sometimes has trouble understanding assignments. <br><br> (h) NOT: Bambang Soetomo studies **hard but** he sometimes has trouble understanding assignments. | When coordinating conjunctions connect independent clauses, they must be preceded by a comma. Without a comma such sentences are called run-on or run-together sentences. They are considered incorrect in formal written English. |
| (i) Jeff **doesn't** plan to leave San Francisco, **nor does** Matt want him to. <br><br> (j) **Not only do** the two have similar interests, **but** they also have similar personalities. | When clauses are joined with negative coordinating conjunctions (*nor, neither, not only*), the clause with the negative coordinating conjunction at the beginning must take question or inverted word order. |
| (k) AWKWARD: I began to miss my family, **and** I was getting more and more depressed, **so** I decided to talk with my advisor. <br><br> (l) BETTER: **In addition to** missing my family, I was getting more and more depressed. **As a result**, I decided to talk with my advisor. | In formal written English, using coordinating conjunctions to connect independent clauses is often considered to be awkward or poor style. Other kinds of logical connectors—sentence connectors and subordinating conjunctions—are more frequently used. In some cases, you may also wish to break up the run-on sentence into two or more sentences. |

## EXERCISE 5

Combine these pairs of sentences to make them less redundant. There is more than one way to combine most of the sentences.

**Example:** Jeff lives in San Francisco. Matt lives in San Francisco.
*Jeff lives in San Francisco, and so does Matt.*
*Both Jeff and Matt live in San Francisco.*

1. Jeff likes cleaning. Matt doesn't like cleaning.
2. Jeff may go home for a visit on his vacation. Jeff may travel to France on his vacation.
3. Matt doesn't plan to return to his hometown to live. Jeff doesn't plan to return to his hometown to live.
4. Jeff likes getting up early. Matt doesn't like getting up early.
5. Jeff always wanted to have a dog. Matt always wanted to have a dog.
6. Matt might take the dog to the park this afternoon. Jeff might take the dog to the park this afternoon.
7. Matt likes dancing at nightclubs. Matt likes meeting friends at nightclubs.
8. Matt comes from a small town in Kansas. Jeff comes from a small town in Wisconsin.

## EXERCISE 6

Connect the numbered pairs of sentences this paragraph with coordinating conjunctions. Make any necessary changes to remove redundancy or to correct word order.

(1) Canada has a large French-speaking minority. The United States has a large Spanish-speaking minority. (2) Many people in Canada speak French. All government publications are printed in both languages. (3) Canada has two official languages. The United States discourages the use of languages other than English for official purposes. (4) In Canada, the French-speaking minority is found primarily in the province of Quebec. In the United States, Spanish-speaking communities are found in New York, Florida, New Mexico, and California.

## FOCUS 4  Problems Using Sentence Connectors

| EXAMPLES | EXPLANATIONS |
|---|---|
| (a) I was getting more and more depressed. **As a result,** I decided to talk with my advisor.<br><br>(b) I was getting more and more depressed; **as a result,** I decided to talk with my advisor.<br><br>(c) NOT: I was getting more and more depressed, **as a result,** I decided to talk with my advisor. | Sentence connectors are used with sentences or independent clauses connected with a semicolon. Do not use them with commas to connect clauses. This produces run-on sentences. |
| (d) Jeff grew up in Wisconsin. **However,** Matt comes from Kansas.<br><br>(e) Jeff grew up in Wisconsin. Matt, **however,** comes from Kansas.<br><br>(f) Jeff grew up in Wisconsin. Matt comes from Kansas, **however.** | Sentence connectors normally occur at the beginning of a sentence, but some can also appear in the middle or at the end. See the chart in Appendix 4 (p. A-8) for more information. |
| (g) Living together has saved both men a lot of money. **Besides,** Matt likes having a roommate.<br><br>(h) NOT: Matt **besides** likes having a roommate.<br><br>(i) NOT: Matt likes having a roommate **besides.** | Other sentence connectors cannot occur in the middle and/or end of a sentence. See the chart in Appendix 4 (p. A-8) for more information. |
| (j) Bambang put a lot of work into improving his writing. **Thus,** he was able to get an A in his composition class.<br><br>(k) He was **thus** able to get an A in his composition class.<br><br>(l) NOT: He was able to get an A in his composition class **thus.** | |

## EXERCISE 7

Correct these run-on sentences from Bambang's essay on page 187. You can correct the punctuation or make two sentences using a sentence connector of similar meaning. Compare your solution to other students' solutions.

1. I still often feel homesick and I miss my family.

   *I still often feel homesick, ~~because~~ and I miss my family*

2. Everything was strange nevertheless I enjoyed the new experiences.

   *Everything was strange. However, I enjoyed the new experiences*

3. The differences weren't interesting, they were boring.

   *The differences weren't interesting Besides, they were boring.*

4. I learned that every person has this kind of experience and it can't be avoided.

   *I learned that every person has this kind of experience However, it can't be avoided*

5. This was good advice, as a result, my culture shock became less but in spite of this I still miss my life in Indonesia.

   *This was good advice. As a result, my culture shock became less, but it spite of, this I still miss my life in Indonesia.*

## EXERCISE 8

These sentences have problems with sentence connectors. Working with other students, identify the problems and correct them.

1. Every person has experience with culture shock. However, I am no exception.

2. Even though I studied however my grades weren't good.

3. In Canada all official government activities are conducted in both French and English. Under such circumstances, students also study both languages in school. Nevertheless, in the United States, there is no official bilingual policy in government operations. Besides, some local governments have policies that prohibit the use of any language other than English for official business.

## FOCUS 5 | Problems Using Subordinating Conjunctions

| CORRECT SUBORDINATION | SENTENCE FRAGMENT | EXPLANATION |
|---|---|---|
| (a) **Because** things were no longer new to Bambang, **he** began to miss his friends and family back home. | (b) NOT: **Because** things were no longer new to Bambang. **He** began to miss his friends and family back home. | Subordinating conjunctions are used with dependent clauses, gerunds, or noun phrases. They cannot be used with sentences. This produces a **sentence fragment,** which is considered grammatically incorrect. |
| (c) **Even though** Bambang Soetomo studies **hard,** **he** sometimes has trouble understanding assignments. | (d) NOT: **Even though** Bambang Soetomo studies **hard. He** sometimes has trouble understanding assignments. | |

| EXAMPLES | EXPLANATIONS |
|---|---|
| (e) **Besides missing his family,** Bambang also misses his friends. | Some subordinating conjunctions cannot be used with dependent clauses. They function as prepositions and are used with gerund or noun phrases instead. Common subordinating conjunctions of this type are: *besides, in spite of, despite, regardless of, due to, as a result of*. |
| (f) NOT: **Besides Bambang misses his family,** he also misses his friends. | |
| (g) Bambang sometimes doesn't do well on tests, **in spite of studying carefully.** | |
| (h) Bambang doesn't do well on tests, **despite his hard work.** | |
| (i) Bambang sometimes doesn't do well on tests, **in spite of the fact that he studies carefully.** | Adding *the fact that* to *in spite of* makes the error in (j) grammatically correct. |
| (j) NOT: Bambang sometimes doesn't do well on tests, **in spite of he studies carefully.** | |

あ!)か1う

# EXERCISE 9

Here are some problems with the form, meaning, or use of subordinating conjunctions that appeared in Bambang's essay. Identify the problems and correct them.

1. Although I have lived in the United States for almost one year. I often feel homesick and miss my family.

   *Although I have lived in the US for almost one year, I often feel homesick and miss my family*

2. Even though I was used to them. Still I wasn't comfortable.

   *Even though I was unsed to them, I still wasn't comfortable.*

3. However I began to miss things in Indonesia. For example food, my friends, the warm climate.

   *However, I began to miss things in Indonesia, for example the food, my friend, the warm climate.*
   
   I miss

4. In addition to he told me about culture shock, my advisor suggested that I should be patient.

   *In addition to telling me about culture shock, my advisor suggest that I should be patient.*

5. Besides I was homesick, I was also having trouble getting used to the way classes are taught in the United States.

   *Besides being homesick, I was also having trouble getting used to the way classes are taught in the US*

6. In spite of the fact that being homesick, I didn't want to go home without completing my education.

   *In spite of being homesick, I didn't want to go home without completing my education.*

7. As a result of my conversation with my advisor. My culture shock got a little better.

   *As a result, my conversation with my advisor. My culture shock got a little better*

8. Despite I was having problems, I didn't stop doing my best.

   *Despite having problems, I didnt stop doing my best*

# Use Your English

### ACTIVITY 1 writing

Write a brief essay describing a personal experience with culture shock. Be sure to connect your ideas with logical connectors and avoid run-on sentences or sentence fragments. Then give it to your teacher. Ask your teacher to indicate places where there are grammatical problems. Follow the same procedure that you used for the Opening Task to analyze your problems and correct your mistakes.

### ACTIVITY 2 speaking

What characteristics would you look for in a roommate? Make a list of things you would like in a roommate and things you would NOT want. Share your list with several other students and decide whether you would be able to get along with each other if you were living together in a new city.

### ACTIVITY 3 speaking

Examine the different meanings that are implied by choosing one connector instead of another.

■ **STEP 1**  With a partner or in a small group, discuss these three groups of sentences. What are the differences in implied meaning?

| | | |
|---|---|---|
| 1. (a) Indian food is spicy, and I love it. <br> (b) Indian food is spicy, but I love it. <br> (c) Indian food is spicy, so I love it. | 2. (a) Although Indian food is spicy, I love it. <br> (b) Although I love Indian food, it's spicy. | 3. (a) Not only is Indian food spicy, but I also love it. <br> (b) Because Indian food is spicy, I love it. |

**STEP 2** The following sentences are illogical. With a partner or in a small group, discuss how the incorrect use of a logical connector makes the meaning of these sentences strange or unclear.

1. I love Indian food, and it is spicy.

2. I love Indian food, so it is spicy.

3. Since I love Indian food, it is spicy.

**ACTIVITY 4 listening**

CD Track 17

*Silly Sally:* **A Game**
Listen to the story about Silly Sally. Silly Sally likes and dislikes various things. There is one single, simple reason for all the things she likes or doesn't like. The purpose of the game is to discover this simple reason.

**STEP 1** As you listen to the description of her preferences, follow along on the chart on the next page, and put a check in the appropriate column. One has been done for you.

**STEP 2** Compare your answers with another student's and try to figure out the secret of her likes and dislikes.

**STEP 3** With your partner come up with one additional example of something she likes and dislikes for each category. Your teacher will tell you if your examples are correct or not. If you think you know the secret of the game, don't tell other students. Just give more examples of the things that Silly Sally likes and doesn't like. Your teacher will tell you if you're correct.

## Silly Sally's Likes and Dislikes

| CATEGORY | LIKE | DISLIKE | CATEGORY | LIKE | DISLIKE |
|---|---|---|---|---|---|
| **styles of food** | | | **movie stars** | | |
| cooking | ___ | ___ | Johnny Depp | ___ | ___ |
| eating | ___ | ___ | Meryl Streep | ___ | ___ |
| Greek food | ___ | ___ | Jennifer Lopez | ___ | ___ |
| Chinese cuisine | ___ | ___ | Brad Pitt | ___ | ___ |
| Brazilian | ___ | ___ | Denzel Washington | ___ | ___ |
| Japanese | ___ | ___ | Whoopi Goldberg | ___ | ___ |
| Moroccan | ___ | ___ | _____ | X | ___ |
| _____ | X | ___ | _____ | ___ | X |
| _____ | ___ | X | **dating** | | |
| **sports** | | | restaurants for dinner | ___ | ___ |
| tennis | X | ___ | restaurants for lunch | ___ | ___ |
| baseball | ___ | ___ | art gallery | ___ | ___ |
| skiing | ___ | ___ | museum | ___ | ___ |
| horseback riding | ___ | ___ | kisses | ___ | ___ |
| hockey | ___ | ___ | hugs | ___ | ___ |
| jogging | ___ | ___ | marriage | ___ | ___ |
| walking | ___ | ___ | engagement | ___ | ___ |
| _____ | X | ___ | _____ | X | ___ |
| _____ | ___ | X | _____ | ___ | X |
| **people** | | | **vacations** | | |
| queens | ___ | ___ | Greece | ___ | ___ |
| princesses | ___ | ___ | Italy | ___ | ___ |
| kings | ___ | ___ | inns | ___ | ___ |
| princes | ___ | ___ | hotels | ___ | ___ |
| Matt and Jeff | ___ | ___ | Philippines | ___ | ___ |
| Peter and Denise | ___ | ___ | Indonesia | ___ | ___ |
| John and Mary | ___ | ___ | travel in the summer | ___ | ___ |
| _____ | X | ___ | travel in winter | ___ | ___ |
| _____ | ___ | X | _____ | X | ___ |
| **fruits and vegetables** | | | _____ | ___ | X |
| beets | ___ | ___ | **animals** | | |
| carrots | ___ | ___ | sheep | ___ | ___ |
| apples | ___ | ___ | goats | ___ | ___ |
| potatoes | ___ | ___ | cats | ___ | ___ |
| oranges | ___ | ___ | dogs | ___ | ___ |
| cauliflower | ___ | ___ | puppies | ___ | ___ |
| _____ | X | ___ | kittens | ___ | ___ |
| _____ | ___ | X | _____ | X | ___ |
| | | | _____ | ___ | X |

## ACTIVITY 5 research on the web

Go on the Internet and use an Internet search engine such as Google® or Yahoo® and enter the keywords "myths of bilingualism." Find a list of common misconceptions about bilingualism and its impact on children. Based on what you read, do you favor a political system that supports and fosters bilingualism, or one that promotes the use of a particular national language? Do you have personal experience with bilingualism yourself? What are the differences between a fluent speaker of a second language and someone who is bilingual in that language and another language? Discuss your ideas with two or three other students and present them to the rest of the class.

## ACTIVITY 6 reflection

Think about ways that your first language affects how you express your ideas in a second language. What are some common connectors in your native language? How does "good style" affect their use? In this unit we learned that although it is grammatically possible to join sentences with coordinating conjunctions, it is not always considered to be "good writing." Think about the words you use to join ideas in your native language. Identify two situations where "good writing" may be different in your first language than it is in English. Present your ideas to the rest of the class.

# UNIT 12

# RELATIVE CLAUSES

## UNIT GOALS

- **Understand restrictive and nonrestrictive modification**

- **Correctly form subject and object relative clauses in different parts of a sentence**

- **Correctly use or delete relative pronouns in different kinds of relative clauses**

- **Use *whose* in relative clauses**

## OPENING TASK
### Which One Is Which?

### ■ STEP 1

Read this article about twins who were separated at birth.

In 1953 two identical male twins were born in Ohio. Their mother was very young, so she gave the children up for adoption. They were separated the day after they were born, and grew up in different parts of the country. One grew up in Ohio and the other grew up in Oregon. Neither one knew he had a twin brother until the one twin moved back to Ohio, where the other twin was living. Then friends of the Ohio twin began to tell him that they had seen a man who looked exactly like him. The Oregon twin met several people who acted as if they knew him, even though he had never met them before. The two men each began doing research, and discovered their backgrounds and the fact that they were twins. They finally met each other in 1998, and the case was even reported on national television news programs.

Many researchers have been interested in this case because they want to see if the two men have any similarities even though they were raised in completely different environments. The researchers have found that

there were, of course, many differences between the two men, but there are also some very interesting similarities: They had both married women with blonde hair and had three children. They had both painted their houses yellow. They both had dogs and shared similar interests and hobbies. They both had jobs that called for a lot of travel.

### ■ STEP 2

Look at the list of differences on the next page between the twins, and use the information to answer the questions that follow.

**Example:** Which twin is married to Bernice?
The twin who has an old-fashioned home is married to Bernice.

202 | UNIT 12

| Here is some information about one twin: | Here is some information about the other twin: |
|---|---|
| People call him "Rosey." | People call him "Red." |
| His house is a modern home. | His house is an old-fashioned home. |
| He is married to a woman named Betty. | He is married to a woman named Bernice. |
| He has three children—all boys. | He has three children—all girls. |
| His children knew that he had been adopted. | His children didn't know that he been had been adopted. |
| He sells plumbing supplies. | He sells advertising space in magazines. |
| He has a large dog named Prince. | He has a small dog named King. |
| His favorite sport is football. | His favorite sport is basketball. |
| He likes to listen to classical music. | He likes to listen to jazz. |

1. Which twin has children that are all girls?

   The twin who _has a small dog named King has children that_ are all girls.

2. Which twin owns a dog named Prince?

   ☀ The twin whom _people call " Rosey " owns a dog named Prince_

3. Which twin sells plumbing supplies?

   The twin whose _favorite sport is football sells plumbing supplies_.

4. Which twin likes classical music?

   The twin whose _favorite sport is football likes classical music._

5. Which twin prefers basketball?

   The twin that _likes to listen to jazz prefers basketball_.

6. Which twin lives in a modern home?

   The twin who _has three children - all boy lives in a modern home_

7. Which twin is married to a woman named Betty?

   The twin whose _children knew that he had been adopted is marrie_...

8. Which twin's children didn't know that he had been adopted?

   The twin who _sell advertising space in magazines his children didn't_...

☀ or 's called "Rosey"

| FOCUS 1 | Restrictive and Nonrestrictive Relative Clauses |
|---------|------------------------------------------------|

| EXAMPLES | EXPLANATIONS |
|----------|--------------|
| (a) Which book do you want?<br>the one **that's under the dictionary.**<br>(b) What kind of food do you like?<br>I like food **that's not too spicy.** | **Restrictive relative clauses** answer the question "what kind" or "which one." |
| (c) Nitrogen, **which is the most common element on earth,** is necessary for all life. | **Nonrestrictive relative clauses** just provide additional information about noun phrases. They do not identify what kind or which one. |

## EXERCISE 1

Underline each relative clause in this passage and circle the noun phrase it modifies. The first two have been done for you as an example.

(1) My friend Charlie has fallen madly in love. (2) He told me he has finally met (the woman) that he has been looking for all his life. (3) He has always been attracted to (women) that are intelligent and independent and that have a good sense of humor and a love of adventure. (4) But Amy, the woman that he has fallen in love with, has all those things and more. (5) Even though physical appearance isn't the most important (characteristic) that Charlie is looking for, he is quite happy his new friend is attractive and athletic. (6) She not only runs and skis, but also goes scuba diving, and has several other (interests) that Charlie also shares.

(7) Charlie was never completely happy with the women that he used to go out with. (8) There was always something that wasn't "right." (9) I used to tell him he was too choosy. (10) The "ideal woman" that he has always been looking for just doesn't exist. (11) No real person can equal the picture that someone has in his or her imagination. (12) But I'm glad he has found someone that he thinks is perfect, because I've never seen him happier.

# FOCUS 2 — Forming Restrictive Relative Clauses

| EXAMPLES | EXPLANATIONS |
|---|---|
| (a) I read a book [Charlie really liked ~~the book~~ *that*.] last week. | The relative pronoun [*that* in Example (a)] replaces the noun phrase in a relative clause in order to avoid repetition. |
| (b) I read a book [**that** Charlie really liked ⟋ ] last week. | When the relative pronoun is in the object position, it is moved to the front of the relative clause. |

Relative pronouns can replace any noun phrase within the relative clause.

| RELATIVE CLAUSE | UNDERLYING SENTENCE | FUNCTION |
|---|---|---|
| (c) I read the book **that** was published last year. | (d) **The book** was published last year. | subject |
| (e) I read the book **that** your professor <u>wrote</u>. | (f) Your professor wrote **the book.** | object |
| (g) I met the person **that** Charlie gave flowers to. | (h) Charlie gave **the person** flowers. | indirect object |
| (i) I met the person **that** Lin told me about. | (j) Lin told me about **the person.** | object of a preposition |
| (k) I read the book **that** was published last year. | Remember that the replaced noun or pronoun of the underlying sentence does **not** appear in the relative clause. |  |
| (l) NOT: I read the book that **it** was published year. |  |  |

In the following article underline the relative clauses. Then restate each relative clause as an independent sentence. The first three have been done for you as examples.

**Examples:** (1) *A new study may interest many people.*

(2) *They conducted a survey with several thousand American women all around the country.*

(3) *These women have common attitudes about men.*

### Scientists Identify Today's "Prince Charming"

(1) Sociologists at Mills College have released a new study <u>that may interest many people</u>, especially men. (2) They reported the results of a survey <u>that they conducted with several thousand American women all around the country</u>. (3) They wanted to examine common attitudes <u>that these women have about men</u>, so that they could identify important characteristics that women think are necessary in a good husband or boyfriend. (4) The study found a number of interesting results, which will probably not surprise most women, but may surprise some men.

(5) The women in the survey generally seem to prefer men who can express their feelings. (6) Most women prefer husbands who they can talk to easily and that they can share their problems with.

(7) There were also several other things that women consider important in a partner. (8) A man's character or personality is more important to many women than the job that he does for a living or the salary that he brings home. (9) Not surprisingly, most women want a husband that will take on an equal share of housekeeping and child-raising duties.

(10) But the most important characteristic is this: Women want boyfriends who they can trust and husbands that they can depend on. (11) Unfortunately, more than 70 percent of the women who answered the questionnaires said they had husbands or boyfriends who lacked one or more of these important characteristics.

# FOCUS 3 | Relative Pronouns

The relative pronouns are *who, whom, which,* and *that*.

| EXAMPLES | EXPLANATIONS |
|---|---|
| (a) The man **who you** told me about last week is over there. | Use *who* and *whom* to refer to humans. In formal written style, use *who* to refer to subjects in relative clauses and *whom* to refer to objects. |
| (b) The man **whom** you mentioned last week is here today. | |
| (c) The man **whom** you told me about yesterday is here to see you. | |
| (d) I read the **book which** Kevin had recommended. | Use *which* to refer to nonhumans. |
| (e) The **man that** wrote this book is a teacher. | Use *that* for humans or nonhumans, but only with restrictive relative clauses. (Review restrictive clauses in Focus 1, page 204.) |
| (f) The **man that** you told me about is a teacher. | |
| (g) I read the **book that** Kevin had recommended. | |
| (h) Abraham Lincoln, **who** was the sixteenth president of the United States, died in 1865. | Do not use *that* as a relative pronoun in nonrestrictive relative clauses. Use only *who, whom,* and *which.* |
| (i) NOT: Abraham Lincoln, **that** was the sixteenth president of the United States, died in 1865. | |
| (j) San Francisco, **which** is on the Pacific Ocean, has a very cool climate. | |
| (k) NOT: San Francisco, that is on the Pacific Ocean, has a very cool climate. | |

## EXERCISE 3

Combine these pairs of sentences by using a relative clause with *that, who, whom,* or *which*.

**Example:** I finally met the woman. Charlie has fallen in love with the woman.

*I finally met the woman that Charlie has fallen in love with.*

1. Last month Charlie fell in love with Amy. He had been introduced to her by some friends.

2. She had a number of positive characteristics. Charlie found these characteristics quite attractive.

3. She has a responsible position in a company. The company produces computer programs.

4. Information technology is a fast-growing field. Charlie is also interested in information technology.

5. Hobbies involve athletics and being outdoors. Both of them like these hobbies.

6. Charlie introduced the woman to his parents. He had been dating the woman for several weeks.

7. She has a wonderful sense of humor. This makes their times together relaxing and enjoyable.

8. From the first time they met, Charlie felt there was a "special understanding" between them. He was unable to explain this understanding.

## EXERCISE 4

Answer these questions using a relative clause ("I like people who . . ."; "People whom I like . . ."). Compare your answers to those of a classmate.

1. What kind of people do you like?

2. What kind of people like you?

3. What kind of food do you like?

4. What kind of leisure activities interest you?

5. What kind of person do you want to marry?

6. What kind of person will want to marry you?

7. What kind of practice is useful in learning languages?

8. What kind of government is the best?

## ■ EXERCISE 5

The following sentences are incorrect. Identify the mistakes and correct them.

1. I read a book that ~~it~~ was published last year.

2. I saw an article that your professor wrote ~~it~~.

3. Jeff and Matt have been living in the city of San Francisco, ~~that~~ *which* is located in California, since 1990.

4. This is the person ~~to~~ whom Charlie gave ~~her~~ flowers.

5. I met the person who Charlie told me about ~~her~~.

6. The teacher that *who* I studied with ~~her~~ has become quite famous.

7. The money that you loaned me ~~some~~ last week is there on the table.

8. The resort that we read about ~~it~~ in the newspaper is becoming more and more popular.

9. The people whom I visited ~~them~~ last year are coming here for a visit.

10. My father, ~~that~~ *who* lives in San Diego, loves sailing.

## FOCUS 4 — Deleting Relative Pronouns

You can delete relative pronouns that function as objects in restrictive relative clauses.

| EXAMPLES | FUNCTION OF RELATIVE PRONOUNS |
|---|---|
| (a) I read the book **that** your professor wrote. <br> (b) I read the book your professor wrote. | direct objects |
| (c) The lady **that** Charlie sent flowers to is on the phone. <br> (d) The lady Charlie sent flowers to is on the phone. | indirect objects |
| (e) I read the book **that** Charlie was so excited about. <br> (f) I read the book Charlie was so excited about. | objects of prepositions |

You can only delete relative pronouns that function as subjects in restrictive relative clauses that contain *be* (either as a main verb or an auxiliary). In such cases both the relative pronoun and *be* are deleted.

| EXAMPLES | EXPLANATIONS |
|---|---|
| (g) I want a book **that was written** by an expert. <br> (h) I want a book **written** by an expert. | relative clauses with passive verbs |
| (i) I think I know that woman **who is carrying** the blue suitcase. <br> (j) I think I know that woman **carrying** the blue suitcase. | relative clauses with progressive verbs |
| (k) I tried to get an autograph from the baseball player **who is beside** the fence. <br> (l) I tried to get an autograph from the baseball player **beside** the fence. | relative clauses with prepositional phrases |
| (m) Anyone **who is foolish enough** to use drugs should be free to do so. <br> (n) Anyone **foolish enough** to use drugs should be free to do so. | relative clauses with adjective phrases |
| (o) Have you read the book **that made** Darryl Brock famous? <br> (p) NOT: Have you read the book **made** Darryl Brock famous? | You cannot delete relative pronouns if they are subjects of a relative clause without *be*. |

## EXERCISE 6

Underline all the relative clauses in this passage. Make sure that you also include the ones that have deleted relative pronouns. The first paragraph has been done for you as an example.

### The War To End All Wars

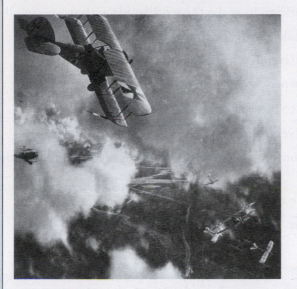

(1) When World War I, <u>which was fought in Europe from 1914 to 1917,</u> was finally over, it was called "the war to end all wars." (2) It was the most destructive war <u>that the world had ever fought until then.</u> (3) Over ten million young men <u>who were sent to battle from both sides</u> were killed or permanently disabled.

(4) The war introduced powerful new weapons the <u>world had never that before seen.</u> (5) The use of the airplane enabled armies on both sides to drop bombs with an effectiveness and precision <u>that had been previously impossible.</u> (6) Heavy casualties were also caused by the wide-scale use of a poison gas, <u>which was called mustard gas, which permanently damaged the lungs of soldiers caught without gas masks.</u>

(7) There were more than 8.5 million deaths. (8) Many people <u>who were fighting this terrible war</u> were killed in battles. (9) But many others died from intestinal diseases <u>which were caused by the unsanitary conditions on the battlefield,</u> or by infections that developed in lungs damaged by mustard gas, <u>which was used by both sides.</u>

(10) The peace established by "the war to end all wars" lasted less than a generation. (11) The most destructive war <u>that the world had ever known,</u> like most wars, didn't solve the political and economic problems <u>that were facing European governments at that time.</u>

(12) Less than twenty-five years after the conflict <u>that everyone hoped would bring world peace,</u> Europe was again at war.

Wherever possible, delete the relative pronouns in these sentences and make any other necessary changes.

**Example:** The kind of people **that** I like are usually people **who** have a good sense of humor.

1. I like people ~~who~~ think about other people's feelings.
2. I like people ~~who~~ are working to make the world a place **that** we can all share.
3. I like people ~~who~~ don't take the work **that** they do too seriously.
4. I don't like people **who** have no sense of humor.
5. I like people **who** don't worry about things **that** other people say about them.
6. I dislike people **who** try to hurt other people's feelings.
7. I dislike people **who** are very concerned with power and position.
8. I like people ~~who~~ question the things **that** they have been taught and the teachers **who** have taught them.
9. I like people ~~who~~ are like me.
10. I like people **who** like me.

## EXERCISE 8

Write five sentences that describe the kind of people you like and five sentences that describe the kind of people you don't like. Compare your sentences with those of a classmate. Describe any common likes and dislikes.

_____

_____

_____

_____

_____

_____

_____

_____

# FOCUS 5 — *Whose* in Relative Clauses

When a relative clause contains a possessive form, *whose* + noun can be used in the same way as relative pronouns.

| EXAMPLES | UNDERLYING SENTENCE | EXPLANATIONS |
|---|---|---|
| (a) I met a man **whose house** was destroyed in the earthquake. | (b) I met a man. **His house** was destroyed in the earthquake. | *Whose* can be used with:<br>• the subject of a relative clause |
| (c) I got a letter from the man **whose house** we visited last week. | (d) I got a letter from a man. We visited **his house** last week. | • the object of a relative clause |
| (e) I spoke to the man **whose party** we got an invitation **to**. | (f) I spoke to a man. We got an invitation **to his party**. | • the object of a preposition |
| (g) I got a letter from the man **whose house** we visited last week.<br><br>(h) NOT: I got a letter from a man **house** we visited last week. | | You can never delete *whose* from a relative clause. It must always be used with a noun. |

## EXERCISE 9

Combine these sentences using *whose*.

**Example:** I got a letter from a man. We visited his house last week.

*I got a letter from the man whose house we visited last week.*

1. Samira met a man. His brother is a well-known geneticist.

2. Jeff and Matt are roommates. Matt's nickname is "Akbar."

3. People may have similar personalities. Their genetic makeups are similar.

4. Nicole took a class from a teacher. She knew his wife in college.

5. Charlie's new girl friend would like to go to the lecture by the mountain climber. She read about his latest climb in *Adventure Magazine*.

6. Matt and Jeff have a dog. Its eyes are different colors.

7. I keep getting phone calls for some stranger. His last name is apparently the same as mine.

8. Charlie finally succeeded in meeting the artist. He had been admiring her work for years.

## EXERCISE 10

Combine the numbered pairs of sentences in this paragraph using relative pronouns or *whose*.

(1) Charlie wants to make some changes in his life. These changes involve both his lifestyle and his social activities. (2) Charlie wants to find a new place to live. The place has to have enough room for a dog. (3) He's looking at a new apartment. The apartment has a balcony, so he can grow some flowers. (4) Charlie also wants to get married to someone. Her political beliefs are similar to his own. (5) He hasn't found anyone yet. No one seems to share his interest in politics and sports. (6) He's thinking of putting a personals ad in a paper. A lot of people advertise in that paper in order to meet others with similar interests and backgrounds.

## EXERCISE 11

Answer these questions, using relative clauses. Compare your answers with one of your classmate's.

**Example:** What kind of food do you like?

*I like food that is not too spicy.*

1. What kind of person do you want to marry?

_____

2. What kind of person should be the leader of a country?

_____

3. What kind of person makes the best teacher?

_____

4. What kind of television programs do you like to watch?

_____

5. What kind of place is the best for a vacation?

_____

6. What kind of house or apartment would you like to live in?

_____

7. What kind of books do you enjoy reading?

_____

8. What kind of students get the best grades?

_____

# Use Your English

## ACTIVITY 1  speaking

■ **STEP 1**  In Exercise 2 you read about some of the things that American women consider important in a husband. Divide into same-gender groups of men and women. In your group discuss the characteristics of "the ideal life partner." Prepare a list of five to ten statements like these: *The ideal partner is someone who takes an equal responsibility for raising the children./The ideal partner is a person whom I can always trust./ The ideal partner is someone whose sense of humor is well-developed.*

What ideals do you all agree on? Are there ideals that are controversial?

■ **STEP 2**  Present your statements to the other groups. Compare the ideals presented by women's groups and the ideals presented by men's groups.

■ **STEP 3**  Discuss these questions as a whole class or in mixed gender groups. What are the important similarities and differences between the statements of the two kinds of groups? Are there some ideals that all men share, no matter what culture they come from? Are there some ideals that all women share, no matter what culture they come from? Are there some ideals that both genders share?

## ACTIVITY 2  writing

Write a brief essay describing personal characteristics in people that you like and dislike. You may wish to look at Exercise 7 for some ideas about the kinds of characteristics other students have identified. Here are some questions you should try to answer in your essay. What kind of people do you like most? What personal characteristics do you appreciate and respect in other people? What personal characteristics do you find distasteful?

## ACTIVITY 3 listening

**CD Track 18**

Listen to the lecture about "hawks" and "doves," and write definitions for the following terms based on the information you heard.

What is a pacifist?
What is a "hawk"?
What is a "dove"?
What is the difference between a war and a revolution?

## ACTIVITY 4 speaking

*Nicknames* are additional names that are given to people to describe some physical characteristic or aspect of their personality.

■ **STEP 1**   Here is a list of some common American nicknames. Working with a partner, decide what characteristics would be likely for someone whose nickname is one of these:

| Blondie | Doc | Sport | Cowboy | Tubby |
|---------|-----|-------|--------|-------|
| Sugar | Gramps | Tiger | Honey | |

■ **STEP 2**   Report your ideas by using sentences like these:

We think that someone whose nickname is Red is probably a person who has red hair. We think that someone whose nickname is Curly is probably a person who has curly hair (or perhaps someone who is bald). We think that someone whose nickname is Sunny is probably a person who has a cheerful, outgoing personality.

■ **STEP 3**   Discuss how nicknames are used in other countries. Do you have a nickname? Why do people call you that name?

## ACTIVITY 5 — research on the web

Some people use the Internet to meet potential partners. Would you ever consider that as a way to meet someone? Google "free online dating" and choose one of the free sites such as www.okcupid.com, www.plentyoffish.com or other Google® listings such as "Christian singles" or "Muslim singles". Be careful to choose a site that does not require you to register personal information, and reflects your interests. Click on "who's on-line" and scan a few of the profiles that you find there. Based on the profiles you have looked at, do you think that online dating would be a good way for you to meet a partner? What sorts of characteristics do people mention there? You may want to do this activity with a classmate.

## ACTIVITY 6 — reflection

The word *daffy* means silly. A *daffynition* is a made-up definition for a word that doesn't really exist. In fact the word *daffynition* is itself, a made-up word.

**STEP 1**    Try to invent daffynitions for the made-up words below. Remember that many prefixes and suffixes in English are good indictors of meaning, so you can use that information as clues for possible meaning or what kind of word (noun, adjective, etc.) it is.

**Example:**   Who or what is a murphler?

> *A murphler is someone who murphles. Murphling is a kind of sport.*

- What are **parahawks**?
- What does **chemicophysiologicalistic** mean?
- What is **antinonsequitology**?
- Define **hypervoraciosity**.

**STEP 2**    Share your daffynitions with the rest of the class. Which one is the most believable? Which one is the most amusing daffynition for each term?

**STEP 3**    Make up some of your own imaginary words and provide definitions for them.

# PRESENT TIME FRAME

## UNIT GOALS

- Distinguish the use of progressive aspect from simple present

- Understand and use nondynamic or stative verbs

- Understand common uses of the present time frame

## OPENING TASK
### Volunteers to the Rescue

*The Water is Rising Pleas*

### ◼ STEP 1

Mary Rae is an account executive for a large advertising agency in New York, but at the moment she is working in New Orleans, participating in a program called "Citizens Care." Citizens Care assigns private citizens who volunteer to help with rescue and reconstruction efforts after natural disasters. Use the information in the chart on the next page to write a paragraph that describes at least five differences between Mary Rae's normal life and her life helping flood survivors of Hurricane Katrina.

**Example:** *Mary Rae normally spends her day as an account executive in a busy advertising firm, but with Citizens Care, she is spending twelve to fourteen hours a day in vigorous physical activity. In New York she supervises twenty-five employees, but in Louisiana, she is only supervising herself. . . . .*

| MARY RAE'S LIFE IN NEW YORK | MARY RAE'S LIFE AT THE CITIZEN CARE CAMP |
| --- | --- |
| Occupation: advertising account executive; visits clients, supervises a 25-person office | Occupation: program participant; rows a boat through flooded streets, removes debris, looks for survivors, brings food to emergency shelters |
| lives in a small apartment | sleeps in a high school gymnasium, spends her days in a boat |
| often eats take-out Chinese food | eats in a Red Cross shelter |
| worries a lot about her career | worries a lot about people who are without food and water, not thinking about her career at all |
| doesn't get much exercise | rows her boat or hauls debris 12–14 hours each day |
| doesn't spend much time outdoors | doesn't spend any time indoors, except to sleep |
| often has trouble falling asleep | falls asleep almost instantly |
| doesn't feel challenged by her daily routine | feels very challenged by each day's activities |
| is somewhat bored with life | is excited about helping those in need |
| feels that she is not learning anything new | feels that she is learning something new every day |
| finds making new friends difficult | finds making new friends easy |

## STEP 2

Compare your paragraph with a classmate's. Did you both use the same verb tenses to describe Mary Rae's life in Louisiana compared to her life in New York?

## STEP 3

Based on Mary Rae's experience, would you ever consider joining a volunteer rescue program? Why or why not?

# Using Simple Present Versus Present Progressive

use

| USE SIMPLE PRESENT TO DESCRIBE: | USE PRESENT PROGRESSIVE TO DESCRIBE: |
|---|---|
| • general statements about recurring habits and skills<br><br>(a)  Mary Rae **works** in New York.<br><br>(b)  She **lives in a small apartment**.<br><br>(c)  She **sleeps** in a comfortable bed. | • actions in progress at the time of speaking<br><br>(d)  She **is working in** New Orleans.<br><br>(e)  She **is living** in a high school gym.<br><br>(f)  She's **sleeping** on the floor. |
| • timeless facts<br><br>(g)  Hurricanes **cause** widespread flooding. | • situations in progress around the time of speaking<br><br>(h)  The floods **are causing** many disruptions in basic services. |
| • permanent situations<br><br>(i)  Mary Rae **lives** in New York. | • temporary situations<br><br>(j)  She's **living** in New Orleans until the project is over. |
| • states and conditions<br><br>(k)  She **thinks** the government should be more active in the rescue effort.<br><br>(l)  She **has** a lot of job responsibilities waiting for her return. | • actions<br><br>(m)  She's **thinking** about ways to get other people to join the project.<br><br>(n)  She's **having** a lot of fun! |

## EXERCISE 1

Choose the correct verb tense (simple present or present progressive) for these sentences. More than one answer may be correct.

1.  Don't turn on the TV. I _____ (talk) to you!

2.  My brother _____ (speak) a little Spanish. Let's ask him to help with hurricane victims that only speak Spanish.

3.  Mary Rae _____ (work) for Citizens Care in New Orleans, so I don't think she can come to the party.

4.  She _____ (report) for work about 7:30 every morning.

5.  Volunteers _____ (clean) the big mess left by the flooding. Please go help them.

6. Mary Rae _____ (do) her best, but she still can't carry as many supplies as other stronger volunteers.

7. I _____ (try) to understand you, but you will have to speak more slowly.

8. Scientists _____ (discover) that many severe floods are caused by human developments of coastal areas.

9. The frequency of hurricanes _____ (get) worse every year.

10. Repairing hurricane destruction _____ (get) easier when you have a lot of people helping.

## EXERCISE 2

Write the correct form of the verb in parentheses (simple present or present progressive).

Ralph (1) _____ (not take) a vacation this summer, because he
(2) _____ (think) that he (3) _____ (have) other more
important things to do. He (4) _____ (teach) computer skills to high school
students, so he (5) _____ (get) three months of vacation, but he
(6) _____ (feel) that teachers (7) _____ (have) a special
responsibility. So he (8) _____ (look) for a temporary volunteer position for
the period of his summer break. He (9) _____ (try) to find work as a
computer programmer. But most relief agencies only (10) _____ (hire)
workers on a long-term basis. Ralph (11) _____ (find) that it is difficult to
locate short-term volunteer positions. He (12) _____ (get) excited about the
prospects of making a real difference in the lives of other people. No matter how hard he
(13) _____ (search), he (14) _____ (begin) to realize that most
programs are looking for long-term volunteers and he may have to take a vacation,
whether he (15) _____ (want) one or not.

## EXERCISE 3

Describe your typical day starting from the time you wake up and ending with going to sleep at night. Write at least eight sentences about things you do on a regular basis. Now describe three things that you are currently doing differently than the way you normally do them, and why you have changed your routine.

**Example:** *I'm living in a dormitory because I have moved to a new city to go to school.*

## FOCUS 2 | Nondynamic (Stative) Verbs

| EXAMPLES | EXPLANATION |
|---|---|
| (a) I **know** that you are unhappy right now.<br><br>(b) NOT: I **am knowing** that you are unhappy right now. | **Nondynamic** or **stative** verbs do not take progressive forms when they describe conditions or states. |

Common Nondynamic Verbs

| SENSORY PERCEPTION | KNOWLEDGE & BELIEF | FEELING & ATTITUDE | LOGICAL RELATIONSHIP | |
|---|---|---|---|---|
| *see* | *agree/disagree with* | *love* | **Cause and Effect** | **Measurement** |
| *hear* | *believe* | *like* | *results in* | *weigh* |
| *feel* | *doubt* | *hate* | *requires* | *cost* |
| *appear* | *feel (believe)* | *dislike* | *depends on* | *measure* |
| *look* | *imagine* | *appreciate* | *means* | *equal* |
| *seem* | *intend* | *prefer* | | **Inclusion** |
| *smell* | *know* | *want* | **Possession** | *contain* |
| *sound* | *recognize* | *need* | *belong to* | *consist of* |
| *taste* | *realize* | *mind* | *possess* | *include* |
| *resemble* | *remember* | | *have* | |
| *look like* | *suppose* | | *own* | |
| | *think (believe)* | | *owe* | |
| | *understand* | | | |
| | *consider* | | | |

## EXERCISE 4

Work with a partner and ask W*h*-questions for the cues given. Your partner should give true answers, and then ask the same questions of you.

**Example:** which parent/resemble most
*Which parent do you resemble most?*
*I resemble my mother more than my father.*

1. what kind of fruit/taste best
2. what way/think/most effective to learn a foreign language
3. how/a sick person/appear
4. what/your MP3 player/contain
5. what/a handshake/mean
6. what activity/your family appreciate/your doing
7. what/learning another language/require
8. how many _____/you/own
9. who/that _____/belong to
10. what/not understand/American culture

## EXERCISE 5

Report your partner's answers from Exercise 4 to the rest of the class.

**Example:** *Yoshiko resembles her mother more than her father.*

1. _____
2. _____
3. _____
4. _____
5. _____
6. _____
7. _____
8. _____
9. _____
10. _____

meaning

<table>
<tr><td colspan="3" style="background:#b3a7d9;"></td></tr>
</table>

## FOCUS 3    Verbs with Both Nondynamic and Action Meanings

Some nondynamic verbs can also be used to describe actions.

| VERB | NONDYNAMIC MEANING | ACTION MEANING |
|---|---|---|
| *have* | (a) Mary Rae **has** an important job in New York. (**possess**) | (b) She's **having** a great time in New Orleans. (**experiencing**) |
| *mind* | (c) She **doesn't mind** hard work. (**object to**) | (d) She's **minding** some lost children this afternoon. (**taking care of**) |
| *see* | (e) I **see** your point. (**understand**) | (f) Peter **is seeing** a specialist about his back. (**consulting**) |
| *think* | (g) I **think** you're right. (**opinion**) | (h) Be quiet! I'm **thinking**. (**mental activity**) |
| *consider* | (i) I **consider** money to be the cause of many problems. (**opinion**) | (j) I'm **considering** going to Hawaii for vacation. (**mental activity**) |
| *depends on* | (k) Athletic ability **depends on** strength and practice. (**requires**) | (l) I'm **depending on** you to help me move next week. (**relying upon**) |
| *be* | (m) She **is** a teacher. (**identity**) | (n) Those children **are being** very noisy. (**behaving**) |
| *feel* | (o) She **feels** that it's important to help the victims of the disaster. (**believe**) | (p) She's **feeling** a little sick today. (**experiencing**) |

Other nondynamic verbs can indicate the **act** of perception or measurement, or the perceptions or measurements themselves.

| VERB | PERCEPTION/MEASUREMENT (NONDYNAMIC MEANING) | ACT OF PERCEPTION/MEASUREMENT (ACTION MEANING) |
|---|---|---|
| *smell* | (q) The flowers **smell** wonderful. | (r) The dog **is smelling** the clothes of the missing boy. |
| *taste* | (s) That cake **tastes** delicious. | (t) Our host **is tasting** the soup to make sure it's not too salty. |
| *feel* | (u) My arm **feels** broken! | (v) The doctor **is feeling** my arm to see if it is broken. |
| *weigh* | (w) Joe **weighs** almost 100 kilos. | (x) The butcher **is weighing** that piece of meat. |

Decide whether the verbs indicated express an action meaning or a nonprogressive meaning and write the simple present or present progressive tense in the blanks. In some cases both answers may be correct.

1. This cloth _____ (feel) really nice.

2. I _____ (consider) applying to Citizens Care.

3. Why did you ask that question? You _____ (be) really rude!

4. I _____ (believe) that Mary Rae _____ (have) a good experience at the Citizens Care program.

5. I don't like this coffee. It _____ (taste) bitter to me.

6. I like people who _____ (mind) their own business and don't try to tell others what to do.

7. Mary Rae _____ (doubt) that she will be able to return to New York right away.

8. It _____ (look) as if the frequency of hurricanes is growing greater every year.

9. Mary Rae _____ (feel) a little guilty about leaving work for so long. But I'm sure they support her efforts to help the disaster victims.

10. Cleaning up after a hurricane _____ (require) a lot of hard work.

11. These days the government _____ (require) people to take drug tests in order to get a government job.

12. The government _____ (be) so slow! I wish someone would make them speed up the rescue operations.

## Uses of the Present Time Frame

**use**

| EXAMPLES | EXPLANATIONS |
|---|---|
| (a) Supply **affects** demand in several ways. If supply **exceeds** demand, the cost of the commodity generally **decreases.** When cost **increases,** demand often **drops.** Decreased demand eventually **results** in decreased supply. | Use present time frame:<br>• to state general truths and relationships in scientific and technical writing |
| (b) Here's how we **make** cookies. First we **mix** a cup of flour and two eggs together in a bowl. Next, we **mix** in some sugar. A cup-and-a half **is** probably enough, but if we **want** sweeter cookies, we **add** at least 3 cups of sugar. | • to describe actions as they are performed in live demonstrations |
| (c) Shimazu **throws** the ball. Martinez **hits** it. He **passes** first base. He's **making** a run to second base. He's out! | • for reporting in radio and television broadcasts such as sporting events |
| (d) One day I'm **walking** down the street. I **see** this guy talking on a pay phone. I **know** he's mad about something because I **can hear** him screaming all the way down the block. So, anyway, when I **get** next to the pay phone, he **stops** shouting and **asks** me if I have an extra quarter. I **tell** him, "Sorry, man," and all of a sudden . . . | • to tell stories orally in informal situations |

## EXERCISE 7

Here are reports of two scientific experiments. Change them into present time so that they are statements of general scientific principles, rather than accounts of specific experiments.

**Example:** *When baking soda is added to vinegar, a chemical reaction occurs.*

### Experiment 1

(1) When baking soda was added to vinegar, a chemical reaction occurred. (2) The baking soda bubbled and $CO_2$ was produced by the combination of elements. (3) When a candle was put next to the container while the chemical reaction was taking place, the flame on the candle went out.

### Experiment 2

(1) We wanted to determine whether gravity affected the rate of acceleration of objects falling through space. (2) Two objects of similar size and shape, but substantially different weights—a cannonball and a volleyball—were dropped from the same height. (3) We found that both objects hit the ground at the same time. (4) This indicated that the attraction of gravity was constant.

## EXERCISE 8

Tell this story aloud, as if you were Mary Rae describing her own experience. Tell it in present time to make it more vivid and less formal. The first two sentences have been done as examples.

**Example:** *There I am, standing in dirty swamp water as deep as my waist, but I'm having a wonderful time! The boat we're rowing has gotten stuck on a log, so somebody has to get into the water and try to lift one end of it.*

There I was, standing in dirty swamp water as deep as my waist, but I was having a wonderful time! The boat we were rowing had gotten stuck on a log, so somebody had to get into the water and try to lift one end of it. I looked into the water. It looked really dark and dirty. I knew there were a lot of poisonous snakes in this area. I knew there were also toxic chemicals and horrible germs. All of a sudden, I realized that I wasn't afraid of any of these things. I had complete confidence in my ability to free the boat and to avoid getting some horrible infection. Without another thought, I jumped into the water and started to pull at the boat. At that moment I knew that there was nothing that I was afraid to do, and nothing that I couldn't do if I put my mind to it.

# Use Your English

**ACTIVITY 1** speaking

Give the class a demonstration of how to do something. This could be how to prepare a favorite food, how to perform some physical activity, or how to make some simple object. While you are demonstrating the activity, tell how it is done.

**ACTIVITY 2** speaking

"How much does that cost?" "How much money do you earn?" "How much do you weigh?" "How old are you?" Most Americans think that these are rude questions to ask anyone who is not a very close friend. In other cultures, people don't consider these to be rude questions but they might hesitate to ask other kinds of questions, such as "How many daughters do you have?" "What do you do—what kind of job do you have?" or even "What kind of house do you live in?" Form a group and talk about what are considered to be rude questions in other cultures that you are familiar with. Make sure you use present time frame to discuss these ideas, since you are discussing general truths about different cultures. Present your findings to the rest of the class. Make a list of potentially rude questions in North American culture that you may want to avoid.

**ACTIVITY 3** writing/speaking

We all learn our basic cultural values when we are very young. A first step in learning about different cultures is learning to identify some of these basic cultural values.

**STEP 1**  Write down at least five things your parents told you that were general truths when you were growing up. Make sure that these things are not orders or requests (such as: *My parents told me to clean my room*), but rather statements about things that are always true (*Big boys don't cry. Good manners are important.*)

**STEP 2**  Compare your list to the lists of several other students. Are any of the statements the same on all your lists? Are there any interesting similarities or differences based on different cultures? What does this tell you about the values your parents tried to teach you? Report your ideas to the rest of the class.

## ACTIVITY 4 — listening

CD Track 19

■ **STEP 1**    Listen to Professor Freemarket's lecture for his Introduction to Economics class, and take notes. You may want to listen to the lecture a second time to make sure you understand the information he describes.

■ **STEP 2**    Use your notes to answer the questions that he asked the class on his weekly quiz.

■ **STEP 3**    Compare your answers to another student's to check the accuracy of your information and the grammatical correctness of what you wrote.

| ECONOMICS 101—DR. FREEMARKET WEEKLY QUIZ #5 | |
|---|---|
| (25 POINTS POSSIBLE) | |
| | |
| 1. | (10 points) Define the Law of Supply and Demand. |
| 2. | (10 points) How does transportation affect the Law of Supply and Demand? |
| 3. | (5 points) What other forces affect the Law of Supply and Demand? |

## ACTIVITY 5 — research on the web

Enter one of these words into the keyword search of *InfoTrac*® *College Edition*: *tsunami, earthquake, hurricane*. Scan the first twenty listings to determine information about the following: What is the most recent disaster of this sort? Where did it happen? Where do these kinds of disasters typically occur? What kind of relief efforts are being made to help the victims?

## ACTIVITY 6 — reflection

Listen to English speakers in conversation with one another and try to notice when they are using present progressive. List three examples of something you heard where the speaker is using present progressive. Decide why he or she chose to use present progressive instead of simple present. Compare your examples with those of another student, and report any interesting similarities or differences to the rest of the class.

# PRESENT PERFECT
## Describing Past Events in Relation to the Present

## UNIT GOALS

- Use the present perfect to understand and express past actions that are related to the present moment by time

- Use the present perfect to understand and express past actions that are related to the present moment by logical relationship or present result

- Understand and express meaning differences with present perfect progressive instead of present perfect tense

## OPENING TASK
### Identifying What Makes You Special

When American students apply to colleges and universities, they often have to write a personal essay about their individual character and achievements and explain what makes them different from the other people who are also applying to the school. Fill out the sample admissions application on the next page, and write a personal essay that identifies some of your characteristics, experiences, and achievements that might be of interest to a university admissions committee.

### ■ STEP 1

To get you started, here are the ideas that Aliona Fernandez used for her successful application to the North American Institute of International Studies. (Her personal essay has been reprinted in Exercise 1 on page 233.) For your essay identify at least one **special** characteristic, **one** experience **that helped you develop that characteristic, and one** achievement **that this characteristic has enabled you to do.**

|  | ALIONA FERNANDEZ | YOU |
|---|---|---|
| Characteristic | flexibility |  |
| Experience | living overseas as a Peace Corps volunteer |  |
| Achievement | she speaks other languages and understands different cultures |  |

### ■ STEP 2

Show your application and essay to another student and compare each of your special characteristics, experiences, and achievements. Decide whose essay would be most effective to use for a university application. Tell your opinion and your reasons to the rest of the class.

# North American Institute of International Studies

## Application for Admission

Applying for: _____ SPRING _____ SUMMER _____ FALL _____ WINTER 20 __

Degree Objective: Undergraduate _____ Graduate _____

　　Major _____ Minor _____

Personal Data: Name _____

Address _____

Telephone _____ Birthdate _____

Sex _____ Ethnic Background _____

Educational Background:

List all secondary and postsecondary schools attended, including language programs.

Name and location of school　　Dates of attendance　　Degree granted　　GPA

_____

_____

_____

_____

_____

Personal Essay / Writing Sample:

All applicants must provide a writing sample. On another sheet of paper, write at least
200 words on the following topic. It must be handwritten, and written *only* by the applicant.
　　*What are some characteristics that make you different from other people you know?*
　　*How have your experiences in life shaped you as a person? What are some*
　　*achievements that you have accomplished that you feel particularly proud of?*

Signature _____ Date _____

All applications must be accompanied by official transcripts in English, proof of finances, and a nonrefundable $60
application fee.

## Choosing Past Time Frame or Present Time Frame

use

We can use both past time frame and present time frame to talk about things that happened in the past.

| PAST TIME FRAME | PRESENT TIME FRAME |
|---|---|
| Use past time frame (in the form of the simple past tense) to show that **a past event has no direct, ongoing relationship to the present.** The event was fully completed in the past or happened at a specific time in the past. | Use a present time frame (in the form of present perfect tense) to show that **a past event is directly related to the present.** The event happened in the past, but **continues to influence the present in some way.** |
| (a) **I lived** in Honduras as a very young child, but I don't remember much about it now. | (b) **I have lived** in four foreign countries, and as a result I am very aware of how cultural differences affect how we perceive reality. |
| (c) I started to fill out the application for the university, but I **didn't finish** it, because I realized I wouldn't be able to afford the tuition. | (d) **I haven't finished** the application for the university yet. I'm still working on the personal essay. |

## EXERCISE 1

Read the following personal essay written by a successful applicant to the North American Institute of International Studies. Underline the verb phrases and identify the tenses that are used. Then discuss these questions with a partner.

- Why did the author use present time in the first paragraph?
- Why did the author use past time in the second paragraph?
- Why did the author use present time in the third paragraph?

## Personal Essay
*by Aliona Fernandez*

(1) One of the characteristics that makes me different from many people is my adaptability. (2) I am flexible and comfortable in new or unusual situations. (3) I think this is because I have had a lot of experience living in foreign countries. (4) This has given me a lot of opportunities to face unfamiliar situations and to learn about unfamiliar customs and beliefs.

(5) My first experience in a foreign country was as a Peace Corps volunteer. (6) I taught English in a small town in a rural area. (7) Life in my town was very simple. (8) Because there was no electricity and rather little contact with the outside world, my life was a lot like living in an earlier century.

(9) I have been to other countries since that first experience, and everywhere that I have traveled has been interesting and educational. (10) As a result of my experiences in other countries, I speak other languages and understand other cultures. (11) I have learned that relationships between people are very much the same, whether they have modern, busy lives, or old-fashioned, more peaceful lives. (12) I have learned to understand different ways of doing things and different ways of looking at the world. (13) Most of all, I have learned that "new" doesn't necessarily mean "better." (14) My experiences have made me adaptable, and this adaptability has allowed me to understand other people and cultures.

## Relationship to the Present: Still True (Present Perfect Tense) Versus No Longer True (Past Tense)

use

Past events relate to the present if they are still true at this time.

| EXAMPLES | EXPLANATIONS |
|---|---|
| (a) **I have lived** in three foreign countries. **I have learned** how to adapt to the local culture. | **Present Perfect Tense:** Use the present perfect tense to show that something is **still true now**. |
| (b) **I lived** in Honduras for three years. **I ate pupusas** every day for lunch. | **Past Tense:** Use the past tense to talk about something that is **no longer true now**. |

## EXERCISE 2

Choose past tense or present perfect tense for the verbs in parentheses. More than one answer may be correct, so be prepared to explain why you chose the form you did. The first one has been done for you.

Bambang Soetomo (1) __came__ (come) to the United States last January to get a degree in mechanical engineering. Since he (2) __was__ (be) in the United States, he (3) __had__ (have) many new experiences. At home in Jakarta, servants (4) __cooked__ (cook) all his food. But here in the United States, Bambang (5) __had__ (have) to prepare food for himself. In Indonesia, a lot of his university classes (6) __required__ (require) the ability to memorize large amounts of information. But here, Bambang (7) __find__ (find) that memorization is not considered to be a very important skill in many of his classes. Of course, he (8) __is__ (be) ready for obvious differences in things like food and social customs, but he (9) __doesn't adjust__ (not/adjust) to the subtle differences. He (10) __learns__ (learn) that knowing about differences and dealing with them are two different things. In fact, he (11) __is__ (be) rather homesick. In Jakarta he (12) __had__ (have) a large group of friends, but here in the States he (13) __meets__ (meet) only a few other Indonesian students, and none of them are in his department. When he (14) __is__ (be) planning his trip to America, he (15) __plans__ (plan) to go home for a vacation after his sophomore year, but he (16) __changed__ (change) his mind since he (17) __got__ (get) here. He (18) __spoke__ (speak) with his father about the possibility of coming home during his first summer vacation. His father (19) __doesn't decide__ (not decide) whether that's a good idea or not.

use

Present perfect is used to describe things that began in the past but continue up to the present moment.

| EXAMPLES | EXPLANATIONS |
|---|---|
| (a) **I have visited** Paris over **a dozen times**. <br> (b) **I've eaten** snake meat **once**, but I'll never do it again! | Use present perfect to describe: <br> • the number of times something has happened |
| (c) Your teacher **has just left** her office. Maybe you can catch her if you hurry to the parking lot. <br> (d) **We've just been talking about** your application. Can we ask you a few questions? | • very recent events with *just* |
| (e) **I've known** Aliona **since** we were in high school. <br> (f) **I've never eaten** snake meat. **Have you ever tried** it? | Use present perfect in sentences: <br> • with *ever*, *never*, or *since* |

## EXERCISE 3

Work with a partner. Take turns asking each other these questions. Ask at least ten questions. You can use the suggested topics or make up questions of your own.

1. Have you ever . . . (ridden a horse, been in love, seen a flying saucer . . .)

2. How many times have you . . . (eaten Chinese food, taken the TOEFL® Test*, driven a motorcycle . . .)

3. Name three things you have never done, but would like to do.

4. Name three things you have done that you don't want to do again.

Then tell the rest of the class about your partner. The class should decide who has asked the most interesting or unusual questions.

*TOEFL is a registered trademark of the Educational Testing Service (ETS). This publication is not endorsed or approved by ETS.

## EXERCISE 4

Choose past tense or present perfect tense for the verbs in parentheses. More than one answer may be possible. The first sentence has been done for you as an example.

My friend Bob is a very happy man. He ∧ just (1) _____found out_____ (find out) that he

(2) _____ (receive) a full scholarship to North American Institute of

International Studies. He (3) _____ (apply) to several graduate programs

in the last few years, but he never (4) _____ (get) any scholarship offers

until six months ago, when he (5) _____ (be offered) a partial scholarship

to North Dakota State. Since then, apparently, the suggestions I gave him about

improving his personal essay (6) _____ (change) his chances. He

(7) _____ (get) two other offers from his second- and third-choice schools.

Most of the scholarship offers (8) _____ (be) small until last week, when

he (9) _____ (get) the letter from NAIIS offering him free tuition plus

room and board. I wonder if he (10) _____ (think about) doing something

nice for the person who helped him with his essay.

## FOCUS 4 — Relationship to the Present: Present Result (Present Perfect Tense)

**use**

Another common way that past events relate to the present is if the past event **continues to affect the present situation in some way.** Use present perfect tense to describe past events that cause a result in the present.

The present result can be stated directly.

| PAST ACTION | STATED PRESENT RESULT |
| --- | --- |
| (a) **I have** already **seen** that movie, | so **I suggest** we go see a different one. |
| (b) He **has been wasting** so much money | that **I don't think** we should give him any more. |
| (c) **I have** always **felt** that teachers were underpaid, | so **I think** we should suggest that our teacher ought to get a raise. |

The present result can be implied.

| PAST ACTION | IMPLIED PRESENT RESULT |
|---|---|
| (d) You **have spilled** juice all over my new tablecloth! | The tablecloth is dirty. |
| (e) John **has obviously forgotten** about our meeting. | He is not at the meeting. |

The present result can also be the speaker's/writer's attitude.

| NOT CONNECTED TO THE PRESENT (PAST TENSE) | CONNECTED TO THE PRESENT (PRESENT PERFECT TENSE) | EXPLANATIONS |
|---|---|---|
| (f) **Did you find** the article you were looking for? | (g) **Have you found** the article you were looking for? Because if not, I think **I know where you can find it.** | The event is connected to the present in the speaker's mind. |
| (h) The White House **released** new figures **yesterday** concerning the economy. | (i) The White House **has released** new figures on the economy in the last quarter. These figures **show** that imports continue to exceed exports by more than 20%. | Reporters often introduce news stories with the present perfect tense to emphasize the connection with the present. |
| (j) The historian Toynbee **often observed** that history repeats itself. | (k) The historian Toynbee **has observed** that history repeats itself, and **I believe that he is correct.** | A writer may mention a past event that has a connection to a point she or he is about to make. |

## EXERCISE 5

Choose the sentence that reflects the most logical continuation of the ideas expressed in the first sentence, based on the tense used in the first sentence. Both sentences are formed correctly.

1. I have told you that I don't like the color green.
   a. My brother didn't like that color either.
   b. So why did you buy me a sweater in that color?

2. Jeff met Matt at a party.

   a. They soon became the best of friends.

   b. They share an apartment in San Francisco.

3. Bambang Soetomo arrived in America about eight months ago.

   a. He has been adjusting to American life ever since.

   b. He is living by himself in an apartment.

4. I have been trying to get in touch with my math professor since last week.

   a. I didn't do well on the last exam.

   b. Whenever I go to her office, she isn't there.

5. I don't think that Denise likes Peter very much.

   a. Have you ever noticed that she avoids looking at him when she speaks?

   b. Did she say anything about her feelings to you at the meeting last week?

## EXERCISE 6

Discuss these questions about the short passages below with a partner and compare your ideas with those of other students.

- Why do you think the speaker chose to use the present perfect tense instead of simple past tense in these sentences?
- How is the past action related to the present: by time relationship, by present result, or by a combination of both?

   1. Scientists have discovered a number of interesting similarities between the atmosphere on Earth and on Titan, one of the moons of Jupiter. They have found significant concentrations of water vapor and other chemicals common on Earth. As a result, they are hoping to send another space probe to Titan later this year.

   2. If I have told you once, I've told you a hundred times: I hate broccoli!

   3. Guess what? We've been invited to Liz's wedding. What should we get her for a gift?

   4. Conservative politicians have often stated that welfare payments to poor families do not help reduce long-term poverty, but recent statistics show that this may not be true.

   5. Shakespeare's reputation as a psychologist has grown in recent years. His plays have always reflected a deep understanding of human motivations.

   6. Has Jill found a summer job? I was talking with my aunt, and she said her office might need a temporary computer programmer.

**use**

| EXAMPLES | EXPLANATIONS |
|---|---|
| (a) **I have been living** with my parents, but I hope to move out once I am accepted to your university. (**temporary**) | Use the present perfect progressive tense (*have/has been* + verb + *-ing*) instead of present perfect to describe something that is: |
| (b) **I have lived** with my parents since they became ill and needed me to help around the house. (**permanent**) | • temporary rather than permanent |
| (c) **I have been talking** to everyone about what to put in my essay, but I don't have a good plan yet. Do you have any ideas? (**repeated occurrence**) | • repeated rather than a single occurrence |
| (d) **I have thought** about the essay, and I have a good idea of what to write. (**single occurrence**) | |
| (e) **I have been working constantly** on my application for the last three hours. I don't know when I'll finish! (**continuous**) | • continuous rather than repeated or recurring |
| (f) **I have tried several times** to work on my application, but I keep getting interrupted. (**repeated**) | |
| (g) **I have been writing** my personal statement. I still have to proofread it and staple it together. (**uncompleted**) | • uncompleted rather than completed |
| (h) **I have written** my personal statement. Let's go celebrate! (**completed**) | |
| (i) Living in foreign countries **has required** a lot of flexibility. | Remember that nonprogressive verbs do not occur with the progressive aspect even when they refer to continuous states. |
| (j) NOT: Living in foreign countries **has been requiring** a lot of flexibility. | |

## EXERCISE 7

Choose the correct form, present perfect or present perfect progressive, for the verbs. More than one answer may be possible.

1. I (a) _____ (read) about the development of early forms of photography, and I (b) _____ (learn) some very interesting facts about it. I would like to continue my research next semester.

2. That baby _____ (cry) constantly since we got here. I wish its parents would do something to make it be quiet!

3. Bob's brother _____ (resent) his getting that full scholarship ever since he heard the news.

4. I _____ (try) to explain that for ten minutes. Aren't you listening?

5. I _____ (try) to explain that every way I know how. I give up!

6. I _____ (work) on this problem all afternoon. It's time for a break.

7. Aliona _____ (expect) the admissions committee to call about her application. That's why she wants to stay home this afternoon.

8. Bob _____ (tell) the committee that he doesn't want to accept the scholarship unless it includes room and board.

9. The college (a) _____ (try) to contact Bob about his scholarship. They (b) _____ (call) at least five or six times.

10. Bob (a) _____ (dream) going to NIIS ever since he read an article about their graduate program in public health. He (b) _____ (become) an expert on it.

## EXERCISE 8

Decide whether the verbs in parentheses should use simple present, present progressive, present perfect, present perfect progressive, or the past tense. Write the correct verb form in the blanks. More than one answer may be correct.

Bambang Soetomo (1) _____ (speak) English quite fluently. I wonder where he (2) _____ (learn) it. He (3) _____ (study) mechanical engineering. He (4) _____ (plan) to go to graduate school once he (5) _____ (get) his B.S. degree. Bambang (6) _____ (live) by himself for the last few months. But he (7) _____ (think) about getting a roommate. He (8) _____ (miss) his friends back home a great deal, and this (9) _____ (affect) his studies. He (10) _____ (hope) that his father will let him come home during the summer, but his father (11) _____ (not decide) yet.

# Use Your English

Find out what important changes your classmates have made in their lives.

- **STEP 1**  Interview three classmates. Ask them the following:

  - Have you changed any habits or routines recently?
  - What kind of changes did you make?
  - Why have you made the changes?
  - How have the changes affected you?

- **STEP 2**  Based on the changes your group has experienced, decide together whether you agree that changes in life are generally for the better. Present your group's ideas and reasons to the rest of the class.

ACTIVITY  **speaking/listening**

Experts in cross-cultural communication have found that North American culture tends to value individualism. As a result, many young children are taught to look for ways that they are different from other people. Most Americans can easily identify several personal experiences and characteristics that make them unique. What about people from other cultures?

- **STEP 1**  Interview three or four people from various cultures and ask them these questions:

  - What experiences have you had that most other people haven't?
  - What things make you different from most other people?

- **STEP 2**  Of the people you interviewed, who was able to think of the greatest number of individual differences?

# ACTIVITY 3 speaking

How do North Americans, as a group, compare to the students you interviewed for Activities 1 and 2?

■ **STEP 1**  Work with three different students than those you interviewed in Activity 1. Two of you should interview three or four North Americans, asking the questions that you used for Activity 1. The second pair should ask the questions you used for Activity 2.

■ **STEP 2**  Compare the responses of the North Americans to the responses of the students you interviewed in those activities.

■ **STEP 3**  Discuss these questions with your group and summarize your ideas for the rest of the class.

- Were there differences between the answers given by North Americans and those of your classmates?
- Were North Americans able to identify their individual differences more readily than people from other cultures?
- Did North Americans feel differently about change than people from other cultures?
- What do the similarities and differences between the answers of various cultural groups tell you about cultural differences?

# ACTIVITY 4 listening/speaking

CD Tracks
20, 21

Which of these two people is most qualified to be accepted for admission to the North American Institute of International Studies?

■ **STEP 1**  Listen to the interviews with each candidate. Using the chart on the next page, identify what the candidates say about their most important accomplishment, their background and experience, and their special abilities.

■ **STEP 2**  Compare your chart with another student's, and listen to the interviews a second time to make sure you have heard all the important information.

| INTERVIEW QUESTIONS | CANDIDATE 1<br>NAME: _____<br>PROGRAM: _____ | CANDIDATE 2<br>NAME: _____<br>PROGRAM: _____ |
| --- | --- | --- |
| What makes you different from other candidates? | | |
| What relevant experience do you have? | | |
| What is an achievement that you're proud of? | | |

■ **STEP 3**    You and your partner should decide which student is a better candidate for admission. Tell your choice and your reasons to the rest of the class.

## ACTIVITY 5 research on the web

■ **STEP 1**    Use an Internet search engine such as Google® or Yahoo® and enter the term "personal essay". You should find listed a number of Web sites of universities and other institutions that provide advice and guidance on writing personal essays for college applications. Visit at least three of these sites and summarize at least five pieces of advice that they provide to prospective applicants. Present that advice to the rest of the class.

■ **STEP 2**    Use the advice you find to revise the personal essay you wrote for the Opening Task of this unit. What changes did you make?

## ACTIVITY 6 reflection

Bring in the front page of a daily newspaper and examine the articles with a partner or in a group. Find examples of sentences written in present time and past time. In what tense are headlines usually written? In what tense are the introductory paragraphs usually written? In what tense is the main part of the article generally written? Can you find a pattern? Why do you think the reporter chose one time frame rather than another? Discuss your ideas with your partner or group, and then present them to the rest of the class.

# FUTURE TIME
## Using Present Tenses, Using *Will* Versus *Be Going To* Versus *Shall*; Adverbial Clauses in Future

## UNIT GOALS

- Understand and use different verb tenses to express actions and states in future time

- Correctly use *will, be going to,* and *shall* and other modals to express future time

- Correctly express future time in adverbial clauses

## OPENING TASK

### Thinking About the Future

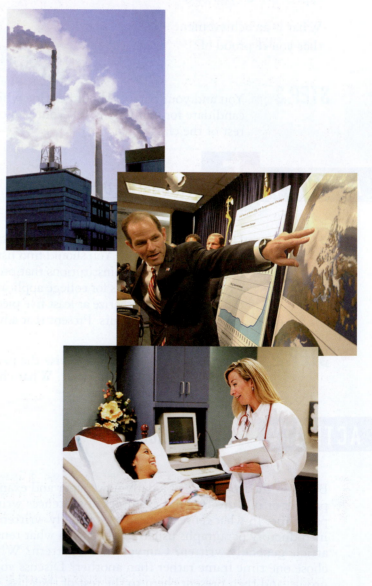

## STEP 1

"Futurists" are people whose job it is to make predictions about the future and look at the way current trends might have unforeseen impacts in the future. They make "projections" of how things might be different in the future, based on things that are happening now. Based on some of the trends listed below, make a projection of how you think life will be different in a hundred years. Write a short paragraph answering the following questions: Do you think that life one hundred years from now will be better or worse than it is today? Why? Consider some of the current trends and issues listed below, and decide how they will affect the lives of people living one hundred years from now.

| Positive Trends | Negative Trends |
| --- | --- |
| Technological improvements | Environmental problems (pollution, acid rain, global warming, decreasing natural resources) |
| New medical treatments | |
| Longer life spans | Population increase |
| Better food crops | New diseases |
| Growth of democratic governments | The growth of terrorism |
| Better communication | Increased traffic |
| More rapid transportation | Increasing government debt |
| Equal status for women | Changing family structures |
| More education | Increasing economic gap between the rich and poor |

## STEP 2

Exchange paragraphs with a partner, and decide which one of you is more of an optimist (someone who generally expects good things to happen) and which one is more of a pessimist (someone who generally expects bad things to happen) about the future of the world.

## STEP 3

Report your decision and some of the reasons to the rest of the class.

## FOCUS 1 — Recognizing Future Time

We can use simple present, present progressive, and modals to talk about future time.

| EXAMPLES | EXPLANATIONS |
|---|---|
| (a) The meeting **begins** at 10:00 every day. | Simple present can describe present time. |
| (b) The conference on global warming **begins** in three weeks. | It can also describe future time. |
| (c) The futurists **are having** problems with their study, so they are postponing their report. | Present progressive can describe present time. |
| (d) They**'re presenting** their report next month. | It can also describe future time. |
| (e) There's a package at the door. It **should** be their report. | Modals can describe present time. |
| (f) When they have finished analyzing the results, they **will** present their recommendations. | They can also describe future time. |

### EXERCISE 1

Do the verbs in these passages refer to future time or present time? Underline the verb phrases. Mark verb phrases that refer to future time with F. Mark verb phrases that refer to present time with P. The first sentence of each passage has been done for you as examples.

1.            P
   (a) School always <u>begins</u> in September in the United States. (b) This coming year, school begins on September 12. (c) Janet's going to start her third year of high school. (d) She's taking chemistry, history, English, and advanced algebra. (e) She might take a theater class, if she can fit it into her schedule.

2.        F
   (a) We'<u>re having</u> a class picnic in just a couple of weeks. (b) As you know, school ends on June 15, and the picnic will be on the next day, so we're already making plans. (c) Most people are being really cooperative. (d) For example, Lucia makes great potato salad, so she's bringing some to the picnic. (e) There should be enough for everyone to have some. (f) But George is being difficult. (g) He says he will come, but he won't bring anything. (h) Will you explain something to me? (i) Will you tell me why George is so stubborn? (j) He really should be more cooperative. (k) Everyone else is bringing something. (i) Why won't he?

| FOCUS 2 | **Present Tenses for Future Planned Events** |  |
|---|---|---|

use

| EXAMPLES | EXPLANATIONS |
|---|---|
| (a) The conference **starts** on a Sunday next month. <br> (b) The futurist **is presenting** his findings next week. <br> (c) Next year **is** the fifth annual conference on global warming. | Use simple present and present progressive tenses to describe future activities that are **already scheduled or planned** to take place in the future. |
| (d) We **will** examine the data if they can get it to us in time for the conference. <br> (e) There **might** be a surprising announcement. | For future events that are **not already scheduled,** use *will* or other modals of prediction (*may, could, might*). |

### EXERCISE 2

Make at least five questions about things that will happen in this class at a future time and have already been scheduled. Ask your questions to another student.

**Example:** *When are we having our next grammar test?*

### EXERCISE 3

Choose the best tense (present, present progressive, or a modal of prediction) for the verbs in the following sentences. Both forms may be grammatically correct, so be prepared to explain your choice.

**Example:** John *'s leaving_____* (leave) for France in a week.

1. The bus _____ (leave) at 6:00 A.M. Don't be late.

2. Filipe _____ (have) a party on Friday. Have you been invited?

3. John doesn't know when he _____ (return) from France.

4. Peter is hoping that Denise _____ (stop) demanding that everyone work so hard.

5. Our teacher's birthday _____ (be) Friday, so we'd better buy her a gift.

6. Perhaps there _____ (be) a test next Friday.

7. There definitely _____ (be) a test next Friday.

8. I _____ (graduate) next June.

## Will Versus Be Going To

**use**

### Will

| EXAMPLES | EXPLANATIONS |
|---|---|
| (a) I'm having trouble with my homework. **Will** you help me? | Use *will*:<br>• for requests |
| (b) I need some milk from the store. Oh, **I'll** get it for you. | • to express willingness or unwillingness |
| (c) Denise **won't** go with us, no matter how much we ask her. | |
| (d) I'm sorry I forgot the book. **I'll** bring it tomorrow, I promise. | • to make a promise |
| (e) Plants **will** die if they don't get enough water. | • to express general truths |

### Be Going To

| EXAMPLES | EXPLANATIONS |
|---|---|
| (f) I'm **going to** go to the party, whether you're there or not. | Use *be going to*:<br>• to talk about intentions |
| (g) We shouldn't go hiking this afternoon. It**'s going to** rain any minute! | • to talk about the immediate future |
| (h) Are you going to Grace's party? I can't. I **am going to** be out of town that weekend. | • to talk about plans that have been made earlier |

### Will and Be Going To

| EXAMPLES | EXPLANATIONS |
|---|---|
| (i) The weather **will** be fine for Reiko's wedding, and everyone**'s going to** have a wonderful time! | Use *will* and *be going to* to make predictions. When *be going to* is pronounced "*gonna*", it is usually more informal than *will*. |
| (j) I'm **going to** paint my apartment. First, I'll get the paint and some brushes. Then I'll get to work. I **might** paint the walls green, but I haven't decided yet. | *Be going to* usually introduces a topic. Following sentences often use *will* and other one-word modals. |

## EXERCISE 4

Decide which form, *will* or *be going to*, should be used in the following sentences. In some cases both answers may be correct.

1. I've got an extra ticket to the football game. (a) _____ (you go) with me? It (b) _____ (be) a great game. Johnson (c) _____ (play) the quarterback. I'm sure he (d) _____ (be) wonderful.

2. I don't know what to do for my vacation. Maybe I (a) _____ (go) to Mexico. I know the plane ticket (b) _____ (be) expensive. Perhaps I (c) _____ (take) the bus to save some money. Your brother's taken the bus before, hasn't he? (d) _____ (you ask) him how the trip was?

3. Lin (a) _____ (finish) her assignment tonight, even if she has to stay up until dawn. It (b) _____ (not be) easy. She has to finish reading *War and Peace*, and then write a ten-page paper. She (c) _____ (probably be) up all night. Maybe her roommate (d) _____ (make) some coffee for her and do the dishes, so that Lin (e) _____ (not have) to worry about anything else.

4. Different plants need different amounts of water. Too much water (a) _____ (kill) certain kinds of plants. Other kinds require daily watering, and they (b) _____ (die) if they don't get it. Setting out a garden (c) _____ (require) some advanced planning to make sure that plants with similar water requirements (d) _____ (be) planted in the same areas.

## FOCUS 4 · Using *Shall*

| EXAMPLES | EXPLANATIONS |
|---|---|
| (a)  I'll go to the conference. <br> (b)  (?) I **shall** go to the conference. <br> (c)  I **won't** do it. <br> (d)  (?) I **shan't** go. | *Shall* is not usually used in American English. Using *shall* to make statements about future actions sounds quite formal and old-fashioned to Americans. The negative contracted form (*shan't*) is almost never used. |
| (e)  **Shall** I tell you my prediction? <br> (f)  **Should** I answer the phone? <br> (g)  **May** I help you? | Use *shall*: <br> • to make offers <br> *Should* or *may* are often used in this context. |
| (h)  **Shall** we dance? <br> (i)  **Shall** we begin with the first exercise? <br> (j)  **Let's** go out for dinner. | • to suggest activities that both speaker and <br> • listener will participate in. <br> *Let's* is less formal and more common. |

### EXERCISE 5

Decide which forms (*will, be going to,* or *shall*) can be used in these sentences.  In some cases more than one form may be possible, so be prepared to explain any difference in meaning or use communicated by the choice of a particular form. Discuss your ideas with a classmate and present them to the rest of the class.

1. _____ we go to a movie tonight?

2. When _____ you graduate?

3. _____ I tell you the answer to the question?

4. He _____ not do it, even though his mother wants him to.

5. Water _____ not flow uphill.

## FOCUS 5    Other Modals in Future Time

Modals (*will, should, may, might, could*) that describe future events also tell about the **probability** of the event. See Unit 16 for more information and practice with predictions about future events.

| EXAMPLES | MEANING | FORM |
|---|---|---|
| (a) There **will** be more people living on the earth in 100 years. | **certain** 100% probability | *will* |
| (b) The average life span of most people **should** increase. | **probable** 65%–80% probability | *should* |
| (c) There **may** be alternative energy sources, but people **may not** be able to afford them. | **quite possible** 35%–65% probability | *may* *may not* |
| (d) The world **might** develop ways to reverse global warming, but they **might not** do it in time to prevent climate change. (e) It **could** rain before we get there. | **somewhat possible** 5%–35% probability | *might* *might not* *could* |
| (f) Life **won't** be the same as it is today. | **certain** 0% probability | *will not* |

## EXERCISE 6

Use a modal to give your opinion about the following questions. Give a reason.

**Example:** What will life be like one hundred years from now?

*Life should be more complex one hundred years from now, because of so many technological developments.*

1. Will there be enough coal and oil?
2. Will there be a decrease in air pollution?
3. Will the overall climate grow warmer?
4. Will the rate of population growth be greater?
5. Will there be increased use of automobiles?
6. Will there be political stability?
7. Will there still be large differences between developing and developed countries?
8. Will there be cures for cancer, AIDS, and other diseases?
9. What will be the problems that people face in the twenty-first century?
10. Will there still be wars between countries?

Make up three questions of your own and ask them to a partner. Compare your ideas about the future to those of your partner. Who is more optimistic about the future?

## FOCUS 6  Future-Time Adverbial Clauses

In future time, adverbial clauses always use present tenses and not modal auxiliaries.

| | |
|---|---|
| (a) I'll present the report tomorrow **when I finish analyzing** the evidence. | (b) NOT: I'll present the report tomorrow **when I will finish analyzing** the evidence. |
| (c) I'm going to watch TV **as soon as I have finished** my homework. | (d) NOT: I'm going to watch TV **as soon as I will have finished** my homework. |
| (e) Hani is planning to have a party **while his parents are visiting relatives in Canada.** | (f) NOT: Hani's planning to have a party while his parents **will be visiting relatives in Canada.** |

### EXERCISE 7

Join the second sentence in each of these pairs to the first sentence using the linking word in parentheses. Make sure to change nouns to pronouns where necessary.

**Example:** I'll go to the movies. I will finish my homework. (after)

*I'll go the movies after I finish my homework.*

1. All my friends will be relieved. The semester will end in a couple of weeks. (when)

2. I'm going to go to the movies every day. I will have finished all the household chores that have been postponed all semester. (after)

3. It will be almost three weeks after the last day of class. Lin will finally get her research paper completed. (by the time)

4. I'm going to read that novel. I'll have some time after the exams. (when)

5. Bob's going to spend every day at the beach. The weather will be sunny. (while)

6. Matt and Jeff will be really tired. They are going to finish their 10-mile hike from the beach. (by the time)

7. Mark and Ann are leaving for Europe. They'll finish their last exam. (as soon as)

8. Doug and Elena are going to get married. They will be on vacation in Mexico. (while)

9. Even our teacher's going to take some time off. She will have finished grading the final papers and correcting the exams. (when)

# Use Your English

### ACTIVITY 1  speaking/writing

What day and time is it at this moment? Imagine what you will be doing **at this exact moment** ten years from now, twenty years from now, fifty years from now. Describe these activities to a partner or write a brief essay about them.

### ACTIVITY 2  speaking

- **STEP 1**    Tell several other students about your vacation plans. Listen to their plans.

- **STEP 2**    Then answer these questions as a group.

  - Whose plans sound like the most fun? Why?
  - Whose plans sound like the most boring? Why?
  - Whose plans sound like the easiest to arrange? Why?
  - Whose plans sound like the best opportunity to practice English?

Decide on one additional category of your own.

- **STEP 3**    Report your answers to the rest of the class.

### ACTIVITY 3  writing

Choose one of the three questions on the next page and write a paragraph or make a presentation expressing your ideas.

- What major **political and economic changes** are going to take place in your lifetime? Describe them and explain why you think they are going to happen.
- What major **social changes** are going to take place in your lifetime? Describe them and explain why you think they are going to happen.
- What major **scientific advances** are going to take place in your lifetime? Describe them and explain why you think they are going to happen.

## ACTIVITY 4 listening/speaking

**STEP 1**

Listen to the two speakers talk about the future. As you listen, note each speaker's predictions and the reasons for those predictions in the chart below. Based on those predictions and reasons, decide whether each speaker is optimistic or pessimistic about the future.

CD Tracks 22, 23

### Speaker 1

| OPTIMISTIC OR PESSIMISTIC? | SPEAKER'S PREDICTION | SPEAKER'S REASONS |
|---|---|---|
| Public health and population | | |
| Life expectancy and nutrition | | |
| Energy and pollution | | |
| Political and economic stability | | |

### Speaker 2

| OPTIMISTIC OR PESSIMISTIC? | SPEAKER'S PREDICTION | SPEAKER'S REASONS |
|---|---|---|
| Public health and population | | |
| Life expectancy and nutrition | | |
| Energy and pollution | | |
| Political and economic stability | | |

**STEP 2**

Imagine that you are one of the speakers. Using the notes you took above, try to give a speech in your own words to a partner explaining why you are optimistic or pessimistic about the future. Your partner should do the same with the other speech. If you wish, add some ideas and reasons of your own.

## ACTIVITY 5    speaking

- **STEP 1**    Organize a debate between optimists and pessimists. Using the Opening Task on page 245, decide whether you are an optimist or a pessimist. Form groups of four or more. Try to have an equal number of optimists and pessimists in each group.

- **STEP 2**    As a group, choose one category of world affairs (see Opening Task for examples). Discuss the current trends related to that category. Add one or two significant additional trends of your own. Optimists will then give reasons why they think the world will be better one hundred years from now. Pessimists will give reasons why they think the world will be worse one hundred years from now.

- **STEP 3**    Present both sets of predictions to the other groups. As a whole class, decide who has presented the most persuasive reasons, the optimists or the pessimists.

## ACTIVITY 6    research on the web

Go on *InfoTrac® College Edition* and enter the term "futurist". Skim at least ten articles quickly to determine what trends futurists are currently looking at and what predictions they are making about those trends.  Choose three that you find interesting and report on these predictions to the rest of the class.

## ACTIVITY 7    reflection

Find three written and three spoken examples of people talking about future activities.  This can be in conversations with native speakers or from a radio or TV program, such as a weather report or a sports program.  Written examples can come from newspaper horoscopes or any news article that talks about future trends.

Identify the forms that the people used to talk about the future event. Did they use present tense or future tenses with *will* or *going to* or other modals?

Report at least one example to the rest of the class.

# MODALS OF PREDICTION AND INFERENCE

## UNIT GOALS

- Understand and use different modals to express predictions in future time

- Understand and use different modals to express logical inferences in present time

- Correctly express predictions and logical inferences in past time

## OPENING TASK

### Solving a Mystery

### ■ STEP 1

Work with a partner. Choose one of the mini-mysteries on the next page to try to solve.

MINI MYSTERIES

MYSTERY #1
A man lives on the fortieth floor of a very tall building. Every day he rides the elevator down to the ground floor. When he comes home he rides the elevator to the twentieth floor, but he has to walk the rest of the way.

Why does he do this?

MYSTERY #2
In a room, a dead woman is hanging by a rope, more than three feet above the floor. There are no windows, and the door has been locked from the inside. The room is empty: no furniture, no ladder. The only thing in the room is a single piece of paper.

What happened to the woman?

MYSTERY #3
A police officer receives an emergency phone call about a terrible automobile accident. A boy and his father have both been very badly injured. The officer has to fill out the report and figure out what happened. The police officer takes one look at the boy and his father, and says "You'll have to find someone else to deal with this. I'm too upset. This boy is my son!"

How can the boy have two fathers?

■ **STEP 2**

Think of five possible explanations. Decide which ones are likely and which ones are not very likely.

■ **STEP 3**

Turn to page A-12 and read the additional clues. Then try to solve the mysteries.

*karaoke*

**FOCUS 1** | **Modals of Prediction**

*meaning*

*use*

Modals of prediction refer to future time. Use them to indicate how likely or possible it is that some future event will happen. (See Focus 3 for information about making predictions in the past time frame.)

| EXAMPLES | FORM | MEANING/USE |
|---|---|---|
| (a) This class **will** end in an hour. | *will* | It will **certainly** happen. We can also use simple present or present progressive to describe these events. |
| (b) We **should** be able to finish the unit by the end of the week. | *should* | It is **likely** to happen. Using *should* for predictions sometimes sounds like advisability. If you aren't sure, use *will probably* to make your meaning clear. |
| (c) We **will probably** finish it in a couple of days. | *will probably* | |
| (d) We **may** need some extra time for review. | *may* *might* *could* | It will **possibly** happen. |
| (e) You'd better study tonight. We **could/might** have a surprise quiz tomorrow. | | |
| (f) We **may not** have one. | *may not* *might not* | It will **possibly not** happen. |
| (g) We **might not** have time for it. | | |
| (h) It **shouldn't** be difficult if you have studied the homework. | *shouldn't* *probably won't* | It is **not likely** that this will happen. Using *shouldn't* for predictions sometimes sounds like advisability. If you aren't sure, use *probably won't* to make your meaning clear. |
| (i) It **probably won't** take too long. | | |
| (j) We **won't** have a quiz tomorrow, because there's no class. | *won't* | It will **certainly not** happen. |

| EXAMPLES | EXPLANATIONS |
|---|---|
| (k) **Will** they finish the quiz by 5:00? Bambang **should finish** on time, but Reiko **might** be a little late. | To ask for predictions about future events, use only *will*, not other modal forms. |

## EXERCISE 1

Make sentences from these cues using modals.

**Example:**   certain: Andy/drive to New York for a vacation.

*Andy will drive to New York for a vacation.*

1. likely: Andy/decide what to do about his car next week. *[should]*
2. certainly not: The car/work well enough for his trip to New York. *[won't]*
3. possible: Andy/get it repaired, if it can be done cheaply. *[may]*
4. not likely: He/have trouble selling it. *[probably won't]*
5. likely: He/be able to get a good price. *[will probably]*
6. possible: Andy's friend Paul/want to buy it. *[might]*
7. possibly not: Andy/sell the car to Paul. *[may not]*
8. possibly not: The car/be in very good condition. *[might not]*
9. possible: Paul/expect a refund if he has troubles with the car. *[could]*
10. certain: Andy/need the money to buy a plane ticket if he doesn't drive. *[will]*

## EXERCISE 2

How likely is it that you will be doing the following activities next Saturday night at 8:00 P.M.?

| | |
|---|---|
| doing English homework | taking a bath |
| watching TV | speaking another language |
| thinking about personal problems | sleeping |
| sitting in a movie theater | writing letters to my family |
| reading a magazine | having a good time with friends |

Work with a partner. Ask questions with *will*. Answer questions with the appropriate modal of prediction.

**Examples:**   *At 8:00 P.M. next Saturday do you think you will be doing English homework?*

*I won't be doing homework on a Saturday night. I might be at a party.*

## EXERCISE 3

Write twelve true sentences about your plans for your next vacation using modals of prediction.

1. two things that you will certainly do

_____

2. two things that you will likely do

_____

3. two things that you will possibly do

_____

4. two things that you possibly won't do

_____

5. two things that you won't likely do

_____

6. two things that you certainly won't do

_____

## EXERCISE 4

Write twelve sentences about how you think life will be at the end of the next century using modals of prediction.

1. two things that will certainly be true

_____

2. two things that will likely be true

_____

3. two things that will possibly be true

_____

4. two things that possibly won't be true

_____

5. two things that won't likely be true

_____

6. two things that certainly won't be true

_____

## FOCUS 2    Modals of Inference

Modals of inference refer to the present time frame. Use them to express a logical conclusion, based on evidence. (See Focus 3 for information about making inferences in the past time frame.)

| EXAMPLES | FORM | MEANING/USE |
|---|---|---|
| (a) The police officer **must** be the boy's mother. | *must* | There is no other possible conclusion from the evidence. |
| (b) There **should** be a good reason why the man walks the rest of the way. | *should* | This is a logical conclusion, based on the evidence we have, but it is possible that there is another conclusion. |
| (c) He **may** want the exercise. <br> (d) The elevator **might** be broken. <br> (e) He **could** want to visit people on the twentieth floor. | *may* <br> *might* <br> *could* | This is one of several possibilities. |
| (f) The officer **may not** be telling the truth. <br> (g) The man **might not** like to ride the elevator up so high so quickly. | *may not* <br> *might not* | This is one of several possibilities. |
| (h) There **shouldn't** be any reason why the elevator wouldn't go up to the top floor. | *shouldn't* | This is not a logical conclusion, based on the evidence we have, but it could be possible. |
| (i) The man is so short he **must not** be able to reach the elevator button for the top floor. | *must not* | This is not a possible conclusion, based on the evidence we have. |
| (j) The officer **couldn't** be the boy's father. <br> (k) A person **can't** have two fathers. | *couldn't* <br> *can't* | This is impossible. |

Make logical conclusions by filling in the blanks with an appropriate modal of inference. Decide whether the logical conclusion you express is:

- the only one possible (*must*) or impossible (*must not/can't/couldn't*)
- more likely than other possible conclusions (*should*) or less likely (*shouldn't*)
- or one of several possibilities (*could/may/might/may not/might not*)

There may be more than one correct answer, so be prepared to explain why you chose the form you did.

1. There's someone at the door. That (a) _____ be my brother; I've been expecting him. But it (b) _____ be the postal carrier, or it (c) _____ even be a salesperson.

2. Someone is ringing the doorbell. It (a) _____ (not) be my brother; he has a key. It (b) _____ (not) be the postal carrier; he doesn't usually ring the bell. It (c) _____ (not) be a friend; all my friends think I'm still in New York. It (d) _____ be a salesperson. Let's not answer it!

3. I hope I can go to the movies with you tonight, but I (a) _____ (not) have enough money. I (b) _____ have enough, because I cashed a check yesterday. But I won't be 100% sure until I buy groceries and see how much money I have left. I really hope I can go. Everyone who has seen that movie says it's really good. It (c) _____ be very funny.

4. Martha looks pretty unhappy. She and George (a) _____ be having another one of their fights. I don't know what the problem is this time. It (b) _____ be because George is always working on his car. It (c) _____ be because Martha wants them to spend every weekend at her mother's house. It (d) _____ (not) be about money, though. That's the fight they had last week. They (e) _____ (not) have a very happy marriage.

5. Where have I put my wallet? It (a) _____ be somewhere! It (b) _____ (not) just disappear by itself. It (c) _____ be on my desk, since that's where I usually put it. But it (d) _____ be in my briefcase, too. I sometimes forget to take it out when I get home.

6. Fiona (a) —————————— (not) need money. She's always eager to pay when we go out for a night on the town. She never seems to have a job. It
(b) —————————— be nice to have enough money without having to work.

7. Frank (a) —————————— have no trouble finding a job when he moves to California. It (b) —————————— take a while, but I know he'll find a good position. He seems unhappy in New York. He (c) ——————————
(not) like living there very much.

## EXERCISE 6

Decide whether the following sentences are predictions or inferences and choose an appropriate modal. Compare your choices with a partner's.

**Examples:**    It _____shouldn't_____ (not) be very difficult to find a parking place today, because it's Sunday, and usually there aren't many people downtown.

Jack _____must not_____ (not) have much money, because he drives a 15-year-old car.

1. Traffic is getting heavy; rush hour ————————— be starting.
2. Commuters ————————— be getting really tired of driving to work in such awful traffic.
3. Experts tell us that traffic ————————— get worse every year unless we do something about the problem.
4. Some people think that traffic ————————— flow more smoothly if we increase the number of highways.
5. But most experts feel that the problem ————————— (not) be solved by building more highways.
6. That ————————— just increase the number of cars on the roads.
7. The traffic problem ————————— begin to improve once we have increased public transportation.
8. This city ————————— (not) have a very efficient public transportation system, because people seem to drive everywhere.

## FOCUS 3  Modals of Prediction and Inference in Past Time

You can make predictions and inferences about things that happened in the past time frame by using **perfect modals**.

### Modal + *Have* + Past Participle

| The woman | must | have | committed | suicide. |

| MODAL | EXAMPLES WITH PRESENT/FUTURE TIME | EXAMPLES WITH PAST TIME |
|---|---|---|
| | Why won't the man ride to the top floor? | How did the woman die? |
| *must* | (a) The elevator **must be** in working order, since he rides down from the top floor every day. | (b) The woman's death **must have been** a suicide. |
| *should* | (c) There **should be** a logical explanation for all these mysteries. | (d) The woman **should have been** able to slide the block of ice out from under her feet. |
| *may* | (e) He **may want** exercise. | (f) She **may have been** mentally ill. |
| *might* | (g) He **might get** sick if the elevator rises too quickly. | (h) She **might have been** having problems. |
| *could* | (i) He **could be** nervous about elevators. | (j) She **could have been** fired recently. |
| *may not* | (k) He **may not like** elevators. | (l) She **may not have seen** any solution to her problems. |
| *might not* | (m) He **might not want** to ride all the way to the top floor. | (n) She **might not have had** anyone to talk to. |
| *shouldn't* | (o) He **shouldn't have** to walk up the rest of the floors. | (p) There **shouldn't have been** anyone else in the room with her, since the door was locked from then inside. |
| *must not* | (q) He **must not be** able to reach the buttons for the top floor. | (r) She **must not have wanted** to continue living. |
| *couldn't* | (s) That **couldn't be** the reason. | (t) The woman's death **couldn't have been** a murder. |
| *can't* | (u) There **can't be** any other explanation. | (v) She **can't have wanted** to go on living. |

## EXERCISE 7

Change this passage to the past time frame.

**Example:**     Denise might not have enough time to finish the project today. That must be
the reason why she isn't at the boss's birthday party.

*Denise might not have had enough time to finish the project yesterday.*
*That must have been the reason why she wasn't at the boss's birthday party.*

(1) Frank might change jobs. (2) He should have no trouble finding a new job.

(3) It might take a while, but he has excellent qualifications and lots of experience.

(4) He must be really unhappy to want to move to a brand new company. (5) He must
not like working in such a big company very much.

## EXERCISE 8

Write the appropriate modal form in the blank. There may be more than one
correct answer.

1. Someone called me up in the middle of the night. They hung up before I could
   answer the phone. It (a) _____ (not be) my brother; he doesn't have a
   telephone. It (b) _____ (be) someone I know, but why would they call
   in the middle of the night? It (c) _____ (be) a wrong number.

2. Where were you last night? I thought you were going to join us at the movies. You
   (a) _____ (have) enough money to go with us, because the tickets
   weren't that expensive. It's too bad you didn't come. I (b) _____ (be)
   able to lend you the money. Or perhaps Peter (c) _____ (pay) for your
   ticket. He's so generous. The movie was really funny. You (d) _____
   (be) disappointed to miss all the fun.

3. Janet looked really unhappy as she was leaving Professor Brown's office. She (a)
   _____ (failed) another exam. I know she's already failed one midterm,
   and she had two more last week. It (b) _____ (not be) her chemistry
   test. I know she was really nervous about it. But it (c) _____ (be) her
   calculus exam. She's really good at mathematics, and I know she studied a lot for it.

4. Peter looked everywhere for the missing documents. They (a) _____
   (not disappear) by themselves. He thought they (b) _____ (be) on the
   desk, where he usually put things he was working on, or they (c) _____
   (be) in his briefcase, too. But when he looked, they weren't in either place. Then he
   remembered working on them at the office. He (d) _____ (leave)
   them there.

5. Who killed Judge Clarence? It (a) _____ (not be) his wife. She was in Switzerland learning how to ski. It (b) _____ (be) his accountant. Apparently there was some trouble with money. But nobody thought his accountant would do such a thing. There were a few clues. His wallet was missing. His brother's fingerprints were found on the candlestick that was used to kill the judge. The murderer (c) _____ (be) his brother, but Detective Grace O'Neill was not convinced. It all seemed too simple. The brother was rich and didn't need the money. The murderer (d) _____ (be) someone else, someone who was actually trying to get the brother in trouble with the law.

## EXERCISE 9

Use modals of prediction and inference to give possible or probable reasons for these situations.

**Examples:**   The window was open. The TV was gone.

*A thief must have broken into the apartment.*

The students are quiet. They're listening carefully.

*They might be taking a test.*

*The teacher could be telling them about their final examination.*

1. The parents are laughing. They're looking at a picture.

2. Mary's waiting at the corner. She's looking at her watch.

3. Altaz was smiling. A doctor was congratulating him.

4. The men were digging holes. They were looking at an old map.

5. A woman was crying. She had just received an envelope in the mail.

6. Denise stays late at the office every night. She tells her boss about it.

7. That man wears old clothes. He doesn't have enough to eat.

8. The police ran to their car. They drove quickly to the house.

# Use Your English

## ACTIVITY  1 writing

- **STEP 1** Watch a television program (comedy or drama) for a few minutes without turning on the sound. You should be able to see, but not to hear, what's going on.

- **STEP 2** Describe at least five interactions between characters. Describe exactly what happened, your interpretation of what happened, and your reasons for thinking so. Make a chart like this.

| DESCRIPTION OF WHAT HAPPENED—WHO DID WHAT? | INTERPRETATION OF ACTION—WHAT WAS THE CHARACTER'S REASON OR PURPOSE? | REASON FOR YOUR INTERPRETATION— WHY DO YOU THINK SO? |
| --- | --- | --- |
| **Example:** One man kept poking the other man in the chest with his finger. | He might have been trying to start a fight. | The other man's expression became more and more angry. |
| Interaction 1 | | |
| Interaction 2 | | |
| Interaction 3 | | |
| Interaction 4 | | |
| Interaction 5 | | |

- **STEP 3** Write a paragraph that describes what you saw and what you think was happening. Be sure to distinguish between things that **might** have been going on versus things that **must** have been going on. Give reasons for all of your interpretations. 16 sentences long/more

## ACTIVITY  2 speaking/writing

Do you have friends or family living in another country? What time is it at this moment in that country? Talk or write about what you think they are doing at this moment.

Look at these pictures of six household items that are no longer used today.

a.

b.

c.

d.

e.

f.

■ **STEP 1**   Work with a partner and discuss what you think each object might have been used for. Give reasons.

■ **STEP 2**   Compare your ideas with those of other students in the class. See page A-12 for answers.

**ACTIVITY** **4** speaking

Number of Children

Love and Romance

Health

Wealth

Do you know how to predict people's future by looking at their palms? Here is a diagram of some of the important "lines" of the palm. If the line is deep and strong, the person should have favorable developments in those areas. If the line is weak or broken, this indicates that the person may have trouble in that area. Using this reference guide, choose a partner and examine his or her palm to make predictions about his or her future. Try to make at least two predictions about what will happen to your partner in the future and two inferences about his or her character or personality.

## ACTIVITY 5 listening/speaking

CD Track 24

**STEP 1** Listen to the conversation of a family trying to solve a mystery. Decide whether each person listed below is a possible suspect, a probable suspect, or not a possible suspect.

| SUSPECT | LIKELIHOOD OF GUILT | EVIDENCE |
|---------|---------------------|----------|
| Mom | could not be guilty | she discovered the cookies were missing |
| Dad | | |
| Nancy | | |
| Eric | | |
| Diane | | |

**STEP 2** Work with a partner to decide who the criminal is. Give reasons to support your decision. The thief must have been _____.

## ACTIVITY 6 research on the web

Go to the Internet to investigate mysteries that have never been solved. Type in the words "unsolved mysteries" into a reliable search engine such as Yahoo® or Google®. Choose one of the mysteries there. Read about it and prepare a brief report about the mystery. Try do develop some possible and probable explanations for the mystery. Can you solve the mystery? Find another student in class who read about the same mystery you did and compare your ideas.

## ACTIVITY 7 reflection

How do you distinguish between a prediction and a logical inference in your first language? Think about how you would indicate the difference between a possibility that you are guessing about and a logical conclusion that you have made on the basis of evidence. If there are other speakers of your language in class, work together with them to make a brief report about how these ideas are expressed in your own language as compared to the structures we use in English.

# HYPOTHETICAL STATEMENTS

## UNIT GOALS

- Correctly identify and understand sentences describing hypothetical or contrary-to-fact situations

- Correctly form hypothetical and contrary-to-fact statements in present, future, and past time frames

- Recognize and use various hypothetical constructions

## OPENING TASK

### If I Ruled the World

Suppose that you had just been made Leader of the Entire World. Imagine that you had been granted the authority and resources to make any kind of changes in world affairs that you would like. You have the power and ability to change the world to fit your vision.

What actions would you take to:

- end world hunger?
- develop renewable energy sources?
- control population growth?
- protect the environment?

- abolish war?
- ensure political stability?
- maintain economic growth?
- _____?

## ■ STEP 1

Choose two or three of the areas listed above and think of one other area where you would like to see changes in the world (for example, access to health care, improving educational levels, ending disease).

## ■ STEP 2

For each general issue outline at least three actions you would take to achieve your desired results, if you had the power and resources to accomplish them.

Problem: _____.
Actions: 1. _____.
         2. _____.
         3. _____.

## ■ STEP 3

Report your plan to the rest of the class. The class will decide whom they would like to choose as President of the Entire World.

## FOCUS 1 | Overview of Hypothetical Meaning

There is an important difference between **hypothetical** and **actual** meaning.

| HYPOTHETICAL STATEMENTS | IMPLIED ACTUAL MEANING | EXPLANATIONS |
|---|---|---|
| (a) If I ruled the world, I would live in a luxurious mansion in Hawaii. | I don't rule the world, so I probably won't be able to live in a luxurious mansion in Hawaii. | Hypothetical statements describe conditions that aren't true or are impossible. |
| (b) If we were in Hawaii right now, we wouldn't have to study grammar. We could be lying on the beach. | We're not in Hawaii—we're in English class. We can't lie on the beach because we're studying grammar. | |
| (c) You should be happy with your life. If I were you, I wouldn't feel so sorry for myself! | You aren't happy with your life. I am not you, but I think you feel too sorry for yourself. | We use hypothetical statements to imply that the opposite situation is actually true. |
| (d) You could have done a better job on your homework. You should have avoided a lot of these careless mistakes. | You didn't do a very good job on your homework. You made a lot of careless mistakes. | |

### EXERCISE 1

Here are some more hypothetical statements. Choose the sentence that expresses their implied meaning:

1. If you had done your homework, you would have gotten an A.
    a. You didn't get an A because you didn't do your homework.
    b. You did your homework, so you got an A.

2. You could have brought a friend to the party.
    a. You had permission, but you came alone.
    b. You brought a friend.

3. You could have been more careful with your homework.
    a. You did your homework carefully.
    b. You were careless with your homework.

4. You should have seen the doctor before you got so sick.
    a. You followed my advice.
    b. You didn't follow my advice.

5. I would have been here early, but the traffic was terrible!
    a. I arrived early.
    b. I arrived late.

6. I wish you had come to the lake last weekend.
    a. You didn't come.
    b. You were there.

7. Let's pretend that we had a new president.
    a. We don't have a new president.
    b. We have a new president.

## FOCUS 2

### Actual Versus Hypothetical Conditionals

| ACTUAL VERSUS HYPOTHETICAL CONDITIONALS | IMPLIED MEANING |
|---|---|
| Actual Conditional: | |
| (a) If I **have** time, I always **clean** the kitchen before I go to work. | I always clean the kitchen when I have time. |
| Hypothetical Conditional: | |
| (b) If I **had** time, I **would** always **clean** the kitchen before leaving for work. | I don't usually clean the kitchen because I usually don't have time. |
| Actual Conditional: | |
| (c) If I **don't have to work, I will come** to your party. | I don't know if I can come, because there's a chance that I may have to work. |
| Hypothetical Conditional: | |
| (d) If I **didn't have to work, I would come** to your party. | I can't come because I have to work. |
| Actual Conditional: | |
| (e) If Denise **was** at the meeting yesterday, I'm sure she **took** very complete notes. | Maybe she was at the meeting and took notes. |
| Hypothetical Conditional: | |
| (f) If Denise **had been** at the meeting, I'm sure she **would have taken** very complete notes. | She wasn't at the meeting, so she didn't take notes. |

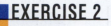

# EXERCISE 2

Match the statements in column 1 with their correct implied meanings in column 2.

| STATEMENT | IMPLIED MEANING |
|---|---|
| 1. If John has the money, he always stops for a cup of coffee on his way to class. | a. He doesn't usually do this, because he usually doesn't have the money. |
| 2. If John had the money, he would always stop for a cup of coffee on his way to class. | b. He always does this whenever he has the money. |
| 3. If I had to work, I wouldn't be helping you with your homework. | c. I may have to work. |
| 4. If I have to work, I won't be able to help you with your homework. | d. I don't have to work. |
| 5. If Bambang took the TOEFL® Test* yesterday, I'm sure he did very well. | e. Bambang didn't take the TOEFL. |
| 6. If Bambang had taken the TOEFL, I'm sure he would have done very well. | f. Maybe Bambang took the TOEFL. |

# EXERCISE 3

Are these sentences hypothetical statements or statements about actual events? If they are hypothetical statements, state the implied meaning.

**Examples:** Those two are always together, so if she attended the meeting, he did, too.
*statement about an actual event*

If the weather hadn't been so cold yesterday, the picnic would have been a lot more fun. *hypothetical statement. Implied meaning: The weather was cold yesterday, so the picnic wasn't much fun.*

1. I would come to your party if I didn't have to work.
2. If Juan went to Hawaii on vacation, he must have spent a lot of money.
3. If Tomas could afford to retire, I'm sure he would have done so by now.
4. I wouldn't tease that dog if I were you.
5. Suppose you had your own private jet. You could take me to Las Vegas for lunch.
6. If they left when they had planned, they should be here any minute.
7. If my brother needed money, he always asked to borrow it from me.
8. If I cook a big casserole for the party, do you think there'll be enough food?

*TOEFL is a registered trademark of the Educational Testing Service (ETS). This publication is not endorsed or approved by ETS.

**FOCUS 3**

# Hypothetical Conditionals in Present and Future Time Frames

| EXAMPLES | | EXPLANATIONS |
|---|---|---|
| **Conditions** | **Results** | Use past-tense verb forms to describe present and future hypothetical conditions. Use *would/could/might* + verb to describe present and future results. |
| (a) If I **had** time, | I **would** always **clean** the kitchen before leaving for work. | |
| (b) If I **didn't have to work**, | I **would come** to your party. | |
| (c) If I **won** the lottery, | I **would give** you a million dollars. | |
| (d) If I already **spoke** English perfectly, | I **wouldn't need** to read this unit. | |
| (e) If we **didn't have to go** to school tomorrow, | we **could stay up** all night tonight. | |
| (f) If John **didn't plan to spend** next year in France, | Mary **might not be** so annoyed with him now. | |

**Using *were* in hypothetical statements**

| EXAMPLES | | EXPLANATIONS |
|---|---|---|
| (g) If my mother **were** here, she would want us all to wash our hands. | (h) If Mary **were** coming to the party, she could bring the potato salad. | *If* clauses in hypothetical conditionals use *were* (rather than *was*) for singular subjects in formal English. *Was* is often used in informal situations. |

**Inverted Hypotheticals**

| EXAMPLES | | EXPLANATIONS |
|---|---|---|
| **Inverted Form** | **Regular Form** | |
| (i) **Were** I in charge of this country, I would make big changes. | (j) **If I were** in charge of this country, I would make big changes. | In formal English, in clauses with a *were* auxiliary, we can indicate hypothetical conditions by omitting *if* and using question word or inverted order. |

## EXERCISE 4

Change these statements of actual condition and result into hypothetical conditionals.

**Example:** Actual condition: I'm not the teacher. Actual result: We have too much homework.

Hypothetical condition: *If I were the teacher, we wouldn't have so much homework.*

1. I don't have a million dollars. I can't afford to buy you a new car.

2. I don't yet speak English perfectly. I still have to study grammar.

3. Doctors have to spend so many years in medical school. Medical care is quite expensive.

4. My mother doesn't know how I am living now. She's not worried about me.

5. I am not president of my country. I don't have influence on world events.

6. I have many good friends. My life is busy and rewarding.

7. The TOEFL Test is a difficult examination. Many people can't do well on it on the first try.

8. There aren't enough places in universities in other countries. Many students come to North America for university study.

## EXERCISE 5

Here are some hypothetical conditions. Add hypothetical results that are true for you.

**Example:** If I could be anywhere in the world at this moment, . . .

*I would be home in bed.*

1. If I were going to attend any American university tomorrow, . . .

2. If I were president of the United States, . . .

3. If my teacher knew how I was studying now, . . .

4. If I were the teacher of this class, . . .

5. If I didn't have to worry about the TOEFL Test, . . .

6. If I went home next week, . . .

7. If I had all the money I needed, . . .

8. If I were the same age as my parents, . . .

## EXERCISE 6

Here are some hypothetical conditions. Add hypothetical results that are true for you.

**Example:**  I would take a vacation . . .

*if I didn't have to get a higher score on the TOEFL.*

1. I wouldn't need to work . . .

2. I would bring my family here for a visit . . .

3. We wouldn't come to school . . .

4. We wouldn't need umbrellas . . .

5. I wouldn't be studying English . . .

6. I wouldn't have to take the TOEFL Test . . .

7. The world would be a much better place . . .

8. I would give my English teacher a thousand dollars . . .

## EXERCISE 7

Work with a partner. Choose five sentences that your partner wrote for Exercises 5 and 6 and rewrite them in nonhypothetical language.

**Examples:**  If I had a million dollars, I would give you a new car.

*My partner doesn't have enough money to give me a car.*

I would take a vacation if I didn't have to finish this project.

*My partner has to finish this project, so she can't take a vacation.*

*My partner can't take a vacation because she has to finish this project.*

## EXERCISE 8

Look over the sentences that you and your partner wrote in Exercises 5 and 6. Which sentences can be rewritten as inverted hypotheticals?

# FOCUS 4

## Hypothetical Conditionals in Past Time Frame

| EXAMPLES | | EXPLANATIONS |
|---|---|---|
| **Conditions** | **Results** | |
| (a) If Denise **had been** at the meeting, | I'm sure she **would have taken** very complete notes. She **wouldn't have minded** sharing them. She **would have let** you borrow them. | Use past-perfect verb forms to refer to past hypothetical conditions. Use *would have/ could have/might have* + verb to refer to past hypothetical results. |
| (b) If William the Conqueror **hadn't invaded** England in 1066, | the English language **would probably have** many fewer words of French origin. | Use *would/could/might* + verb to refer to present or future hypothetical results. |
| (c) If I **had been born** in 1890, | I surely **wouldn't be** alive today. | |
| (d) If we **hadn't saved** enough money last year, | we **wouldn't be able to take** a vacation next summer. | |

### Inverted Hypotheticals

| EXAMPLES | | EXPLANATION |
|---|---|---|
| **Inverted Form** | **Regular Form** | |
| (e) **Had I known** that you were coming so late, I wouldn't have waited. | (f) **If I had known** that you were coming so late, I wouldn't have waited. | In formal English, in clauses with a *had* auxiliary, we can indicate hypothetical conditions by omitting *if* and using question word or inverted order. |

## EXERCISE 9

Do these sentences indicate statements of past possibility, or hypothetical events that did not actually happen?

**Examples:** I didn't see him, but he could have been there. *past possibility*

If John had been at the concert, he would have been able to explain how the composer was able to get those effects. *hypothetical event*

1. My brother could have loaned me the money, but he's too cheap.

2. Assuming that the plane was on time, it should have landed a little while ago.

3. I don't know what the problem is. They should have been here by now.

4. You should have asked for a receipt when you bought those clothes.

5. Tiffany might have worked a little harder on this report. It's pretty careless.

6. The thief might have gotten in through the window. It's unlocked.

## EXERCISE 10

Change these nonhypothetical statements of condition and result to hypothetical conditionals.

**Example:** I wasn't alive one hundred years ago. I have been able to fly all over the world.

*If I had been alive one hundred years ago, I wouldn't have been able to fly all over the world.*

1. My parents didn't speak English when I was a baby. I have to learn it in school.

2. English became a language of international business after World War II. Most developing countries require students to study it in high school.

3. Modern English developed from several different languages: French, German, Latin, Dutch, and even Norwegian. As a result, the grammar and spelling rules are very irregular.

4. England was invaded by France in 1066. Many French words replaced the traditional Anglo-Saxon ones.

5. English society changed a great deal after the French invasion. Modern English grammar is more similar to French grammar than to German grammar.

## EXERCISE 11

Complete these sentences with past-time hypothetical results that are true for you.

**Example:** If I had been born one hundred years ago, _____

*I wouldn't have had a chance to travel around the world.*

1. If my family had used English at home when I was growing up, _____
   _____

2. If World War II had ended differently, _____
   _____

3. If the grammar of English hadn't developed from so many different languages,_____
   _____

4. If advanced computer technology hadn't been developed, _____
   _____

5. If I had never studied English, _____
   _____

## EXERCISE 12

Add present or future time results to the following sentences.

**Examples:** If I had been born one hundred years ago . . .

*I probably wouldn't be alive today.*

*my great-grandchildren might be entering the university in the next few years.*

1. If I had been born in another country . . .
2. If World War II hadn't ended over fifty years ago . . .
3. If my parents hadn't wanted me to learn English . . .
4. If computers hadn't become so inexpensive and widely available . . .
5. If I had already gotten a score of 650 on the TOEFL . . .

## EXERCISE 13

Here are hypothetical results. Add appropriate past-time conditions.

**Example:** I wouldn't have had a chance to travel around the world . . .

*if I had been born one hundred years ago.*

1. I wouldn't have asked you to join us . . .
2. I would not be studying English now . . .
3. English grammar would be much more regular . . .
4. Fax machines wouldn't be so popular . . .

5. America wouldn't be spending so much money on the military . . .

6. Transoceanic telephone calls wouldn't be possible . . .

7. There wouldn't have been such major political changes in Eastern European countries . . .

8. Modern antibiotics might not have been discovered . . .

9. Life today would be much more difficult . . .

10. I wouldn't have to answer this question . . .

## EXERCISE14

Look over the sentences that you and your partner wrote in Exercises 11, 12, and 13. Choose five sentences to rewrite as inverted hypotheticals.

## EXERCISE 15

Work with a partner. Choose five sentences that your partner wrote for Exercises 11, 12, and 13 and rewrite them in nonhypothetical language.

**Examples:** I wouldn't have asked you to join us, if I had known you were going to be so rude.

*I asked you to come because I thought you would be more polite.*

If I had been born one hundred years ago, I wouldn't have had a chance to travel widely.

*A hundred years ago people like me didn't have a chance to travel widely.*

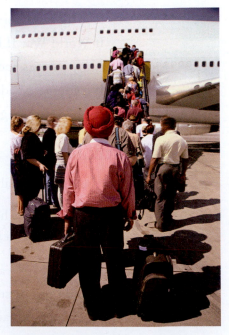

# FOCUS 5    Mixing Hypothetical and Actual Statements

use

We sometimes combine actual conditions and hypothetical results.

| ACTUAL CONDITION | HYPOTHETICAL RESULT |
|---|---|
| (a) I had to work last night. | **Otherwise**, I would have come to your party. |
| (b) Peter brought a doctor's excuse to explain his absence. | **Otherwise**, Denise would have accused him of being irresponsible. |
| (c) It's going to rain tomorrow. | **Otherwise**, we could have the luncheon outside. |

| HYPOTHETICAL RESULT | ACTUAL CONDITION |
|---|---|
| (d) I would have come to your party last night, | **but** I had to work. |
| (e) Denise would have accused Peter of being irresponsible, | **but** he brought a doctor's excuse to explain his absence. |
| (f) We could have the luncheon outside, | **but** it's going to rain tomorrow. |

## EXERCISE 16

Here are some actual conditions. State a hypothetical result by using *otherwise* or *but*.

**Example:** I'm not rich.

*I'm not rich. Otherwise, I would loan you the money you asked for.*

*I would loan you the money you asked for, but I'm not rich.*

1. I don't have a million dollars.
2. I don't yet speak English perfectly.
3. Doctors have to spend many years in medical school.
4. My mother doesn't know how I am living now.
5. My father is not the leader of my country.
6. I have many good friends.
7. Many students come to the United States for university study.
8. The weather forecaster has predicted heavy rain for tomorrow afternoon.

## Using Hypotheticals for Unlikely Possibility and for Sensitive Topics

use

Use hypothetical statements to indicate unlikely possibilities.

| STATEMENT | IMPLIED MEANING |
|---|---|
| **Likely Possibility (Nonhypothetical)** | |
| (a) If we **get** some free time, we **can go** to the movies. | There is a strong possibility that we may get free time. |
| **Unlikely Possibility (Hypothetical)** | |
| (b) If we **got** some free time this weekend, we **could go** to the movies. | The possibility of free time is not strong, but we are discussing it anyway. |
| (c) If I **had** free time, I **would go** to the movies. | There is no possibility of free time, but this is what would happen if there were a possibility. |

Use hypothetical statements to discuss potentially "sensitive" topics more easily and diplomatically.

| STATEMENT | IMPLIED MEANING | EXPLANATION |
|---|---|---|
| **Nonhypothetical** | | |
| (d) **Will** you ever leave your husband? | I think you might do this. | |
| **Hypothetical** | | |
| (e) **Would** you ever leave your husband? | This is not a real situation, just an example. I don't really think that you would do this. | Using hypothetical indicates that the speaker does not believe the listener would actually consider doing the thing being discussed. |

## EXERCISE 17

Decide whether these statements are likely or unlikely possibilities for you, then make a hypothetical or nonhypothetical sentence that reflects that.

**Example:** marry someone from another country

    a. likely possibility—something that might actually be possible for me

    *If I marry someone from another country, I will probably become a citizen of that country.*

    b. unlikely possibility—something that I don't think will ever be possible for me

    *If I married someone from another country, my parents would be very disappointed.*

1. go to Las Vegas for the next vacation
   a. likely possibility  b. unlikely possibility

   _____

2. pass the TOEFL Test the next time I take it
   a. likely possibility  b. unlikely possibility

   _____

3. become president of your country
   a. likely possibility  b. unlikely possibility

   _____

4. have eight children
   a. likely possibility  b. unlikely possibility

   _____

5. buy a new car within the next three months
   a. likely possibility  b. unlikely possibility

   _____

6. join the army
   a. likely possibility  b. unlikely possibility

   _____

7. get sick later today
   a. likely possibility  b. unlikely possibility

   _____

8. look for a new place to live
   a. likely possibility  b. unlikely possibility

   _____

9. have free time before class tomorrow
   a. likely possibility  b. unlikely possibility

   _____

10. win the lottery
    a. likely possibility  b. unlikely possibility

    _____

11. appear on television sometime in my life
    a. likely possibility  b. unlikely possibility

    _____

# Using Hypotheticals to Imply That the Opposite Is True

use

Use hypothetical statements to talk about things that didn't actually happen.

| STATEMENT | IMPLIED MEANINGS |
|---|---|
| (a) You could have brought a friend. | You had permission, but you came alone. |
| (b) You could have been more careful with your homework. | You had the ability to be careful, but you didn't do it. |
| (c) You should have seen the doctor. | You didn't see the doctor. |
| (d) You might have cleaned the house before my mother got here. | The house was still dirty when she arrived. |

## EXERCISE 18

Restate these sentences in nonhypothetical language. Compare your answers with those of a partner.

**Example:** You should have been there.

*You weren't there.*

1. You shouldn't have gone to so much trouble!

_____

2. We could have been seriously injured in that bus accident.

_____

3. You might at least have invited her to the party.

_____

4. You should be happy that I was able to come at all.

_____

5. She wouldn't have gone even if she had been invited.

_____

# FOCUS 8 | Using Hypotheticals with *Wish* and Verbs of Imagination

**use**

We use hypothetical statements with *wish* to talk about situations that are not true or not likely to become true.

| STATEMENT | IMPLIED MEANING |
| --- | --- |
| (a)  I **wish** you **had come** to the lake last weekend. | You didn't come. |
| (b)  I **wish** you **liked** Chinese food. | You don't like it. |
| (c)  I **wish** you **would come** to my party. | You refuse to come. |

We use hypothetical statements with verbs that indicate imagination.

| STATEMENT | IMPLIED MEANING |
| --- | --- |
| (d)  **Let's imagine** that we **had** a new president. | We know this is not a real possibility. |
| (e)  **Pretend** that you **could** fly. Do you think you **would** still own a car? | This is an impossible situation. |
| (f)  **Suppose** we **went** to Europe next summer. How much do you think it **would** cost? | We are only talking about it now; we're not making an actual plan. |

Read the following paragraph. Underline the hypothetical statements. Rewrite the sentences using nonhypothetical language. The first hypothetical statement has been done for you as an example.

**Example:** *(3) For example, Sir Isaac Newton decided to take a nap under an apple tree, and as a result he was hit on the head by a falling apple.*

(1) Many important scientific developments have happened by accident. (2) Discoveries have often been made because someone was in the right place at the right time, or because someone made a mistake and got an unexpected result. (3) For example, <u>if Sir Isaac Newton hadn't decided to take a nap under an apple tree, he wouldn't have been hit on the head by a falling apple.</u> (4) It was this event that gave him the idea about the Law of Gravity. (5) If Sir Alexander Fleming hadn't left a sandwich on a windowsill of his laboratory and forgotten about it, he wouldn't have discovered the fungus or mold that contains penicillin. (6) Had Christopher Columbus correctly calculated the actual size of the earth, he would never have tried to reach Asia by sailing west. (7) If that hadn't happened, the European discovery of the New World might have occurred in 1592, instead of 1492.

# Use Your English

**ACTIVITY 1 speaking**

We often use hypothetical language to discuss very controversial topics. Choose one of the following topics:

- Should drugs be legalized?
- Should people of the same sex be allowed to marry?
- Should human embryos be used for stem-cell research?
- Should doctors be allowed to assist people to commit suicide?

■ **STEP 1**  Form a group with three other students in the class to discuss your opinions on the issues:

- What is your opinion? Pro or con?  What are your reasons?
- What three things might happen if the government allowed it?
- What three things might happen if government didn't allow it?

■ **STEP 2**  Based on your discussion, your group should answer these two questions:

- What is the strongest reason in favor of keeping the current policy?
- What is the strongest reason against?

Present your topic, your position, and your reasons to the rest of the class.

**ACTIVITY 2** writing

There is a saying "Hindsight is 20/20," which means it's always easier to see things clearly and make the right decisions after something has happened and you can see the results. Think about some things that you would have done differently if you had known then the things that you know now. Choose one of the topics. Then write a short essay about this topic or make a presentation to the rest of the class.

- Things you wish you had done that you didn't do. For example: *I wish I had studied harder when I was in high school.*

- Things you wish you hadn't done that you did do. For example: *I wish I hadn't spent all my time watching television instead of exercising.*

**ACTIVITY 3** writing/speaking

If you could have three wishes, what would they be, and why would you wish for them?

**STEP 1**    Write down your three wishes.

**STEP 2**    Compare your answers to those of someone else in class. What do someone else's wishes tell you about his or her life? What do your wishes tell someone else about you?

**STEP 3**    Make one statement about why you think your partner made the wishes that he or she did. Tell that statement to your partner, but not to the rest of the class.

## ACTIVITY 4 reflection

Listen to native speakers talking to each other. (This can be a live conversation or something on TV or radio.) Identify three examples of hypothetical statements. Write down:

(1) the situation, (2) what was said, (3) the nonhypothetical meaning if there was one, and (4) why you think the speaker chose to use hypothetical in that particular situation. Share your examples with two or three other students, and together choose one to present to the rest of the class.

## ACTIVITY 5 speaking

■ **STEP 1** Think about what you would do if you were faced with the following problems.

- Your parents don't approve of the person you want to marry.
- Your friend and you both work at the same company. You feel very loyal to the company, but you discover your friend has stolen some of the company's money.
- You have fallen in love with the husband or wife of your best friend.
- Your best friend needs to borrow some money "for a serious emergency"—but he won't say what that emergency is. You had been planning to use that money to buy a birthday present for your boyfriend or girlfriend. Your friend needs the money right away, and the birthday celebration is also today. You can't get any more money: only what you have now.

■ **STEP 2** Discuss your solutions in a small group. Together decide on one or two suggestions for what people can do if they are faced with any kind of difficult problem.

## ACTIVITY 6 writing/speaking

Identify some things you would and wouldn't do for ten million dollars, and compare them to those of other people in class. Ideas to consider: Would you tell a lie? Would you betray a friend? Would you give a child up for adoption? Would you become a citizen of another country? Would you leave your family? What would you refuse to do, even if you were offered ten million dollars?

## ACTIVITY 7 listening

CD Track 25

Listen to the conversation between Peter and Denise. Then choose the sentence that correctly describes the situations that they talked about.

1. a. Peter didn't hear the announcement because he wasn't at the meeting.

   b. He heard the announcement because he was at the meeting.

2. a. The meeting wasn't important.

   b. The meeting was important.

3. a. Peter thinks Denise did good work.

   b. He thinks she was careless.

4. a. Peter finished the project in plenty of time.

   b. He didn't finish it in plenty of time.

5. a. Denise told Peter that she hadn't gone over the figures.

   b. Denise didn't tell Peter that she hadn't gone over the figures.

6. a. She didn't check the figures.

   b. Maybe she checked the figures.

7. a. There were many mistakes.

   b. There weren't many mistakes.

8. a. Denise said that she wanted to get Peter fired.

   b. Denise said that she didn't want to get Peter fired.

# ACTIVITY 8 research on the web

Go on the Internet and use a search engine such as Google® or Yahoo® and enter the keywords "hypothetical questions". You will find a number of Web sites that talk about hypothetical questions. Look at several of the sites and make a list of ten interesting questions you found there.

**STEP 1**  Work with a partner to choose three of the most interesting questions to report to the rest of the class.

**STEP 2**  With another pair of students try to develop a definition of what hypothetical questions consist of and how they might be useful in generating ideas or discussions.

# ACTIVITY 9 reflection

What if Columbus had never sailed to America? What if Great Britain had never been a colonial power? What if communism had replaced capitalism worldwide? What if the United States had not decided to invade Iraq?

Choose a famous event in history and decide what might have happened if that event had **not** taken place. How would life today be different? Write a paragraph or make a brief presentation to the rest of the class.

# SENSORY VERBS, CAUSATIVE VERBS, AND VERBS THAT TAKE SUBJUNCTIVE

## UNIT GOALS

- Correctly understand and use sentences with sensory verbs

- Correctly understand and use sentences with causative verbs

- Correctly understand and use sentences with verbs followed by subjunctive *that*-clauses

## OPENING TASK

### Parenting Techniques

Think about the way your parents raised you. How did they reward your good behavior or punish your bad behavior? What kind of responsibilities did they give you?

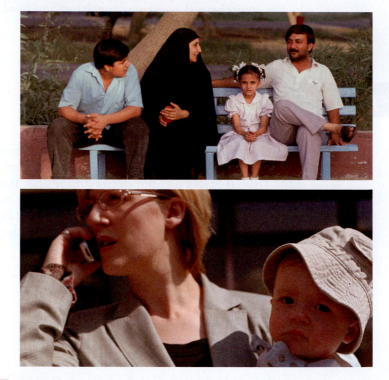

### ◼ STEP 1

Complete the chart on the next page to identify some of the parenting techniques your parents used. Identify some things they saw you doing that they wanted to change or encourage. Decide whether their techniques were effective, and whether you would use (or are using) them to raise your own children. Examples have been provided.

| Behavior | Parenting Techniques Your Parents Used | Effective? Yes/No | Would/Do You Use This Technique? Yes/No/Why |
|---|---|---|---|
| My mother heard me yelling at my younger brother. | **Discipline/Punishment** <br> 1. sent to my room <br><br> 2. <br> 3. | 1. no <br><br><br> 2. <br> 3. | 1. No. My children have toys in their rooms so it's not really an effective punishment. <br> 2. <br> 3. |
| My father saw me helping my baby sister. | **Responsibilities** <br> 1. gave me more chances to take care of her <br> 2. <br> 3. | 1. yes <br><br> 2. <br> 3. | 1. Yes. It was good practice for being a parent myself. <br> 2. <br> 3. |
| My mother caught me trying to feed my vegetables to the dog. | **Rewards/Motivations** <br> 1. gave me ice cream and candy when I ate my vegetables <br> 2. <br> 3. | 1. yes <br><br><br> 2. <br> 3. | 1. No. I don't want to use food as a reward for good behavior. <br> 2. <br> 3. |

## ■ STEP 2

Form a small group with three or four other students, and compare the information you have written in your charts. Based on your discussion, your group should make ten recommendations for parents. Start five of them with "Parents should have their children . . ." **Start five recommendations with** "Parents shouldn't make their children . . ."

## ■ STEP 3

Compare your group's recommendations to those of other groups. Compile a list of recommendations that the entire class agrees upon. Begin your recommendations with "Good parenting requires that . . ."

form

| FOCUS 1 | Overview |
|---------|----------|

The verbs that are dealt with in this unit are followed by simple verb forms or present participles that describe a second action.

| TYPES OF VERBS | EXAMPLES |
|----------------|----------|
| **Sensory Verbs** (*see, hear,* etc.) | (a) I **saw** the mother **spank** her child. <br> (b) I **heard** the child **crying**. |
| **Causative Verbs** (*make, let,* etc.) | (c) My parents **made** me **go** to bed at 8:00 on school nights. <br> (d) They **let** me **stay** up late on Fridays and Saturdays. |
| **Subjunctive *that*-Clause Verbs** (*demand, recommend,* etc.) | (e) Good parenting **demands that** parents **be** consistent with discipline. <br> (f) Educators **recommend that** a parent **try** to explain the reasons for punishment to children. |

## EXERCISE 1

Underline the simple verb form or participle that **follows** the highlighted verbs in the passage below. The first one has been done for you as an example.

Ideas about the best way to raise children differ a great deal from culture to culture. In some cultures, if a mother **hears** her baby <u>crying</u>, she will immediately go to pick it up and try to **get** it to stop. But in other cultures people **insist** that a mother ignore her child, because they feel that if you don't **let** a baby cry, it will become spoiled. In some cultures, any adult who **sees** a child misbehaving will **make** the child stop, but other cultures **prefer** that only the parent be allowed to discipline a child. In some cultures, people **have** slightly older children help take care of their younger brothers and sisters, but in other cultures people rarely **let** children be responsible for their brothers and sisters unless they are at least twelve or thirteen years old.

In the United States, most parents prefer to get a child to behave by persuasion rather than force. You rarely **see** parents spank their children in public, and schools don't usually **let** teachers use physical punishment as discipline. Parents who are seen hitting their children may even be reported to the police. American child-care experts **recommend** that children be given responsibility from a relatively early age. As a result, many parents **let** their small children make their own decisions about what kind of clothes they want to wear, or what they want to eat. They prefer to get children to obey instead of **making** them obey.

## FOCUS 2 | Sensory Verbs

| EXAMPLES | EXPLANATIONS |
|---|---|
| (a) Mary **heard** the children **laughing**. <br> (b) **I saw** the child **take** the cookies. | Sensory verbs use either a **present participle** (verb + *ING*) or the **simple form** of a verb to express the second action. Depending on which is chosen, the meaning differs. |
| (c) Bob heard the children **breaking** the bottles, so he called their parents. <br> (d) I saw the child **leaving** school before class was over, so I ran to catch her. <br> (e) The teacher watched the children **overturning** the chairs and **setting** them outside. | Use a present participle to describe actions that are: <br> in progress (c) <br><br> unfinished (d) <br><br> repeated (e) |
| (f) Bob saw the children **take** the cookies and **put** them in their pockets. <br> (g) I saw the child **leave** school before class was over, so I'm sure she's not coming to the conference with her teacher. <br> (h) The teacher watched the children **overturn** the chair and **set** it outside. | Use the simple form of a verb to describe actions that are completed (f and g) <br><br><br> or happen just once (h) |
| (i) I saw the child's bicycle **lying** by the side of the road. <br> (j) NOT: I saw the child's bicycle **lie** by the side of the road. | Use present participles with verbs of position (*lie, stand, sit,* etc.), if the thing that performs the second action cannot move by itself. |
| (k) We **caught** the child **taking** cookies out of the jar. <br> (l) NOT: We caught the child **take** cookies out of the jar. <br> (m) We **found** the child **sleeping** in front of the TV. <br> (n) NOT: We found the child **sleep** in front of the TV. | Use present participles with verbs of interception (*find, catch, discover,* etc.), where the second action is interrupted or not completed. |

## EXERCISE 2

Answer these questions by using sensory verbs with a second action.

**Example:** What can you see at a disco?

*You can see people dancing.*

1. What can you hear at a concert?
2. What can you see at a skating rink?
3. What can you smell at a bakery?
4. What can you hear at the beach?
5. What can you see at a shopping mall?
6. What can you hear at a playground?
7. What can you hear in an English class?
8. What can you see at a gym?

## EXERCISE 3

Restate the lettered sentences in these paragraphs as sensory verbs followed by a participle or simple form of a verb.

**Example:** Here is what Tom saw: (a) Three boys were swimming in the river. (b) They were splashing and playing. (c) One of them shouted that it was time to go. (d) They picked up their towels and left.

*(a) Tom saw three boys swimming in the river. (b) He watched them splashing and playing. (c) He heard one of them shout that it was time to go. (d) He watched them pick up their towels and leave.*

1. Here is what Doris observed: (a) A man came into the bank. (b) He got in line. When he reached the teller's window, he handed her a piece of paper and a brown paper bag. (c) The teller was putting money in the bag, when a loud alarm began to ring. (d) Guards rushed in, but the man had escaped through the side entrance.

2. When Mrs. McMartin looked out the window, this is what she saw: (a) There were a few children playing on the swings. (b) Others were climbing on the monkey-bars. (c) One little boy was running very fast around and around the playground. (d) Suddenly he fell down. (e) He screamed in pain. (f) All the other children looked around to see where the noise was coming from. (g) One child ran toward Mrs. McMartin's office.

3. Here is what I saw, heard, and felt during the hurricane. (a) The wind grew louder. (b) The windows and doors shook. (c) The trees swayed in the garden outside. I thought the house was moving. (d) A tree crashed against the house. (e) There was a sound of breaking glass upstairs. I went upstairs. (f) Rain was pouring through the broken window. (g) A strong wind blew into the room. (h) The wind howled louder and louder.

## EXERCISE 4

Decide on which form of the verb to use, based on the context. Circle your answer. In some sentences both forms may be correct.

**Example:** I saw smoke (come/coming) from the storeroom, so I called the fire department.

1. I hear the phone (ring/ringing), but I'm not going to answer it.

2. Brian heard the phone (ring/ringing), but by the time he reached it, the person at the other end had hung up.

3. The principal watched the students (take/taking) the test, so she was sure there had been no cheating.

4. Matt felt himself (get/getting) angry as he and Jeff argued about who should do the dishes.

5. On my way to the store I saw Morris (ride/riding) his new bike.

6. As Mary listened to the radio (play/playing) her favorite song, she began to cry and hurried out of the room.

7. I heard the workers (leave/leaving) earlier today. I'm sure they haven't returned yet.

8. We could all smell something (burn/burning). Apparently somebody had tossed a lit cigarette into the waste paper basket.

9. As the hurricane grew stronger, they heard many branches of the big oak tree (snap/snapping) and (fall/falling) to the ground.

10. John was relieved when he saw his lost wallet (sit/sitting) next to his checkbook on the shelf.

11. Deborah heard Evan (cry/crying), so she went in to see what was wrong.

12. When we arrived we found the dog (wait/waiting) at the door for us.

## FOCUS 3  Causative Verbs

Many causative verbs are followed by infinitives. But a few common causative verbs (*make, let, have, help*) are followed by the simple form of the verb. Causative verbs show how much force or persuasion is necessary to cause a person to perform an action. They are listed here from most forceful to least forceful.

| CAUSATIVE VERB + INFINITIVE | CAUSATIVE VERB + SIMPLE FORM OF THE VERB |
|---|---|
| (a) Parents should **force** naughty children to stand in the corner. | (b) Parents should **make** naughty children **stand** in the corner. |
| (c) Parents should **get** their children **to read** instead of watching TV. | *no synonym or substitute for this form* |
| (d) Parents should **employ or hire** a doctor to **examine** their children at least once a year. | (e) Parents should **have** the doctor **examine** their children at least once a year. |
| (f) Good parents should **allow** their children **to play** outside on sunny days. | (g) Good parents **let** their children **play** outside on sunny days. |
| (h) Good parents **help** their children **to learn** good manners. | (i) Good parents **help** their children **learn** good manners. (*help* can occur with either form) |

## EXERCISE 5

Underline the causative verbs and circle the infinitive or base form of the verb that follows. One has been done as an example.

(1) Kilroy hated his life in the army from the very first day. (2) When he arrived at Fort Dix for basic training, a drill instructor <u>had</u> him (join) all the other new recruits on the parade ground. (3) The officers made them stand in the hot sun for several hours, while clerks filled out forms. (4) They wouldn't allow the new recruits to joke, or talk to each other, or even to move their heads. (5) Then they had Army barbers cut their hair so short that Kilroy felt like he was bald. (6) An officer ordered Kilroy to report to a long building called Barracks B, along with about twenty other men. (7) The sergeant

at Barracks B had each man choose a bed. (8) He let them put their personal possessions in lockers next to each bed. (9) Kilroy helped the man in the next bunk make his bed, and that man helped Kilroy to do the same thing. (10) The sergeant then required the recruits to sweep the floors and clean the bathrooms. (11) Kilroy had wanted to join the army to learn how to be a soldier, but now he was beginning to worry that the army would only teach him how to be a janitor.

## EXERCISE 6

Decide whether you think the policies suggested below are good ideas or not. Make statements with *should* or *shouldn't*. Then give a reason with *because*.

**Example:** *Parents should let their kids play actively every day, because vigorous physical exercise is important for growing bodies.*

| CAUSER | CAUSTIVE VERB | DOER OF ACTION | ACTION |
|---|---|---|---|
| **Example:** | | | |
| *parents* | *let* | *kids* | *play actively* |
| 1.  parents | make | children | go to bed at 6:00 |
| 2.  teachers | help | students | learn things by themselves |
| 3.  police | allow | people | break laws |
| 4.  people | have | a dentist | examine their teeth regularly |
| 5.  dog owners | let | pets | run around freely |
| 6.  a government | require | all citizens | take drug tests |
| 7.  a good manager | allow | employees | do whatever they like |
| 8.  a good manager | motivate | employees | do their best |

## EXERCISE 7

Match the verbs listed in Group A with the verbs in Group B which have the same or similar meaning.

| GROUP A | | GROUP B | | |
|---|---|---|---|---|
| let | get | convince | assist | employ |
| help | make | hire | encourage | force |
| have | | require | permit | allow |

# EXERCISE 8

Use the chart below to make sentences about what governments should expect citizens to do and what citizens should expect governments to do. Choose three actions from each category and make sentences that express your real opinions. Write two sentences that express each opinion: one with a causative verb followed by a simple verb and one with a verb + infinitive.

**Example:** **causer:** government  **doer:** citizens  **action:** vote in regular elections

*Governments should let their citizens vote in regular elections.*

*Governments should allow their citizens to vote in regular elections.*

| CAUSER | DOER | ACTION |
|---|---|---|
| government | citizens | pay taxes<br>read any books and magazines they wish<br>be of service to the nation<br>meet national goals<br>defend the country |
| citizens | government | be responsive to their wishes<br>work without corruption<br>establish national goals<br>maintain law and order<br>provide for basic defense |

1. _____

_____

2. _____

_____

3. _____

_____

4. _____

_____

5. _____

## FOCUS 4 — Passive Causative Verbs

form

use

The causative verbs *make* and *help* can be made passive, especially when the causer or agent of the action is obvious or not stated, or is a law or an institution. When the verbs *make* and *help* are passive, they must be followed by an infinitive, not the base form of the verb.

| PASSIVE CAUSATIVE VERBS | ACTIVE CAUSATIVE VERBS |
|---|---|
| (a) Children should **be made to brush** their teeth before bedtime. | (b) Parents should **make** their children **brush** their teeth before bedtime. |
| (c) Children should **be helped to learn** good table manners. | (d) Parents should **help** their children **learn** good table manners. |

Other causative verbs (*get, have, let*) cannot appear as passive verbs in causative sentences. If the agent is unknown or unimportant, we must express the passive sentence with another causative verb + infinitive that has the same meaning.

| | |
|---|---|
| (e) NOT: Children should **be gotten** to read. | (f) Children should **be inspired** to read not forced. |
| (g) NOT: Teachers should **be had** to teach. | (h) Teachers should **be employed** to teach, not baby-sit. |
| (i) NOT: Children shouldn't **be let** to stay up too late. | (j) Children shouldn't **be allowed** to stay up too late. |

### ■■ EXERCISE 9

Decide whether the causative verbs in these sentences can be made passive without omitting important information or being ungrammatical. If so, write the passive version of the sentence.

**Examples:** The law requires parents to send their children to school.

*Parents are required to send their children to school.*

The doctor got the patient to take the bitter tasting medicine.

*No change possible*

1. Tradition doesn't allow people to smoke in church.
2. Lack of time forced Kilroy to return to the barracks before the movie was over.
3. The law requires everyone who works to pay some income taxes.
4. People shouldn't let their dogs run free around the neighborhood.
5. We had the janitor clean up the mess.
6. When I was a child my mother didn't allow me to play in the street.

form

## FOCUS 5 — Verbs of Urging Followed by Subjunctive *that* Clauses

| EXAMPLES | EXPLANATION |
|---|---|
| (a) The teacher **suggested** that the child **spend** more time on his homework.<br><br>(b) NOT: The teacher **suggested** that the child **spends** more time on his homework. | Certain verbs of urging (*advise, ask, demand, desire, insist, propose, recommend, request, require, suggest, urge*) are followed by a *that* clause. The verb of the *that* clause must appear in simple form. |
| (c) The children **demanded** that their father **give** them candy.<br><br>(d) NOT: The children **demanded** that their father **gives** them candy. | |

### EXERCISE 10

Are these sentences correct or incorrect? For incorrect sentences, identify the mistake and fix it.

1. The students were got to do their homework.
2. The sergeant made the recruits to march for several hours.
3. A tailor was had to shorten my pants.
4. Parents shouldn't let their children watch too much television.
5. I had the waiter to bring the food to the table.
6. They encouraged all their children be independent.
7. We heard the protesters come closer and closer, so we left the area.
8. Companies should be required to provide their employees with health insurance.
9. The baby sitter made the children to fall asleep by singing quietly.
10. Kilroy had his hair to be cut.
11. The judge demanded that he was punished.
12. The army requires that every new soldier gets his hair cut very short.
13. My parents heard our coming in late from the party.

# Use Your English

## ACTIVITY 1 · writing/speaking

Seeing is the sense that we rely on most. But when we are deprived of sight, our other senses become sharper. Test your other senses through the following activity.

### ■ STEP 1

Go to a place you know well. It could be this classroom, or a favorite room in your house, or someplace outdoors. Close your eyes and keep them closed for three minutes. Listen for the sounds that you can hear, both inside and outside. Are there any smells that you notice? Are they pleasant or unpleasant? What can you feel? Is it hot, cold? Make a list of things you have noticed about this place that you never noticed when your eyes were open. Try to think of at least three things for each of these categories:

I heard . . . I smelled . . . I felt . . .

### ■ STEP 2

Compare your list with several other people's lists. As a group, decide what other kinds of things escape your attention when you can rely on eyesight for information about the world around you. Present your ideas to the rest of the class.

## ACTIVITY 2 · speaking/writing

In the previous activity you had an opportunity to experience the world as a blind person does. How are blind people able to move around independently? In what ways do they compensate for lack of sight? How do they get information about where they are and where they are going? Consider deaf people, who cannot hear. How are they able to communicate with each other and the rest of the world?

In a small group discuss ways that people with sensory handicaps can compensate for those handicaps. Use your experience in the previous activity, and any other experiences you have had with people who are blind or deaf. Present your ideas in a written or oral report.

## ACTIVITY 3  speaking/writing

There is a proverb in English that says. "You can catch more flies with honey than you can with vinegar." What do you think are the best ways to get someone to do something? Support your ideas by describing a situation when someone convinced you to do something you didn't want to do. How did that person convince you? Were you glad you did it or not?

## ACTIVITY 4 listening/writing

Here are some general statements about human nature.

- People are usually in too much of a hurry.
- Children are spontaneous.
- Teenagers like to spend time together in groups.
- Older people are usually slower than younger people.

Do you think such generalizations are true or not? Test the validity of such generalizations by doing the following:

**STEP 1**　Choose a generalization that you want to test. It could be one of the statements listed above, or some other generalization. You may want to test a generalization that involves cultural differences, such as *North Americans are very outgoing* or *Asians are studious.*

**STEP 2**　Go to a place where you can watch lots of people. A shopping mall, a cafeteria, a busy corner—these are all good places. Watch how people behave. Look for examples of behavior that reflect the generalization you are testing. Find as many examples as you can that either support or contradict the generalization, and write a paragraph describing what you have observed. Here's an example:

*They say that most people are friendly, and I have found that this seems to be true. At the mall yesterday I saw many people smiling at each other, I saw two people meet by chance. They must have been old friends because I saw them hug each other. I heard many people laughing and joking. I heard many of the salespeople say "Have a nice day" to customers. I saw one family arguing with one another, but strangers tended to be polite.*

**ACTIVITY 5** speaking

What routine jobs do you hate? Pretend that you don't have to worry about money. What things would you have other people do for you?

■ **STEP 1**   Decide on five to ten personal tasks that you would have someone else do, if money were no problem. (For example: *If money were no problem, I would have somebody else do my homework.*)

■ **STEP 2**   Compare your list to those of other students in class. Based on your discussion, decide what the three most unpopular tasks are that people have to do.

**ACTIVITY 6** speaking

If you were the leader of the country, what things would you change?

- What laws would you establish for people to follow?
- What would you require people to do?
- What privileges would you allow people?
- What things would you not allow them to do?
- How would you get people to support you?

Think of at least three answers to each of these questions. Then tell the class why they should let you be their leader. Take a vote to see who is the most convincing candidate.

## ACTIVITY 7 listening/speaking/writing

In the radio, TV, and movie business the term "sound effects" is used to refer to the noises that are added to make the program or movie seem more real. You will hear some common sound effects that are used in radio and TV broadcasts or movies.

CD Track 26

▪ **STEP 1**   After you hear each sound, write a description of what you heard.

**Example:** *I heard a dog barking.*

▪ **STEP 2**   Once you have identified all the sounds, compare your descriptions to those of another student to make sure you both interpreted the sound effects in the same way. Together, use your descriptions to write the story suggested by the sounds.

## ACTIVITY 8 listening

Listen to the conversation between Matt and his doctor, and answer the following questions. You may need to listen to the conversation more than once. The first question has been answered for you as an example.

CD Track 27

1. What does Dr. Wong recommend that Matt do? She recommends that _he change his eating habits_____.

2. How does she suggest that Matt do this? She suggests that . . .

3. What is the problem Matt has with following her advice? His roommate Jeff, . . .

4. How does Jeff insist that food be cooked? He insists that . . .

5. What does Dr. Wong urge that Matt demand? She urges that . . .

6. What other solution does Dr. Wong suggest? She suggests that . . .

## ACTIVITY 9 research on the web

Opinions on the best way to raise children vary widely from culture to culture and from family to family. Go to the Internet and use a search engine such as Google® or Ask® or Yahoo® to research this topic. Enter the term "child rearing" or "childrearing" and look for contrasting examples of how people think children ought to be raised. Some Web sites offer advice to parents about a variety of common problems parents have with their children. Find information about how children are raised differently in different cultures, or what the different viewpoints are regarding physical punishment. Prepare a brief report on a subject of interest for the rest of the class.

## ACTIVITY 10 reflection

■ **STEP 1** What should a teacher do in order to help students learn to speak English? *Teachers should have students do homework every night. Teachers should help students guess the meaning of unfamiliar vocabulary*, etc. Think of at least five recommendations for teachers to help their students become more fluent.

■ **STEP 2** Now think about things that students can do to help each other learn better: *Students should try to speak English with each other even outside of class. Students should work together to understand grammar*, etc. Think of at least five recommendations for students to help their fellow students become more fluent.

■ **STEP 3** Compare your ideas with those of two or three other students and present two or three of the best suggestions to the rest of the class.

# ARTICLES IN DISCOURSE

## UNIT GOALS

- **Correctly distinguish generic and particular statements**

- **Correctly understand and distinguish specific and nonspecific reference in particular statements**

- **Use correct articles with specific, nonspecific, and unique nouns**

## OPENING TASK
### Proverbs

A dog is man's best friend.

Other Common American Proverbs:

*Time is money.*

**A fool and his money are soon parted.**

Experience is the best teacher.

*An idle mind is the devil's playground.*

Absence makes the heart grow fonder.

The leopard cannot change its spots.

*Actions speak louder than words.*

**Beauty is only skin-deep.**

Every cloud has a silver lining.

*Time heals all wounds.*

Spare the rod and spoil the child.

**Money is the root of all evil.**

*You are known by the company you keep.*

## STEP 1

Proverbs are well-known sayings that express general truths. On the previous page are some common American proverbs. Choose one that you agree with, and think of an example from your own life (or the life of someone that you know) that proves the truth of that proverb.

## STEP 2

Write a paragraph about that example. Show why the proverb is true from your own experience. The first proverb has been done for you as an example.

### A DOG IS MAN'S BEST FRIEND

I once had a dog named Poppy. She was a very faithful friend. Every afternoon when I came home, the dog would greet me with kisses and a wagging tail. I liked the wagging tail, but I didn't enjoy the kisses very much. Even so, she was always glad to see me, and I was happy to see her, too.

There was a time in my life when I was feeling very lonely. I didn't think I had any friends. Every day I came home to an empty house with an empty heart. But Poppy was always at the door waiting for me. She seemed to know whenever I was sad or lonely, and at those times she would be extra friendly. One time she even gave me a "gift": an old bone. Somehow she knew that I was especially sad. She must have thought the bone would cheer me up.

Those bad times passed eventually, but they would have been a lot more difficult without my faithful companion, Poppy. She proved to me that a dog really is a wonderful friend.

## FOCUS 1 | Overview of Determiners

Most noun phrases in English require a determiner.

| EXAMPLES | EXPLANATIONS |
|---|---|
| | Determiners can be: |
| (a) We need **this** pen. **That** pen is out of ink. | • **Demonstratives**<br>(see Unit 20 for more information) |
| (b) **Peter's** information surprised us more than **his** appearance. | • **Possessives**<br>(see Unit 21 for more information) |
| (c) Denise has **few** friends. She doesn't make **much** effort to meet people. | • **Quantifiers**<br>(see Unit 22 for more information) |
| (d) Denise has **a** new position. She has **some** work to do. She feels **the** work is quite important. | • **Articles**<br>(see Focus 2 for more information) |
| (e) NOT: Here is **a this** pen.<br>(f) NOT: **That my** pen is green. | There is only one determiner of these types in each noun phrase. |

Many nouns can have both a countable and a noncountable meaning.

| NONCOUNT MEANING | COUNT MEANING |
|---|---|
| (g) They grow **coffee** and **tea** in Sumatra. | (h) We ordered **two coffees** and **a tea** in addition to dessert. |

The form of most determiners depends on whether you think of the noun as being countable or noncount, singular or plural.

| EXAMPLES | EXPLANATIONS |
|---|---|
| one bottle/two bottles<br>one dollar/two dollars<br>one man/two men<br>one chair/two chairs | If you think of a noun as countable then you must indicate singular or plural. |
| milk  (one gallon of milk/two gallons of milk)<br>money (one dollar/a hundred yen)<br>furniture (two pieces of furniture) | If you think of a noun as noncountable then you must use a unit word in order to talk about specific quantities.<br>Noncountable nouns have no plural form. |

## EXERCISE 1

Underline and identify the determiners in the sample paragraph of the Opening Task. Are they demonstratives, possessives, quantifiers, or articles? Are the nouns count or noncount, singular or plural? List them below.

_____

_____

_____

_____

_____

_____

_____

_____

## FOCUS 2    Overview of Articles

There are two kinds of articles: definite and indefinite.

### Definite Articles (used for specific reference)

| EXAMPLES | EXPLANATIONS |
|---|---|
| the pencil/the pencils<br><br>**the** information | There is only one form for definite articles: *the*. *The* can be used with any kind of noun: countable, singular and plural, and noncountable. |

### Indefinite Articles (used for nonspecific reference)

| EXAMPLES | EXPLANATIONS |
|---|---|
| **a** book          **a** shiny apple<br>**a** church      **a** university<br>**a** hotel | *a/an*: Used with singular count nouns. *A* precedes nouns (or their modifiers) that begin with a consonant sound. |
| **an** apple          **an** uncomfortable situation<br>**an** honest man<br>**an** easy lesson      **an** hour | *An* precedes nouns (or their modifiers) that begin with a vowel sound. |
| (a) Please get me **some pencils**.<br>(b) I've invited **some friends** for dinner.<br>(c) I have **some ideas** about the party.<br>(d) Would you like **some rice**?<br>(e) **Some water** got on my notebook.<br>(f) I'm looking for **some information**.<br>(g) Everyone needs **friends**.<br>(h) **Teachers** want **students** to succeed.<br>(i) **Ideas** can come from anywhere.<br>(j) **Rice** is eaten all over Asia.<br>(k) **Water** is necessary for life.<br>(l) I'm looking for **information** about public transportation. | *some*: Used with plural count nouns and noncount nouns.<br>*Some* indicates a nonspecific quantity or amount.<br>Use no article (Ø) with nouns that are nonspecific or generic.<br>See Focus 3 for information in using Ø to make generic statements.<br>See Focus 4 for information about nonspecific statements that do not refer to a quantity or amount and other rules regarding some versus Ø. |

NOTE: See Appendix 5 for a chart that reviews the process for deciding how to choose the correct article for most situations in English.

**EXERCISE 2**

Decide which articles (*a, an, the, some, Ø*) can **NOT** be used with the following noun phrases.

1. pencils
2. water
3. apple
4. university professor
5. hourly employee
6. motherhood
7. bread
8. fast food
9. test

---

| FOCUS 3 | Using Articles in Generic and Particular Statements |

use

There are different rules for using articles depending on whether we are making a **generic** statement or a **particular** statement. So the first step in choosing the correct article is to understand the difference between these two kinds of statements.

| GENERIC STATEMENTS | PARTICULAR STATEMENTS |
|---|---|
| Generic statements describe concepts and ideas. They refer to general categories of things. | Particular statements describe real situations. They refer to individual members of a category. |
| (a) **Bicycles** are an excellent means of transportation. (a category) | (b) They went shopping for **bicycles** yesterday. (particular things they wanted to buy—they didn't buy all the bicycles in the world) |
| (c) **An angry customer** is a frightening sight. (a category of person) | (d) We saw **an angry customer** complaining about the high price of tickets. (a particular person—not all customers are angry) |

*Continued on next page*

*Continued from previous page*

| GENERIC STATEMENTS | PARTICULAR STATEMENTS |
|---|---|
| (e) **The lion** is found throughout Africa. (a category of animal) | (f) I saw **the lion** at the circus. (a particular animal—not all lions are in the circus) |
| (g) **Some people** never fall in love. (a category of people) | (h) **Some people** are joining us for dinner. (particular people, not a class of people) |
| (i) **Information** is increasingly communicated by electronic rather than printed media. (a category of things that are communicated electronically) | (j) Please give me **some information** on medical treatments for heart disease. (particular written or spoken facts) |

Both definite and indefinite articles can be used to express generic statements. The following examples are listed from most common to least common.

| EXAMPLES | EXPLANATIONS |
|---|---|
| (k) **Lions** are mighty creatures. (l) **Rice** is eaten throughout Asia. | Ø **with plural count or noncount nouns** is the most common way to make generic statements. |
| (m) **A lion** is a mighty creature. | *A/an* **with singular count nouns** is less common, but also acceptable. |
| (n) **The** lion is a mighty creature. | *The* **with singular count nouns** is also possible, but sounds very formal to most native speakers. |

NOTE: Article usage in particular statements is explained in the rest of the focus boxes of this unit.

Decide whether these sentences are (*G*) generic statements (describing classes or categories) or (*P*) particular statements (describing members of a category).

**Examples:**

   **G**      **Computers** are cheaper now than they were ten years ago.

   **P**      **Computers** for the new lab are being donated by a company in San Jose.

_____ 1. I wanted to buy **some mangoes** for the fruit salad, but they were too expensive!

_____ 2. **Mangoes** are a fruit found in most tropical places.

_____ 3. I saw **a doctor** about my cough.

_____ 4. **A doctor** is someone who has received training in medical science.

_____ 5. **Computers** have completely changed the way we live.

_____ 6. Don't go to that store for **computers**. They're cheaper at Radio Hut.

_____ 7. **Many people** don't like spicy food.

_____ 8. There weren't **many people** at Reiko's party.

_____ 9. If you really want to know how John is feeling, don't ask the doctor, ask **the nurses**. They will have better information.

_____ 10. There is a shortage of **nurses** in American hospitals today.

_____ 11. Raul is starting **a new company**.

_____ 12. **A company** needs to make sure that it is earning a profit.

## EXERCISE 4

Write one generic statement and one particular statement for each of the cues listed here. The first one has been done for you as an example.

**Examples:**   **Generic:** *Bicycles are a cheap and efficient means of transportation.*

               **Particular:** *Both Billy and his sister got bicycles for Christmas.*

1. bicycles
2. a new car
3. the English language
4. transportation
5. tea
6. salespeople
7. books
8. hard work
9. Chinese food
10. trouble

| FOCUS 4 | Specific Versus Nonspecific Nouns |
|---|---|

In particular statements, article use is determined by whether a noun is specific or nonspecific.

| SPECIFIC NOUNS | IMPLIED MEANING | EXPLANATION |
|---|---|---|
| (a) Please give me **the** red pen. | There is only one red pen. | Specific nouns require definite articles. Specific nouns refer to an identified object. **Both** the speaker and the listener know specifically which object is being talked about. |
| (b) Please pass **the** tea. | There is a teapot right here. | |

| NONSPECIFIC NOUNS | IMPLIED MEANING | EXPLANATION |
|---|---|---|
| (c) Please give me **a** red pen. | There are several red pens. Any red pen is O.K. | Nonspecific nouns require indefinite articles. A noun is nonspecific when **either** the speaker or the listener or both do **not** know specifically which object is being referred to. |
| (d) Let's go to **a** restaurant and have **some** tea. | We don't know which restaurant it will be, or what kind of tea we will have. | |

| EXAMPLES | IMPLIED MEANING | EXPLANATIONS |
|---|---|---|
| (e) I bought **a new car**. | You haven't seen it yet. | Use indefinite articles (*a/an, Ø, some*) when: |
| (f) I had **some cookies** with lunch today. | I know which cookies I had, but you don't. | • the speaker has a specific mental image of the noun, but the listener doesn't. |
| (g) There are **students** in my class who always do their homework. | I know which ones they are, but you don't. | |
| (h) I hear you bought **a new car**. What kind is it? | You know, but I don't. | Use indefinite articles (*a/an, Ø, some*) when: |
| (i) You said you were holding **some mail** that came for me. | You know what kind and how much mail there is, but I don't. | • the speaker doesn't have a specific mental image or idea, but the listener does. |
| (j) Mary tells you **secrets** that she never tells me. | You know which secrets, but I don't. | |

*Continued on next page*

| EXAMPLES | IMPLIED MEANING | EXPLANATIONS |
|---|---|---|
| (k) I hope you have **a wonderful time** on your vacation. | We don't know what events will make it a wonderful vacation. | • neither the speaker nor the listener has a specific mental image. |
| (l) Let's get **some spaghetti** when we go out tonight. | We don't know what kind of or how much spaghetti we're going to get. | |
| (m) We're supposed to bring **dessert** to the picnic. | We haven't been told a specific kind of dessert to bring. | |

## EXERCISE 5

Decide whether the nouns in the sentences below are specific or nonspecific. Is the noun phrase identified for the speaker, the listener, or both? Write the number of the sentence on the appropriate line below. The first two have been done for you.

Both listener and speaker know which one: _____

Listener knows which one, but speaker doesn't: _____

Speaker knows which one, but listener doesn't: _____2_____

Neither listener nor speaker knows which one: _____1_____

1. Do you want to go to **a movie** tonight?

2. The O'Neills just bought **a beautiful new house**. You really ought to see it. I'm sure you'll think it's wonderful.

3. I want you to meet **a friend** of mine. You both have the same interests.

4. Did you have fun at **the party**?

5. Let's have **some friends** over for dinner on Saturday.

6. I heard Ali has **a new girlfriend**. What's she like?

## EXERCISE 6

Choose the correct implied meaning for each of these sentences. (*I* refers to the speaker. *You* refers to the listener.)

1. The student from Japan is here to see you.
   a. There are several students from Japan who had appointments.
   b. There is only one student from Japan who had an appointment.

2. Let's go to a restaurant.
   a. We've already decided which restaurant to go to.
   b. Let's choose a restaurant.

*Continued on next page*

3. Some friends are coming to dinner.

    a. You know who's coming to dinner.

    b. You don't know who's coming to dinner.

4. Let's invite the neighbors to dinner.

    a. You know which neighbors will be invited to dinner.

    b. You don't know which neighbors will be invited to dinner.

5. You should see a doctor about that cough.

    a. I am thinking about a specific doctor.

    b. Any doctor should be able to help you.

## EXERCISE 7

Add the appropriate article (*a/an, the, some,* or Ø) in the blanks. There may be more than one correct answer.

1. I didn't bring _____ roses that you asked for. I completely forgot them.

2. Sally wanted to buy _____ new dress, so she's gone out to find one.

3. _____ teacher was here to see you. I think it was your English teacher.

4. Did you give _____ musicians a nice tip? They certainly played beautiful music for your party.

5. Would you like _____ cold iced tea?

6. How did you enjoy _____ Chinese food last night?

7. I have _____ problems that I don't want to talk about.

8. John sent Mary _____ card for her birthday, but she says she never received it.

9. (a) _____ bank where Dora works was robbed by
   (b) _____ masked man with (c) _____ gun.
   By the time (d) _____ police officer arrived, it was too late.
   (e) _____ robber had disappeared.

use

| EXAMPLES | EXPLANATIONS |
|---|---|
| (a) There once was **a** little old man who lived in **a** house by **a** river. **The** shack was rather dirty, and so was **the** man. | A noun is usually used with an indefinite article the first time it is mentioned because it is *nonspecific*: it is the first time the listener has encountered it. |
| (b) I once had **a** big black dog and **a** little white dog. **The** black dog kept itself very clean, but **the** white dog loved to roll in mud. | In later sentences the same noun is used with a definite article because it has become *specific*: both the speaker and the listener now know exactly which noun is being talked about. |
| (c) I had **a dog** named Poppy. Every afternoon when I came home **the dog** would greet me with **kisses** and **a wagging tail**. I liked **the wagging tail**, but I didn't enjoy **the kisses** very much. | A noun becomes specific:<br>• **by direct reference.**<br>(The noun is repeated.) |
| (d) If you have **a dog** as **a pet**, you can always look forward to going home because of **the kisses** and **the wagging tail** that are there to greet you when you arrive. | • **by indirect reference.**<br>(The noun itself is not repeated, but the reference is still clear from the context.) |
| (e) I read **an interesting book. The author** suggested that all life came from visitors from another planet. **The first chapter** tells stories of visitors from outer space that are found in many different cultures. | |

Write articles (*a/an, Ø, some, the*) in the spaces. More than one answer may be correct.

1. A fool and his money are soon parted.  I have (a) _____ foolish
   friend who is really careless with (b) _____ money. He has
   (c) _____ good-paying job, but he doesn't even have
   (d) _____ bank account. He says he doesn't need one because he
   spends his salary right away. He gets (e) _____ paycheck once
   (f) _____ week. (g) _____ money is always gone
   before (h) _____ week is over. I can't tell you what he spends it on.
   And you know what? Neither can he!

2. You can't make a silk purse out of a sow's ear.  I saw (a) _____
   interesting play last night. (b) _____ actors were excellent, and
   (c) _____ scenery was beautiful. However, (d) _____
   play itself was unfortunately really badly written, and actually rather stupid. Half
   (e) _____ audience left at intermission.

3. Spare the rod and spoil the child.  Little Billy doesn't like (a) _____
   school. He's not doing well, and he's really rather lazy.  He says
   (b) _____ teachers are boring. He doesn't like doing
   (c) _____ homework. He much prefers to watch
   (d) _____ cartoons on TV. As (e) _____ result, his
   teachers aren't very happy with (f) _____ way he performs in class.
   If he doesn't take (g) _____ responsibility for doing
   (h) _____ assignments, he may have to repeat
   (i) _____ same grade next year. Some people would say that he needs
   a good spanking.

**Repeating the Indefinite Article**

use

There are certain situations in which the usual rule of replacing an indefinite article with a definite article after the first time it is mentioned is not followed.

| EXAMPLES | | EXPLANATIONS |
|---|---|---|
| (a) There once was **a** little old man who lived in **a** house by *a river*. **The** house was rather dirty, and so was **the** man. Although *there was a river* right next to **the** house, **the** old man had to walk quite far to get clean drinking water. | | • Sentences with *there is/there are*. |
| (b) I once had **a** dog. Her name was Poppy. She was **a** good dog. | **Implied Meaning**: She was a member of the category "good dogs." | • Sentences that identify someone or something as a member of a category. |
| (c) You know John. He's **a** teacher. | **Implied Meaning**: He's a member of the category "teachers." | |
| (d) John is **a** teacher. John and Fred are teachers. | | Do not use *some* for plural nouns that identify things as part of a group. |
| (e) NOT: John and Fred are **some** teachers. | | |
| (f) Paris is **a** city. Paris, Rome, and Munich are cities. | | |
| (g) NOT: Paris, Rome, and Munich are **some** cities. | | |

Add the correct article to the blank spaces in these sentences.

I once had (1) _____ experience that proved to me that

(2) _____ idle mind is (3) _____ devil's playground. Miss

Kersell was my eighth grade science and math teacher. She was (4) _____

very strict teacher and wouldn't allow any misbehaving in class. To my friend Billy, this

presented (5) _____ irresistible challenge. He found math and science very

easy, so he was frequently bored in class. As (6) _____ result, he would try

to play (7) _____ tricks on her without getting caught. It was

(8) _____ challenge that he could never resist, especially when he didn't

have anything else to do. One day we were taking (9) _____ arithmetic

quiz. It was (10) _____ easy quiz, but I have never been good at

arithmetic, so it was taking me (11) _____ long time. However Billy had

finished (12) _____ quiz in just (13) _____ few minutes.

I heard (14) _____ strange noise coming from the back of the room. It was

(15) _____ noise like no other I had ever heard. Someone in

(16) _____ front of the class began to giggle. Then there were

(17) _____ giggles in the back. Soon

there was (18) _____ laughter

everywhere. Miss Kersell was furious and looked

everywhere to find out where (19)

_____ noise was coming from. Billy

had found (20) _____ way to make

(21) _____ strange noise by rubbing

his foot against (22) _____ leg of his

chair.

## FOCUS 7  Unique Nouns

There are certain nouns that are specific for both the speaker and the listener the first time they are mentioned. These are called **unique nouns**.

| EXAMPLES | EXPLANATIONS |
|---|---|
| (a)  I hear someone knocking at **the** door. <br> (b)  **The** sun is too hot. Let's sit in **the** shade. | Unique nouns are used with definite articles. We do not need to "introduce" them in a specific context. |

| Unique Nouns | Implied Meaning | A noun can be unique: |
|---|---|---|
| (c)  We were all having dinner. We were sitting around **the table**, and I asked my brother to pass **the butter**. | There was only one table and one dish of butter. | • because of a particular situation or setting. |
| (d)  "How did you do on **the exam** yesterday?" "Terrible! **The questions** were really difficult!" | The speakers both know which test is being discussed. | |
| (e)  I hope you remembered to ask **the neighbors** to pick up **the mail** while we're on vacation. | We've previously decided which neighbors we will ask to pick up the mail. | |

| | |
|---|---|
| (f)  **The sky** is so beautiful tonight. **The moon** is bright. | • because it is a universal reference (there is only one) |
| (g)  **The street that John lives on** is lined with trees. <br> (h)  First we went to a hotel where **the man at the desk** told us we had no reservations. <br> (i)  **The book the teacher told us about** is available at **the bookstore across the street**. | • if it is immediately identified by a relative clause or prepositional phrase |

Why do you think the highlighted nouns in the following sentences are unique? Decide whether they have been specified:

a. by being mentioned previously by direct or indirect reference (identify the reference)
b. by a specific context/situation (identify the context or situation)
c. by a universal context or situation
d. by being immediately identified by a relative clause or prepositional phrase (identify the modifier)

1. An idle mind is **the devil's** playground.

2. I saw a great movie last night. **The camera work** was fantastic.

3. **The newspaper** said it was going to rain tonight.

4. **The tallest mountain** in **the world** is on **the border** between Nepal and China.

5. **The place** we went last year is great for a vacation.

6. Let's go to **the club** for dinner tonight.

7. **The teacher** said we have to finish **the assignment** before Friday.

8. **The town** that I grew up in was quite small.

9. **The noise** Billy made was like no other noise I had ever heard before.

10. What did **the doctor** say about **the medicine** you've been taking?

## EXERCISE 11

Write the appropriate article (*a*, *an*, *the*, or Ø) in the blanks. There may be more than one correct choice.

Peter Principle believes that every cloud has (1) _____ silver lining. He is (2) _____ very optimistic person. He thinks that (3) _____ problem is really (4) _____ opportunity in disguise. As (5) _____ result, he is always happy and reasonably content with (6) _____ things that (7) _____ life has given him. (8) _____ people like being around him, because he's (9) _____ cheerful, positive person. Denise Driven is just (10) _____ opposite. She always looks on (11) _____ dark side of (12) _____ things. If she encounters (13) _____ problem, she sometimes blames it on (14) _____ fact that she is (15) _____ woman in (16) _____ man's world. She believes that (17) _____ world isn't (18) _____ fair place, and she in particular has always had (19) _____ bad luck. Although she's not

(20) _____ optimistic person, she doesn't spend much time feeling sorry for herself. She rarely has time to listen to anyone's troubles or tell you about (21) _____ troubles she is facing. But whenever (22) _____ friend does something nice for her, she always suspects that the person actually has (23) _____ hidden motive. She believes that every silver lining has (24) _____ cloud.

## ■ EXERCISE 12

Write the appropriate article in the blanks. There may be more than one correct choice.

The tall person in this picture is one of (1) _____ most beautiful people I know: (2) _____ woman by (3) _____ name of Big Sue. She proves (4) _____ truth of (5) _____ saying "Beauty is only skin deep." Perhaps people who don't know her well would say that she is not (6) _____ beautiful person. I guess that compared to (7) _____ movie star or (8) _____ fashion model she isn't that attractive. But anyone who knows her well thinks that she has (9) _____ beautiful and courageous spirit. Her beauty is in her personality. She has (10) _____ deep, booming laugh that makes other people laugh with her. She's not self-conscious about her size. She makes (11) _____ jokes about it. She was (12) _____ person who invented (13) _____ name "Big Sue." She says there are plenty of Sues in (14) _____ world, but only one Big Sue. If she gains (15) _____ few pounds she

doesn't worry. She just says "There's more of me to love." She is (16) _____ incredible dancer, and moves around (17) _____ dance floor with (18) _____ grace and style. She is (19) _____ wonderful comedian. She can tell (20) _____ stories in (21) _____ way that has (22) _____ people falling down with laughter. She has (23) _____ friends all over (24) _____ world. She has turned down (25) _____ dozens of proposals for marriage. People can't help falling in love with her, once they get to know her well. But she's not in (26) _____ hurry to find (27) _____ husband. She says "I'll wait till I'm old and skinny. Right now I'm having too much fun."

Write the appropriate article in the blanks. There may be more than one correct choice.

When I first went to (1) _____ university, I learned the truth of the proverb "Absence makes (2) _____ heart grow fonder." It was (3) _____ first time I had lived away from home. I was surprised to discover how homesick I got, even after just (4) _____ few days. When I lived with my family, my brother and I used to fight about everything. He wanted to watch one TV program and I wanted to watch another. We fought about whose turn it was to do certain chores like feeding (5) _____ dog, sweeping (6) _____ garage, cutting (7) _____ grass, and taking out (8) _____ garbage. We argued about whose turn it was to use (9) _____ car on Saturday night. (I was allowed to use it one week, and then he was allowed to use it on (10) _____ other.) However when I moved away, I realized that there were (11) _____ lot of things about my brother that I missed. I began to forget about all (12) _____ tricks he used to play on me. I started to remember only (13) _____ happy times we had spent together. By (14) _____ time (15) _____ year ended and I went back to spend (16) _____ summer at home, I was really anxious to see him again.

# Use Your English

## ACTIVITY 1 speaking/writing

Describe an object that you found once, and what you did with it. Compare your story with the stories of other people in the class. Can you create a proverb that talks about finding objects, and what should be done with them? (For example, "Find a penny, pick it up, all day long you'll have good luck.")

## ACTIVITY 2 speaking

A time capsule is a metal or concrete box (usually about one cubic meter) that is sometimes built into the floor or walls of a building. The designers of the time capsule fill it with objects that they think are important, or interesting, or characteristic of the time when the building was built.

■ **STEP 1**   Imagine that you are organizing a time capsule to be placed in a skyscraper being built today. The building is expected to remain standing for several hundred years. What objects would you place in the time capsule, and why would you choose those particular objects?

■ **STEP 2**   Work with several other people and decide on the contents of a time capsule that will not be opened for at least 500 years. Present your list of items and your reasons for choosing them to the rest of the class.

## ACTIVITY 3 writing

What are three things that everybody needs? Write a short composition describing your three choices and why you think everyone should have them. Start your essay with: *"There are three things everyone needs: . . ."*

## ACTIVITY 4 · speaking

Here are four pictures. What story do you think they tell? Tell your story to a partner or write it down for your teacher to correct.

## ACTIVITY 5 · speaking

Think about the meaning differences that are implied when we use articles. For example, we would use "a Bible" to describe the physical book you can find in many motel rooms or bookstores in the United States, but "the Bible" when we refer in a more abstract way to the book Christians believe in. Similarly we distinguish between "a Koran" and "the Koran", the book Muslims believe in.

With a partner or in a small group consider some of these other distinctions. What difference is implied by choice of articles? Discuss when you would use one article rather than the other.

| a law/the law | a truth/the truth | a government/the government |

Present your ideas to the rest of the class.

## ACTIVITY 6 listening

CD Tracks 28, 29, 30

Listen to the example and short conversations and then choose the statement from the pairs listed below that can be correctly implied from the conversation.

**Conversation 1**

_____ There is one ACME sales representative.
_____ There are several ACME sales representatives.
_____ There is one vice president.
_____ There are several vice presidents.

**Conversation 2**

_____ There is only one snack bar in the building.
_____ There are several snack bars in the building.
_____ John has already decided what he is going to eat.
_____ John hasn't decided what he is going to eat yet.
_____ Mary already knows what snack John will bring her.
_____ Mary doesn't know what John will bring her from the snack bar.

**Conversation 3**

_____ This is the first time Bob and Betty have discussed the idea of a party.
_____ They've discussed the party before.
_____ They have already decided who they are going to invite.
_____ They haven't decided who they are going to invite.
_____ They have already decided which restaurant to go to.
_____ They haven't decided which restaurant to go to.

## ACTIVITY 7 research on the web

Every country has different proverbs. In America we say "Don't bite off more than you can chew," to remind people not to be too ambitious or try to do too many things at once. In Afghanistan the same idea is expressed by this proverb: "You can't hold two watermelons in one hand."

■ **STEP 1** Go on the Internet and use a search engine such as Google® or Yahoo® and type in the word "proverbs". You will find a number of Web sites that contain proverbs from many different countries. Find three pairs of proverbs from different cultures. Each pair should express the same idea in two different ways.

■ **STEP 2** Share each message and its two different proverbs with the rest of the class.

# REFERENCE FORMS IN DISCOURSE

## UNIT GOALS

- Correctly understand and use determiners and demonstrative pronouns

- Correctly understand and communicate differences in reference by using determiners

- Correctly understand and communicate differences in focus and emphasis by using determiners

## OPENING TASK

### *This, That, or It?*

■ **STEP 1**

Work with a partner. Read the dialogue on the next page and look at how the words *it, this*, and *that* are used in the first part of the dialogue. Discuss why you think one form is used rather than another. With a partner, replace the blanks in the dialogue with reference forms (*it, this*, and *that*). Finally, complete the last few lines of the dialogue.

■ **STEP 2**

Form a group with one or two other pairs of students. Compare your dialogues. Discuss any differences you had in choosing appropriate reference forms to fill in the blanks.

■ **STEP 3**

As a group, decide on three general observations about when to use *it* instead of *this* or *that*. Share your ideas with the rest of the class.

## STEP 4

Finally, as a group, decide on the best way to end the dialogue and have two of your members perform the dialogue for the rest of the class.

**Denise Driven:** Mr. Green has informed me that you're not going to be here this afternoon. **That's** outrageous, Peter! What about the Davis contract? **It's** due first thing Monday morning.

**Peter Principle:** Well, my son's in a play at school. **It's** his first big role. He's one of the Three Wise Men.

**Denise Driven:** He certainly didn't learn **that** role from his father! Is some stupid school play more important than your job?

**Peter Principle:** You'd better believe **it!** Besides, I spoke with Mr. Green. I told him **it** would get done sooner or later.

**Denise Driven:** If he believes **that**, he'll believe anything. **That's** what makes me so annoyed, Peter. **This** isn't the first time you've left work early. You're always asking for permission to take time off, and I am left having to do all the work. I'm getting tired of _____ Peter. _____ **is** all I can do to keep this office running professionally!

**Peter Principle:** I'm sure Mr. Green would be happy to give you time off, too. Just ask for _____ Denise. _____ is all you have to do.

**Denise Driven:** _____'s not the point. _____'s true that most of us would probably rather be playing instead of working. But some of us have a sense of responsibility and a respect for hard work.

**Peter Principle:** _____'s true. My responsibility is to my son, and I respect the hard work he's put into learning his lines. _____'s not easy when you're only 8 years old.

**Denise Driven:** Don't give me _____ nonsense, Peter. I don't appreciate _____

**Peter Principle:** _____'s your trouble, Denise. You need a little nonsense in your life. _____

**Denise Driven:** _____

**Peter Principle:** _____

**Denise Driven:** _____

**Peter Principle:** _____

form    meaning

use

## FOCUS 1 | Overview of Demonstratives

Demonstratives can be used as determiners or as pronouns.

| EXAMPLES | EXPLANATIONS |
|---|---|
| (a) Does **this** laptop belong to you? | Demonstrative determiner |
| (b) Yes, **that** is mine. | Demonstrative pronoun |

The form of the demonstrative depends on whether the thing being referred to is singular or plural, and near or far.

| | NEAR | FAR |
|---|---|---|
| Singular | (c) You take a look at **this** Web site.<br><br>(e) **This** is amazing. | (d) Does **that laptop** belong to you?<br><br>(f) Is **that** yours? |
| Plural | (g) **These problems** aren't new, Peter.<br><br>(i) If you want other examples of Peter's careless reports, look at **these**. | (h) **Those workers** don't take time off the way you do.<br><br>(j) **Those** are the sloppiest reports I have ever seen! |

| EXAMPLES | EXPLANATIONS |
|---|---|
| (k) Please sit in **this** chair **(by me.) That** chair **(over there)** is broken. | Near and far distinctions can be determined by:<br>• physical distance. |
| (l) I've been to dinner with two co-workers in the last week, but **this** one (today) with Peter is much more enjoyable than **that** party Denise had (a few days ago) at the club. | • time distance. |
| (m) What are we going to do about **this** budget deficit, Peter? | • whether the speaker feels involved with the situation or distanced from it. |
| (n) I don't know, Denise. **That's** for you to worry about, not me! | |

| EXAMPLE | EXPLANATION |
|---|---|
| (o) There once was **a** workaholic who worked in **an** insurance company. Every day **this woman** would go to **a** file on her computer. **This file** was where she kept track of what time each of her co-workers arrived. | Use demonstratives with nouns that have been specified by being mentioned previously (see Unit 19 for more information). |

A demonstrative is not usually repeated to refer to the same item. A personal pronoun (*he, it, etc.*) or a definite article (*the*) is used instead.

| | |
|---|---|
| (p) Have you seen **these** figures? **They** are quite alarming. | (q) NOT: Have you seen **these** figures? **These** are quite alarming. |
| (r) **This** is the problem Denise was talking about. **It** will continue to get worse if we don't find a solution. | (s) NOT: **This** is the problem Denise was talking about. **This** will continue to get worse if we don't find a solution. |
| (t) I brought up **that** problem at the meeting. **The** problem was discussed but not solved. | (u) NOT: I brought up **that** problem at the meeting. **That** problem was discussed but not solved. |

## EXERCISE 1

Add appropriate demonstratives (*this, those, etc.*), personal pronouns (*he, it, etc.*), or articles (*a/an, the*) in the blanks. More than one answer may be possible. The first one has been done for you as an example.

1. When Denise came to Mr. Green with her complaints about Peter, he realized that they had talked about (a) ___these/those___ issues before. He told her there was no point in discussing (b) ___them___ any further.

2. I got these new file folders on sale. I'd like you to take a look at (a) _____. Which of (b) _____ folders do you like better, (c) _____ red one or (d) _____ green one? What about (e) ____ larger folders? Which do you prefer? (f) _____ one or (g) _____ one?

3. I got a new computer for my birthday. (a) _____ was a gift from my boss. I'm glad she got (b) _____ laptop instead of another kind. (c) _____ will be much more practical.

4. The report that Peter submitted had to be done over. (a) _____ didn't follow any of the guidelines Mr. Green had explained when he had first assigned Peter to do (b) _____ report. (c) _____ guidelines were not simple, but (d) _____ had to be followed in order to get the vice-president's approval on (e) _____ report. (f) _____ decision made Peter rather upset, but Mr. Green had made (g) _____ guidelines quite clear.

5. Where did you get (a) _____ fountain pen? (b) _____ is really beautiful. (c) _____ looks like (d) _____ came from Europe. Is (e) _____ silver?

---

| **FOCUS 2** | **Demonstratives for Reference** |

use

| EXAMPLES | EXPLANATIONS |
|---|---|
| (a) Everyone started laughing. **This** made Denise very angry. | There are two kinds of demonstrative reference: |
| (b) I knew you were going to be late! **That's** why I wanted someone else to make the presentation. | • **backward-pointing reference**: where demonstratives refer to information that has been previously mentioned |
| (c) **This** is why I don't like Peter: He doesn't come to work on time, he doesn't check his work, and he takes no responsibility. | • **forward-pointing reference**: where demonstratives refer to information that is about to be introduced. |
| (d) I can use **these** kinds of software: Word, Excel and PowerPoint. | |

Using a particular demonstrative form depends on whether it refers forward or backward in the text.

| EXAMPLES | EXPLANATIONS |
|---|---|
| (e) **This** is why I didn't finish the report: I had a terrible case of the flu. <br><br> (f) I had a terrible case of the flu. **This** is why I didn't finish the report. | *This/these* can be used to point both forward or backward. |
| (g) I had a terrible case of the flu. **That** is why I didn't finish the report. <br><br> (h) Denise is a workaholic. **That** is why nobody wants to work with her. | *That/those* are usually only used for backward pointing reference (except with modifiers that follow a noun—see Focus 4). |

## EXERCISE 2

What do the demonstratives refer to in these sentences? Circle the demonstratives in these passages, and draw an arrow to what each one refers to. Is it an example of forward-pointing or backward-pointing reference? The first passage has been done for you as an example.

1. Most people find it difficult to sleep during the day and work at night. (This) is why people who work "swing shift" (as (that) work schedule is called) are usually paid a higher wage than (those) who work during the day.

2. We hold these truths to be self-evident, that all men are created equal, and have a right to life, liberty, and the pursuit of happiness.

3. Let me make this perfectly clear: No new taxes!

4. Frank said that he wanted to leave New York because he was tired of big city life. But I don't think that was the real reason for his move to California. The real reason was that his wife wanted to live in a place with warmer winters. At least, this is what Stuart told me.

5. These soldiers must report to Barracks B: Private Rebecca Adams, Private Mary Collins, and Corporal Marsha Powell. These soldiers have been assigned to patrol duty: Sergeant Kitty Westmoreland and Corporal Mary MacArthur. Those are your orders, soldiers.

6. The causes of the American Civil War were not very different from those of other wars that have taken place between different regions of any country. This is one of the things that can be learned by studying history.

7. The chemical composition of baking soda is similar to that of any compound containing sodium. This is what allows baking soda to enter into a chemical reaction with any compound containing acid, such as those found in vinegar or even orange juice.

8. Management techniques of many American companies now tend to resemble those used in Japan much more than they did a few years ago. This is due to the success those techniques have had in raising worker productivity.

## FOCUS 3    *This/That Versus It*

| EXAMPLES | EXPLANATIONS |
|---|---|
| "Did you hear the news? Denise didn't get the promotion?"<br><br>(a) "I knew **it**! That woman is so unpleasant to work with." (*Implied Meaning*: I'm not surprised!)<br><br>(b) "I knew **that**. Mr. Green told me last week." (*Implied Meaning*: I'd already heard that news.) | Both demonstrative pronouns (**this/that**) and personal pronouns (**it**) refer back to ideas or items in previous sentences, but there is often a difference in emphasis or implied meaning. |
| They say that Denise is getting a raise.<br><br>(c) Has Peter heard about **this**? (*Implied Meaning*: Has this important information been told to Peter?) | Using *this/that* emphasizes that the idea being referred to is the most important information in the new sentence. |
| They say that Denise is getting a raise.<br><br>(d) I don't *believe* **it**! (*Implied Meaning*: That's unbelievable!) | Using *it* indicates that some other part of the sentence (the subject or verb) is the most important information. We do not generally use pronouns to talk about significant new information. |

In some cases we **must** use *that* instead of *it*.

| EXAMPLES | EXPLANATION |
|---|---|
| (e) Don't leave your laptop in the lobby. Someone might steal **it**.<br><br>(f) Don't worry. I'm smarter than **that**.<br><br>(g) NOT: I'm smarter than **it**. | This is especially true in cases where *it* could refer to a physical object (*the car* or *the dog*) rather than the general idea or situation. |
| (h) Denise is planning to file an official complaint about Peter.<br><br>(i) I was afraid of **that**! No wonder she was asking me what time he came in this morning.<br><br>(j) NOT: I was afraid of **it**! | |

## EXERCISE 3

Decide which form, demonstrative pronoun (*this/that*) or personal pronoun (*it*), to put in the blanks. In most sentences, both forms are possible, but native speakers would tend to choose one form instead of the other to indicate a particular emphasis. Compare your choices with those of other students and your teacher.

1. Someone took your wallet? I was afraid _____ would happen!

2. I'm glad Peter's wife hasn't had her baby yet. She was afraid _____ would happen while her husband was out of town.

3. I'm sorry you had to spend such a beautiful, sunny Saturday in the office. _____ isn't really fair, is it?

4. I assume you have all heard the news about Denise. _____ is why I have asked you here to this meeting.

5. I love the wonderful California climate. _____ is why I moved here.

6. Did you say the Republicans are involved in another financial scandal? Are you completely sure of _____?

7. I just know Mary's dating someone else. I'm sure of _____!

8. If you don't take advantage of this great opportunity, I know you'll regret _____ in the future.

9. Don't worry about making such a mess. _____ really doesn't matter.

10. Don't worry about making such a mess. _____ is why I put newspapers over everything.

11. **A:** You said "seventeen." Don't you mean "seventy"?

    **B:** Oh yes, _____'s what I meant.

12. Don't complain to me. _____ is why we have a complaint department.

use

## FOCUS 4 — *That/Those* with Forward-Pointing Reference

| EXAMPLES | EXPLANATIONS |
|---|---|
| (a) **Those who cannot learn from history** will repeat the mistakes made in the past.<br><br>(b) I'm not very fond of dogs, but **those that are well behaved** are O.K.<br><br>(c) The boss only gives raises to **those he really likes**. (**whom** has been omitted)<br><br>(d) This report is really confusing I can't tell the difference between **that which is supposed to be profit** and **that which is supposed to be loss**. | *That* and *those* can be used for forward pointing reference only when they occur with:<br>• relative clauses. |
| (e) Compare your paragraph to **that of another student** in the class.<br><br>(f) This problem will have to be solved by **those in charge**. | • prepositional phrases |

## EXERCISE 4

Identify the demonstratives that are followed by modifying clauses or phrases in these passages. Not all sentences contain these structures.

1. There is an old proverb that says fate helps those that help themselves.

2. Please put those on Denise's desk.

3. My co-worker is very fussy about using certain kinds of computer programs. He won't touch these, but those he likes will be quickly downloaded onto his hard-drive.

4. Those in the stock brokerage business think that this is a bad time to invest.

5. One must learn to distinguish between that which is necessary and that which is only desirable.

6. Those who can't tell the difference between the colors teal and aquamarine shouldn't become interior decorators.

7. That is not my responsibility. You'll have to speak to those in charge of that part of the operation.

8. I read about that in the newspapers.

# Special Uses of Demonstratives

**use**

### Using *This*/*These* with Nonspecific Nouns

| EXAMPLES | EXPLANATIONS |
|---|---|
| (a) I'm walking down the street, and I see **this** man on the corner. He's talking with **these** two other guys. | In very informal speech or written narratives we can use *this* and *these* in place of indefinite determiners (*a, an,* and *ø*) to introduce nouns for the first time. |

### Using *That* to Refer to Humans

| EXAMPLES | EXPLANATIONS |
|---|---|
| (b) **That** man over there is married to **that** woman in the red dress. | **That** is not usually used to refer to humans, except when the speaker is pointing to the person. |
| (c) Were you talking to **that** boy again? I told you not to speak to him! | When *that* is used in other kinds of reference, it usually indicates the speaker is annoyed, or is insulting the person being referred to. |

## EXERCISE 5

Make this paragraph more informal by replacing the underlined articles with demonstratives. Are there some articles that can't be replaced with demonstratives? Decide which demonstratives are appropriate for the remaining blanks.

I went to (1) a  party where I met (2) some rather strange people. They had all read (3) an article in the newspaper about (4) a new invention that was supposed to help people lose weight. Mary, the hostess, was the strangest of all. She went around the room, asking all the guests to put on (5) some very dark glasses. Apparently (6) _____ is supposed to help people eat less. Now I ask you: Why does a person go to all the trouble of giving (7) a party if she doesn't want her guests to eat? (8) _____ 's Mary for you! She'll believe anything she reads in the paper.

# Use Your English

## ACTIVITY 1 speaking/writing

Here is a puzzle. Can you punctuate it so that it makes sense?

**that that is is that that is not is not isn't that it it is**

There are four sentences in the correct answer. The solution is on page A-12.

## ACTIVITY 2 writing/speaking

Write a dialogue like the one in the Opening Task on page 329. Work with a partner. First, decide what the argument will be about. Then write your dialogue. Try to use some of the phrases that Peter and Denise used. Perform your dialogue for the rest of the class.

## ACTIVITY 3 speaking

Tell a story in informal spoken English. Use the present time frame and demonstratives (*this* and *these*) instead of indefinite articles. See Exercise 5 for an example to get you started.

## ACTIVITY 4 research on the web

Go on the Internet and use a search engine such as Google® or Yahoo® to find information about how common products differ from one country to another. For example: How does the coffee of Guatemala differ from that of Sumatra? How are automobiles from Japan different from those made in the United States? How does rice grown in India differ from that grown in China? Find comparative information on three different products and make a brief presentation in either written or spoken form.

# ACTIVITY 5  listening

CD Track 31

Denise and Peter are arguing again. Listen to their conversation and answer the questions below in your notebook. You may need to listen to the conversation more than once. Use *it* or *that* in your answers. The first question has been answered for you as an example.

1. When did Denise finish the Davis contract?
   *She finished it late last night.*

2. What did Denise think of Peter's offer to help?

3. When did Denise write her official complaint to Mr. Green?

4. How does Denise react when Peter offers to show her pictures of his son's play?

5. What does Denise threaten to do with the computer terminal if Peter doesn't stop telling her to be less serious about work?

6. Why does Peter decide to leave the office to take his children to the beach?

7. What effect does Denise think that firing Peter would have on the office?

Compare your answers to those of another student in the class.

# ACTIVITY 6  reflection

Discuss these pairs of sentences with a partner or in a small group. Can you identify a difference in implied meaning? Why do you think native speakers would use one form rather than the other? In what situations would one form be more appropriate than the other? What difference in intonation might be used in one sentence rather than the other? Can you think of a rule or strategy for learning and remembering which form is the correct one to use in each set of examples?

| | | |
|---|---|---|
| I can't believe you said it!<br>I can't believe you said that! | That's what she said.<br>It's what she said. | Try it. You'll like it.<br>Try this. You'll like it. |

| | |
|---|---|
| This is what's going to be on the test.<br>That's what's going to be on the test. | She really doesn't like that.<br>She really doesn't like it. |

Present your ideas to the rest of the class. Pay special attention to the reference forms you are using in your presentation. Be sure to use all three reference forms in your presentation (for example: *This is what we decided about the first pair of sentences . . . That is the most important part of the sentence . . . It's difficult to decide . . .* etc.).

# POSSESSIVES

## UNIT GOALS

- Correctly identify and use possessive forms (possessive determiners, possessive pronouns, possessive phrases and, possessive nouns)

- Know when to use possessive nouns and when to use possessive phrases

- Correctly understand the various meanings of possessives

## OPENING TASK

### What's Wrong with This Picture?

How observant are you? How accurate is your memory? Look at the picture below for exactly thirty seconds, then cover the picture. There are at least fifteen strange things about the picture. For example, the legs of the table seem to be a person's legs. The little girl's hair is very unusual. Notice as many other strange things as you can, and then, without looking at the picture again, write complete sentences describing the strange things. When you are finished, compare your answers with a partner's, and then together check the picture to complete the list of strange things.

**What's strange about . . .**

the boy's hat? _____

the girl's hair? _____

the dog's tail _____

the dog's nose _____

the girl's tricycle _____

the girl's shoes _____

the boy's shoes _____

the hands of the clock _____

the fringe of the couch _____

the handle of the door _____

the top of the table _____

the cover of the book _____

the knobs of the TV _____

the drawers of the dresser _____

the legs of the table _____

# FOCUS 1 — Possessive Forms

| EXAMPLES | EXPLANATIONS |
|---|---|
| | There are four kinds of possessive forms: **Possessive determiners:** |
| (a)  **Their** dog has a really long tail. | (*my, your, his, her, its, our, their*) Possessive determiners precede the noun. |
| (b)  His hair is covered by a cap, but **hers** appears to be made of snakes. | **Possessive pronouns:** (*mine, yours, his, hers, its, ours, theirs*) Possessive pronouns can take the place of a noun phrase. |
| (c)  The fringe **of the couch** looks like human fingers. | **Possessive phrases:** (*the leg **of the chair**, the end **of the story***, etc.) Possessive phrases are formed by adding the preposition *of* to the noun phrase. Possessive phrases follow the noun. |
| (d)  **The boy's** shoes are swim fins, and the **girl's** have curly toes. | **Possessive nouns:** (*the **student's** answers, the **children's** laughter, those **babies'** cries, **Elvis'** cousin,* etc.) Possessive nouns are formed by adding *'s* (pronounced **apostrophe -*s***) to a noun, or simply adding an apostrophe to nouns or proper nouns ending in -*s*. |

Underline and identify all the possessive structures in the following passage. Then label each one: (a) possessive determiner, (b) possessive pronoun, (c) possessive phrase, or (d) possessive noun? The first paragraph has been done for you as an example. Do all the structures you identified describe possessive relationships?

(1) Have you ever tested <u>your memory</u>? (2) There have been many studies of <u>people's</u> ability to remember things. (3) These studies have found that there are two types <u>of memory</u>: short-term memory and long-term memory.

(4) Short-term memory depends on the "length" or number of items that someone needs to remember. (5) A person's ability to remember a series of numbers for more than a minute is limited to about twelve or fourteen digits. (6) An individual's ability to remember strings of unconnected words seems to average about eight items. (7) Most people's performance on such memory tests will drop quickly if they are tested again, even after only a few hours' time.

(8) Long-term memory seems to be determined by the item's usefulness to the person being tested. (9) For example, people do a better job of remembering one of Shakespeare's sonnets if they can apply the "message" of the poem to some part of their own lives. (10) The more important a piece of information is to a person's life, the longer and more accurately it can be retained.

1. _your memory – possessive determiner_    6. _____
2. _people's – possessive noun_    7. _____
3. _of memory – possessive phrase_    8. _____
4. _____    9. _____
5. _____    10. _____

## Possessive Nouns Versus Possessive Phrases

**use**

| EXAMPLES | EXPLANATIONS |
|---|---|
| (a) **The little girl's** hair appears to be made of snakes. <br> (b) The hair **of the little girl** appears to be made of snakes. | Possessive noun (*'s*) mean the same thing as nouns with a possessive phrase (*of* . . .), but one form is usually preferred over the other in specific situations. |
| (c) the **boy's** cap <br> NOT: the **cap of the boy** <br> (d) the **dog's** tail <br> NOT: the **tail of the dog** | Use possessive nouns (with *'s*) for: <br> • most animate (living) nouns |
| (e) the **razor's** edge <br> (f) the **train's** arrival | • objects that perform an action |
| (g) the **moon's** orbit <br> (h) the **river's** mouth <br> (i) the **earth's** atmosphere | • natural phenomena |
| (j) the top **of the table** <br> NOT: the **table's** top. <br> (k) the fringe **of the couch** <br> NOT: the **couch's** fringe <br> (l) the cause **of the problem** <br> NOT: the **problem's** cause | Use possessive phrases (with *of* + noun phrase): <br> • for most inanimate (nonliving) nouns |
| (m) the dog **of a rather strange local family** <br> NOT: **a rather strange local family's** dog | • when the possessive noun phrase is very long |
| (n) the hat **of the girl's older brother** <br> NOT: **the older brother's girl's** hat | • when a multiple possessive is long |

## EXERCISE 2

For each noun + possessive, write the best possessive form in the blank in the sentence. Add articles where necessary.

**Examples:**  hat/boy: _____The boy's hat_____ has a propeller.

cover/*Time* magazine: Being on _____the cover of Time magazine_____ made Elvis Presley even more famous.

1. results/investigation: _____ were reported in the newspaper.

2. restaurant/Alice's mother: We had dinner at _____.

3. ability/individual: _____ to remember something depends on how important the information is.

4. rights/women: Suffragettes were early activists in the battle for _____.

5. opening/novel: _____ begins with the famous words, "Call me Ishmael."

6. take-off/rocket: _____ was quite an amazing spectacle.

7. music/Elvis Presley: _____ has been heard all over the world.

8. discovery/penicillin: Sir Alexander Fleming was responsible for _____.

9. children/a very famous American movie star: I went to school with _____.

10. rotation/earth: _____ is what causes night and day.

## EXERCISE 3

Change the cues in parentheses to the correct possessive constructions. Add articles where necessary.

Last week Matt went shopping to get a present for his roommate, Jeff. It was (1) _____ (Jeff/birthday), and he wanted to buy a really "unusual" gift. He drove (2) _____ (Jeff/car) downtown. When he got there he realized that the (3) _____ (shopping district/center) was already quite crowded, and every (4) _____ (store/ parking lot) seemed to be full. He was in a hurry, so he decided to park in front of a hotel. He thought the (5) _____ (hotel/doorman) looked annoyed, but he wasn't really paying much attention. He visited several stores. In (6) _____ (one of the stores/window) he saw the perfect gift: a statue of a cowboy. In (7) _____ (cowboy/hand) there was a container for toothpaste, toothbrush, and razor. He thought that the statue would look perfect in (8) _____ (their apartment/bathroom). He bought it and hurried back to where he had parked. The car was gone! At first Matt thought it had been stolen, but then he realized that it had probably been towed away. He called the police, and they verified that the car was at the station. When he got there, he found that (9) ———————— (the car/front fender) had a dent, and there was a big scratch on (10) ———————— (the car/side). Matt had to pay for the (11) ———————— (repair/cost) and the towing charges. Jeff got a very expensive birthday present, and Matt got a long-overdue lesson about traffic laws and parking regulations.

meaning

| **FOCUS 3** | **Meanings of Possessive Forms** |
|---|---|

Possessive forms can be used to describe other kinds of meaning besides belonging to someone or something.

| EXAMPLES | EXPLANATIONS |
|---|---|
| (a) Please give me ten **dollars'** worth of unleaded gasoline.<br>(b) That leather coat cost me a **week's** pay.<br>(c) This book represents three **years'** work. | We also use possessive forms to indicate:<br>• amount or quantity |
| (d) The **index of a book** is the best place to start when you're looking for specific information.<br>(e) The **team's captain** scored the goal. | • part of a whole |
| (f) Scientists are still trying to discover **the cause of cancer.**<br>(g) **The streets of New York** can be dangerous at night.<br>(h) **Margaret's friend** is blind. | • a general relationship or association |
| (i) We learned about **the exports of Australia** in our international business class.<br>(j) **Joan's conversation** with the doctor caused her some concern. | • origin or agent |

## EXERCISE 4

**By yourself:** Read the following article about Elvis Presley and underline all the possessives or expressions with "of". The first paragraph has been done for you.

**With a partner:** Compare your answers. Find at least two examples of possessives that convey each of the following meanings, and write those examples in the space next to the meanings listed.

a.  quantity or amount _____

b.  part of a whole _____

c.  general relationship or association _____

d.  origin or agent _____

e.  actual possession _____

f.  phrases with *of* that should not be _____
    considered possessive

### THE KING OF ROCK AND ROLL

(1) The most-visited residence in the United States is, <u>of course</u>, the White House, in Washington, D.C., the home <u>of the President of the United States</u>. (2) But the second most visited residence may surprise you. (3) It is Graceland Mansion in Memphis, Tennessee, the home <u>of Elvis Presley</u>, the "King" of <u>Rock and Roll</u>. (4) <u>Presley's</u> influence on the popular music <u>of America</u> was profound. (5) He was one <u>of the first blues artists</u> to make rock and roll popular with the middle class <u>of the United States.</u> (6) And <u>Elvis's</u> swinging hips and sexy voice made him the dream boyfriend <u>of an entire generation of teenage girls</u>. (7) <u>Presley's</u> historic appearance on a 1958 broadcast of The Ed Sullivan Show caused an uproar. (8) His singing could not be heard because of the screams of his adoring fans. (9) And Presley's famous swinging hips were not seen at all, because of the objections of TV broadcasters, who felt his wild movements weren't suitable for family television. (10) Presley rapidly became America's most popular male singer of all time. (11) He made dozens of records and many films. (12) Everywhere he went crowds of screaming, adoring fans showered him with gifts, love, and devotion.

(13) But his personal life was marked by tragedy. (14) By the time he died in 1977, everyone had heard the rumors of his troubles with alcohol and drugs. (15) They had read about his failed marriage in the movie magazines. (16) His suspicions about his friends' loyalties and motivations had made a "living nightmare" of his life. (17) He died a prisoner of his own popularity.

(18) In spite of his death, Elvis is still called "The King of Rock and Roll." (19) Graceland Mansion is visited by hundreds of adoring fans every day. (20) His records continue to be popular, and there are several radio stations that play nothing but Presley's music.

(21) Some people even believe that he is still alive and living in disguise. (22) There continue to be rumors that his mysterious death was just a trick to allow him to escape from the prison of his fame and his fans' adoration. (23) Many people still believe that he is living a quiet life with a new name and a thick beard to hide his famous face. (24) Today the Memphis post office still receives hundreds of letters addressed to Elvis at Graceland from fans who still await "The King's" return.

## EXERCISE 5

Underline the possessive forms in the following sentences. There may be more than one possible interpretation. With a partner, discuss which of the following meanings the possessive forms indicate:

a. an amount or quantity
b. a part of a whole
c. a general relationship/association
d. an origin or agent
e. actual possession

                            *b*                           *c*

**Example:** The <u>streets of San Francisco</u> are famous for <u>their</u> steep hills.

1. Scientists are studying the effects of alcohol on an individual's memory.

2. The wines of France are among the best in the world.

3. The teacher's assistant will hand back the homework.

4. That concept was introduced in the book's first chapter.

5. Chicago is four days' drive from Los Angeles.

6. An investigation of short-term memory has shown that items of personal importance are more easily remembered.

7. The top of the table looked like a small patch of grass.

8. Matt's roommate likes ice cream.

9. Beethoven's symphonies still thrill listeners.

## EXERCISE 6

Are these sentences correct or incorrect? If they are incorrect, identify the problems and correct them.

1. The fame of Elvis Presley spread across America.
2. The table's top was covered with grass.
3. The child of Bambang's classmate was sick with the flu.
4. Gladys' well-known next-door neighbor's dog's barking annoyed the entire neighborhood.
5. The scientists' studies' results indicate that memory is affected by such things as weather and time of day.
6. Memory's investigations have shown that the ability of people to remember things declines with age.
7. Rock and Roll's King died in 1977.
8. Elvis's death's circumstances are somewhat mysterious.

## EXERCISE 7

Ask a classmate for his or her opinions on these topics, and the reasons for those opinions. Report your partner's answers to the rest of the class.

**Example:** best place to sit in a classroom

**You:** *Where's the best place to sit in a classroom?*

**Your partner:** *The front of the class is better if you're a good student, but the back of the class is better if you want to sleep.*

1. most important part of the semester (beginning, end, or middle)
2. favorite object that belongs to someone else
3. most important period of history
4. favorite piece of music

Ask two additional questions of your own that use possessive forms.

5. _____

_____

6. _____

_____

# Use Your English

Work with a partner to fill in the missing parts of the diagrams. Student A, look at diagrams A and C below. Student B, look at Diagrams B and D on page A-12. Diagram A contains elements not contained in Diagram B. Student A, help your partner complete Diagram B by verbally describing Diagram A. Student B should help Student A complete Diagram C, which is incomplete by verbally describing the diagram D. Student A should not look at Diagrams B and D. Student B should not look at Diagrams A and C.

**Diagram A**

**Diagram C**

ACTIVITY **2** writing/speaking

Check your short-term memory. Study the picture below for thirty seconds. Then close your book and describe to a partner what has happened to the car and its passengers. Your partner should look at the picture while you describe it and check your description for accuracy.

Your partner should also check the accuracy of your use of possessive forms.

## ACTIVITY 3 listening/speaking

■ **STEP 1**    As you listen to the geometry class lecture, use the information to draw the diagram that is described by the speaker. Once you have finished, listen to the lecture again to check that you have completed your diagram correctly.

CD Track 32

■ **STEP 2**    Compare your diagram with two or three others. As a group, decide on the correct answer to the two questions the speaker asks at the end of the lecture.

## ACTIVITY 4 research on the web

 Go to the Internet and use an Internet search engine such as Google® or Yahoo® to find information on a famous person who is no longer alive. Write a short description of that person. What are the things that made him or her famous? Be sure to describe his or her accomplishments, childhood, important experiences, and influence on society.

## ACTIVITY 5 reflection

Write two paragraphs—one that describes some interesting things about your extended family (including grandparents, uncles, aunts, in-laws etc.), and one that describes your favorite room in your house. Compare your paragraphs with those of another student. Identify the possessive forms that you used in your description. Together, select five examples of possessive forms you used in your descriptions to present to the rest of the class. Tell why you used the form you did, and what meaning was communicated by the possessive (amount or quantity, part of a whole, a general relationship or association, an origin or agent, actual possession). If possible, pick one example for each possessive meaning.

# UNIT 22

# QUANTIFIERS, COLLECTIVE NOUNS, AND COLLECTIVE ADJECTIVES

## OPENING TASK

### Statistics about International Education

The Institute for International Education publishes statistical information about international educational exchange. Work with a partner. Examine these charts on the enrollment of international students in educational institutions in the United States. Using that information and your own knowledge, answer these three questions:

- What fields of study do international students pursue in the United States?

- What kinds of locations do they choose to study at?

- Which parts of the world do students come from?

CHART A: FOREIGN STUDENTS BY FIELD OF STUDY

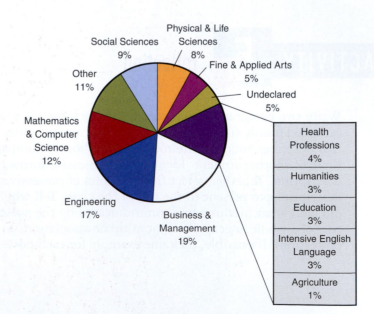

**CHART B: FOREIGN STUDENTS BY DESTINATION**

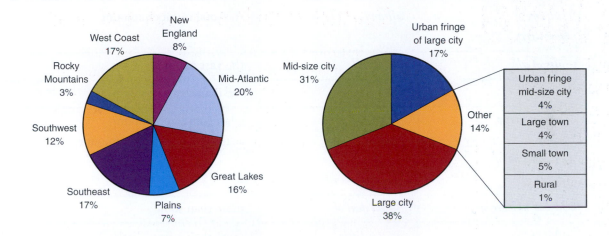

West Coast 17%
New England 8%
Rocky Mountains 3%
Mid-Atlantic 20%
Southwest 12%
Great Lakes 16%
Southeast 17%
Plains 7%

Mid-size city 31%
Urban fringe of large city 17%
Other 14%
Large city 38%

Urban fringe mid-size city 4%
Large town 4%
Small town 5%
Rural 1%

**CHART C: FOREIGN STUDENTS BY ORIGIN**

N. America Oceania 5.5%
Latin America 12.2%
Middle East 5.6%
Europe 13.0%
Africa 6.7%
2003/04
Asia 66.9%

N. America Oceania 5.6%
Latin America 11.7%
Middle East 5.9%
Europe 13.3%
Africa 6.7%
2002/03
Asia 66.6%

form    meaning

## FOCUS 1    Overview of Quantifiers in English

| QUANTIFIERS<br>Listed in decreasing order from all (100%) to none (0%) | | PHRASES OF QUANTITY<br>AND AMOUNT WITH<br>SIMILAR MEANING |
|---|---|---|
| **AFFIRMATIVE QUANTIFIERS** | | |
| Used with<br>count nouns | Used with<br>noncount nouns | |
| *all/any*<br>*each/every* | *all/any* | the total number/amount |
| *almost all* | *almost all* | the vast majority |
| *most* | *most* | the majority |
| *a great many*<br>*many*<br>*lots of/a lot of*<br>*plenty of* | *a great deal of*<br>*much*<br>*lots of/a lot of*<br>*plenty of* | a large number/amount<br>a substantial number/amount |
| *a good number of* | *a good deal of* | more than some |
| *quite a few*<br>*quite a number of* | *quite a little*<br>*quite a bit of* | more than a few/a little |
| *some/any*<br>*a (certain/large/small)*<br>    *number of* | *some/any*<br>*a (certain/large/small)*<br>    *number of* | an indeterminate number or amount |
| *a few several* | *a little* | a small number/amount |

| **NEGATIVE QUANTIFIERS** | | |
|---|---|---|
| Used with<br>count nouns | Used with<br>noncount nouns | |
| *not all/every* | *not all* | an unspecified number are not/do not |
| *not many* | *not much* | a small number/amount |
| *few* | *little* | an insufficient number/amount |
| *hardly any*<br>*almost no/none* | *hardly any*<br>*almost no/none* | the vast majority are not/do not |
| *no/none/not any* | *no/none/not any* | the total number/amount are not/do not |

| EXAMPLES | EXPLANATIONS |
|---|---|
| (a) **Most international students** study business or technical subjects. | You can use quantifiers:<br>• as determiners with noun phrases |
| (b) **A few** study humanities or fine arts. | • in place of noun phrases to describe number or amount |

## EXERCISE 1

**STEP 1** In the following passage, underline the quantifiers and circle the noun phrases they modify. The first sentence has been done for you as an example.

**STEP 2** Are there quantifiers that do not appear with noun phrases? What sentences do they appear in, and what do they refer to?

**Example:** *Clause 1 of the first sentence has a quantifier that does not appear with a noun phrase:* **many**. *It refers to* **people** *or* **experts**.

### Medical Education in the United States

(1) Even though American medical education is considered by many to be the best in the world, (2) there are relatively few spaces in American medical schools, and a substantial number of Americans are forced to go overseas to get their basic medical training. (3) As a result, not all the doctors practicing in the United States have received their training from American medical schools. (4) In fact, quite a few have been educated in other countries. (5) However, all physicians must have clinical experience and pass qualifying examinations in order to receive a license to work in the United States.

(6) Most doctors currently working in the United States have completed their practical training in an American hospital or clinic. (7) Every hospital in this country accepts a few recently graduated medical students each year, (8) including graduates from many foreign medical schools. (9) While some popular hospitals receive a great many applications for each available space, (10) a number of hospitals in rural areas may receive only a few. (11) This period of practical training is called a "residency," and most last for two years. (12) A few are longer; some are shorter, depending on the specialization of the doctor.

(13) Many doctors study for an extra year before they begin their residency in order to become a specialist in a particular area of medicine. (14) No doctor is an expert in every area of medicine, but some doctors have more than one specialty. (15) Each area of medicine has its own period of residency and its own qualifying examinations.

## EXERCISE 2

Based on the information you read in Exercise 1, write sentences that describe the training of medical doctors in the United States. Then write another set of sentences that describe medical training in a second country that you are familiar with.

1. Most doctors . . .
2. Not all doctors . . .
3. All doctors . . .
4. A few doctors . . .
5. No doctors . . .
6. Many doctors . . .

## EXERCISE 3

Use quantifiers to paraphrase the highlighted phrases of quantity or amount.

**Example:** **The vast majority of students** pass their qualifying examination on the first try.

*Almost all students pass their qualifying examination on the first try.*

1. **The vast majority of medical students** in the United States already have bachelor's degrees.
2. **An indeterminate number of students** have more than one major.
3. There are **a small number of scholarships** for international students.
4. It takes **a large amount of money** to fund a university education.
5. **A small number of students** apply to only one university for admission.
6. **An unspecified number of applicants** don't achieve scores that qualify them for university admission on exams such as TOEFL® Test*, GRE, or GMAT.
7. **The majority of international students** apply for admission to more than one university.
8. **A large number of students** study English before they begin their academic studies.

*TOEFL is a registered trademark of the Educational Testing Service (ETS). This publication is not endorsed or approved by ETS.

# FOCUS 2 Affirmative and Negative Quantifiers

| EXAMPLES | EXPLANATIONS |
|---|---|
| (a) Do **all** international students have similar educational backgrounds? <br><br> (b) **Many** have different backgrounds. **Most** have graduated from high school, although **a few** haven't. | Affirmative quantifiers can usually be used in both affirmative and negative statements and questions. |
| (c) NOT: **Few** doctors **don't** have medical degrees. <br><br> (d) BETTER: **Almost all** doctors **have** medical degrees. | Negative quantifiers have a negative meaning, and usually do not occur in sentences with negative verbs. |

Negative quantifiers often imply that the amount or number is insufficient.

| AFFIRMATIVE QUANTIFIERS (A Small Amount) | NEGATIVE QUANTIFIERS (Not Enough) |
|---|---|
| (e) **A few** doctors have studied non-Western medicine. <br><br> (**Some** doctors have studied it.) | (f) **Few** doctors have studied non-Western medicine. <br><br> (**An insufficient number** have studied it.) |
| (g) There's **a little** money left after the bills are paid. <br><br> (There is still **some** money for other things.) | (h) There's **little** money left after the bills are paid. <br><br> (There is **not enough** money for other things.) |

## EXERCISE 4

Decide whether to use *few* or *a few, little,* or *a little*. Compare your answers to those of a partner.

1. The students were discouraged because _____ people passed the examination.

2. Even very good students sometimes have _____ difficulty gaining admission to a good university.

3. I can loan you some money, but I've only got _____ dollars.

4. They were working in the laboratory for so long that now there's _____ time to get ready for the quiz.

5. There are _____ scholarships available for first-year medical students, so a medical education is expensive.

6. He put _____ effort into studying for examinations, and as a result, didn't pass on the first try.

7. The average medical student usually applies to at least _____ places for residency.

8. Bambang had _____ trouble finding a university. Several schools were willing to accept him.

## EXERCISE 5

Using the following negative quantifiers, make true statements about the statistics on international education that you studied in the Opening Task on pages 356–357.

| few | not all | little | hardly any | no |
| --- | --- | --- | --- | --- |

_____

_____

_____

_____

_____

_____

_____

_____

_____

form

| FOCUS 3 | Singular and Plural Quantifiers |
|---|---|

| EXAMPLES | EXPLANATIONS |
|---|---|
| (a) **All doctors know** basic first-aid techniques. **Most have** studied them in medical school. <br><br> (b) **Every doctor knows** basic first-aid techniques. **Each has** studied them in medical school. | Most quantifiers are used with plural count nouns, but a few have a singular form. |
| (c) **Each student was** asked a question. <br><br> (d) **Every student wants** to do **his or her** best in this class. | *Each* and *every* are only used with singular count nouns. |
| (e) **No student has** ever taken this test more than once. <br><br> (f) **No doctors** in this country **are** allowed to practice without a license. | *No* can be used with both singular and plural nouns. |
| (g) When Bambang and Yanti took the TOEFL, **both students** got high scores on **their** first try. <br><br> (h) **Both were** worried about doing poorly on the exam, but **neither has** to take it again. <br><br> (i) They applied to the same two universities; **both universities have** accepted Yanti, and Bambang is willing to go to **either university** that **accepts** him. | *Both, either,* and *neither* are used in situations where there are only two nouns being described. *Both* is considered plural, but *either* and *neither* are considered to be singular. |

## EXERCISE 6

Change these statements with plural count nouns to statements with *any, each,* or *every*. Remember to make any other necessary changes to preserve the meaning of the original sentence. More than one answer may be correct.

**Example:** *All doctors know basic first aid.*

*Every doctor knows basic first aid.*

*Any doctor knows basic first aid.*

1. All doctors must complete their residencies within two years.
2. All parents want their children to succeed in life.
3. Peter spends all free weekends at the beach.
4. All the people who came to the examination brought calculators.
5. A wise student takes advantage of all opportunities to gain practical experience.

## EXERCISE 7

Complete these sentences with true information.

1. Each student in this class . . .
2. Every teacher I have had . . .
3. Any English class . . .
4. No student . . .
5. No teachers . . .

## EXERCISE 8

Use each of the quantifiers *both, either,* and *neither* to make true statements about similarities between each of the following categories.

1. two students in your class
2. two other people that you know
3. you and a good friend

---

| FOCUS 4 | Using Quantifiers with *Of* |

use

Quantifiers usually refer to nonspecific nouns (nouns that describe how many or how much, rather than identifying a specific item). But you can also use quantifiers with specific noun phrases, by adding *of* to the specific noun phrase. (See Unit 19 for more information and practice with specific and nonspecific reference.)

| GENERIC/NONSPECIFIC REFERENCE | SPECIFIC REFERENCE |
|---|---|
| (a) **Any TOEFL practice book** will give you examples of the questions on the test. | (b) **Any of the TOEFL practice books** that our teacher has recommended will give us test-taking strategies. |
| (c) **Most students** want to get good grades. | (d) **Most of the students** whom Donna teaches have college degrees. |
| (e) **Several teachers** have studied overseas. | (f) **Several of the teachers** at this university have studied overseas. |

Note that *all* can be used for generic reference and specific with or without *of*.

(g) **All students** hate to take tests.

(h) **All the students** in this class hate tests.

(i) **All of the students** in this class hate tests.

Note *no* should be used for generic reference and *none of* for specific reference.

(j) **No books** will guarantee a passing score on TOEFL.

(k) **None of the books** that we have studied will guarantee a passing score on TOEFL.

## EXERCISE 9

Decide whether to use a *quantifier* or *quantifier + of* for these sentences.

1. (All) _____ books and notebooks on your desk must be removed before beginning the examination.

2. (Almost all) _____ students are anxious at examination time.

3. (Most) _____ TOEFL practice books contain exercises.

4. You won't need (much) _____ your warm clothing if you go to medical school in the Philippines.

5. (A great deal) _____ the population of China still believes in traditional medicine.

6. (Some) _____ the information in the report about international students studying overseas was incomplete.

7. Bambang doesn't need (any) _____ my help.

8. Bambang wasted (little) _____ the money his parents gave him for books on frivolous things.

9. The students at the café learned that (no/none) _____ classmates failed the test!

use

| | |
|---|---|
| **FOCUS 5** | **Quantifiers: Special Cases** |

| EXAMPLES | EXPLANATIONS |
|---|---|
| (a) How **much** money do you have? | *Much* is used in questions and negative sentences. |
| (b) **Not much**. We'd better stop at the bank and get a little. Are there any banks around here? | |
| (c) I'm having **a lot of** trouble with finding a school. | *A lot (lots) of* is usually preferred in affirmative sentences. |
| (d) NOT: I'm having **much** trouble with finding a school. | |
| (e) **Much of the financial support** for study in the United States comes from the students themselves. | *Much* is **not** usually used in affirmative statements unless it is a specific reference (used with *of*). |
| (f) Is it true that **no students** failed the test? | *No* cannot be used in place of a noun. *None* is used instead. |
| (g) That's correct. **None** did. | |
| (h) Did **every** student pass the exam? | *Every* cannot be used to replace a noun phrase without using *one*. |
| (i) **Yes, every one** did. | |
| (j) NOT: Yes, **every** did. | |

## EXERCISE 10

Using the information in the article in Exercise 1, answer these questions with complete sentences, using quantifiers in place of noun phrases.

**Example:**   Where are most doctors trained?

*Most are trained here in America, but some study medicine overseas.*

1. Do all doctors in the United States have to pass qualifying examinations?

_____

2. How much money does it take to get a medical education in the United States?

_____

3. How much competition is there for admission to American medical schools?

_____

4. How many doctors have more than one specialty?

_____

5. How many residency positions do most medical students apply for?

_____

6. How many Americans study at medical schools overseas?

_____

7. How many foreign students are enrolled in American medical schools?

_____

8. How many doctors are experts in every area of medicine?

_____

### EXERCISE 11

Choose the correct form in these sentences.

1. I feel sorry for Bambang. He's so shy and he has (few/a few/quite a few) friends he can talk to if he has problems.
2. Hardly any people (came/didn't come) to the meeting.
3. Your teacher went to (quite a bit of/a bit of/only a bit of) trouble to get those tickets, so you must remember to thank him.
4. (Not every/Not all/None of) students like to go dancing on Saturday nights.
5. Do you have (many/much/every) time to help me?
6. Sure I do. I've got (a lot/lots of).
7. Why are Bambang and Yanti so sad? (Both/Neither/None) passed the qualifying exam.
8. Learning English takes (several/a certain amount of/any) practice.

---

**form**

| FOCUS 6 | Collective Nouns |
|---------|------------------|

One category of collective nouns refers to groups of people or animals.

| EXAMPLES | | EXPLANATION |
|----------|--|-------------|
| a **troupe** of dancers<br>two **teams** of ball players<br>several **committees** of experts<br>a **delegation** of officials | a **flock** of birds<br>that **herd** of goats<br>**packs** of dogs<br>a **swarm** of insects<br>a **school** of fish | These collective nouns function like other count nouns. You can use them alone or with *of* + *a noun phrase*. They can have both singular or plural forms. |

A second kind of collective nouns refers to social or political categories.

| EXAMPLES | | EXPLANATION |
|---|---|---|
| the government<br>the middle class<br>the media<br>the opposition<br>the arts community | the administration<br>the aristocracy<br>the public<br>the establishment | They always occur with *the*. Their grammatical form is singular:<br>NOT: **a** public, **a** media<br>NOT: the **publics** of the United States |

Although the form of this kind of collective noun is singular, it can be used with either singular or plural verbs and pronouns.

| SINGULAR | PLURAL |
|---|---|
| Using singular verbs and pronouns usually implies that the group operates as a whole. American English tends to use singular forms with singular collective nouns. | Using plural verbs and pronouns focuses on the individual behavior of the members of the group. British English tends to use plural forms with singular collective nouns. |
| (a) The committee of experts **has** decided to release **its** findings next week. | (b) The committee of experts **have** decided to release **their** findings next week. |
| (c) **The aristocracy has** opposed any challenge to **its** economic privileges. | (d) **The aristocracy have** opposed any challenge to **their** economic privileges. |
| (e) **The middle class** in America **has** begun to protest the accelerating decline in **its** standard of living. | (f) **The middle class** in America **have** begun to protest the accelerating decline in **their** standard of living. |

| EXAMPLES | EXPLANATION |
|---|---|
| (g) The beginning class **likes its** teachers to give **it** lots of homework.<br>(h) The beginning class **like their** teachers to give **them** lots of homework.<br>(i) NOT: The beginning class **likes their** teachers to give **them** lots of homework. | Although either singular or plural can be used, it is bad style to change from singular to plural within a single sentence or single reference. |

## EXERCISE 12

In the following sentences, underline each collective noun and any pronouns and verbs which refer to it. Decide why the author chose to consider the collective noun singular or plural.

**Example:**   The French Revolution was caused in part by the refusal of <u>the aristocracy</u> to give up <u>its</u> social privileges.

*Reason: Reference to a single social class—not a collection of individuals.*

1. The victorious team all waved to their supporters while the crowd roared its approval.

2. The media is aware of the important role it plays in American presidential elections.

3. The herd of sheep bleated nervously to its shepherd as a pack of wolves made their way through the forest.

4. The military continues to fight further reductions in its funding.

5. The middle class is facing a greater tax burden than it has ever faced before.

6. A rash of new developments have made a great change in the government's priorities, and it is just beginning to respond to them.

## EXERCISE 13

Decide whether the collective nouns in these sentences should be used with singular or plural verbs and pronouns, and choose the correct form. Although both choices may be grammatically correct, there may be a clear preference for one form instead of the other, so be prepared to explain why you have chosen the forms you did.

1. The staff took a vote about what kind of holiday party (it/they) (want/wants). (It/They) decided to rent a hall and hire a band.

2. The college administration (want/wants) a basketball team that (is/are) able to win enough games to place (itself/themselves) in the final play-offs.

3. The rowing team raised (its/their) oars as (its/their) boat crossed the finish line.

4. The advanced grammar class never like to turn in (its/their) homework right after a long vacation. (It/They) prefer(s) to finish all assignments before (it/they) leave(s) for vacation.

5. The crowd showed (its/their) approval by letting out a deafening roar.

6. The opposition voiced (its/their) disapproval of the policies the government had released in (its/their) latest report, by making more than three dozen speeches in Parliament.

## FOCUS 7  Collective Adjectives

form    meaning

| EXAMPLES | EXPLANATION |
|---|---|
| (a) **The rich** get richer and **the poor** get poorer. | ***The* + adjective** can be used to refer to a group that is defined by a particular characteristic. These structures are plural, and the verbs and pronouns reflect this. |
| (b) These laws are designed to protect **the young** and **the helpless** from exploitation. | |
| (c) **The elderly are** making **their** opinions a growing force in American politics. | |

## EXERCISE 14

Rewrite each *the* + adjective construction below as a noun + relative clause.

**Example:**   The French aristocracy didn't care about the poor.

   *the poor = people who were poor.*

1. A few years ago, Britney Spears was very popular with the young.
2. Dear Abby writes an advice column in the newspaper for the lonely and the confused.
3. Nelson Mandela is an important hero for the oppressed.
4. Bambang and Yanti became doctors so they could help the sick.
5. The government should establish more comprehensive programs to help the underprivileged.

## EXERCISE 15

Are these sentences correct or incorrect? If they are incorrect, identify the problem and correct it.

1. None of doctors are allowed to practice without a license.
2. I watched the flock of birds as it landed in the field across the road.
3. Few students never pass their qualifying exams.
4. The rich is always trying to avoid giving its money to pay taxes.
5. Quite a bit of time that doctors spend in their residencies is clinical training.
6. Students usually apply to several of universities for admission.
7. The herd of sheep was frightened by a pack of wolves, and it bleated nervously in their pen.
8. We had much trouble with the examination this morning.
9. A great many of traditional medicines are still used in rural areas.

# EXERCISE 16

Circle the correct form of the underlined phrases below.

## The Problem of Homelessness in America

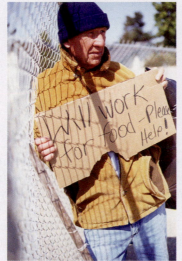

(1) The homeless <u>are/is</u> an increasing problem in most American cities. (2) The homeless <u>consist/consists</u> of several different categories of people. (3) The first category <u>consist/consists</u> of the mentally disabled. (4) In the early 1980s the Reagan administration ended most of <u>its/their</u> funding for treatment programs for the mentally ill. (5) As a result, quite a few mental hospitals were closed, and many of the mentally ill <u>was/were</u> released, and left to make <u>its/their</u> own way. (6) A substantial number <u>have/has</u> been unable to establish normal lives, and, as a result, <u>it/they</u> <u>has/have</u> ended up living on the streets.

(7) A second category of the homeless <u>is/are</u> the unemployed. (8) Typically, the unemployed <u>is/are</u> part of the homeless for a relatively short period of time— usually less than a year. (9) Some of <u>it/them</u> <u>have/has</u> lost <u>its/their</u> jobs; or the factories where <u>it/they</u> worked were closed without warning. (10) As a result, <u>it/they</u> didn't have enough money to pay rent. (11) Many of the unemployed <u>has/have</u> also ended up living on the streets or sleeping in <u>its/their</u> automobiles. (12) But the majority of the people in this category of the homeless <u>is/are</u> able to find housing again, once they have found other jobs.

(13) A third category of the homeless <u>is/are</u> the people who <u>is/are</u> addicted to drugs or alcohol. (14) Like the mentally ill, this category of homelessness <u>represent/represents</u> a persistent social problem. (15) The unemployed can hope for better times, and <u>is/are</u> usually able to escape from poverty and life on the streets, but the government <u>has/have</u> been very slow in giving <u>its/their</u> support to programs that help the mentally disabled or the addicted work on <u>its/their</u> recovery.

# Use Your English

**speaking**

English used to have many different collective nouns to refer to specific animals. These nouns usually indicated a quality or characteristic that these animals had: a *pride* of lions (because lions are proud), a *parliament* of owls (because owls are wise), a *leap* of leopards (because leopards leap)

Such collective words are rarely used in modern English. But sometimes for humorous reasons, people will invent collective words to apply to a particular group of people. Here are some examples: a sweep of cleaning ladies, a hustle of salesmen, a splash of swimmers

Working with a partner, decide on some humorous collective terms for some of these categories of people:

| flight attendants | English teachers | puppies/kittens | accountants |
|---|---|---|---|
| lawyers | magicians | computer programmers | real estate agents |

**ACTIVITY 2** **speaking/writing**

There is a joke that says, "A camel is a horse that was designed by a committee." Some management experts think that committees generate a product that is better than one made by a single individual. Others feel that committees tend to be inefficient and badly organized.

Based on your experience, identify the strengths and weaknesses of working in a committee. What are the advantages (Pro) of having a group work together on a single task? What are the disadvantages (Con)?

**Example: Pro:** *A committee is able to assign tasks to each member, so the work can be divided.*

**Con:** *A committee doesn't reach decisions quickly because each member has to agree about the issue before they can take action.*

First decide how you are going to do this activity. By yourself or in a group? Then decide on at least three advantages and disadvantages and present your ideas to the rest of the class as a list of pros and cons.

## ACTIVITY 3 speaking

Should the rich pay more taxes or higher penalties (for traffic tickets, etc.) than the poor? Why do you think so? Discuss your ideas in a small group, and present a report on your group's opinion to the rest of the class. Your report should use phrases like "Our group feels that . . ."

## ACTIVITY 4 writing/speaking

Have you ever seen a political demonstration? Where and when did it occur? What was the demonstration about? What did the crowd do? What did the police do? Write a description of what happened.

## ACTIVITY 5 speaking

**STEP 1** Conduct a poll of your classmates to find out about their educational backgrounds. How many years of school do they have? What subjects have they studied? Did most of them enjoy school? Decide on two more questions to ask them.

**STEP 2** Present your information by constructing pie charts similar to the ones in the Opening Task of this unit.

## ACTIVITY 6 listening/ writing

Conduct a public opinion poll on some aspect of current events.

**STEP 1** In a group, choose some topic of current interest from the news, and develop a list of five to eight questions to determine how people feel about this issue.

(*Continued on next page*)

- **STEP 2**    Poll your classmates, and also interview ten to fifteen people outside of class.

- **STEP 3**    Devise a graphic representation of your results similar to the charts in the Opening Task of this unit.

- **STEP 4**    Using your charts, make a presentation of your findings to the rest of the class. Report any interesting differences between the opinions of your classmates and the people you interviewed outside of class.

- **STEP 5**    Make a short written report of your findings with your group. Have some members check the information and have others check the grammar.

ACTIVITY 7   listening

- **STEP 1**    Listen to the brief news reports and answer the following questions. You may need to listen to each report more than once.

CD Tracks 33, 34, 35

**Report 1**

1. What happens every year on March 19th?

_____

2. Who provides publicity about this event?

_____

3. Who else arrives on March 19th besides the swallows?

_____

**Report 2**

1. What did the Canadian government ask the committee to do?

_____

2. What is being anxiously awaited by the press and the public?

_____

**Report 3**

1. What is different about the theater company described in this report?

   _____

2. When was it founded?

   _____

3. What effect has the company had?

   _____

■ **STEP 2**    Compare your answers with a classmate's.

 **ACTIVITY 8**    research on the web

 **Option A:** Go to the Internet and find the home pages for several teams of a sport that you are interested in. It could be soccer, American football, baseball, hockey, or basketball, for example. Prepare a brief written or oral report that discusses the sport you have chosen. What are the strengths and weaknesses that most teams have in common? Which ones have a better chance of winning and why? What characteristics make some teams better than others?

**Option B:** Go on the Internet and find the home pages for several famous performing troupes or groups (for example, opera, drama, circus, dance, or orchestra). Prepare a brief written or oral report that identifies what characteristic(s) these troupes have in common that make them famous, and if you feel that reputation is justified.

**ACTIVITY 9**    reflection

Work with one or two other students and make a list of common errors that you hear learners of English making in their conversations. Try to identify some mistakes that all students make, and then mention other English language problems that many students might have trouble with, as well as problems that some have but others might not have trouble with. What is one feature of the English language that none of your classmates find difficult? Prepare a brief written or oral presentation about "The Troublespots of English" using both affirmative and negative quantifiers.

# UNIT 23

# PAST TIME FRAME
## Using Adverbs and Aspect to Indicate Time Relationships

## UNIT GOALS

- Use correct sequence of tenses in past time to indicate time relationships

- Correctly understand and use clauses with *when* and *while* in past time

- Correctly understand and use progressive and perfect aspect in past time

## OPENING TASK
### I'll Never Forget . . .

Everyone has had an unforgettable moment of one kind or another. Write a paragraph or tell a partner about a moment that you will never forget. You can tell about a time when you heard about or experienced an important world event or something more personal in your own life.

**Examples:**

- *I will never forget the moment I heard the newscast about the Berlin Wall being torn down.*
- *I will never forget the day my wife told me that I was going to become a father.*
- *I will never forget the day my father told me that my family wanted me to go overseas for my university education.*

Your description should include what you were doing at the time, what you had been doing, and how you reacted. You may want to read the example on the next page to help you organize your ideas.

I will never forget the day I lost my family in Disneyland. The flight had been a long one and when we finally got there my three kids (and my husband) were so excited. They wanted to go everywhere at once. The kids ran across Main Street to say hello to Mickey Mouse. I thought my husband had gone with them, and I stopped for just a moment to get a drink of water. Suddenly, I heard some loud music and turned around to see what was happening. I saw a marching band, electric floats and many people in costumes marching down the street. As soon as it passed I realized that my kids and my husband had disappeared! I started shouting their names as loudly as I could, but they were nowhere to be seen.

I knew I had to go find my family. I tried to catch up with the parade as quickly as possible. This wasn't easy, because the street was really crowded. I asked one of the cartoon characters if there was a lost children office. He told me where to go and when I got there, I saw several children but not my family. After several minutes, I heard my husband's voice calling my name. Our daughters were with him, but not our son. We finally found him watching a clown show by the Magic Castle. He hadn't even noticed the rest of us weren't with him. Now that we were finally back together, I made all of them promise to stay together, and for a little while the kids were keeping as close to me as they could, but they soon began to run around again. That's the last time I'm taking them to Disneyland until I can tie them together with a piece of rope!

**Overview of Time Relationships in Past Time Frame**

**use**

| EXAMPLES | EXPLANATIONS |
|---|---|
| (a) He **walked** up the stairs. He **turned** the knob, and **opened** the door. | Time relationships in past time can be indicated by: <br><br> • sequence <br> Things happened in the order they are mentioned. |
| (b) **As he entered the room,** he realized something was different. **Before he had a chance to turn around,** he knew something was missing. **In a moment,** he realized what it was. | • adverbial information <br> Adverbial clauses and phrases describe the order in which things happened. |
| (c) The television **had disappeared.** The antenna wires **were hanging** from the wall. He **had been watching** TV a few hours ago, but now there **was** nothing there. | • perfect and progressive aspect <br> Choice of a particular verb tense and aspect describes the order in which things happened. |

### EXERCISE 1

Work with a partner to examine how time relationships are indicated in these passages. Passage 1 has been done for you as an example.

**STEP 1**  List the highlighted verbs in the order that they occurred.

**STEP 2**  Tell how you think that the order was indicated (by sequence, adverbials, or using perfect or progressive verb tenses). Sometimes there is more than one indication. Passage 1 has been done for you on the next page as an example.

Passage 1

I'll never forget the day my apartment got broken into. As I **entered** the room, I **realized** something was different. Before I **had** a chance to turn around, I **knew** something was missing. In a moment, I **realized** what it was. The television **had disappeared.** The antenna wires **were hanging** from the wall. I **had been watching** TV a few hours ago, but now there **was** nothing there.

| STEP 1  WHAT IS THE SEQUENCE OF EVENTS? | STEP 2  HOW IS THE ORDER OF EVENTS INDICATED? |
|---|---|
| 1. I had been watching TV | 1. perfect progressive; adverbial (a few hours ago) aspect |
| 2. the TV had disappeared | 2. perfect aspect |
| 3. the wires were hanging from the wall | 3. progressive aspect |
| 4. there was nothing there | 4. adverbial (now) |
| 5. I entered the room | 5. sequence aspect |
| 6. I realized something was different | 6. sequence aspect |
| 7. I knew something was missing | 7. sequence aspect |
| 8. I had a chance to turn around | 8. adverbial (before) aspect |
| 9. I realized what it was | 9. sequence, adverbial (in a moment) aspect |

**Passage 2**

Jeff will never forget the time the earthquake hit San Francisco. He **was** still in his office. He **had been trying** to finish a project before he left for the day. Suddenly, the building **began** to move. Books **fell** off their shelves. People **were screaming**. Although it seemed as if things were moving for several minutes, the actual time was just fifteen seconds. Even before the building **stopped** moving, people were trying to get out as quickly as possible. This wasn't easy for people who **had been working** on the higher floors of the building. The electricity **had gone off** the moment the earthquake struck, so no elevators **were working**. Most people **ran** down emergency stairs in darkness and **got** out to the street.

**Passage 3**

Detective Smith will never forget the day he made the announcement of his first big arrest. Last Tuesday, **he reported** that he **had uncovered** a large amount of stolen property from a warehouse in the southern part of the city. The warehouse **had been** under surveillance for some time. A suspiciously large number of people **had been seen** going in and out of the building. Once Detective Smith **had obtained** a search warrant, he **entered** the warehouse in the middle of the night and **discovered** large amounts of electronic equipment and other supplies. He **announced** that this discovery **may lead** to the solution of a number of robberies.

## When, While, and Progressive Aspect in Past Time

use

### Using *when*

| EXAMPLES | TIME SEQUENCE | EXPLANATIONS |
|---|---|---|
| (a) When the books **fell** off the shelf, Jeff **hid** under his desk. | First the books fell off the shelf; then Jeff hid under his desk. | If you use *when* to connect two clauses with simple past tense verbs, the action described in the *when*-clause happened before the action in the main clause. |
| (b) When the books **fell** off the shelf, Jeff **was hiding** under his desk. | First Jeff hid under his desk; then the books fell off the shelf. | Use past progressive with the main clause to describe situations where the action described in the main clause happened before the action described by the *when*-clause. |

### Using *while*

| EXAMPLES | EXPLANATIONS |
|---|---|
| (c) While the books **fell** off the shelf, Jeff **hid** under his desk. | *While* indicates that the action was **in progress at the same time** as the action described by the verb in the main clause. |
| (d) While the books **were falling** off the shelf, Jeff **was hiding** under his desk. | We can use either past progressive or simple past, since *while* makes the meaning clear. |

## EXERCISE 2

Answer these questions about the example passage in the Opening Task on page 377.

1. What had the author been doing when she realized her children were missing?
2. What happened to the children when she left to get a drink of water?
3. What was happening in the park when she first couldn't find her children?
4. What did she do when she couldn't find them?
5. What happened when she reached the lost children office?
6. What was her son doing when they found him?
7. What happened when the family finally got together?

## FOCUS 3 · Other Uses of Progressive Aspect

**use**

| EXAMPLES | EXPLANATIONS |
|---|---|
| | Use progressive aspect to express: |
| (a) When my kids disappeared **I was trying** to get a drink of water. | • actions that were in progress or uncompleted |
| (b) As soon as the parade passed I **was constantly calling** out the names of my children. | • actions that were repeated or continuous |
| (c) For the first hour after I found them, my kids **were keeping** as close to me as they could, they soon began to run around again. | • temporary situations |

## EXERCISE 3

Identify all the past progressive verb forms in the example passage of the Opening Task and tell why you think the author chose to use past progressive.

## EXERCISE 4

Circle the appropriate form of the verbs in parentheses. There may be more than one correct choice. The first sentence has been done for you as an example.

---

### The Search for the Northwest Passage

(1) The St. Lawrence Seaway, the waterway that (links /is linking) the Great Lakes of North America with the Atlantic Ocean, was discovered by explorers who (looked /were looking) for the Northwest Passage. (2) Geographers at that time (believed/were believing) that there was a water course that (connected/was connecting) the Atlantic and Pacific oceans. (3) Throughout the sixteenth and early seventeenth centuries, both England and France constantly (sent/were sending) one expedition after another to attempt to find the passage. (4) Early explorers (investigated/were investigating) every large inlet and river along the entire eastern coast of North America.

(5) Even though they never (found/were finding) the Northwest Passage, these early explorers (made/were making) a valuable contribution to the knowledge of North American geography. (6) While they (explored/were exploring) the coast they (made/were making) many other very useful discoveries. (7) Not only the St. Lawrence Seaway, but also Hudson Bay, Chesapeake Bay, the Hudson River, and the Delaware River all (were discovered/were being discovered) by explorers who actually (looked/were looking) for something else.

---

## FOCUS 4 | Using Perfect Aspect in Past Time Frame

**use**

You can use both **adverbials** and **perfect aspect** to indicate that a particular action happened before others.

| ADVERBIALS | PERFECT ASPECT |
|---|---|
| (a) **Before** we left on the trip, we checked the car thoroughly.<br><br>(b) **After** we checked the oil, we made sure the tires had enough air. | (c) But we **hadn't gotten** more than a few miles when we realized that we **had forgotten** something: We **had left** our suitcases on the front porch. We **had been worrying** so much about the mechanical condition of the car that we left without thinking about its contents. |

We don't usually use both adverbials and perfect aspect in the same sentence, and tend to avoid the past perfect tense if the time sequence is clear from other information.

| EXAMPLES | EXPLANATIONS |
|---|---|
| | In general, we indicate time relationships with perfect aspect only when it is necessary: |
| (d) He **had seen** the movie, and **therefore** didn't want to go with us. | • to communicate a logical connection between the two events |
| (e) They **started** the project when **I arrived,** but they **had finished** it when **I left.** | • to clarify a time relationship |
| (f) **I had finished** all my homework before I went to Jane's party. | • to describe an action that was fully completed |
| (g) They **told** me that the doctor **had just left.** | • to change the time frame in reported speech. |

## EXERCISE 5

With a partner, examine how adverbials and aspect are used to indicate time relationships in the following passages.

- For each sentence, identify the verb phrases that happened **before** the verb phrases listed in the first column of the chart, and write them in the "Time Before" column.
- Then decide whether each time relationship is indicated by adverbials, by aspect, or by both. Record that information in the "How Indicated" column.
- Compare your answers with those of another pair of students.

The first two sentences in each passage have been done for you as examples.

1. I'll never forget our horrible vacation. (1) Before we left on the trip, we checked the car thoroughly. (2) After we checked the oil, we made sure the tires had enough air. (3) But we hadn't gotten more than a few miles when we realized that we had forgotten something: We had left our suitcases on the front porch. (4) We had been worrying so much about the mechanical condition of the car that we left without thinking about its contents.

| VERB PHRASE | TIME BEFORE | HOW INDICATED |
|---|---|---|
| 1. we left on the trip | we checked the car | adverb (before) |
| 2. we made sure the tires had enough air | | |
| 3. we realized that . . . | | |
| 4. we left without thinking about its contents | | |

2. European historians will never forget the impact of the Black Plague in the fifteenth century, which brought a new social and economic order to Europe. (1) By the end of the fourteenth century, the population of Europe was about a third smaller than it had been at the beginning of the century. (2) It was one of the few times in history when the population had actually decreased. (3) This smaller population was caused by repeated outbreaks of bubonic plague that had swept through the continent several times during the century, (4) and by the time the century had ended, this disease had caused some fundamental changes in society. (5) So many people had died that the traditional feudal landlords were forced to intermarry with wealthy merchant families instead of the aristocracy. (6) People who had previously only had the opportunity to make a living as farmers or serfs were able to become craftsmen and artisans. (7) The plague had killed so many people that the traditional social boundaries were wiped out, and this created a period of great social mobility and economic change.

| VERB PHRASE | TIME BEFORE | HOW INDICATED |
|---|---|---|
| 1. the population was one third smaller | than it had been at the beginning of the century | adverbial (By the end of the fourteenth century) aspect |
| 2. it was one of the few times in history | | |
| 3. the smaller population was caused by repeated outbreaks of plague | | |
| 4. this disease had caused some fundamental changes in society | | |
| 5. landlords were forced to intermarry with wealthy merchants | | |
| 6. people were able to become craftsmen and artisans | | |
| 7. this created a period of great social mobility and economic change | | |

## EXERCISE 6

Use past perfect in these sentences only if it is necessary to the meaning of the sentence. Otherwise use simple past or past progressive.

1. Peter (a) _____ (went) to talk with Mr. Green about the fight he
   (b) _____ (have) with Denise earlier in the day.

2. As soon as the building (a) _____ (stop moving), Jeff
   (b) _____ (try) to call Matt, but the telephones
   (c) _____ (stop working).

3. It was too late to put out the fire because it _____ (grow) too big for anything to control.

4. I (a) _____ (look) everywhere for my wallet, but I
   (b) _____ (not find) it anywhere. It (c) _____ (disappeared).

5. Denise (a) _____ (go) to Peter's office to complain about his attitude, but he (b) _____ (leave) early to take his children to the circus.

6. Mary (a) _____ (be) extremely worried about John since she
   (b) _____ (not receive) any letters from him in over a month.

---

**FOCUS 5**

## Perfect Progressive Aspect in Past Time Frame

use

| PERFECT PROGRESSIVE ASPECT | PERFECT ASPECT | |
|---|---|---|
| **Continuous:** | **Repeated:** | Use perfect progressive aspect instead of perfect aspect in past time frame to describe actions that are: |
| (a) I'll never forget our unlucky ski-trip. It **had been snowing for three hours**. Unless they cleared the roads soon, it was likely that we would have to spend the night in our car. | (b) I'll never forget our unlucky ski trip. It **had snowed several times** since we arrived, but there still wasn't enough snow for skiing. | • continuous instead of repeated |
| **Uncompleted:** | **Completed:** | • uncompleted instead of completed |
| (c) I'll never forget the weekend I visited my aunt in New York. I **had been visiting** my aunt all morning when she suddenly became quite ill and asked me to drive her to the hospital. | (d) I'll never forget the weekend I visited my aunt in New York. I **had visited** my aunt all morning so I was free to spend the rest of the afternoon at the museum. | |

## EXERCISE 7

Fill in the blanks with the appropriate form of the verbs (past perfect or past perfect progressive) in parentheses.

1. When the earthquake struck, Jeff was still in the office because he _____ (try) to finish a project before he left for the day.

2. Denise _____ (look) for a reason to complain about Peter even before he took time off from work to see his son's school play.

3. By the beginning of the fifteenth century, the bubonic plague _____ (cause) some fundamental social and political changes.

4. The police _____ (keep) the warehouse under surveillance for some time when they finally obtained a search warrant and investigated.

5. They first became suspicious because so many people _____ (go) in and out of the warehouse at strange hours of the day and night.

## EXERCISE 8

Fill in the blanks with the appropriate form of the verbs in parentheses (simple past, past perfect, or past perfect progressive). More than one answer may be correct.

1. I (a) _____ (work) on my homework for about twenty minutes when I (b) _____ (overhear) the TV broadcast announcing Rabin's assassination.

2. Jeff (a) _____ (experience) several minor earthquakes, but he (b) _____ (be) still surprised by the strength of this one.

3. Nancy (a) _____ (be) not really happy with what she (b) _____ (do) so she (c) _____ (decide) to look for another job.

4. European explorers (a) _____ (try) to reach Asia, when they (b) _____ (land) in the New World "by accident."

5. When Jeff (a) _____ (get) to the street, he (b) _____ (see) that hundreds of other people (c) _____ (leave) their offices and (d) _____ (stand) out on the street wondering what to do.

## EXERCISE 9

Fill in the blanks with the correct forms of the verbs in parentheses (present, present perfect, simple past, past perfect, past progressive, or past perfect progressive). There may be more than one correct answer.

George Washington (1) _____ (be) the first President of the United States, and (2) _____ (serve) as the leader of American troops during the War of Independence. According to a famous story, when George (3) _____ (be) a young boy and (4) _____ (learn) how to use farming tools, his father (5) _____ (give) him a hatchet for his birthday. George (6) _____ (be) anxious to use the hatchet, so he (7) _____ (run) out of the house and (8) _____ (chop) down a cherry tree in his father's garden.

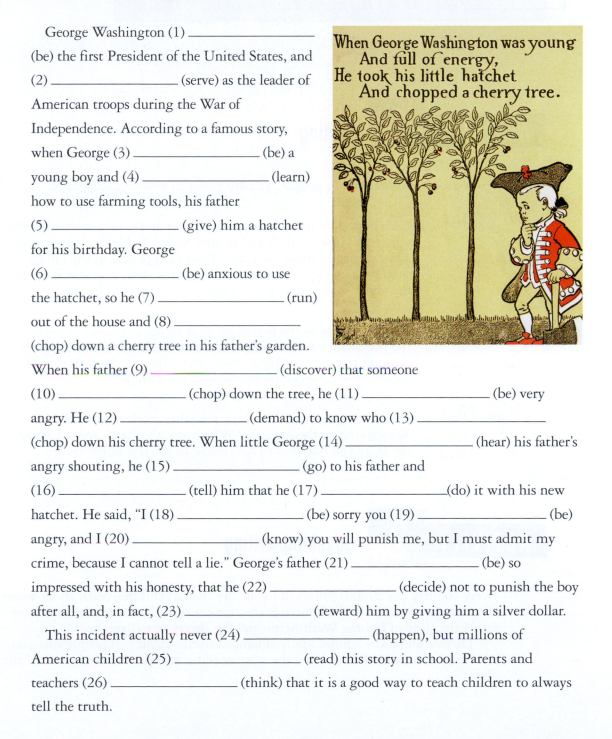

When his father (9) _____ (discover) that someone (10) _____ (chop) down the tree, he (11) _____ (be) very angry. He (12) _____ (demand) to know who (13) _____ (chop) down his cherry tree. When little George (14) _____ (hear) his father's angry shouting, he (15) _____ (go) to his father and (16) _____ (tell) him that he (17) _____ (do) it with his new hatchet. He said, "I (18) _____ (be) sorry you (19) _____ (be) angry, and I (20) _____ (know) you will punish me, but I must admit my crime, because I cannot tell a lie." George's father (21) _____ (be) so impressed with his honesty, that he (22) _____ (decide) not to punish the boy after all, and, in fact, (23) _____ (reward) him by giving him a silver dollar.

This incident actually never (24) _____ (happen), but millions of American children (25) _____ (read) this story in school. Parents and teachers (26) _____ (think) that it is a good way to teach children to always tell the truth.

# Use Your English

**ACTIVITY 1 writing**

Form groups of three to five people. You are going to write a group story.

**STEP 1** Each person should take a piece of paper and start a story with this sentence: "It was a dark and stormy night. Suddenly, (your teacher's name) heard a terrible scream." Then each person in the group should write for three minutes. When the three minutes is up, fold the paper so that only the last sentence or two can be read.

**STEP 2** Pass your story to the person on your right, and take the paper of the person on your left. Then each person should write for three minutes to continue that person's story. Repeat the process until the papers have gone completely around the group.

**STEP 3** Unfold the papers and read the resulting stories to each other. Which story is the funniest? Which story is the clearest? Choose the story you like best to read aloud to the rest of the class.

**ACTIVITY 2 speaking/writing**

Every country has famous stories in its history that all children learn about when they are growing up. In the United States, for example, all school children have heard the story of George Washington and the cherry tree (Exercise 9).

Do you know any similar kinds of famous stories about real people that you were told as a child? Write down the story or tell it to a partner or the rest of the class.

## ACTIVITY 3 listening

CD Track 36

Listen to the story of one person's unforgettable experience and answer the questions below.

1. What was the speaker doing when she heard the news about John F. Kennedy ( JFK)?

   _____

2. What did the speaker do when she heard the news about JFK?

   _____

3. What were her classmates doing when they heard the news about JFK?

   _____

4. What did they do when they heard the news about JFK?

   _____

## ACTIVITY 4 research on the web

Go on the Internet to http://www.infoplease.com and search for "disasters", or use a search engine such as Google® or Yahoo® to find information on past or historical disasters.

Spend some time looking through the Web site and make a report about a historical disaster that occurred in a part of the world you are interested in. Write an "eyewitness" account of the disaster as if you had actually been one of the survivors.

## ACTIVITY 5 reflection

Work with a partner. Read the story of your partner's unforgettable experience that was written for the Opening Task of this unit. Construct a time line of your partner's experience, identifying what he or she had been doing, what they did when the unforgettable thing happened, and what happened afterwards. Make suggestions about how to make the sequence of events clearer by using perfect aspect instead of adverbials. Ask your partner to do the same thing with your story.

# MODALS IN PAST TIME

## UNIT GOALS

- Correctly use *could* versus *was able to* to describe abilities in past time

- Correctly use *would* versus *used to* to describe habitual actions in past time

- Correctly use *would* versus *was going to* to describe future events in past time

## OPENING TASK
### Identifying the Benefits of Growing Older

### ■ STEP 1

**Think about these questions:**

- In what ways are you different than you were in the past?

- What are some things that you used to do but don't do anymore?

- What are some things that you do now, but you couldn't or wouldn't do five or ten years ago?

- How do people change as they grow older?

## STEP 2

Discuss your ideas with two or three other students in the class. Your group should decide on two general ways that people's lives change for the better as they grow older, and present those ideas to the rest of the class. You can read the paragraph below as an example of the kind of changes you may want to consider.

### GROWING OLDER

Growing older makes people less worried about what other people think. In high school I used to be really shy. I would avoid talking to people, and I couldn't express my ideas in class without feeling very uncomfortable. I guess I was afraid that people were going to laugh at me, or that they would think I was strange. In high school people were supposed to "fit in." They weren't allowed to be different. So I used to wear the same kind of clothes and try to behave the same way as everybody else. I felt I had to be "one of the crowd." Now that I am older, I can stand up in front of other people and tell them what I think. I certainly couldn't do that in high school. I wear clothes because I like them, not because other people like them. I think I'm much more independent and self-confident than I used to be in high school.

## Overview of Modals in Past Time Frame

form   meaning

use

| MEANING/ USE | ONE-WORD MODALS | EXAMPLES | PHRASAL MODALS | EXAMPLES |
|---|---|---|---|---|
| necessity | | | *had to* | (a) I **had to** do my homework before my parents would let me watch TV. |
| permission | *(No one-word modals for these uses.)* | | *was allowed to* | (b) I **wasn't allowed to** watch TV until I finished my homework. |
| advice/ obligation | | | *was supposed to* | (c) I **was supposed to** be in bed by 9:00 on school nights. |
| ability | *could* *couldn't* | (d) I **could** spend my summer vacations just playing with my friends. | *was able to* | (e) I **was able to** amuse myself by day dreaming. |
| habitual actions | *would* *wouldn't* | (f) When I was little I **would** pretend I was a pirate. | *used to* | (g) I **used to** be afraid of the dark. |
| future events in past time | *would* *wouldn't* *might* *might not* *(mightn't)* | (h) I hoped that I **would** grow up to be a famous person who **might** become president. | *was going to* *was about to* *was to* | (i) I **was about to** leave for college when I realized how much **I was going to** miss my family. |

## ■■ EXERCISE 1
■■

Decide whether the modals in these sentences are requests in present time or questions about past habits and abilities.

1. Could you tell me how to improve my English?

2. Would you cry when your mother punished you?

3. Could you ride a bicycle when you were 5?

4. Would you mind putting out that cigar?

5. Do you think you could tell that joke without laughing?

6. When you were little, would you always do everything your parents wanted?

form

use

| FOCUS 2 | Expressing Necessity, Permission, and Advisability in the Past Time |
|---------|-----------------------------------------------|

| EXAMPLES | EXPLANATION |
|----------|-------------|
| | Use phrasal modals in the past time frame to describe: |
| (a)  When I was a child, my brothers and sisters and I **had to** do a number of chores. | • necessity |
| (b)  If we didn't, we **weren't allowed to** watch TV. | • permission |
| (c)  I **was supposed to** wash the dishes on Mondays. | • advisability |

## EXERCISE 2

Make five statements about things you **were allowed to do** when you were a child. Make five statements about things you **weren't allowed to do**.

## EXERCISE 3

Work with a partner, and ask if he or she was allowed to do the things you talked about in Exercise 2.

**Example:** *When you were a child, were you allowed to stay out after dark?*

Identify one privilege that was the same for both of you, and report it to the rest of the class.

## EXERCISE 4

Make five statements about things that you **had to do** when you were a child. Make five statements about things that you **were supposed to do** when you were a child but didn't always do.

## EXERCISE 5

Work with a partner, and ask if he or she had to do the things you talked about in Exercise 4.

**Example:** *When you were a child, did you have to come home before dark?*

*When you were a child, were you supposed to do your homework before you could watch TV?*

Identify one responsibility that was the same for both of you, and report it to the rest of the class.

meaning

| FOCUS 3 | Ability in Past Time: *Could* Versus *Was Able To* |
| --- | --- |

| EXAMPLES | EXPLANATIONS |
| --- | --- |
| (a) I **could** amuse myself all summer long.<br>(b) I **was able to** amuse myself all summer long. | In statements of general ability (skills that exist over time), there is no difference in meaning or use between *could* and *was able to*. |
| (c) Jeff **was able to** get two tickets to the concert.<br>(d) NOT: Jeff **could** get two tickets to the concert. | In statements of specific ability (specific events or actions), use *was able to*. |
| (e) Matt stood in line for over an hour, but he **couldn't** get tickets.<br>(f) Matt stood in line for over an hour, but he **wasn't able to** get tickets. | In negative statements of specific ability both *couldn't* and *wasn't able to* can be used. |

## EXERCISE 6

Fill in the blanks with *could* or *be able to*.

**Example:** ___Were you able to go___ to Joan's party?

No, I . __couldn't/wasn't able to__ But I __was able to__ send her a birthday card.

1. Matt (a) _____ get tickets to the concert. However, he (b) _____ (not) find them when it was time to go to the auditorium.

2. Peter (a) _____ convince his boss to let him do anything he wanted. As a result, he (b) _____ stay home from work last week.

3. Professor Katz (a) _____ speak Russian. Because of this, she (b) _____ translate the ambassador's speech to the United Nations last week.

4. Bambang (a) _____ (not) get a high enough score on the TOEFL® Test*, so he enrolled in an English course. He still (b) _____ (not) get the score he needed last semester, but he succeeded this semester.

## EXERCISE 7

1. Which of the following activities were you able to do ten years ago? Use complete sentences to identify things that you could do ten years ago and things that you couldn't do.

ride a bike _____                          run a mile in eight minutes _____

speak fluent English _____                 drive a truck _____

understand American films _____            support my family _____

play a musical instrument _____            shop for food in a foreign country _____

read and write English _____               swim _____

speak a second language _____              play soccer _____

drive a car _____                          translate things into English _____

2. Describe two other things not listed below that you could do ten years ago and two other things that you couldn't do.

---

* TOEFL is a registered trademark of the Educational Testing Service (ETS). This publication is not endorsed or approved by ETS.

### ■ EXERCISE 8

Underline the structures that describe past abilities in these short passages. Why do you think the author decided to use the form he did?

1. (a) Matt stood in line for four hours, but he wasn't able to get tickets for the concert. (b) When he got home, Jeff could tell that he was frustrated and a little angry. (c) He wanted to cheer Matt up, but he couldn't do much to improve Matt's mood.

2. (a) Nigel was a genius. (b) He was able to do many things that other children his age couldn't do. (c) He could solve complicated mathematical equations. (d) He could write poetry and quote Shakespeare. (e) He was even able to get into college when he was only 14 years old. (f) But he couldn't make friends with other children his own age.

---

| FOCUS 4 | Habitual Actions in Past Time: *Would* Versus *Used To* |
|---------|---------------------------------------------------------|

use

| EXAMPLES | EXPLANATIONS |
|----------|--------------|
| (a) I **used to** live in Washington, D.C. <br> (b) Every day I **would** go jogging past all the famous monuments. <br> (c) No matter how hot or cold it was, I **would** run around the Tidal Basin and along the Mall. | Habits and regular activities in the past are described by using *used to* and *would*. *Used to* is often used in the first sentence to establish the topic. *Would* is used in other sentences to supply the details. |
| (d) When I was a child I **would wait** at the bus stop for my father to come home. <br> (e) When I was a child I **used to wait** at the bus stop. | Habitual **activities** can be expressed by both *would* and *used to*. |
| (f) When I was a child I **used to have** lots of toys. <br> (g) When I was a child I **had** lots of toys. <br> (h) NOT: When I was a child I **would have** lots of toys. | Habitual **states** must be expressed by *used to* or simple past tense. We do not use *would*. |

## EXERCISE 9

Below is a list of things many children do.

1. From this list choose five things that you used to do when you were a child.

2. Choose five things that you didn't use to do.

3. Think of three additional examples for each category.

4. Describe these activities in complete sentences. Be sure to use the correct form for verbs that describe habitual states rather than activities. You should create eight sentences describing things you used to do as a child and eight sentences about things you didn't used to do.

| | |
|---|---|
| believe in ghosts | have a secret hiding place |
| be afraid of the dark | play with dolls |
| eat vegetables | like going to the doctor |
| play "cops and robbers" | enjoy going to school |
| pretend to be able to fly | obey older brother or sisters |
| ride a bicycle | cry when hurt |
| spend the night at a friend's house | |

## EXERCISE 10

Work with a partner, and ask questions about the things you described in Exercise 9.

**Example:** *When you were a child, did you ever pretend that you could fly?*

Report some of your partner's answers to the rest of the class.

## FOCUS 5 | Future in Past Time Frame

| EXAMPLES | EXPLANATIONS |
|---|---|
| (a) My parents got married almost fifty years ago. In 1957 my father first met the woman that he **would marry** a few years later. From that very first day my father knew that he **was** eventually **going to marry** her. | The past time frame often includes references to future events. The actual time of these events may be in the past (in relation to **now**), but it is in the future in relation to our moment of focus. The moment of focus in Passage (a) is "that very first day" in 1957. |
| (b) Although Lincoln **wasn't to become** president until 1860, he started running for political offices quite early in his career. At that time he had no idea that he **was going to have** three unsuccessful attempts before he **would** finally **win** his first election. | In passage (b) the moment of focus is when Lincoln "started running for political offices." We use the one-word and phrasal modals for future activity in their past tense forms (*would, was/were going to,* and *was/were to*). See Unit 15 for more practice with these modals in the present and future time frames. |
| (c) Matt used to hope that he someday **would** have a job where he **might** travel around the world. Perhaps he **could** even have a chance to live in another country. | "Past tense" one-word modals (*might, would, could*) of future activity can be used to talk about future events in the past time frame. |

| EXAMPLES | EXPLANATIONS |
|---|---|
| | *Was going to* is preferred over *would*: |
| (d) Elizabeth didn't have much time to get ready for the dance She **was going to** do all her errands in a single afternoon. First she **would** pick up her dress. Then she **would** get her hair done. That **would** leave her the rest of the afternoon to get ready. | • to introduce a topic |
| (e) Yuri didn't want to leave the house. It **was going to** rain any minute. | • to indicate immediate future |
| (f) At first my parents **weren't going to** let me stay up late, but I convinced them to let me do it.<br>(g) Oh, here you are! I **was going to** call you. But now I don't have to.<br>(h) We **were going to** go skiing tomorrow, but there's no snow, so we'll just stay home instead. | • to describe unfulfilled intentions—intended actions that did not actually take place |

## EXERCISE 11

Underline all the modal structures that refer to future events or intentions in these paragraphs. The first sentence of each passage has been done for you as examples.

1. (a) When I was a child I used to dream that I <u>would have</u> a bright future. (b) I thought I was going to be a doctor or a movie star. (c) I would have a university medical degree. (d) I would have a job where I could do what I wanted, and wouldn't have to go to an office every day. (e) I was going to be famous, and I was definitely going to have lots of money. (f) I would have a big house in Hollywood and ten children.

2. (a) Nora <u>was going to spend</u> a month in Japan before she started her new job, which <u>was to begin</u> in six weeks. (b) She was going to fly to Japan last Monday, but a strange thing happened as she was about to leave for the airport. (c) Suddenly she had a strong sensation that she shouldn't get on the plane. (d) She had a strange feeling that there might be an accident or that there would be some other problem. (e) She knew that she could take a flight later in the week, so that's what she decided to do. (f) It's a good thing she did, because the plane she was going to take crashed into the ocean.

## EXERCISE 12

Do these sentences describe unfulfilled intentions or future activities in the past time frame? In sentences that describe future activities, substitute *would* for *was/were going to*.

**Example:** Nora and Jim aren't here right now. They said they **were going to** be studying at the library.

*It describes future activity. They said they would be studying at the library.*

1. I **wasn't going to** mention the money you owe me. But since you brought it up, I guess we should talk about it.

2. My teacher **wasn't going to** postpone the test, so we studied for the entire weekend.

3. The committee organized the refreshments for the party. Mary **was going to** bring cookies. John **was going to** take care of beverages.

4. I'm not finished painting the house. Jim **was going to help,** but I guess he had something else to do.

5. **Were you going to** send me a check? I haven't received it yet.

6. I never thought this party **was going to** be so much fun.

7. We **weren't going to** extend our vacation, but the weather was so nice that we decided to stay for a few more days.

## ■■ EXERCISE 13

Decide which form, *would* or *was/were going to*, should be used in the following sentences. In some cases both answers may be correct.

1. As soon as Charlie heard about Maria's party he decided that he
   (a) _____ (not go). Sophie (b) _____ (be) there, and
   she and Charlie didn't get along. He was afraid that she (c) _____
   (probably want) to tell everyone about how they used to be engaged to be married.

2. Last week Jeff stood in line for five hours to get a ticket to the opera, but he knew it
   was worth the long wait. It (a) _____ (be) a great performance.
   Pavarotti (b) _____ (sing) the part of Falstaff. Jeff had heard him
   before so he was sure it (c) _____ (be) wonderful.

3. Naomi didn't know what to do for her vacation. Perhaps she
   (a) _____ (go) to Mexico. The plane ticket (b) _____
   (be) expensive, but she didn't want to travel by herself on the bus.

4. When I talked to Lin last Sunday night she wasn't planning on getting much sleep.
   Her project was already a week late, and she couldn't ask the professor for another
   extension. She (a) _____ (finish) her assignment, even if she had to
   stay up until dawn. It (b) _____ (not be) easy. She had to finish
   reading *War and Peace* and then write a ten-page paper. She (c) _____
   (probably be) up all night.

5. We performed a very difficult experiment in our chemistry class the other day.
   I was very nervous because we had to put just the right amount of chemicals
   into a solution in order for the reaction to occur. Too much phosphorous
   (a) _____ (cause) the wrong reaction. If there was too little, nothing
   (b) _____ (happen) at all. If I (c) _____ (do) the
   experiment correctly, it (d) _____ (be) necessary to measure very,
   very carefully.

# Use Your English

## ACTIVITY 1 writing/speaking

- **STEP 1** In the Opening Task on page 387 you read about ways in which people change for the better as they grow older. Now think about ways that people change for the worse. Make a list of things that you can no longer do that you used to be able to do. These may be activities or privileges. If you wish, compare your list to those of other students in the class.

- **STEP 2** Write a paragraph or give a short speech to the rest of the class describing one general way that people's lives change for the worse as they grow older. Be sure to provide examples to support your ideas.

## ACTIVITY 2 speaking

In 1989 political changes in Eastern Europe resulted in important changes in worldwide economics, politics, and military alliances. On September 11, 2001, the terrorist attack on the World Trade Center caused similar unexpected changes in world affairs.

What predictions did people make about world events before these changes occurred? What things are happening now that seemed impossible a few years ago? In a small group, develop two lists: *Things people thought were going to happen that no longer seem likely to happen* and *Things that are happening now that people never thought would happen, Present your lists to the rest of the class.*

## ACTIVITY 3 writing

Write a short paragraph about one or more of these topics:

- Bad habits that you used to have, but don't have anymore
- A time when you were going to do something but weren't allowed or weren't able to do it
- How your life has turned out differently from your expectations (things you thought were going to happen that didn't, and vice versa)

# ACTIVITY 4 listening

## STEP 1

CD Track 37

Listen to the short lecture on science fiction and match the predictions listed below to the authors who imagined them, by writing the initials of the author (JV—Jules Verne; HGW—H.G. Wells; GO—George Orwell; or AH—Aldous Huxley) next to the prediction. Then put a check by those predictions which have actually come true, and compare your answers with a partner's.

The government will control all aspects of people's lives. Anyone who tries to disagree with the government will be put in prison.

Many people will own airplanes.

There will be exploration of the moon.

People will be able to travel through time.

Children will be raised in state-run nurseries instead of in individual families.

There will be a single world language.

People will use solar power to get energy.

Aliens from Mars will invade and conquer the Earth but will eventually die from common bacterial infections.

Scientists will discover a way to make people invisible.

People will be watched by police, by hidden cameras, and by microphones.

Children will be born through artificial means.

There will be movies that are so realistic that people will think they are actually happening.

There will only be three or four huge governments, and they will constantly be at war with each other.

The use of mind-altering drugs will be widespread and encouraged by the government.

## STEP 2

Based on the information you learned from the lecture, discuss the following question in a small group and present your opinion and your reasons to the rest of the class. Which writer did the most accurate job of predicting the future?

## ACTIVITY 5 writing/speaking

First think about these questions: How has the social role of women changed? What things were your grandmothers not allowed to do, simply because they were women? What things wouldn't women consider doing fifty years ago that are commonplace today? Then write a paragraph or make a presentation to the rest of the class discussing the five biggest differences between women's lives fifty years ago and today.

## ACTIVITY 6 research on the web

 Go on the Internet and use a search engine such as Google® or Yahoo® to search for "mistaken predictions". You will find a number of articles that talk about events people thought would happen but didn't. Some topics focus on predictions about technological developments or medical breakthroughs that turned out not to have happened. There are even articles that discuss the most common predictions that turned out not to be true. Prepare a brief report that describes three mistaken predictions that interest you. Tell what people thought would happen and what actually happened.

## ACTIVITY 7 reflection

How are you progressing in your English skills?

- Identify three mistakes that you used to make that you don't anymore. (For example: "I used to confuse *confusing* and *confused*.")
- Identify three concepts that you didn't used to be able to express that you now can. (For example: "I didn't used to be able to distinguish hypothetical from real statements.")
- Identify three "compensation" strategies that you used to use that you no longer need. (For example: "I used to avoid passive constructions.")
- Identify three things that you hoped you would be able to do by now that you are still not able to do. (For example: "I had hoped that I would be able to understand everything my roommate says without having to ask him to repeat it.")

Compare your answers with those of two or three other students. Identify common accomplishments and common goals you still want to achieve and report them to the rest of the class.

## UNIT GOALS

- Correctly indicate meaning in statements of indirect quotation and reported speech

- Know when to make necessary changes in verb tenses and reference forms

- Correctly report statements questions and commands when using indirect quotation

- Distinguish between formal and informal patterns of quotation, paraphrase, and reported speech

## OPENING TASK
### What Are They Saying?

Look carefully at this series of pictures. It is a record of a conversation between Jack and Jean.

1.

2.

3.

4.

■ STEP 1

**What do you think these people are talking about? Write down the exact conversation that you think occurred between them.**

Picture 1

Jack: _____

Jean: _____

Jack: _____

**Picture 2**

Jean: _____

Jack: _____

Jean: _____

Jack: _____

**Picture 3**

Jean: _____

Jack: _____

**Picture 4**

Jean: _____

Jack: _____

Jean: _____

Jack: _____

## ■ STEP 2

Compare your conversation with that of another student. Discuss what you thought they were talking about in each picture and why you thought that. Your discussion might be something like this:

> **You:** "In the first picture I thought that Jack was telling Jean that he had something important to tell her."
>
> **Your partner:** "Oh really? I thought that he was trying to introduce himself for the first time. Why did you think he already knew her?"
>
> **You:** "Because they're sitting rather close together."

## ■ STEP 3

Report the three most interesting differences between your two conversations (and your reasons for thinking so) to the rest of the class.

form    meaning

use

## FOCUS 1    Overview of Direct Versus Indirect Quotation

When we report information that was spoken, written, or thought at some time other than the current moment, we can use direct quotation or indirect quotation.

- **Direct quotation** is the **actual words** that were spoken, written or thought. Direct quotation occurs in informal spoken English and appears most commonly in fiction.

- **Indirect quotation** (also referred to as "**reported speech**" when we are reporting spoken language) expresses the **meaning** of what was said or thought or communicated rather than the actual words.

We can use these patterns to describe thoughts, ideas, and feelings of others that were thought but not actually spoken. Indirect quotation is most frequently used by reporters and writers in news reports and nonfiction writing.

| DIRECT QUOTATION | INDIRECT QUOTATION |
|---|---|
| (a) Jack said, "I'm feeling really sick." | (b) Jack said that he was feeling really sick. |
| (c) Jean thought, "I wonder if Jack is OK because he doesn't look well." | (d) Jean wondered if Jack was OK because he didn't look well. |
| (e) A famous historian once wrote, "Western history shows repeated examples of great empires going into decline when uncontrolled military spending exceeds expenditures for other needs." | (f) A famous historian once observed that Western history showed repeated examples of great empires going into decline when uncontrolled military spending exceeded expenditures for other needs. |
| (g) So Jack's all, "Yeah, I guess I'm really sick," and he goes, "Okay I'm going to the doctor right away." | (h) So Jack admitted that he was really sick and promised that he was going to the doctor right away. |

**Direct quotation:** In direct quotation, quotation word order changes depending on whether the quotation is a statement, a question or an imperative. In formal written English we use quotation marks ("...") to indicate direct quotation. When the quotation follows the reporting verb, it is commonly preceded by a comma. In some contexts we can use a colon

| EXAMPLES | EXPLANATIONS |
|---|---|
| (i) The doctor told Jack, "I'm afraid we'll have to do more tests." | Direct quotation of a statement |
| (j) The doctor asked Jack, "Have you been having these headaches for a long time?" | Direct quotation of a question |
| (k) The doctor told Jack, "Take these pills three times a day, and please stop drinking coffee." | Direct quotation of a command or request |

In casual spoken English we use can use reporting words such as *go* or *be like* to indicate direct quotation of something that has been spoken or thought.

| EXAMPLES | EXPLANATIONS |
|---|---|
| (l) The doctor **goes**, "Well, buddy, I'm afraid we'll have to do more tests." | Casual spoken direct quotation of a statement |
| (m) And Jack **was like**, "Oh my gosh, have I got cancer or something?" | Casual spoken direct quotation of a question |
| (n) So the doctor **was all**, "Could you just relax? Put this thermometer in your mouth." | Casual spoken direct quotation of a command or request |

**Indirect Quotation:** In indirect quotation, certain changes need to be made in time frame, reference forms, and word order, depending on whether the quotation is a statement, question, or imperative. These changes are outlined in the rest of this unit.

Underline the indirect quotation patterns in the following passage that tell what the narrator heard or thought. The first one has been done for you as an example.

(1) When I was a child I often wondered <u>where babies come from</u>. (2) My parents always told me that they had found me under a cabbage leaf. (3) I knew that probably wasn't true, since I realized there were lots of new babies in my neighborhood and no cabbage plants at all. (4) For several years I thought my parents had actually bought my younger sister at the hospital. (5) I figured hospitals were places that sold babies to any couple that wanted one. (6) This was because when my mother came back from the hospital after giving birth to my sister, I heard her remind my father that he had to be sure to pay the bill before that week was over. (7) I was a little jealous of my new sister, and I hoped my father would forget to pay and that the hospital would decide to take her back and sell her to someone else. (8) It wasn't until several years later that I found out babies were neither bought nor found.

| FOCUS 2 | Indirect Quotation and Change of Time Frame |
|---|---|

When using indirect quotation, because we are describing something that has already occurred (the speaking, thinking, or reporting), we use past time frame and modal forms of the verb phrases of what we are reporting.

**To refer to present time frame:** Use past verb forms instead of present.

| DIRECT QUOTATION | INDIRECT QUOTATION |
|---|---|
| (a) Jack said, "I'm really sick. I **am having** terrible headaches. I'm **going to try** to see my doctor this afternoon, if I **can get** someone to drive me to her office." | (b) Jack acknowledged that he **was** really sick. He reported that he **was having** terrible headaches and **was going to try** to see his doctor yesterday afternoon, if he **could get** someone to drive him to the doctor's office. |

**To refer to past time frame:** Use past perfect verb forms instead of past.

| DIRECT QUOTATION | INDIRECT QUOTATION |
|---|---|
| (c) Last Tuesday Jean saw Jack. Here is what he said: "My headache **was getting** worse all the time, so **I went** to the doctor yesterday. She **took** my temperature. She **prescribed** some pills. My condition **has improved**, but I still **haven't gone** back to work yet." | (d) When Jean spoke to Jack last Tuesday he told her that his headache **had been getting** worse, so he **had gone** to the doctor the day before, on Monday. She **had prescribed** some pills. Jack felt that his condition **had improved**, but when Jean spoke to him he still **hadn't gone** back to work. |

**Modal forms in indirect quotation:** Use past modal forms instead of present.

| DIRECT QUOTATION | INDIRECT QUOTATION |
|---|---|
| (e) "**I will try** to see my doctor this afternoon, if **I can** get someone to drive me to her office." | (f) He said that he **would try** to see his doctor yesterday afternoon, if he **could** get someone to drive him to the doctor's office. |

| INSTEAD OF: | USE: |
|---|---|
| *may* | *might* |
| *can* | *could* |
| *shall* | *should* |
| *will* | *would* |

## EXERCISE 2

Here is the response Mr. Green made when he talked with Denise. Write a paragraph describing the outcome that reports all his statements. Start your paragraph with *Mr. Green decided that*. . . . Use *Mr. Green suggested that* . . . and *Mr. Green thought that* . . . later in the paragraph.

Mr. Green said, "The personnel officer will be asked to speak to Peter. If Peter can't get to the office on time, he will just have to take an earlier bus. He may not be crazy about getting up at 5:30, but he will have to do it if he wants to keep his job. Personnel won't talk to Peter about the other problems he may be having, though. One of Peter's friends in the office can deal with him directly about his lack of responsibility. Peter probably won't change much, but he may be more willing to listen to the complaints if he can get the information from someone he likes and respects."

## EXERCISE 3

Denise Driven had a meeting with her boss, Mr. Green, to complain about Peter Principle's work in the office. Here are some of the complaints that Denise made about Peter. Report her complaints, using the cue given.

**Example:** "I've been getting more and more annoyed by Peter's behavior."

Denise reported that . . .

*Denise reported that she had been getting more and more annoyed by Peter's behavior.*

1. "Peter needs to be more serious about work."

   Denise felt that . . .

2. "Peter came to work fifteen minutes late for the second time in a month."

   Denise was angry that . . .

3. "Peter is going to leave the office early to see his child perform in a school play."

   She complained that . . .

4. "He is always whistling in the office."

   She didn't like the fact that . . .

5. "He has made rude comments about my personal life."

   She was upset that . . .

## EXERCISE 4

Here are other complaints Denise had about Peter. How do you think she stated her complaints? Use her probable actual words and direct quotation.

**Example:** She reported that she had been getting more and more annoyed by Peter's behavior.

*"I have been getting more and more annoyed by Peter's behavior."*

1. She observed that he didn't always finish projects on time.

2. She pointed out that he told too many jokes at staff meetings.

3. She complained that he refused to come into the office on Saturdays.

4. She reported that he had told her that he was going to miss an important meeting because he had promised to take his children to the circus.

5. She resented that he constantly allowed his personal life to interfere with his work obligations.

## FOCUS 3  Other Reference Changes in Indirect Quotation

In indirect quotation we must change pronoun forms in order to keep the same meaning.

| EXAMPLES | IMPLIED MEANING |
|---|---|
| (a)  Jack said, "**I** am sick." | Jack is sick. |
| (b)  Jack told me that **I** am sick. | I am sick—not Jack. |
| (c)  Jack told me that **he** was sick. | Jack is sick. |

Compare the pronouns in these two passages.

| DIRECT QUOTATION | INDIRECT QUOTATION |
|---|---|
| (d)  Jack told me, "**You** will be happy to know that **my** condition has improved, but **I** still haven't gone back to **my** office yet." | (e)  He said that **I** would be happy to know that **his** condition had improved, but **he** still hadn't gone back to **his** office yet. |

If there is some confusion about what the pronoun or possessive determiner refers to, it may be necessary to substitute the actual noun.

| DIRECT QUOTATION | INDIRECT QUOTATION |
|---|---|
| (f)  Jack said, "I asked **my** brother Peter to bring **his** wife to the party." | (g)  Jack asked **his** brother Peter to bring **his**—**Peter's**—wife to the party. |

You may also need to change demonstratives and adverbials to keep the same meaning.

| DIRECT QUOTATION | INDIRECT QUOTATION |
|---|---|
| (h)  On Saturday Maria said, "Please come **here** for lunch **this afternoon**." | (i)  On Saturday Maria asked me to go **there** for lunch **that afternoon**. |
| (j)  Jack said, "I went to the doctor **yesterday**." | (k)  Jack told me that he had gone to the doctor **(on) the previous day**. |

Here are some examples of other common changes (→) in reference that may be required when reporting with indirect quotation.

| | | | |
|---|---|---|---|
| *this/these* → *that/those* | | *tomorrow* → *the next day* | |
| *here* → *there* | | *two days from today* → *two days from then* | |
| *today/tonight* → *(on) that day/that night* | | *two days ago* → *two days earlier* | |
| *yesterday* → *(on) the day before/the previous day* | | | |

## EXERCISE 5

Peter's co-worker had a conversation with him at the water cooler on Wednesday. The following Monday, he told Denise what Peter had told him. Report the things that Peter told him. Use the cues given.

**Example:** "My kids have an invitation for your kids."

*Peter said that his kids had an invitation for my kids.*

1. "My kids are having a birthday party at my house on Saturday." Peter said.
2. "My kids have invited your kids to come to their party." Peter said.
3. "I've asked my friend to bring her three girls." Peter added.
4. "I've hired a clown to entertain all our kids." Peter announced.
5. "While our kids are watching the clown, my wife and I can prepare the cake and ice cream for your kids." Peter predicted.
6. "I asked Denise's secretary to tell her about the party, because she wanted me to work all weekend." Peter mentioned.
7. "My family is more important to me than Denise's project." Peter admitted.

## EXERCISE 6

Answer these questions using the information found in the direct quotations. Use indirect quotations in your answers.

**Example:** Ali told me: "I came here to get some groceries, but the store's closed until tomorrow."

Why didn't Ali buy groceries while he was out? *Ali said that he had gone there to get some groceries, but the store was closed until the next day.*

1. Peter told me, "I am coming to the meeting this afternoon."

   Do you know if Peter is planning to be at this meeting?

2. Mary said, "My father may be able to take this letter directly to the Immigration Office later today."

   When you saw Mary last week who did she say was going to take the letter and when would it get there?

3. Bambang announced, "I have already completed all the assignments I have for my classes this week."

   How come Bambang was playing video games on Wednesday night?

4. The doctor said, "The results of your test will be here by tomorrow morning."

   What did the doctor tell you the day before yesterday?

## FOCUS 4 — When No Tense Changes Are Required in Indirect Quotation

In certain situations, English speakers do not always make the tense and modal changes we have practiced here. These situations occur when we are reporting in the following categories:

| CATEGORY | DIRECT QUOTATION | INDIRECT QUOTATION |
|---|---|---|
| • things that are always true | (a) My father always used to say, "Time **is** money." | (b) My father always believed that time **is** money. |
| • things that are still true | (c) Jean told me, "Jack **is still living** with his parents after all these years." | (d) Jean observed (that) Jack **is still living** with his parents after all these years. |
| • hypothetical statements | (e) Peter said, "If I **had** the money, I **would make** a donation to the club, but I **am** a little short on cash this month." | (f) Peter admitted that if he **had** the money, he **would make** a donation to the club, but that he **is/was** a little short on cash this/last month. |
| • statements that were made only a very short time ago | (g) Bambang told me, "I **can't** understand a word you're saying." | (h) He **just** said that he **can't** understand a word **I'm** saying. |
| • future events that have not yet occurred | (i) Diane said, "I **am going** to Hawaii next month." | (j) Diane announced that she **is going** to Hawaii next month. |
| • casual speech using direct quotation with such words as *be all, be like, go,* etc. | (k) Jack was all, "This doctor's bill is way too expensive." | (l) So Jack said this doctor's bill is way too expensive. |

## EXERCISE 7

Decide whether tense changes are required in the following sentences when they are stated as indirect quotation. If a tense change is not required, state the reason. Example: Shakespeare once observed, "Love is blind." *No change. Timeless truth—still true*

1. A student in my geography class reported, "Not all the people who live in China speak Chinese as their first language."

2. My brother told me, "I wouldn't need to borrow money from you all the time if I had a better paying job."

3. It was only a minute ago that I asked, "Are you paying attention?"

4. Jeff told Matt, "I couldn't get any tickets for the concert."

5. Yesterday Denise said, "If I were you, I would plan things a little more completely before you leave for vacation next week."

## FOCUS 5 — Reporting Verbs and Indirect Quotation

Many reporting verbs used for indirect quotation have restrictions about what other information must be included.

| | |
|---|---|
| (a) Jack **admitted that** he should have gone to the doctor before his symptoms got so bad. | Many reporting verbs are followed by *that* clauses. Verbs in this category include: *admit, announce, comment, complain, confess, explain, indicate, insist, mention, point out, remark, reply, report, said, shout, state, swear, whisper.* That can usually be omitted without loss of meaning. These verbs are not used with indirect objects. |
| (b) The doctor **explained (that)** Jack had to take the medicine for a full two weeks, even if he began to feel better. | |
| (c) Jack **replied** he would. | |
| (d) The doctor **assured Jack that** he would start to feel better soon. | Some reporting verbs require an indirect object to precede the *that* clause. Verbs in this category include *tell, assure, convince, inform, notify, persuade, remind.* Many of these verbs can also be used with infinitive constructions, and verbs of this sort follow Pattern 2 (verb + infinitive constructions). (See Unit 6, Focus 5 and Appendix 3 for a review of these forms.) |
| (e) Jean **reminded Jack that** he needed to take his pills with plenty of water. | |
| (f) Jean **reminded Jack to take** his pills on an empty stomach. | |
| (g) Jack **promised (the doctor) (that)** he would take the pills until they were finished. | Other reporting verbs can be used with or without indirect objects before the *that* clause. Verbs in this category include *advise, answer, ask, promise.* |
| (h) The students **asked the teacher** to give them the answer. | |
| (i) The students **asked that** the test be postponed until next week. | |
| (j) The doctor **recommended that Jack take** the pills before bedtime. | Some verbs of urging require the subjunctive *that* clause. (See Unit 18, Focus 5 for more information on these verbs.) |

## EXERCISE 8

Most of these sentences are incorrect. Identify the problem and rewrite them so that they are grammatical. Some of the sentences are correct. Which ones are they?

1. Peter admitted Mr. Green he and Denise didn't get along.

2. Mr. Green told he wanted both of them to try harder to cooperate.

3. He asked that they work together on another project.

4. He explained them how important the project was.

5. Mr. Green insisted them to work together.

6. He convinced them that working together would be beneficial.

## FOCUS 6  Word Order and Indirect Quotation

In indirect quotation, different word order is used for reporting statements, questions, and imperatives.

| EXAMPLES | EXPLANATIONS |
|---|---|
| (a) The doctor told Jack (**that**) he was afraid they would have to do more tests. | *That* introduces reported statements. *That* is often omitted in informal contexts and conversation. |

Questions in indirect quotation require changes in word order: Indirect quotation uses statement word order, whether it is reporting a statement or a question.

| DIRECT QUOTATION | INDIRECT QUOTATION |
|---|---|
| (b) "Am I late?" | (c) Peter asked **if he was late**. |
| (d) "Do you need money?" | (e) Jean wanted to know **whether I needed money**. |
| (f) "How much do you need?" | (g) She asked **how much I needed**. |

**Adding question markers:** We use different patterns depending on whether the question being asked is a *yes/no* question or *wh*-question.

| EXAMPLES | EXPLANATIONS |
|---|---|
| (h) Mr. Green wanted to know **if** Denise could bring her notes to the meeting. | ***Yes/no* questions:** We can use either *if* or *whether (or not)* to report *yes/no* questions. *If* is preferred for *yes/no* questions. |
| (i) He wanted to know **whether** she could bring her notes to the meeting. | |
| (j) He wanted to know **whether or not** she could bring her notes to the meeting. | |
| (k) I applied for a job. They wanted to know **where I had worked, when I worked there, how many years of experience I had**, and **what kind of previous experience I had had** in sales. | ***Wh*-Questions:** We use a *wh*-question word to report *wh*-questions. |

**Embedded questions:**

| | |
|---|---|
| (l) Can you tell me **what your zip code is?** | Direct *yes/no* and *wh*-questions sound more polite if they are embedded in a conversational frame such as "Do you know . . . ," or "Can you tell me . . . ," or "I wonder . . . ." It is not necessary to change the tense of the questions from present to past. |
| (m) Do you know **what time the store opens?** | |
| (n) I wonder **if Dr. Tang is able to come to the phone.** | |

## EXERCISE 9

Here is a list of interview questions that were common in American businesses thirty or forty years ago. Some of them are no longer asked by employers these days. In some cases the law prohibits asking such questions.

Restate the questions as statements about old-fashioned hiring practices by adding such reporting phrases as "A number of years ago employers used to ask . . . ," "They wanted to know . . . ," "They often asked prospective employees to tell them . . . ," and other similar phrases you can think of.

Which questions do you think are still being used?

1. Are you married or single?
2. Does your wife work outside the home?
3. How many children do you have?
4. Are you a Communist?
5. Do you go to church?
6. How old are you?
7. Why do you want to work for this company?
8. Do you use drugs?
9. What is your racial background?
10. How much experience do you have?

## EXERCISE 10

Change this report of a job interview into the list of questions that the interviewer actually asked. The one underlined is done for you.

**Example:** *Where did you graduate from high school?*

Bob applied for a summer job as a computer programmer in a large company. (2) The head of the Personnel Office interviewed him. (3) <u>She wanted to know where he had graduated from high school</u>, and if he had ever studied in a college or university. (4) She wanted to know if he had ever been arrested, or whether he had ever needed to borrow money in order to pay off credit card purchases. (5) She wanted to know how fast he could type and what kind of experience he had had with computers, and whether he was more proficient in COBOL or BASIC. (6) She asked him what companies he had worked for in the past. (7) She wanted to know what his previous salary had been. (8) She wanted to know why he was no longer working at his previous job. (9) She asked him if he would voluntarily take a drug test. (10) He began to wonder if he really wanted to work for a company that wanted to know so much about his private life.

## EXERCISE 11

Make these direct questions more polite by making them embedded questions using phrases such as "Do you know," "Can you tell me," or "I wonder."

1. What time does the test begin?
2. Is the bookstore open yet?
3. Can Peter come with us to the party?
4. How do I get to Carnegie Hall?
5. Where can I find a cheap apartment?

# Commands and Requests in Indirect Quotation

**use**

| EXAMPLES | EXPLANATIONS |
|---|---|
| (a) Doctor to patient: "Take these pills."<br>(b) The doctor **told me to take** these pills. | To report commands, use verbs like *tell* or *order* + infinitive. Many other reporting verbs of this sort follow Pattern 2 (verb + infinitive constructions). See Unit 6, Focus 5 and Appendix 3 for a review of these forms. |
| (c) Jack: "Can you help?"<br>(d) Jack **asked Jean to help** with the dishes. | To report requests or invitations, use verbs such as *ask* or *invite* + infinitive. |
| (e) The doctor told me **not to stay** up late or sit in a cold place.<br>(f) Jack asked Jean **not to expect** him at the party. | Negative commands and requests are reported with *not* + infinitive. |

## EXERCISE 12

Rewrite these indirect commands and requests as direct quotations.

**Example:** On his first day in the army, Kilroy was told to report to the drill field by the master sergeant.

*The master sergeant told Kilroy, "Report to the drill field."*

1. Another officer assigned him to clean the area for nearly an hour.

2. The officers ordered all the new recruits not to talk to each other.

3. They were told to stand at attention until their papers had been processed.

4. Kilroy asked to go to the bathroom, but this request was denied.

5. Finally the processing was over, and they were ordered to return to their barracks.

6. Several other recruits invited Kilroy to join them in a game of cards.

7. He told them he was too tired, and asked them not to be too noisy since he wanted to sleep.

# Use Your English

**ACTIVITY 1** speaking/writing

Work with a different partner from the one with whom you worked on the Opening Task. Together, write a conversation that matches the photos in the Opening Task. Act out your conversation for the rest of the class. Other students should write a paraphrase of your conversation using reported speech.

**ACTIVITY 2** listening/speaking/writing

Listen to a news broadcast on television. Report one story that you heard on that broadcast to the rest of the class. Start with some sort of statement like this: *I heard on the news that . . ., It was announced that . . .,* etc.

**ACTIVITY 3** listening/speaking

Play a game of "*Telephone.*" Here's how to play:

Form two or more teams of ten people each. Student 1 should make a statement to Student 2 very quietly, so that only Student 2 can hear what was said. Student 2 then reports what was said to Student 3 using reported speech (*Student 1 told me that . . .*). Student 3 tells Student 4 and so forth. When the last student receives the report, he or she should announce the message to the rest of the class. Compare how close that message is with what was originally said by Student 1. The team that has the closest and most accurate report wins a point. Student 2 starts the next round.

**ACTIVITY 4** writing

Write a paragraph discussing some of the misconceptions about life that you had when you were a child. Describe what you thought, and why you thought it. See Exercise 1 on page 404 for an example.

## ACTIVITY  5   writing

Tell about a time when you had an important conversation with someone. Perhaps you learned some important information about yourself or someone else. Perhaps you found out about a decision that had a big effect on your life in some way. Perhaps you got some valuable advice.

■ **STEP 1**    First, tell the **story** of the conversation. Write down who it was with and where and when it took place. Then try to write the conversation word-for-word.

■ **STEP 2**    Next, write a paragraph telling what you learned from this conversation, and why it was important for you. You may want to begin your paragraph with *When I was . . . , I learned that. . . .*

## ACTIVITY 6   listening

CD Track 38

Based on the short news broadcast you hear, complete the following sentences with the actual words that were probably used by the speaker.

1. The Police Department representative announced, "_____ "

2. He admitted, "_____ "

3. He predicted, "_____ "

Use the sentences you have written to perform the announcement.

## ACTIVITY 7   research on the web

Go onto the Web and use an Internet search engine such as Google® or Yahoo® to research a common illness or physical complaint that is of interest to you. It could be something like "the common cold" or "asthma" or even "dry skin" or something that you might possibly consult a doctor about (like "losing weight" or "better sleep").

    Visit three or four Web sites and summarize the recommendations you find there; imagine that you got these recommendations from a doctor and report to the rest of the class what the "Web doctor" told you to do.

## ACTIVITY 8 — speaking

To *eavesdrop* means to secretly listen to someone else's conversation. Go to a public place, like a restaurant, a shopping mall, or a bus station, and eavesdrop on someone's conversation. It's important not to let people know what you're doing, so pretend to read a book, study your English grammar, read a magazine in another language (people might think that you don't understand English), or pretend to write a letter.

■ **STEP 1**      Report what the people were talking about, and tell or write two or three things that they said to each other.

■ **STEP 2**      What reporting words did you hear people use? Did the people you listened to use casual direct quotation ("So he goes…" "I'm like…") ?

■ **STEP 3**      Report three interesting things about their lives, or about English, that you learned as a result of this experience.

## ACTIVITY 9 — reflection

Form a group with three other students. Discuss strategies that you use or could use to learn all the different forms that indirect quotation takes in English. Report to another group the strategies that came up in your group and say whose strategy it was.

**Example:** *Marco said that he memorized the different forms of modal verbs in the present and in the past.*

# APPENDICES

## Appendix 1A

**Present Time Frame:** Use Present Time to talk about general relationships. Most scientific and technical writing is in Present Time. Anything that is related to the present moment is expressed by Present Time, so newspaper headlines, news stories, and spoken conversations, jokes, and informal narratives are often in Present Time.

| FORM | MEANING | USE | EXAMPLE |
|---|---|---|---|
| SIMPLE PRESENT<br>*I/you/we/they* +<br>simple form of verb<br>*he/she/it* + *-s* form<br>of verb | true in the past,<br>present and future | general relationships<br>and timeless truths<br>permanent states<br><br><br>habitual and<br>recurring actions | (a) Time **changes** the way people live.<br>(b) Bob **has** two brothers and one sister.<br>(c) Bob **works** in the library every afternoon. |
| PRESENT PROGRESSIVE<br>*am/is/are* + present<br>participle<br>(verb + *-ing*) | already in progress<br>now or around this<br>time | actions in progress<br><br>repetition or<br>duration<br><br>temporary states<br>and actions<br><br>uncompleted<br>actions | (d) Bob **is studying** for a midterm at this moment.<br>(e) Bob **is taking** a biology class this semester.<br>(f) Bob's brother **is living** with his father for the summer.<br>(g) **He is** still **looking** for a cheap apartment. |

| FORM | MEANING | USE | EXAMPLE |
|---|---|---|---|
| PRESENT PERFECT *have/has* + past participle (verb + *-ed* or past participle of irregular verbs) | began, in the past but related in some way to the present | past events related to now by time<br><br>past events related to now by logical relationship | (h) Bob **has visited** Canada twice, so he won't join the tour to Quebec.<br>(i) Bob **has gotten** very good at the computer, so he doesn't need to take another class. |
| PRESENT PERFECT PROGRESSIVE *have/has* + *been* + present participle (verb + *-ing*) | in progress before and including the present | repeated and/or continuous actions | (j) Bob **has been spending** his weekends at home since he started living in the dorm.<br>(k) Bob **has been singing** in a chorus ever since he was in high school. |

## Appendix 1B

**Past Time Frame:** Use Past Time to talk about things that are not directly connected to the present moment. Most fiction, historical accounts, and factual descriptions of past events are in Past Time.

| FORM | MEANING | USE | EXAMPLE |
|---|---|---|---|
| SIMPLE PAST verb + *-ed* or irregular past form | at a certain time in the past | states or general relationships that were true in the past<br><br>habitual or recurrent actions that took place in the past<br><br>specific events that took place in the past | (a) Tuberculosis **was** a common cause of death 50 years ago.<br>(b) Robert Lee **worked** 12 hours a day for low wages.<br>(c) Robert Lee **went** to work in a factory at age 14. |

| FORM | MEANING | USE | EXAMPLE |
|---|---|---|---|
| **PAST PROGRESSIVE** *was/were* + present participle (verb + *-ing*) | in progress at a certain time in the past | interrupted actions<br><br>repeated actions and actions over time | (d) Robert **was studying** in high school when his father died.<br>(e) Robert **was** always **trying** to get promotions at the factory. |
| **PAST PERFECT** *had* + past participle (verb + *-ed* or past participle of irregular verbs) | before a certain time in the past | actions or states that took place before other events in the past | (f) His father **had been** dead for several weeks when Robert quit school and started working to help his mother. |
| **PAST PERFECT PROGRESSIVE** *had been* + present participle (verb + *-ing)* | in progress until a certain time in the past | continuous versus repeated actions<br><br>uncompleted versus completed actions | (g) Robert **had been working** for 12 hours when the foreman told him to go home.<br>(h) Robert **had been hoping** to complete school when he had to find a job to help his family. |

## Appendix 1C

**Future Time Frame:** Use Future Time for anything that is scheduled to happen or predicted to happen in the future. Notice that two tenses (simple present and present progressive) that are used in Present Time Frame can also be used to talk about future plans or scheduled events.

| FORM | MEANING | USE | EXAMPLE |
|---|---|---|---|
| SIMPLE PRESENT | already scheduled or expected in the future | schedules | (a) The plane **leaves** at 6:30 tomorrow. |
| PRESENT PROGRESSIVE | | definite future plans | (b) **I am spending** next summer in France. |
| SIMPLE FUTURE one-word (*will/might/etc.*) or phrasal modals (*be going to*) + simple verb | at a certain time in the future | predictions about future situations | (c) Roberta is **going to take** a vacation on the moon. (d) She **will** probably **get** there by space shuttle, and she **might stay** on an observation platform. |
| FUTURE PROGRESSIVE future modal + *be* + verb + *-ing* | in progress at a certain time in the future | future events in progress | (e) 100 years from now Roberta **will be living** on the moon. |
| FUTURE PERFECT modal + *have* + past participle (verb + *-ed* or past participle of irregular verbs) | before a certain time in the future | events happening before other future events | (f) Scientists **will have visited** the moon long **before** tourists **will be** able to. |
| FUTURE PERFECT PROGRESSIVE modal + *have* + *been* + verb + *-ing* | in progress until a certain time in the future | repeated and/or continuous actions | (g) When Roberta retires on Earth she will probably not be used to the earth's level of gravity because she **will have been living** on the moon for several years. |

# APPENDIX 2  Passive Verb Forms

| ASPECT: | SIMPLE | PROGRESSIVE | PERFECT | PERFECT PROGRESSIVE* |
|---|---|---|---|---|
| TIME: Present | TENSES: is/are studied<br><br>is/are given | am/is/are being studied<br>am/is/are being given | has/have been studied<br>has/have been given | has/have been being studied<br>has/have been being given |
| Past | was/were studied<br><br>was/were given | was/were being studied<br>was/were being given | had been studied<br><br>had been given | had been being studied<br><br>had been being given |
| Future | will be studied<br><br>will be given | will be being studied<br>will be being given | will have been studied<br>will have been given | will have been being studied<br>will have been being given |

* Although perfect progressive passive forms are theoretically possible in English, such forms are **very** rarely found in speech or writing.

# APPENDIX 3   Overview of Verbs Followed by Infinitives and Gerunds

## VERB PATTERNS THAT ARE FOLLOWED BY INFINITIVES

| | |
|---|---|
| **(a)** Norman **decided to specialize** in African stamps when a friend **offered to give** him some stamps from Ghana. | Pattern 1:<br>verb + infinitive |
| **(b)** A friend **advised Norman to order** rare stamps from commercial companies, and **encouraged him to be** persistent. | Pattern 2:<br>verb + noun phrase + infinitive |
| **(c)** Norman **likes to send** stamps to other people and also **likes other people to send** stamps to him. | Pattern 3:<br>verb (+ noun phrase) + infinitive |

## VERB PATTERNS THAT ARE FOLLOWED BY GERUNDS

| | |
|---|---|
| **(a)** Charlie **can't help falling** in love with a new woman every week.<br>**(b)** The doctor told me that I've got to **quit smoking**. | Pattern 1:<br>verb gerund |
| **(c)** Doctors **advise reducing** fats in one's diet. (It's good advice for everyone.)<br>**(d)** The doctor **advised me to reduce** fats in my diet. (She gave this advice to me specifically.) | Pattern 2:<br>verb $\begin{cases} + \text{gerund} \\ + \text{noun pharse} \\ + \text{infinitive} \end{cases}$ |
| **(e)** I **don't mind sleeping** late when I get the chance, and I **don't mind** other people **doing** it either. | Pattern 3:<br>verb (+ noun phrase) + gerund |

## VERBS THAT ARE FOLLOWED BY INFINITIVES

| Pattern 1 | Pattern 2 | Pattern 3 |
| --- | --- | --- |
| appear | advise | expect |
| refuse | remind | arrange |
| seem | persuade | want |
| agree | urge | intend |
| claim | encourage | consent |
| care | convince | ask |
| deserve | force | need |
| decide | forbid | |
| demand | command | |
| pretend | order | |
| hesitate | allow | |
| offer | permit | |
| tend | invite | |
| learn | trust | |
| neglect | cause | |
| wait | tell | |
| | warn | |
| | teach | |
| | hire | |

## VERBS THAT ARE FOLLOWED BY GERUNDS

| Pattern 1 | Pattern 2 | Pattern 3 |
| --- | --- | --- |
| can't help | advise | appreciate |
| keep on | encourage | anticipate |
| recommend | urge | dislike |
| suggest | forbid | don't mind |
| deny | allow | enjoy |
| consider | permit | resent |
| admit | invite | consider |
| give up | cause | delay |
| avoid | teach | postpone |
| quit | | excuse |
| practice | | imagine |
| include | | miss |
| resist | | tolerate |
| | | understand |

| MEANING CATEGORIES | BEGINNING OF THE CLAUSE | MIDDLE OF THE CLAUSE | END OF THE CLAUSE |
|---|---|---|---|
| ADDITION | *additionally*<br>*also*<br>*in addition* | *also*<br>*in addition* | *also*<br>*in addition*<br>*too as well* |
| EMPHASIS/ INTENSIFYING | *actually*<br>*as a matter of fact*<br>*besides*<br>*furthermore*<br>*indeed*<br>*in fact*<br>*moreover* | *actually*<br>*as a matter of fact*<br>*furthermore*<br>*indeed*<br>*in fact*<br>*moreover* | *as a matter of fact*<br>*indeed*<br>*in fact* |
| CONTRAST | *despite this*<br>*however*<br>*on the other hand* | *however*<br>*on the other hand* | *despite this*<br>*however*<br>*on the other hand* |
| CONCESSION | *despite this*<br>*even so*<br>*in spite of the fact*<br>*nonetheless* | *nonetheless* | *despite this*<br>*even so*<br>*in spite of the fact*<br>*nonetheless*<br>*regardless*<br>*though* |
| REASON | *with this in mind*<br>*for this reason*<br>*therefore* | *therefore* | *therefore*<br>*with this in mind*<br>*for this reason* |
| RESULT | *accordingly*<br>*as a result*<br>*consequently*<br>*thus* | *accordingly*<br>*as a result*<br>*consequently*<br>*therefore*<br>*thus* | *accordingly*<br>*as a result*<br>*consequently* |
| CONDITION | *providing*<br>*if*<br>*then*<br>*under such circumstances* | | *under such circumstances* |
| | *next*<br>*then*<br>*first, second, etc.* | *and*<br>*next*<br>*then*<br>*first, second, etc.* | *next*<br>*first, second, etc.* |

## APPENDIX 5 The Basic Rule for Choosing the Correct Form of the Article

1. What is the form of the noun? Noncount or count? Singular or plural?
2. Is the noun used to make a generic reference or particular reference?
   Does it describe a class of things or does it refer to a particular item?
3. If it refers to a particular thing, is the reference specific or nonspecific?

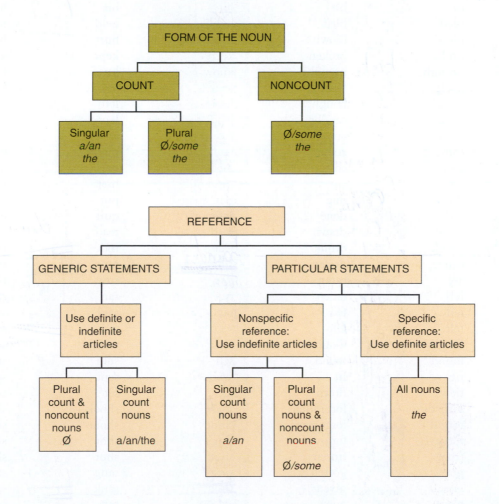

| SIMPLE FORM | PAST TENSE FORM | PAST PARTICIPLE | SIMPLE FORM | PAST TENSE FORM | PAST PARTICIPLE |
|---|---|---|---|---|---|
| become | became | become | grow | grew | grown |
| begin | began | begun | hang | hung | hung |
| bend | bent | bent | have | had | had |
| bet | bet | bet | hear | heard | heard |
| bind | bound | bound | hide | hid | hidden |
| bite | bit | bit | hit | hit | hit |
| bleed | bled | bled | hold | held | held |
| blow | blew | blown | hurt | hurt | hurt |
| break | broke | broken | keep | kept | kept |
| bring | brought | brought | know | knew | known |
| build | built | built | lead | led | led |
| buy | bought | bought | leave | left | left |
| catch | caught | caught | lend | lent | lent |
| choose | chose | chosen | let | let | let |
| come | came | come | make | made | made |
| cost | cost | cost | mean | meant | meant |
| cut | cut | cut | meet | met | met |
| dig | dug | dug | put | put | put |
| do | did | done | quit | quit | quit |
| draw | drew | drawn | read | read | read |
| drink | drank | drunk | ride | rode | ridden |
| drive | drove | driven | ring | rang | rung |
| eat | ate | eaten | rise | rose | risen |
| fall | fell | fallen | run | ran | run |
| feed | fed | fed | say | said | said |
| feel | felt | felt | see | saw | seen |
| fight | fought | fought | seek | sought | sought |
| find | found | found | sell | sold | sold |
| fit | fit | fit | send | sent | sent |
| fly | flew | flown | set | set | set |
| forbid | forbade | forbidden | shake | shook | shaken |
| forget | forgot | forgotten | shine | shone | shone |
| forgive | forgave | forgiven | shoot | shot | shot |
| freeze | froze | frozen | shut | shut | shut |
| get | got | gotten | sing | sang | sung |
| give | gave | given | sink | sank | sunk |
| go | went | gone | sit | sat | sat |
| grind | ground | ground | sleep | slept | slept |

| SIMPLE FORM | PAST TENSE FORM | PAST PARTICIPLE | SIMPLE FORM | PAST TENSE FORM | PAST PARTICIPLE |
|---|---|---|---|---|---|
| slide | slid | slid | swing | swang | swung |
| speak | spoke | spoken | take | took | taken |
| speed | sped | sped | teach | taught | taught |
| spend | spent | spent | tear | tore | torn |
| split | split | split | tell | told | told |
| spread | spread | spread | think | thought | thought |
| spring | sprang | sprung | throw | threw | thrown |
| stand | stood | stood | understand | understood | understood |
| steal | stole | stolen | wake | woke | woken |
| stick | stuck | stuck | wear | wore | worn |
| sting | stung | stung | weave | wove | woven |
| strike | struck | stricken | weep | wept | wept |
| swear | swore | sworn | win | won | won |
| sweep | swept | swept | wind | wound | wound |
| swim | swam | swum | write | wrote | written |

# ANSWER KEY
# (for puzzles and problems only)

## UNIT 11

### Answer to Activity 4 (page 199)

Secret: Silly Sally only likes things with double letters.

## UNIT 16

### Additional Clues for Opening Task (pages 256–257)

| MYSTERY 1 | MYSTERY 2 | MYSTERY 3 |
|---|---|---|
| The man is very, very short. | There's a big puddle of water in the room, and the paper is a delivery bill from an ice company. | The police officer is a woman. |

### Answer to Activity 3 (page 268)

(a) Candle snuffer; (b) Antique screwdriver; (c) Cherry pit remover; (d) Blender;
(e) Bread slicer; (f) Meat chopper

## UNIT 20
### Answer to Activity 1 (page 342)

That that is, is. That that is not, is not. Isn't that it? It is!

## UNIT 21

### Activity 1 (page 354)

Diagram B

Diagram D

# CREDITS

## Photo Credits

p. 0: © Royalty-Free/Corbis

p. 1: (Top) © Brownie Harris/CORBIS, (Bottom) © Colin Anderson/Getty/RF

p. 12: (Top) © Frederic Larson/San Francisco Chronicle/Corbis, (Bottom) © SORBO ROBERT/CORBIS

p. 13: (Left) © STOCK IMAGE/Alamy, (Right) © Stockbyte/Getty/RF

p. 15: © Jim Sugar/CORBIS

p. 25: ©IndexOpen/RF

p. 28: © Photos.com/RF

p. 37: © Joe McDonald/CORBIS

p. 46: (Top) © Adam Woolfitt/CORBIS, (Bottom) © Charles & Josette Lenars/CORBIS

p. 55: © Michael Prince/CORBIS

p. 59: © Photos.com/RF

p. 60: © Photos.com/RF

p. 64: © Jeff Greenberg/Alamy

p. 76: © STOCK IMAGE/PIXLAND/Alamy/RF

p. 86: © Norman/zefa/Corbis

p. 89: © Virgo Productions/zefa/Corbis

p. 94: © Robert Fried/Alamy

p. 99: © IndexOpen/RF

p. 103: (Top Left) © IndexOpen/RF, (Bottom Left) PhotoObjects.net/RF, (Bottom Right) © IndexOpen/RF

p. 106: (Left) © Ingram Publishing/Getty/RF, (Right) © Stockbyte/Getty/RF

p. 110: © IndexOpen/RF

p. 113: © IndexOpen/RF

p. 120: © Royalty-Free/Corbis

p. 124: © Bruce Ayres/Stone/Getty

p. 130: © Digital Vision/Getty/RF

p. 137: © Yellow Dog Productions/Taxi/Getty

p. 146: © Steve Vidler/SuperStock

p. 156: (Top Left) © IndexOpen/RF, (Top Right) © Photos.com/RF, (Bottom Left and Right) © Photos.com/RF

p. 182: © Henry Westheim Photography/Alamy

p. 191: © Photos.com/RF

p. 202: © Seth Kushner/Stone/Getty

p. 209: © IndexOpen/RF

# INDEX

5 ⑦